THE SEXIEST MAN ALIVE

THE SEXIEST MAN ALIVE

A BIOGRAPHY OF

WARREN BEATTY

ELLIS AMBURN

HarperEntertainment
An Imprint of HarperCollins*Publishers*

HarperCollins books may be purchased for educational, business, or sales promotional use. For information please write: Special Markets Department, HarperCollins Publishers Inc., 10 East 53rd Street, New York, NY 10022.

FIRST EDITION

Designed by Mary McAdam Keane

Printed on acid-free paper

Library of Congress Cataloging-in-Publication Data

Amburn, Ellis.
  The sexiest man alive : a biography of Warren Beatty / by Ellis Amburn.
    p. cm.
  Includes bibliographical references and index.
  ISBN 0-06-018566-X
  1. Beatty, Warren, 1937– 2. Motion picture actors and actresses—United States—Biography. I.Title

  PN2287.B394 A83 2002
  791.43'28'092—dc21
  [B]

                                                            2001051554

02 03 04 05 06 ❖/RRD 10 9 8 7 6 5 4 3 2 1

To Dorris Halsey
a friend for life

CONTENTS

WARREN BEATTY "UNCLOTHED" (PART I: SHARON WASHINGTON)

IT WAS A TYPICALLY bright, mild Southern California day, warm enough for Warren Beatty to have the top down on his chocolate 450 Mercedes convertible. Diane Keaton sat by his side as they sped along Sunset Boulevard in the heart of Beverly Hills. At Beverly Glen, they stopped for a light. As they waited for it to change, a youthful, exotic-looking black woman pulled up beside them. Warren didn't notice her, but Diane smiled and said, "Hi." At first, eighteen-year-old Sharon Washington, a broadcasting-school student who'd shortly win a production-assistant job with syndicated radio DJ Rick Dees at L.A. station KIIS, didn't realize who the famous driver of the Mercedes was. And Warren didn't take any notice of Sharon at all. When she finally looked around at him, Sharon was entranced and couldn't stop staring. Just then, the light changed. Warren peered over his sunglasses and shot a dazzling smile at Sharon as he steered into the turning lane and headed north on Beverly Glen. Interviewed two decades later, Sharon remembers what flashed through her mind: "Oh, my God, it's Warren Beatty again. Could this be fate? Somehow, some way I'm going to meet him."

This marked the third time in as many weeks she'd seen Beatty, who at the time was still one of the world's leading movie stars, and her yearning to meet him had grown with each sighting. "After seeing him on Sunset," Sharon said in 2000, "I was having dinner one night with a friend, who'd brought along her boyfriend. This guy said he was staying at the Beverly Hillcrest Hotel, but had thought of getting a room at the Beverly Wilshire, where Warren Beatty and Joe Namath were staying. He didn't because he liked it a little more low profile. Suddenly, I saw my chance to meet Warren Beatty. I said, 'I know it sounds crazy, but I'm going to call the Beverly Wilshire and leave a message for him to call me.'"

Over the next two weeks, she rang the hotel four times, leaving messages. Early one Saturday afternoon, she was watching television in her apartment in Culver City when Warren called. "Is this Sharon Washington?" he asked in a voice that was hushed and intimate. When she replied, "Yes," he said hesitantly, "This is Warren, Warren . . . Beatty." Sharon was momentarily speechless. Then Beatty asked, "Do I know you?"

Fearing that if she told the truth, he'd dismiss her as just another groupie and hang up, she said, "Yes." But then she thought, I'm not going to make something up. "Well, kind of," she sputtered, "but not really."

"Okay, slo-o-o-w down," he said. "Tell me what you're trying to say."

After she explained how she'd seen him three times, he didn't hang up. Instead he wanted to know all about her. When he asked why she had called, she answered honestly. "I'm not big on writing fan letters, but I knew I had to contact you because I feel there's something between us that could mesh."

"Okay," Beatty said matter-of-factly. "Describe what you look like."

"I'm five foot four, a hundred and two pounds. My hair is dark brown, and I have big eyes, thick eyebrows, long lashes, dimples, and a slender frame."

An hour and fifteen minutes of lively conversation followed. "This guy loves the telephone," she explains. "He asked me all about myself. I told him acting didn't interest me as a career, but I'd always been fascinated by the entertainment industry. Eventually I'd end up working at the William Morris Agency in Beverly Hills."

Toward the end of the conversation, Beatty asked Sharon if she'd do him a "favor."

"What's that?" she inquired.

"Would you mind dropping off a photo of yourself?"

She agreed, and added that since she'd recently been doing some modeling, she had a professional portrait. Before hanging up, he asked about her family and wanted to know how she got along with them. She told him fine, and he said he'd wait for her picture.

Without wasting a minute, Sharon rushed from Culver City to the Beverly Wilshire, a regal, rococo structure at the intersection of Rodeo Drive and Wilshire Boulevard. In the lobby, she handed the envelope containing her photo to the concierge. She drove back to Culver City a half hour later, just as it was just beginning to get dark. Five minutes after she opened her door, Warren called and said he was looking at her picture. "My God, you certainly described yourself perfectly," he said. "The picture is exactly the way I thought you'd look."

He wanted to see her in person. A few days later, he called and gave her the telephone number of his house on Mulholland Drive. He wanted to know more about why she'd contacted him and what had attracted her to him.

"It's not just one thing," she said. "I just see us communicating as friends."

"Be more specific."

It was difficult, because she was focused on having a relationship, not just a roll in the hay. But his voice was warm, cozy, and insistent, and after they talked a while, a certain intimacy was achieved. Finally, she felt comfortable enough to admit to him, after he kept pressing for input regarding her attraction to him, "Well, I do have sexual fantasies about you."

"Give me an example."

"I see us on a date. What you're wearing is very preppy . . . blue jeans . . . a powder-blue cardigan sweater with a little insignia on it . . . a shirt with a pin-striped collar. I always think of you as a football player like you were in *Heaven Can Wait*. Then I see us unclothed, being intimate."

She recalled in a 2000 interview,[1] "It's not like we got into this heavy conversation, like, 'Are we going to go all the way or not?'. He seemed to understand how nervous I was. There were several more calls after that, during which he explained that he was about to go to Europe, to work with Diane Keaton in *Reds*, a film he was also directing. Finally, he called and asked me to come to the hotel."

To make sure she'd have time to bathe and make up, she told him to stay on the phone and ran to the bathroom to draw her bathwater, all the time thinking, I'm going to see him. I'm really going to see him. Back on the phone, she said she'd be there in an hour.

He called back while she was soaking in the tub and asked, "What are you doing?"

"Getting dressed," she lied, fearing if she said she was bathing, it would sound like she was assuming they were going to have sex, and she thought this would make her appear too eager.

Ironically, she was doing precisely what Warren wanted her to be doing. "I was hoping you were freshening up," he said.

"Actually, I am," Sharon admitted. After they hung up, she finished bathing and prettied herself up before driving to Beverly Hills. When she arrived at the hotel, the desk clerk told her Warren's quarters could be reached by taking a service elevator to an upper floor. "When I got there it was like an attic," she recalls. "It didn't look like something you'd see in a beautiful hotel. Frankly, it was grungy. So I was like, 'Whoa! This is . . . different.'

"As I walked down the hall, I suddenly saw Warren Beatty standing outside his door. What blew me away was that he was wearing exactly what I had described him wearing in my fantasy. He was very warm. He said, 'Hi,' and took my hand, and he walked me into his suite, which was covered with mirrors, even in the bathroom."[2]

Sharon was on the brink of discovering what most women in the world[3] wanted to know at that time—exactly what Warren Beatty was like in bed, and what he looked like "unclothed," as she put it. She would learn these secrets and much more as they indulged their desires and fantasies that day. She would experience his essence, his imaginative eroticism, his willingness to inspire others to enact their private dreams, his obliviousness to risk in seeking amorous adventure in the AIDS era, his scrupulous attention to a sex partner's responses, drawing his greatest pleasure from discovering what turned her on, and, finally, his cold rejection of any woman who wanted a continuing relationship.

Woody Allen once said that if he were reincarnated, he'd like to come back as "Warren Beatty's fingertips."[4] Sharon Washington knows the feel of those fingertips—as did many other women whose associations with Warren have only recently come to light: Jackie Kennedy Onassis, H.R.H. Princess Margaret, Barbara Harris, Lillian Hellman, Princess Elizabeth of Yugoslavia, Linda Eastman McCartney, Inger Stevens, Dewi Sukarno, Vanessa Redgrave, Jean Seberg, Susannah York, Brooke Hayward, Jaid Barrymore, and Maria Callas. Altogether, fifty-seven liaisons were documented during his four decades as Hollywood's leading Don Juan. In one context or another, he has been linked with Julie Christie, Cher, Brigitte Bardot, Candice Bergen, Jessica Savitch, Connie Chung, Diane Sawyer, Joni Mitchell, Carly Simon, Joan Collins, Barbra Streisand, Jane Fonda, Natalie Wood, Lana Wood, Leslie Caron, Diane Keaton, Michelle Phillips, Mamie Van Doren, Britt Ekland, Madonna, Barbara Hershey, Goldie Hawn, Barbara Minty, Margaux Hemingway, Elle Macpherson, Dayle Haddon, Carol Alt, Sippi Levine, Isabelle Adjani, Kate Jackson, Justine Bateman, Robin Menken, Daryl Hannah, Mary Tyler Moore—and, finally, Annette Bening.[5]

All would know his fingertips better than they would ever know his heart, a heart he doesn't even know himself because his emotional life has been busy rather than deep, and has generated more heat than light, unencumbered by any genuine passion. He is a dedicated pragmatist and apart from one-night stands, his women have either received an Oscar or an Oscar nomination, or they're rich, or socially or politically prominent. His strict public-relations policy is never to appear in public or act with anyone of lower social or professional status.

He is an amorous adventurer, a bit of a rascal, and a heartless seducer in the classic tradition of Gabriel Téllez's seventeenth-century antihero, Don Juan, depicted in Mozart's opera *Don Giovanni*, and in film roles by John Barrymore, Douglas Fairbanks Sr., Errol Flynn, and Fernandel. Of one of his best movies, *Shampoo*, Beatty said, "I wanted to explore contemporary sexuality through the medium of a Don Juan. A Don Juan doesn't get that way out of a misogynist feeling or the idea that he's a latent homosexual who's seducing all these women because he really wants to seduce men, impotence, or the desire to degrade women. He just wants to fuck because he likes to fuck."[6]

It's a bravura statement, the kind we used to love him for, but today it betrays a condition of human illness. One marvels that with such a complex sexual nature, he has managed to survive almost seventy years without a single scandal. Given his profligate sex life, that alone qualifies him as one of the shrewdest figures on the public scene. Unlike most Don Juans—who are known for their sexual stamina and little else—Warren is a spectacularly gifted actor, director, negotiator, and political fund-raiser.

Since the 1970s, he has seriously been talked about as a potential candidate for the governorship of California, the U.S. Senate, the vice presidency of the U.S., and the presidency. His political career has been sabotaged by the curious dynamics of his personal search for a hero. Drawn to father figures, he always sets them up as mentors only to knock them down, for he is far too competitive to acknowledge superior experience or ability on the part of others. In politics, he habitually backed losers—Hubert Humphrey, Eugene McCarthy, George McGovern, and Gary Hart—until his endorsement became tantamount to the kiss of death. When his own turn for the presidency came around, his insecurity made him back away. His uncontested genius lies in his innovations as an auteur of cinema, from *Bonnie and Clyde* in the 1960s to *Bulworth* in the 1990s. He has helped redefine Hollywood, changing it from the formula grind factory of the old studio days into a legitimate, if short-lived, producer of art.

Bonnie and Clyde was one of two genuine landmarks in movie history in 1967. The other was Mike Nichols's *The Graduate*. Both were harbingers of the New Hollywood—a renaissance in American filmmaking that culminated with the successes, in the following decade, of Martin Scorsese, Steven Spielberg, Peter Bogdanovich, Francis Ford Coppola, Stanley Kubrick, Dennis Hopper, Woody Allen, Bob Fosse, Arthur Penn, John Cassavetes, Alan J. Pakula, Bob Rafelson, Hal Ashby, William Friedkin, Robert Benton, Robert Altman, and George Lucas. As originators of a stunning new style of filmmaking, *Bonnie and Clyde* and *The Graduate* were often equaled by the New Hollywood films that came afterward, but never surpassed.

In the new cinema Beatty helped create, people mattered more than plot, the traditional linear narrative line was replaced by a higher aesthetic logic, old sexual and moral rules were boldly broken, and the conventional Hollywood upbeat fadeout was junked in favor of reality. For the first time, there was a sense of fun and inventiveness in American movies, and artistic rather than commercial considerations prevailed in filmmaking. Actors were chosen for their talent rather than looks, leading to the casting of such masters as Dustin Hoffman, Robert De Niro, Al Pacino, Richard Dreyfuss, Robert Duvall, Harvey Keitel, Donald Sutherland, Elliott Gould, and Jack Nicholson. The standardized Lana Turner plastic-blond cliché of Hollywood beauty was supplanted by earthy and substantive heroines like Diane Keaton, Mia Farrow, Jane Fonda, Faye Dunaway, Ellen Burstyn, Dyan Cannon, Barbra Streisand, and Jill Clayburgh.

Though they could all outact Beatty, in some degree they all owe their careers to his iconoclasm and the forces that have driven him as man and artist: hunger, lust, restlessness, eternal questing, recklessness, insatiable passion, indestructable courage, and incurable curiosity. His life and his oeuvre are inextricably intertwined, so that you wouldn't have one exactly the way it is without the other. Nor would Hollywood have evolved as it did after *Bonnie and Clyde* had Warren Beatty lived his life any differently.

All over within a mere ten years, the New Hollywood left many technological legacies. Also, the breakthrough in censorship was permanent. But the industry soon fell into artistic bankruptcy, never again to regain the aesthetic level it had achieved. The generation of Beatty, Nicholson, and Hopper and the revolution they spawned represent a peak in movie history unmatched since, and equaled only by the silent masterpieces of D. W. Griffith and Charlie Chaplin and the sound classics of Cecil B. DeMille, David O. Selznick, John Ford, David Lean, Federico Fellini, Ingmar Bergman, and Orson Welles.

In 2000, the Academy of Motion Picture Arts and Sciences gave Warren its ultimate honor, the Irving G. Thalberg Award—a lifetime-achievement prize—in recognition of the consistently high quality of such Beatty films as *Splendor in the Grass*, *Bonnie and Clyde*, *Shampoo*, and *Reds*. A few critics, like the Turner network's Robert Osborne, felt he didn't deserve the award because many of his films, like *The Only Game in Town*, were terrible. In an interview on CBS's *Saturday Early Show*, Osborne attributed Warren's conquest of the Thalberg to "a kind of boys'-club situation. Hollywood is honoring him as one of its own," he said, and the charge has some basis in fact.

More interested in negotiating than acting, Warren often turned down great roles offered to him in his prime, including *Butch Cassidy and the Sundance Kid*, *The Way We Were*, *Last Tango in Paris*, and *Misery*. He let them go to Robert Redford, Marlon Brando, and James Caan. As an auteur, a rebel who came along in the 1960s at the exact time the old studio system was collapsing and introduced new ways of moviemaking that were desperately needed, Beatty richly deserved the Thalberg. He fascinates us not only as an artist, but as a canny, brash businessman who cultivated powerful mentors and learned how to manipulate Hollywood, all while conducting one of the most spectacular, if erratic, love lives of any personality of his generation. He wooed and won the most desirable women of his time, and this book is a huge plunge into his sometimes public but far more often secret world.

THE SEXIEST MAN ALIVE

CHAPTER ONE

GROWING UP INSECURE: 1937–1960

WARREN BEATTY spent an unusually long period as a single man and didn't marry until he was in his mid-fifties. One of his closest friends, Richard Sylbert, the gifted designer who became production chief at Paramount, explains the anomaly this way: "He's an actor. The definition of acting is to be emotionally frozen at six to twelve years of age, when you're wearing your mother's dresses in the attic."

Another old friend and associate, "Sarah Porterfield," a movie technician who has worked on a few of Warren's films, blames Warren's complicated relationship with his famous sister, Shirley MacLaine. Porterfield met Warren some thirty years ago at the Daisy, a hip Sunset Strip hangout. Interviewed in 2000, Porterfield referred to "problems" between Warren and Shirley and added, "The women in his life gotta be real high profile. He likes the show, the trophy on his arm. Annette Bening [the woman he finally married] had an Oscar nomination for *The Grifters*, and she looks like his sister."[1] No one has ever accused them of incest, but both brother and sister have always been intrigued with each other. On March 1, 1976, Shirley told a *People* magazine reporter, who labeled her "Mac the Mouth," "I'd love to see what Warren's got that all the other girls are so mad about." And Warren once said, "My sister was my first big crush."[2]

Shirley MacLean Beaty was born April 24, 1934. Her brother, Henry Warren Beaty (he added the extra "t" when he became an actor, pronouncing it "Bay-ty," *not* "Bee-ty") came along three years later, on March 30, 1937. They grew up together in Virginia, Shirley as a tomboy, a ham, a scene stealer at home, and Warren was moody and withdrawn. There was one thing in which he excelled, then as now. "He was always prettier than me, even at the age of three," Shirley says.

Not everyone agreed that Warren was pretty. At home, where Shirley was known as that "little dancin' gal" because of her early determination to be a ballerina, Warren was called "Little Henry" because of his unfortunate resemblance to the imbecilic-looking cartoon character of that name. From the start, Shirley resented her little brother's bid for attention, and a lifelong sibling rivalry ensued. "Warren spent most of his time as a baby yelling," she says, "and with growing finesse, and sometimes astounding precision, has been doing so ever since."[3]

She was a pretty good yeller herself. Whenever she felt ignored, she turned into a hellcat, screaming and biting herself until she drew blood.[4] She had to "erupt," she later explained, in order to "arouse [her stolid mother's] passion." It "required ever increasing levels of drama on my part to elicit a response," she added. A doctor told her mother to train a water hose on Shirley to shut her up.

Show business coursed through the blood of both children, their grandmother, a teacher, having specialized in what used to be known as "elocution."[5] Both their parents were frustrated performers, whose sad lives had bogged down in a quagmire of failure, bitterness, and twisted values. Ira Owens Beaty, a boozer from Front Royal, a small town in Virginia, showed the hurtful effects of an upbringing by a domineering mother, and once said, "I was born tired, and every morning I have a relapse."[6] Big and bossy, he'd been a violinist, drummer, and bandleader before meeting and marrying a quiet, thin Canadian, Kathlyn MacLean, in Baltimore, where she taught dramatics at Maryland College and acted in little theaters. Ira, a realtor, had gone to Johns Hopkins University in the same city. Kathlyn had also taught acting in Nova Scotia and West Virginia.

Settling in Richmond, Virginia, the couple gave up their thespian dreams, and settled for respectable middle-class Baptist family life. Warren later said his mother had stopped teaching to become "kind of a . . . housewife."[7] His father's drinking problem got worse.

Ira managed to salvage some of his show-business dreams by entertaining at home. A good storyteller, he could hold a roomful of people rapt spinning an anecdote, and his wife was an effective sidekick. Warren recalls that acting "was really something that I was aware of at an early age. The fact that I later became an actor is not exactly accidental." Of her parents, Shirley added, "They were like a vaudeville team at home, and Warren and I would sit there and watch." But there was a downside. Instead of picking up confidence and showbiz chops from their parents, the children sometimes were tongue-tied, embarrassed by their parents' showing off, fueled by Ira's drinking. Brother and sister became somewhat standoffish and one of their ambitions in life was to conquer their shyness.[8]

"The frustrating spectacle of people who hadn't [made anything of themselves], who had been afraid to, and were bitterly disappointed in themselves as a result, had been crippling to us in many ways as we grew up," Shirley once remarked, "but, on the other hand, their failures and frustrations had been so clear that Warren and I had a precise blueprint of how *not* to be."[9]

Although the Beaty house was well kept and furnished with tasteful antiques, a strict Baptist atmosphere made it difficult for children who wanted to romp and play. When Warren's model car collection was scorned as clutter, he stopped playing with the cars. Every Saturday the siblings went to the movies and stayed until the last feature was shown, or as long as they could sit still. Sometimes they'd go behind the theater building and listen to the amplified voices from the screen inside, savoring the screams from *Frankenstein Meets the Wolfman* and the WWII torture epic *The Purple Heart*. By five years of age, Warren was imitating Charles Boyer and Milton Berle. "I was a lonely sort of kid," he recalled. "You begin to cut yourself off from people . . . I wasn't interested in what other kids did."

Ira's drinking[10] possibly created an emotional void at the center of the family. "My dad internalized most of his tumultuous emotions and suppressed them with liquor," Shirley recalled. Warren "shut everyone out,"[11] she added, and withdrew into himself. Both were traumatized by a perceived lack of love, and

Shirley resorted to loudmouthed rambunctiousness. By twelve, she was five feet seven inches and could fight and play baseball better than most boys (she had a .425 batting average). She hated dolls.

Warren, on the other hand, was socially recessive, a book reader, piano player, and inveterate loner. Decidedly nonathletic, he inevitably became the target of neighborhood bullies. He knew nothing about fighting and was unable to defend himself. Years later, one of his Hollywood peers, Marty Davidson, co-director of the Sylvester Stallone film *The Lords of Flatbush*, offered an insight into the forces that frequently turn outcasts like Warren into movie moguls. He cited David Geffen, with whom he grew up in a tough Brooklyn neighborhood and who later became the richest and most powerful man in Hollywood. "If you threw a baseball like a girl, you were called a faggot and you were in trouble," said Davidson, a close friend of Warren's. "[David Geffen] was not one of the guys. . . . He was on the outside, with a lot of pain and a lot of 'I'll get them later' in his attitude. . . . Guys who were nerds . . . do well in show business later on. Guys like Geffen, Jeffrey Katzenberg . . . They're driven by something very deep."[12] Though Warren was too good-looking in adulthood ever to be described as a nerd, his childhood legacy of insecurity and fear would give him much in common with the executives who later helped found the New Hollywood.

When Shirley saw the kind of punishment Warren was taking and how helpless he was to defend himself, she stepped into the fray and fought off his tormentors. "I'd beat up the boys who were trying to hurt him," she boasted. Warren looked up at his sister with big, wondering eyes and asked, "What do I do now?" He didn't need to worry; Shirley sent the bullies packing. For a while he was safe in the neighborhood, until one day his sister deserted him after realizing she wasn't getting any dates because she was considered too butch. She started acting more gracefully, and let Warren fend for himself. She gave up baseball, later commenting, "I had sense enough to know that *that* wasn't very feminine." Her personal popularity grew and soon she was elected to the cheerleading squad, a huge honor in southern secondary education. Before long she had all the dates she could handle. As for her beleaguered little brother, she said, "I finally let Warren learn to defend himself. He's been all right ever since."

Warren, who grew up with some neurotic doubts about his masculinity, wasn't so sure. "My childhood was very strongly and very positively affected by women," he observed, "my mother, my sister, my aunts, my great-aunts, cousins, all of whom were women—and I was fortunately not smothered by them."

Male influences on Beatty were scarce. His father taught him to read at five, but their closeness seems to have ended there. Ira was dead set against either of his children pursuing their artistic aptitudes; if show business hadn't worked for him, it wouldn't work for them, or so he reasoned. Shirley once stated that she most emphatically did not want to be like her father. "We sensed our parents' unrealized potential," she said, "and didn't want that to happen to us." Once, Ira drunkenly stumbled home and set the house afire; often, he passed out in front of the TV set while "The Star-Spangled Banner" played.[13]

Looking back years later, Warren and Shirley disagreed about the nature and quality of their upbringing. Warren said their parents raised Shirley with "a good, healthy, early feminist point of view," but Shirley maintained, "We sat for twenty years, warily watching each other grow up in so conventional a household in so conventional a town that it was a cliché. . . . Everything Warren and I are and represent is anti-Establishment, because we are products of the Establishment. Later on, we both sought some expert scientific help— psychiatric." On another occasion she attributed their differences to the fact that "we both love being king of the mountain. . . . It takes time to work out child-hood rivalries."[14]

Their parents continued to cavort like vaudevillians at home. Though Shirley disdained their antics, Warren eventually became convinced that they "were determined that Shirley and I would be disciplined in some means of self-expression." Indeed Shirley later said her mother gave up her dream of becoming a recognized actress because she wanted "to be a mother more."

Though obedient and well behaved at home, Warren and Shirley were wild in the neighborhood, their pranks bordering on juvenile delinquency as they stole from stores, set off fire alarms, dumped garbage on their neighbors' lawns, and limped across busy thoroughfares, pretending to be handicapped, stopping traffic. They collapsed at intersections, lying prostrate until someone tried to help them, at which point they jumped up and fled. "Warren and I breathed the breath of rebellion into each other," Shirley said, "a kind of conniving rebellion to beat the system. At home we were good; outside we really lived."[15]

Suddenly, just as they seemed about to become likely candidates for reform school, they developed a consuming passion for the comedy team of Martin and

Lewis. They saw every picture that Jerry Lewis and Dean Martin ever made. "At one point," Shirley says, "[we] drove our parents crazy by cupping our hands and screeching around the house holding huge, invisible grapefruits the way we had seen Dean and Jerry do in *At War With the Army*." Within a few short years, Shirley would be co-starring with Martin and Lewis in *Artists and Models*.

One unalloyed gift the Beaty children received from their parents was an intense interest in what Shirley later called "the power, meaning, and manipulation of [national] politics." Both parents were passionately involved in the course of world events, and the children found this concern for international affairs "contagious." To Warren and Shirley, who listened to President Roosevelt's Fireside Chats, politics and show business were intertwined. They realized, as Shirley put it, "that really fine politicians were good performers. They knew how to communicate their feelings." Their father insisted that anyone who could dominate the screen could rule nations, whether they were qualified or not. He believed in the power of charisma, and foresaw the changes that would come about in the Kennedy and Reagan eras, when political campaigns were waged on network television. Politicians would need above all to be effective performers.[16]

In the mid-1940s, the Beaty family moved to Arlington, Virginia, and Ira worked as principal of an elementary school. The family settled in the Dominion Hill section, and Warren's peers started mocking him for being nonathletic. He avoided them by taking refuge in a large closet that had a window and a light fixture, where he wrote and read for hours at a time. Since Arlington was just outside Washington, D.C., he fantasized about politics. "My childhood ambition was to be president of the United States," he said. "At seven, I decided to be governor of Georgia. At eight, I decided to become an actor. People become actors because of a need within themselves."[17] On another occasion he said, "People go into the theater because they have *neuroses*."[18] The incomplete person he was describing was himself.

"I met him in the ninth grade," says Jo Ann Wacaster Ratterree, in an interview in 2001. "We went to Swanson Junior High School in Arlington. I was going into English class one day, and there he was, redoing the *Texaco Star Theater*, imitating Milton Berle. He kept it up until we settled down and class began. My girl friend Nancy Mailer, whose family owned Mailer Seafood on the Potomac, had a crush on Warren. Nancy was a cute brunette, but not as popular as the girl Warren went with, whose name was Ann Read." Asked to describe Ann, Jo Ann calls her "very sweet." Photographs taken at the time show her to be a lovely, dark-haired, dark-eyed Jackie Kennedy type. Warren once said he'd assumed he'd marry the first girl he had sex with, and stay with her the rest of his life. He soon got over that illusion. "He was a flirt," says Ann Read. "When we got to high school, he immediately started dating senior girls."[19]

At Washington-Lee High School in Arlington, Virginia, he had his pick of the girls, and the boys respected and liked him. "I can't remember," said Shirley, "when he stopped looking like Little Henry and started looking like Superman." Whenever it happened, the ugly duckling had grown into a swan—a good-looking, six-foot-one, 205-pound varsity football center, with a beefy body and a heroic, broad-browed head, but his feeling of incompleteness as a human being persisted. It could only be fixed from the inside, by character development, not by football, which he took up out of a need to convince himself and others of his maleness. Though he became a gridiron star, he remained the same needy person inside. His determined effort to establish his gender didn't stop at football. He also went out for baseball and track. He became one of the best jocks in school, so full of himself that one of his teachers scolded him for being conceited, vain, and cocky.

His first love was theater, but he neglected it and didn't appear in any school shows because, as he later explained, "I was too occupied in proving myself a male."[20] In 1962, recalling his adolescent years at Washington-Lee, he said, "I got most of my acting ambitions temporarily pounded out of me in high school football." Like most American males, especially adolescents, he didn't grasp the essential fluidity of gender. Cramming himself into a restrictive macho straitjacket resulted in some emotional disfigurement of his personality.

As with many beautiful people, Warren came out barely on the plus side of the very fine line that separates physical ugliness from beauty. If he'd resembled the boiled-looking Little Henry as a child, he could at times look like Frankenstein in adolescence, with his massive forehead, flat-top haircut, and strange squinty eyes. The squint came from nearsightedness, and would eventually require thick "Coke bottle" eyeglasses. Later, after becoming a movie star, he carefully monitored his lighting as well as camera angles, distance, and shutter speed. "Warren tried to give cameras only his right profile," reveals screenwriter Joe Eszterhas. There could be no question that from the proper angle, and in good lighting, Warren's gray-green eyes, long lashes, elegant nose, creased cheeks, full sensuous lips, and muscular chest and arms were a case of nature perfecting itself. And no one knew it better than Warren himself. According to Eszterhas, Warren in adulthood surrounded himself with mirrors, even ones that provided a good view of himself on the toilet. "In a town filled with narcissistic actors," Eszterhas said, "Warren Beatty, I knew firsthand, won the prize in the Cracker Jack box."[21]

In his high-school class photo in the Washington-Lee yearbook, *The 1955 Blue and Gray,* Warren was noticeably better looking than most of his male classmates, but he was by no means the handsomest boy. "The Class of '55 was the largest up to that time—over five hundred," says Jo Ann Ratterree, and it included a remarkable number of heartthrobs of both sexes. Warren had far more than good looks. "He played the hell out of a piano," recalls Jo Ann. "I don't know whether I found him attractive. I worked and didn't run in his circle, which was football players and cheerleaders. He was friendly and nice to everybody, always spoke to you in the halls. I don't remember ever hearing anyone criticize him. I liked him as a person, but I didn't want to date him."[22]

From adolescence on, Warren's behavior was wildly contradictory. "He would come to my house, sweep in and give me a big theatrical kiss," recalled the mother of one of his friends. "He gave the impression of being self-confident; actually, he was essentially a loner, never wanting to be committed and tied down."[23] To some observers, he appeared not to like people, but needed them to assuage a voracious sex drive. One of his classmates, who asked not to be identified, said that "he was a virgin until he went to Hollywood." In Joe Eszterhas's later description, Warren was "a self-involved snob [who] held himself aloof and superior."[24] Whatever the case, when he finally figured out how to get sexual relief and confirm his manhood—which needed reinforcement on a daily basis—he would develop a philosophy he called "sequential polygamy."[25] Though it satisfied him for a while, it eventually backfired. Sexual surfeit did not, ultimately, lead to contentment, but always left him hungry and wanting more. His total absorption with proving his masculinity and relieving libidinal pressure, in fact, reduced him to emotional starvation.

Sexual notches in his belt would never give him the assurance he sought, for he failed to realize that a genuine sense of self-esteem can only come from giving rather than taking, not from sexual or professional conquests. Part of his emotional nature was mysteriously missing, but clues could be found in his hav-ing had a father who was a heavy drinker and a mother who, for some reason, did not express her feelings.[26] As a result, he grew up with no experience of love, apart from the sporadic affection of his scattered, erratic sister.

Many insecure, emotionally stunted males turn into misogynists and women beaters, but Warren, whose character had been formed by women, and whose basic orientation in life was feminine, would never be accused of striking a woman. "If a boy starts off liking women," he once remarked, "there's no rea-son he shouldn't continue to feel that way." Women were inextricably bound up in the basic drive of his life, which was for power and manipulation. As Sharon Washington and others would later attest, he was constantly monitoring his part-ner's responses during the sex act, questioning, analyzing, and searching to dis-cover what turned his sex partner on. Though he learned how to please women, his own sense of incompleteness would remain, and soon it would be time to move on to another woman and another vain search for affirmation.

Though emotionally a mess in his adolescent days, he formed many posi-tive habits. As a football hero he always had to be in condition, so he learned to eat healthily and keep fit. A friend who knew him for over a decade once said, "I've never seen him consume anything gastronomically incorrect—take a drink, eat a piece of meat, a dessert, even a bite of cheese."[27]

According to one high-school girlfriend, now Mrs. Ann Colgan, Warren said "the only reason he would marry would be to have a child—and that would be to satisfy his ego," and it's conceivable his dependence on his sister prevent-ed him from forming meaningful attachments with other girls.[28] Former gossip columnist and TV personality Rona Barrett observed of Warren and Shirley during a 2000 interview, "Oh, they had their moments . . . really. They had their moments. Why did they have their moments? I believe it was very deep-rooted and very psychological. I'm not quite sure that they know specifically why it is, but I do believe there was tremendous competition, whether they would admit it or not, and it has to do with their early days together. What was expected of Shirley and what was expected of Warren contributed to this uneasy relation-ship. Maybe a part of Shirley was jealous of Warren for his ability to be very free. This is not to say that Shirley didn't have her own multi-relationships after she broke up with her husband, even though they didn't get a divorce. But she always kept it private. Warren always picked on people who made it very public."

Warren's fame as a football center, No. 61, was widespread throughout the area. "I didn't miss a game," says Jo Ann Ratterree. "We had pep rallies before the games, and we screamed our heads off. I started dating my future husband, Gene, at the Thanksgiving game." John Phillips, subsequently of the Mamas and the Papas, went to a rival school in Alexandria, but was acutely aware of " 'Mad Dog Beaty' . . . a rugged footballer."[29] In 1954, his senior year, Warren was elected president of his class. He was also named "Best All Around," an honor he shared with a girl named Jo Schilling. In the yearbook section devoted to the most popular students, the best all-around couple is shown striding through the student body, Miss Schilling dressed in a pleated, plaid "New Look" skirt and saddle oxfords with bobby sox, and Warren, looking much brawnier than in his later days as an actor, conservatively attired in a V-neck pullover, dark gabardine slacks, and dark shoes. In keeping with his all-around status, the jock was toting an armload of textbooks. His cheery, open smile was in marked contrast to the sulky expression he'd shortly cultivate as a matinee idol.

Though he was a starter on the football team, the Generals, he was not cited in the yearbook as the team's most outstanding athlete. But he did make it onto the list of the six most honored General gridders, and he made the all-suburban team. His drive to match or outdo his sister was partly responsible for his career as a high-school hero. Shirley had become an overachiever, getting only four hours of sleep a night in order to take ballet lessons and practice cheerleading. "I had this obsession about being a ballerina," she recalled, though her large feet and height of over six feet *en pointe* obviated a career in classical dance.[30] Nor was she conventionally pretty. But there could be no question that she possessed two powerful assets for stardom: a pair of showgirl legs that seemed to start at her shoulders, the kind of legs seen at the Copa, the Latin Quarter, the Winter Garden, the Lido, the Moulin Rouge—and, of course, in Hollywood musicals.

When Shirley graduated from high school and left home, at eighteen, for a career as a Broadway hoofer, Warren was fifteen years old. In New York, leasing a sixty-seven-dollar-a-month fifth-floor walk-up apartment at 116th Street and Broadway, she went on casting calls, worked in summer theater in Lambertville, New Jersey, promoted refrigerators in a traveling trade show, and performed in the chorus of *Oklahoma!* Since everyone was mispronouncing Beaty (as Bee-ty) and were just as likely to mispronounce MacLean, she dropped the former and changed the spelling of the latter. During an audition, Richard Rodgers personally picked her for the chorus line in *Me and Juliet*, which opened at the Majestic Theater on May 23, 1953. Within a year she met Steve Parker, a thirty-three-year-old ex-paratrooper who'd fought in WWII. Smitten with his rugged handsomeness and raging ambition to succeed as a show-business entrepreneur in Asia, she became his mistress. They got married a year later, when she was twenty-one, and she continued working as a chorine, convinced she'd found her niche in musical comedy. Though her singing voice was strident, grating, and unmelodic, she had those legs—and endless ambition and energy.

Back home in Arlington, Virginia, news of Shirley's New York breakthrough had the effect of galvanizing her younger brother's show-business hopes. Years later, attempting to trace his artistic influences, Warren remarked, "I watched my mother direct, my father play the violin, and Shirley dance." Watching Shirley would soon turn into a spectacular fireworks display; stardom for her was unusually quick in coming. Hired for the chorus of the Broadway musical *The Pajama Game*, Shirley was assigned to understudy the dancing lead, Carol Haney. One fateful night, Haney stumbled and sprained her ankle, and Shirley went on for her, playing the part for several weeks. Warren was seventeen when he caught the show and announced that Shirley was "wonderful," adding, prophetically, that she was much more than a dancer. Ex–Warner studio chief Hal B. Wallis, now an independent producer, was also in the audience, and he promptly gave Shirley a film contract. Months later, Haney missed another performance, and again Shirley substituted for her. This time, Alfred Hitchcock's New York scout saw her and alerted his boss. Shirley, strutting her stuff in Bob Fosse's showstopping number "Steam Heat," struck the legendary director as a perfect candidate for the kooky lead in his forthcoming film *The Trouble With Harry*. She subsequently filmed *Artists and Models* for her discoverer, Hal Wallis.

The two pictures, both popular, marked the beginning of one of Hollywood's epic careers, one that would begin with perky ingenue roles, showgirl flash, and Rat Pack slapstick; mellow into resonant, haunting pathos in *The Apartment* and *Some Came Running*; and culminate in moving tragicomedy in *Terms of Endearment*, *Guarding Tess*, and *Postcards from the Edge*. "We were still in junior high when Shirley hit it big," says Jo Ann Ratterree. "Warren started yakking about her. He was really proud of his big sister."

Warren became an uncle when Shirley and Steve Parker had a daughter, Stephanie (Sachi). Their marriage, however, though it lasted twenty-eight years, proved a dud. "Before our marriage, sex between Steve and me had been terrific," Shirley recalled. "Afterward, not at all."[31] In Hollywood, she was quickly absorbed into Frank Sinatra's clique, becoming the Rat Pack's beloved but sexually untouchable mascot. "Frank and Dean [Martin's] crowd acted more like adolescent boys around me than swinging seducers," she said. Because the "intensity" of her parents' union had left her gasping for "more breathing room," she never remarried. Warren too had been afflicted by his parents' suffocating relationship, she said, adding, "I can't imagine Warren with children."[32]

Football and being a teenage dreamboat weren't enough for Warren, who said, "I was sick of it. It was a drag. Some things you want to do . . . and some things you do to prove something. The important thing is doing what you enjoy, not because you get a reaction from others." He soon tempered his adolescent effort to establish his masculinity and overcome his shaky childhood as a wimp protected by his big sister. He could no longer suppress his real nature, which was sensitive and artistic. Unlike most athletes in American high schools, who steer clear of the drama department, Warren showed considerable bravery in eschewing the jock crowd and at last casting his lot with the far less popular fine-arts students. He began by rehearsing Eugene O'Neill plays in the basement of his parents' red-brick Colonial home.

Though artistic self-expression is the usual motive behind a career in acting, Warren's embodied a thirst for power. "I never thought I would be an actor," he said. "I was interested in the theater as a place to control, to manipulate."[33] In the summer of 1954, just prior to his senior year at Washington-Lee, he went to the National Theater in Washington and got a job as a guard at the stage door, where his main duty was to keep alley rats from scurrying into the theater. "Maybe it wasn't a job *in* the theater," he laughed, "but it was a job *near* the theater."

Helen Hayes, then regarded as the first lady of the American stage, was appearing at the National in Thornton Wilder's *The Skin of Our Teeth*, a World War II play that was a parable about the end of the world. It struck fifties audiences as particularly relevant because of the Cold War, Eisenhower conformity, the McCarthy-army inquisition, H-bomb tests, and fallout shelters. This revival of the play came only a few years after one of Warren's future heroes, director Elia Kazan, ratted out all his buddies by cooperating shamelessly with the U.S. House Un-American Activities Committee in its persecution of artists wrongfully accused of disloyalty. The Communist witch hunt focused on Hollywood and left scars that would weaken the industry until an entirely new generation of filmmakers, spearheaded by Warren, Mike Nichols, and others, created the New Hollywood in the late sixties and seventies.

Though Warren was offered ten college scholarships following his gridiron exploits, he turned them down, later explaining that jocks "get their teeth knocked down their throats, their noses splashed over their faces." He graduated in the class of '55, with no intention of pursuing a career in sports, either college or professional, and determined to save his fabulous face for millions of imagined fans to worship. His father tried to get him to become a lawyer, and even attempted to enlist Shirley's help in warning Warren about the pitfalls and uncertainties of an actor's life.[34] That, of course, was a mistake, since Shirley was an example of overnight stardom. Besides, she had a belief about her brother: "He'll do something," she thought. "And it will be his way, just as I am going off to do something my way. But I knew that, whatever it was, somehow it would continue to be a joint plan against the established way of doing things."[35]

In September 1955, he enrolled in the School of Speech and Drama at Northwestern University, in the Chicago suburb of Evanston, Illinois, alma mater of Patricia Neal, Ann-Margret, and Charlton Heston. While insisting vaguely that he eventually "intended to go into law and then politics,"[36] he sang in a campus show, worked on improving his elocution, and dated an undergraduate, Ellie Wood, who later married Jennifer Jones's son, Robert Walker Jr.

After his freshman year, he dropped out, convinced that he was ready to act professionally, and that acting couldn't be taught anyway. He managed to pass his courses, but, according to the registrar's office, "he didn't do so great."[37] He, like many actors bound for stardom, was too impatient to pursue Northwestern's excellent liberal-arts curriculum, one that would have provided him with the humanities background he sorely needed. Most actors are not especially well educated. They forgo cultivating their intellects in favor of storming the stage and igniting audiences. And they pay a price. Though Marilyn Monroe, the predominant star of the fifties, wanted to play Grushenka in Dostoyevsky's *The Brothers Karamazov*, she could never completely make the transition from sexpot to serious actress. This was due not only to her having no real range of emotion, but also to her sparse knowledge of literature.

Warren, like Monroe, was a beautiful dropout who for years would succeed on the strength of a kinetically magical screen persona. His limited emotional range, coupled with a lack of higher education and its gifts of vocabulary, richness of allusion, and logical thought, would ill prepare him for demanding roles. His impatience forced him to follow in Shirley's footsteps. He went to New York and worked as a dishwasher, often subsisting on peanut butter sandwiches. For the first few weeks, he stayed with an uncle who lived outside New York City,[38] and later rented a "junk heap" of an apartment for twenty-four dollars a month on West Sixty-eighth Street. Finally, he was able to put together a few gigs, playing piano at dives in Manhattan and Long Island, and for a while he worked at Clavin's, a fashionable lounge on East Fifty-eighth Street. He modestly described his musical ability, which a lovesick Joan Collins later praised to high heaven, as "sloppy jazz. Not really very good . . . well, not rinky dink—just sloppy." He admitted he wasn't "any Carmen Cavallaro—just a half-baked piano player."

"None of us working in Broadway shows knew that Warren wanted to be an actor," recalled actor/writer Arnold Margolin, who was starring as Peter Van Dann, opposite Susan Strasberg, in the hit Broadway play *The Diary of Anne Frank*. "He was a shy kid, and all we knew for sure was that he wanted to play the piano. He hung out with an actor named George Firth, who later wrote the book for the Sondheim musical *Company*, and then the three of us started hanging out together. He wasn't known for making out with girls at all, not yet, that is."

Warren started studying acting with Marlon Brando's drama coach, the legendary Stella Adler, whom Warren called "the greatest teacher of them all." A member of the Group Theater, she'd appeared in Clifford Odets's *Awake and Sing* with John Garfield and Morris Carnovsky, but somehow lost her nerve as an actress. In 1934 she went to Paris, where she met the great Russian director Stanislavsky, founder of Method acting. Bringing the lessons of the master back to America, she taught students like Warren how to concentrate, and she gave them sense-memory exercises (for example, sewing with an phantom needle) to hone their performance skills. Stella believed that an actor could *become* his character, and make his emotions real, not by burrowing inward, as Lee Strasberg taught at the Actors Studio, but by means of a process of what she called externalization. The actor, she taught, should empathize with and construct a character from the outside, adhering strictly to the playwright's setting and time frame. The play's "given circumstances," its physical action, supplied the key.

Through these catalysts, the actor could find his interpretation, putting aside his own experiences and letting his "creative imagination" take over, filling in his character's past history. "Your life is one-millionth of what you know," Stella said. "Your talent is your imagination; the rest is lice. Acting is action; action is doing. Find ways to do it, not to say it." Her students often heard her scream, "Don't act! Stop acting!"

Brando was nineteen or twenty when he studied with her. Devastatingly handsome, quite unlike the rotund giant he became later on, Brando dated Stella's daughter Ellen, but it was Stella he loved, and he attributed his Broadway breakthrough in *A Streetcar Named Desire* in the late 1940s to her genius as a teacher. "If it hadn't been for her," Brando said, "maybe I wouldn't have gotten where I am—she taught me to read, she taught me to look at art, she taught me to listen to music." Stella Adler flirted with every man she met, especially male acting students who were muscular and sexy, and she routinely had flings with them. "It was love," said her protégé David Diamond, describing her relationship with the young Brando. Brando himself said, "She imparts a most valuable kind of information—how to discover the nature of our own emotional mechanics and therefore those of others." Though she was married to director Harold Clurman, she let Marlon spend as much time as he wanted in their apartment, and she wore nothing but her "peignoir," Diamond recalled, "but it's always open, the tits half out with nothing on underneath." She referred to Brando as this "puppy thing," and sagely predicted he'd "be the best young actor on the American stage."

She also adored Warren, and it was Adler's endorsement that gave him "arrogant self-confidence," he recalled. This was a quality that many would come to detest, but it gave Warren, in lieu of experience and education, the courage that would propel him through future successes as an actor, dealmaker, director, and politico. Courage would never hurt him either in his quest for "enormous amounts of money."[39]

He won a bit part playing the piano on the daytime soap *Love of Life*, and spent most of his time with actress Diane Ladd, future wife of Bruce Dern and mother of Laura Dern. Though Diane relished Warren's brash certitude, one of her roommates, Rona Barrett, considered it overbearing brazenness. "I had three roommates at that time, including Diane Ladd and a model named Judy Loomis," Rona said in an interview in 2000. "And then, we had friends who came in and out like Suzanne Pleshette. Susie was actually more of an occasional roommate. When she'd have a fight with her parents and not go back home to West End Avenue or whatever, she'd come and stay with us for a while, though never on a regular basis. We had this little Pullman kitchen, and in the bedroom, four beds in each corner. Whoever came in first took the bed at the back. Everybody knew that my father was in the food business, so he would bring me weekend food for us to eat, wondering why I was living there and not at home. We'd make these enormous pots of spaghetti and meatballs and leave it there for all the gypsies. Everybody on Broadway who was hungry and had no money came to us—not that we had any money either.

"One morning at about two or three o'clock, there was a knock at the door. I was the one closest to the living room, so I went to the front door and asked, 'Who is it?' An ominous voice replied, 'Open up!' I asked again who it was, and a man said, 'Open up. Open the door. I'm gonna rape you.' 'No, you're not,' I said. 'Who is it?' I finally opened the door, and it was Warren. He had come to get something to eat and to see Diane. Diane came running in and said, 'Oh, my God. It's only *Warren*.' We became good friends from that moment on." In her autobiography, Rona added that Warren said, "This is it, baby! You're finally gonna lose that fuckin' cherry!"

In the interview she continued, "He played a mean piano and was very cute . . . the kind all females like to mother. He liked being mothered. Except afterward, he'd complain that his girlfriends were too possessive. Warren is afraid to find out who and what he is. As his own sister, Shirley MacLaine, said to me about him: 'He empathizes—from the waist down only.' "[40]

Predictably, by late 1956, like so many attractive young persons who find Manhattan's fast lane too much for them, he wrecked his health. "He's a whore," Rona wrote in her memoir. "He's very spoiled and selfish. He only does what he wants to do when he wants to do it."[41] But retrospect or nostalgia had mellowed her view of Warren by the time of the 2000 interview. "He always was adorable," she said. "He was starving to death. He lived down in Hell's Kitchen. He was struggling like all of us. I used to ask all my friends, 'What is it about him?' He's just very charming, very attentive, and impossible to get a commitment out of, which is why I think he never married up until recently."

Suddenly stricken by an attack of hepatitis, he retreated to his parents' home, and Ira and Kathlyn nursed him back to health over a period of several months. When he returned to New York in February 1957, he told friends he had no interest in acting, and yet accepted roles on daytime soap operas, CBS's *Studio One* and *Playhouse 90*, and NBC's *Suspicion* (the episode was called "Heartbeat"). He also played both a young man and the young man's older self in *One Step Beyond* with Joan Fontaine. He won the lead in *The Curly-Headed Kid* for Kraft Theater and NBC.

In 1958 he met director Robert Altman while doing a bit part in an Ernest Kinoy teleplay about a man with heart trouble, played by David Wayne. Then came the TV sitcom *The Many Loves of Dobie Gillis*. "*Dobie* was shot at the old Fox/Western studios in the heart of Hollywood," recalls designer Donfeld. "The huge facility occupied both sides of Western Avenue at the corner of Sunset Boulevard (several of the soundstages were later felled to make room for another seedy California corner mall). Warren was co-starring in *Dobie* with Dwayne Hickman (Dobie) and Tuesday Weld (as Thalia Menninger, the object of their mutual affection). Beatty played an aristocratic classmate of Hickman and Weld's. I remember very well the day he walked onstage. Magic is the only word I can think of to describe him. But Tuesday was singularly unimpressed with young Warren during their scenes—unlike the rest of the company and/or half of Hollywood."

In a foreshadowing of Warren's White House ambitions, his character, Milton Armitage, runs for junior-class president against Dobie, and tells Weld's Thalia, "How can I lose the election? I'm handsome, cultured, debonair, attractive, manly. I'm in politics seriously. I owe it to my class—the ruling class. I won't mince words. This junior-class presidency is merely the beginning. A finger exercise, so to speak. I'm going onward and upward."

Weld looks at him and says something that might also have been a forecast of things to come: "You cannot win the election. You're perfect. And people don't vote for perfect people."[42] Nevertheless, in real life, Warren would become ardently political in 1960, when he cast his first vote for John F. Kennedy for president. Later in the decade, he would work for Robert F. Kennedy's election in the Democratic presidential primaries. Tuesday Weld went on to distinguished work in such films as *The Cincinnati Kid* and *Pretty Poison* and to a stormy personal life. "She once tried to run down actor Gary Lockwood with her car," wrote *Time*. "When he jumped on the hood, she sped down Sunset Boulevard trying to shake him off while he pleaded with her through the windshield." Weld also had a tempestuous marriage to comic actor Dudley Moore.[43]

In the late 1950s, Warren met fellow aspiring thespian and future diva

Barbara Joan Streisand, who was still spelling her first name with three *a*'s. The meeting took place in summer 1958 in Clinton, Connecticut, where Warren was performing in Charlotte Harmon's Clinton Playhouse. Barbara had come to Clinton to work as a baby-sitter for her acting coach Allan Miller and his wife, Anita. One evening, Warren invited himself to the Millers' house, ostensibly to help Barbara baby-sit. Though she'd had a good-looking boyfriend, she'd never seen anyone quite so pink and glowing as Warren, and she cooked him a spaghetti dinner. In contrast, the Brooklyn-born Streisand was rather plain and hook-nosed, but she had sensational legs and an aura of sensuality that mesmerized Warren. He was twenty, and she was sixteen and a student at Brooklyn's Erasmus Hall High School. In the beatnik style of the era, she sported a black pixie haircut and wore a black sweater, black skirt, and black stockings and carried a black leather bag. On her face she wore pasty white makeup and hot pink lipstick, and her nails were painted purple.

The Morticia Addams look scared the kids at Erasmus Hall, according to classmate Cynthia Roth, but Barbara continued to dress in her eccentric style "to show everybody that I didn't care what they thought of me." Her attitude sprang from a childhood of rejection. Her courageous father, Manny, who taught truants and delinquents at a vocational high school, died the year of Barbara's birth after receiving a morphine injection for an epileptic seizure. Taken in by her grandparents, she grew up in a one-bedroom flat in the rough Bedford-Stuyvesant section. Her mother, Diana, who went to work as a bookkeeper after her husband's death, had little inclination or energy to offer Barbara affection or emotional support, so when the grandparents were unavailable, Barbara was parked with friends and distant relatives.

Virtually an orphan, she was terrified she'd end up "alone in the world"[44] because she wasn't pretty, and kids at the yeshiva on Willoughby Street called her "Cross-eyes." Her left eye was a shade lazy and tended to focus on her nose. "Big beak" was another name she endured, and "Mieskeit"—Yiddish for ugly. Soon, the unlucky child copped a defensive, imperious attitude, one that would win her few friends, either in childhood or later.

In 1951 her mother, now forty, married Louis Kind, a piece sewer in the garment industry who also owned several buildings. Not long after the marriage, Diana gave birth to Barbara's half-sister, Rosalind (later the singer Roslyn Kind). Barbara's stepfather doted on Rosalind and completely ignored Barbara.

After she entered Erasmus Hall, Barbara's life didn't change for the better until April 22, 1956, her fourteenth birthday, when she was given a ticket to *The Diary of Anne Frank* at the Cort Theater. She related to the story of a bright young Jewish girl suffocating in an attic and dreaming of a glamorous life. From that day on, Barbara knew she wanted to be an actress. She also taught herself to sing by miming the recordings of Johnny Mathis and listening to Mabel Mercer, the high priestess of saloon singers, whose records taught Barbara to project lyrics with dramatic flair.

She took the school's English honors course, called Radio Dramatics, and acquired some acting experience in summer stock at Malden Bridge Playhouse in Malden Bridge, New York. Occasionally, she'd cross the East River and drift into mid-Manhattan's theatrical milieu. Though Barbara was too preoccupied with her teeming ambition to be popular, when she enacted the nurse in *Romeo and Juliet* in class, doing it as a comedy monologue, some thought her extraordinarily talented. She was "*fabulous*," recalled classmate Jane Soifer. Soon Barbara had a steady beau, Teddy, who was black; she was probably the first girl at Erasmus, or almost anywhere else in the U.S., to go biracial. Later, she developed a crush on classmate and future world chess champion Bobby Fischer. They lunched together every day, but he showed more interest in *Mad* magazine than in her.

Always quick and bright, she was an outstanding student with a 91 average, though her true interests lay in the acting classes she began to take in Manhattan with Method coach Allan Miller, who ran his own workshop on West Forty-eighth Street. "She was stagestruck and life-struck," said Anita Miller. "She had a voracious mind. She wanted to know what everything was, what everything meant. She was like someone who had been starved."

She was starved no longer after meeting Roy Scott, a short, rugged twenty-three-year-old who was the best-looking man in the workshop. "She was very plain," Scott recalled, "but I found her wondrous in her own way, with her big, beautiful eyes . . . a doe, a fawn." Still convinced she was ugly, mostly because of her big nose, Barbara permitted herself to be groomed into attractiveness, inspired by Roy's flattery and forceful lovemaking. Inevitably, she became attached to him, but he was making it with many other girls as well. Roy found her to be somewhat conventional sexually, but the more they got together in his eight-dollar-a-week Park Savoy apartment on Fifty-eighth Street, the more erotically "inquisitive" she became. "She was growing up, dawning," he said, "learning to be a woman."

Warren had no doubt about that when they met. They talked about the theater, but both were also drawn to politics, and Barbara deeply cared about children and about people's welfare in general. Warren wanted to have sex, but, already having undergone sexual initiations with a Brooklyn black and a Method muscle boy, she was by no means a pushover.

"She seemed to be a person of strong moral convictions," Warren later said. "One of her convictions seemed to be that with the recent loss of my virginity, I might be experiencing too much of a good thing." As two intelligent, independent-minded fifties rebels, they enjoyed each other, but wouldn't consummate their relationship for another thirteen years. Nonetheless, Warren was grateful to have found a free spirit in the pre-women's-lib 1950s; Barbara was "critical [and] encouraging," he recalled. "She had energy, she was funny, she was uninhibited by conventions or tradition, she was sexy, she was honest."

Back in Manhattan, Barbara landed a role, appearing at the Garret, a rickety, forty-seat, fifth-floor walk-up performance space under the Third Avenue El, at Forty-ninth Street. Also in the cast, playing a lesbian, was Joan Molinsky, who'd shortly change her name to Joan Rivers. In one scene, Rivers proclaimed her passion for Barbara. "She rejected me," Joan later told me. "I pulled a knife on her and tried to kill her—and then myself."[45] The show folded when the Garret was declared a fire hazard.

On January 26, 1959, Barbara graduated from Erasmus Hall. Almost seventeen, she now spent all of her spare time watching Broadway shows, especially *The Sound of Music*, and memorizing every move of musical star Mary Martin, then the queen of Broadway. Soon she was singing at the Lion, a gay bar in Greenwich Village, where the boys cheered her pure, clear voice and the magic spell she wove with a lyric. When posters featuring her were prepared, she told club manager Burke McHugh, "I want to take an *a* out of 'Barbara.' Who needs it? The name's pronounced Bar-bra. So that's how I want you to spell it: B-a-r-b-r-a."[46] According to her friend Bob Schulenberg, an artist who taught her how to use eyeliner and contour her cheeks, "Barbra had almost exclusively gay friends."[47] As they would later do for Bette Midler and Madonna, gays made Streisand a cult figure in the Village, packing the Bon Soir on Eighth Street and the Ninth Circle near Sheridan Square, cheering her unique renditions of "Cry Me a River" and "Lover, Come Back to Me." When she moved uptown to the

Blue Angel, on East Fifty-fifth Street, she graduated from Village kook to sophisticated cabaret chanteuse, and from there it was just a short hop to Broadway and her breakthrough as Miss Marmelstein, the harried stenographer, in Harold Rome's *I Can Get It for You Wholesale*. Though it was a small part, she stole the show, rolling around the stage in a chair on casters while belting her big song. Like Warren, she was interested in directing, and she enraged *Wholesale* director Arthur Laurents by directing herself.

Meanwhile, Warren's star also was rising. He had continued to work in summer and winter stock at the Gateway Theater on Long Island and the North Jersey Playhouse in Fort Lee, playing leads in *A Hatful of Rain*, *Compulsion*, *The Happiest Millionaire*, and *Visit to a Small Planet*. The most important single career break of his life came one night when playwright William Inge, the Pulitzer Prize–winning author of *Come Back, Little Sheba*, *Picnic*, and *Bus Stop*, and Joshua Logan, the director of *South Pacific*, *Mister Roberts*, and *Picnic*, came to Fort Lee. Both were struck by Warren's moody sensuality, and at this crucial point in Warren's life, they held his fate in their hands. Inge was gay, Logan bisexual. That does much to explain how a young man with very little talent and no technique to fall back on, but with stunning beauty, supercharged sexual chemistry, and a jock's instinctive ability to look sexy, talk sexy, and act sexy, rose to superstardom in mid-twentieth-century America.

One of Broadway's most successful and distinguished playwrights, Bill Inge had begun as a drama critic at the *St. Louis Star-Times*. After interviewing Tennessee Williams prior to the Chicago tryout of *The Glass Menagerie* in 1944, Inge and Williams, according to the latter's biographer Donald Spoto, "had an impromptu and intense sexual affair, never resumed in their later friendship." One reason for the end of the affair was Inge's emergence a few years later as Williams's rival on Broadway. Williams's role in connection with Inge gradually evolved from lover to writing advisor, and from successful Broadway peer to fierce competitor and envious detractor.[48] He resented Inge's success as the author of a steady succession of dramatic box-office triumphs and did not want to share his crown as the king of Broadway with anyone, but after *Picnic* in the fifties and through *The Dark at the Top of the Stairs*, no one writing drama could match Inge's success, not even Williams or Arthur Miller.

"Bill Inge was in love with Warren Beatty on sight," Josh Logan once recalled.[49] "Warren's career was assured. 'I absolutely must have him,' Bill said. He decided to star this complete unknown on Broadway." Despite Inge's obsession with Warren, it was Logan who employed the actor first, flying him to the West Coast for a screen test opposite Jane Fonda in *Parrish*, a tale of teenage love and woe. Nearly half a century after Warren's arrival in California, casting director Marvin Paige recalled over dinner at Georgio's Pizza Pasta in Studio City in 2000, "I picked up Warren at the airport when he first came to L.A. He was eating cold hot dogs. I took him to his sister's place, somewhere in the Valley, maybe Sherman Oaks."

On one of his first nights in Los Angeles, Warren performed an act of homage to the film capital that would only have occurred to a lifelong movie fan. He took a long walk through the streets that ascend from the flats of West Hollywood and Beverly Hills—tree-lined thoroughfares like Elm and Roxbury that begin to wind and swoop north of Sunset Boulevard. He gazed longingly at the stately homes of the stars and dreamed of one day owning one himself. Like most devoted movie fans, he was a scholar of Hollywood history, and he yearned to claim his place in the ongoing epic of the movies.

The screen test with Jane Fonda was a love scene, and it went so well that Warren and Jane continued kissing long after the director repeatedly called "Cut."[50] Jane already had a boyfriend, twenty-seven-year-old Alexander (Sandy) Whitelaw, who worked in production. One day Sandy arrived unexpectedly and knocked on Jane's door. "Warren?" Jane called out, and Sandy testily replied, "No, it's not Warren. It's Sandy." A violent fight ensued, and Sandy smashed a mirror. Suddenly, Warren arrived and strolled in through the open door. He calmly drew the agitated Sandy aside. "Listen," he said, "I know exactly what you're feeling. Once I threw a bed out of a window in Philadelphia in a similar situation. I'll just go take a walk while you guys get this thing settled."[51] Jane's relationship with Whitelaw soon ended, but she and Warren remained friends.

Parrish hit a snag when Logan couldn't get Vivien Leigh and Clark Gable for the roles of Warren's parents. Also, Logan disliked the finished script so much he asked Warner Bros. to reassign it. Ultimately, Claudette Colbert played the mother in the film, and Troy Donahue got Warren's part. Logan agreed to direct *Tall Story*, in which he hoped to cast Warren and Jane Fonda. Warner Bros., however, preferred Anthony Perkins, who'd already made a name for himself on Broadway, as John Kerr's replacement in *Tea and Sympathy*. Warren was out of the movie, but Jane stayed in, making her film debut.

Warren still remained a contender among the attractive new generation of actors who'd been pouring into Hollywood throughout the 1950s—Rock

Hudson, Troy Donahue, George Nader, Tom Tryon, Richard Beymer, Paul Newman, George Hamilton, Tony Perkins, Rod Taylor, Ray Danton, Stuart Whitman, Tab Hunter, James Dean. All hoped to supplant such aging but durable matinee idols as Gable, William Holden, James Stewart, and John Wayne. Much of the new crop of movie beefcake was represented by a gay agent named Henry Willson, who'd once been David O. Selznick's talent scout. Pretty, willowy Nan Morris, later the wife of Edward G. Robinson's son, was Henry Willson's associate, and knew most of the young hopefuls. "Warren hung out at the Daisy," Nan recalls, referring to the popular discotheque owned by Jack and Sally Hansen, who also owned Jax, the famous Beverly Hills shop that reinvented women's slacks. At the Daisy, according to writer Dominick Dunne, "you could slip out to the garden in back for a snort or a toke. The smell of pot was often in the air. The young and the rich twisted and boogied away the nights in a town famous for going to bed early. The skirts were short. The girls were beautiful. The guys were handsome. . . . It was a nightly party."[52]

After seeing Warren at the Daisy, Nan told Henry Willson, "Warren's going to be the hottest thing in this town." Henry replied, "He's been blackballed. I heard it through the grapevine. Jack Warner is mad as hell at Warren for turning down a movie. Warner thought he had signed Warren up, but he hadn't."

According to Hollywood journalist Jim Bacon, "Rock Hudson had an affair with Henry Willson.[53] Many of Willson's clients did." Nan recalls, "I was on the fast track at Henry Willson's, drinking, having fun, dating a folksinger, hanging out at the Unicorn. Henry was representing all the hot new actors, giving them new names and telling them how to dress and behave—Rock Hudson, Rory Calhoun, R. J. Wagner, Guy Madison, and Troy Donahue. Troy stalked me for a while, but I was running around with Johnny Mathis and Richard Beymer, though Richard was dating Diane McBain. Elvis Presley also was around Hollywood at this time."

In the late fifties, Beymer seemed a cinch to become the biggest star of them all, grabbing plum roles in *The Diary of Anne Frank* and *West Side Story*, but suddenly his career folded. "He was a Pisces, very reclusive to begin with," says Nan. "Hal Gefsky was his agent at that time, and he sold Richard's contract to another agency. Richard was so disappointed he stopped acting, having lost his momentum at a crucial point."

Warren helped Nan out after Troy Donahue became her boyfriend and started behaving erratically. Born Merle Johnson Jr., the blond, blue-eyed

Donahue had studied journalism at Columbia University, and in Hollywood he felt underappreciated as an intellect. "Troy was volatile and suicidal," recalls Nan, "drinking too much, with the studio working him too hard. I spent two years fighting and carrying on with him. All he had on his mind was lying in the sun, getting a great tan. I urged him to get out and make something of himself." Though she adored Troy, he was so jealous that he frightened Nan, and she spent the night at Rona Barrett's. Tracking her down, Troy yelled, "Is Nan there?" "No, Troy . . . call back in an hour," Rona said. At daybreak, he broke down the door and dragged Nan by her ankles from the bed into the living room. Rona called the police. Nan and Troy made up, and they were sitting at a table in a joint on the Strip one night when Warren came in.

"Warren walked over to our table and started trying to intimidate Troy," Nan remembers. "I said, 'Warren, please leave.' " He did, and Nan later went outside and sat with him in a car and talked. He asked her for a date, but she explained she was still with Troy. "When I'm with somebody, I don't step out," she told him, but they later became friends. "I liked the way he outsmarted the big guys and didn't get destroyed," she says. When her affair with Troy finally ended, "Warren moved me out," she recalls. Years later, Troy explained his dilemma in Hollywood: "I was too good-looking—people didn't take me seriously."[54] He went on to TV fame in *Surfside 6* and *Hawaiian Eye*, then fell into obscurity. At his death of a heart attack in 2001, he was survived by a son, daughter, and fiancée, opera singer Zheng Cao.

After Troy, Nan met and married Eddie Robinson, and thereafter went under the name Nan Morris-Robinson. In an interview in 2000, she described Robinson as "beautiful, a genius with an IQ of 167, and very sensitive." Within hours of their first meeting, Eddie introduced her to some of his friends and said, "I want her to be my wife if she'll have me." After they married, he couldn't stand for Nan to be out of his sight. She loved him, but Eddie was beyond help. Though one of the most likable of Hollywood's bright young men of the fifties, he was overwhelmed by his father's fame and fell into alcoholism and drug addiction. After taking a dose of Antabuse to get off alcohol, he choked on food and died at the age of thirty-nine.

Warren's disappointment at Warner led to a new opportunity. His *Parrish* test was seen by Metro-Goldwyn-Mayer, and the studio put him under contract at four hundred dollars a week. He checked into the Chateau Marmont off Sunset Boulevard—the hip place to stay, then as now. He idled away his days at the Marmont pool, crashing industry A-list parties, using Shirley MacLaine's name as his calling card. Sometimes he charmed the guests with his piano stylings in the manner of Art Tatum and Erroll Garner. He owned few clothes but always looked dapper in an open-collared, loose shirt and gabardine trousers. "He looked like he was being kept," said Rita Stone, then a nightclub singer, later an assistant to Sam Peckinpah. "I remember when he first came out here," says Rita. "Nobody knew what he did. He never worked but was always out with gorgeous women. He looked like he was studying everybody—very quietly."

One night in 1959, Warren and Jane Fonda were dining at La Scala in Los Angeles. He started scanning the room for likely bedmates, as if Jane, a world-class beauty, wasn't enough. He spotted a green-eyed, dark-haired vamp at another table. She was Joan Collins, future star of *Dynasty,* who had just lost the title role of *Cleopatra* to Elizabeth Taylor. She appreciated the attention of Fonda's flirty escort. When she unblinkingly returned Warren's gaze, he lifted his glass to her and smiled, and his eyes roamed over Collins's exceptional figure. "She's got eyes that are big pools [and] the kind of face that will get more beautiful the next fifteen or twenty years," he later observed.[55] With a 38–23–37 figure gracing her five-foot-five frame, Collins was 126 pounds of British dynamite.

A companion at Joan's table said, "That boy who's looking at you is Shirley MacLaine's brother, Warren something or other." Joan later described Warren as having "blondish, slightly curly hair, worn rather longer than was fashionable, a square-cut Clark Kent type of jaw with a Kirk Douglas dimple in the chin—rather small greenish eyes, but a cute turned-up nose and a sensual mouth. . . . He wore a blue Brooks Brothers shirt and a tweed jacket." Despite the pimples she noticed on his face, Joan found him "appealing and vulnerable," and her interest was "somewhat piqued."[56] Jane was "quite pretty," in Collins's estimation, if "a bit full in the face." She doubted that Fonda would photograph well. Jane had already been advised, by a Warner executive, to have her back teeth removed and her jaw surgically broken and rebuilt to emphasize her high cheekbones. Studio chief Jack Warner also thought Jane was flat-chested and told her to get some falsies.[57]

At La Scala that night, Collins noted that Jane "was hanging onto Warren's every word . . . [but] out of the corner of my eye I saw Warren looking me over occasionally." A week or so later, he was playing the piano at a party given by Debbie Minardos Power, Tyrone Power's widow, at her house in the flats of Beverly Hills, when he saw Collins again. She looked campy and adorable in her outrageous getup—gray flannel boy's Bermuda shorts, gray knee socks, sneakers, and a green Brooks Brothers shirt. The outfit was a breather from the sexpot costumes she was wearing while filming *Seven Thieves*, in which she played a stripper. She'd just ended an affair with Loew's Inc. heir Arthur Loew Jr., and she was on the prowl for an able young lover. She stood watching Warren, but he was engrossed in playing his own renditions of such jazz greats as George Shearing and Oscar Peterson. After hovering over the piano for two hours to get his attention, she finally left.

The next day he rang her from the Chateau Marmont and asked her to dinner. Impressed that he'd wangled her telephone number without their ever having exchanged a word, she consented. She already had a studio-arranged date with Gardner McKay for a cocktail party, but she figured out a way to see both men during the course of the evening. McKay was a six-foot-four actor who'd recently been hailed by *Life* as the handsomest man in the world, but he struck no sparks with Joan. At the appointed time, she met McKay as planned, and they went to the cocktail party. She excused herself at 8 P.M., and went home to change into something less formal for her date with Warren.

He was waiting in his rented Chevrolet at the corner of Rodeo Drive and Santa Monica Boulevard when he saw her pull up in her rented yellow Ford, looking delectable in jeans and a shirt. Did she like "Mexican?" he asked, and she quipped, "Mexican what?" He replied, "Food, of course. I thought we'd go to the Casa Escobar—they make terrific margaritas." She got into his Chevy and they drove into the Santa Monica Boulevard traffic, relaxing with each other and feeling jolly and impish. Joan later revealed that she found him even handsomer than she'd originally thought, and despite his pimply complexion, his eyes were weirdly compelling. Like Sharon Washington years later, Joan noticed his hands on the steering wheel, and later wrote that they were "beautiful."

At dinner, over enchiladas and guacamole, he confided that he wanted the lead in *A Loss of Roses*, the new Inge play,[58] because he "was sitting out in California doing nothing."[59] Though supportive of his ambition, Joan, who believed in astrology, was more interested in the fact that he was an Aries, born on the same day, March 30, as her previous lover, Sydney Chaplin. Later that night, with more testosterone than even the concupiscent Collins could imagine, Warren gave new meaning to the word compatible, making nonstop love to her with a stamina she'd never before experienced. She was delighted, if somewhat exhausted, and it would never have occurred to her to describe Warren's lovemaking pejoratively, as producer Julia Phillips later did, when she called him a "priapic rammer."[60] Finally, Joan staggered from the bed and later told a friend, "In a few years, I'll be worn out."[61] So addicted was she to Warren that Twentieth Century-Fox suspended her twice for refusing roles in order to be with him.

When Metro assigned him to *Strike Heaven in the Face*, Warren flatly turned down the film and borrowed money to buy his way out of his despised contract. The inspired move paved the way for his big break. One day, his agent told him about the new William Inge movie, *Splendor in the Grass*, which was then being cast. "MCA sent Warren over to me as I was about to go into production with a picture," Inge recalled. "He seemed . . . just perfect . . . marked for success . . . the kind of boy everyone looked at knowing he was going to make it big. . . . As it turned out, we didn't start the picture right away, so I began casting for my play *A Loss of Roses*. I asked to see him again for that. Danny Mann, the director, liked him immediately. He went right into the play." In an uncanny stroke of luck, his co-star was Shirley Booth, the most popular dramatic actress on Broadway, who'd enchanted audiences in *Come Back, Little Sheba*, *Time of the Cuckoo*, and *Desk Set*.

Inge thought the young actor too shy to last long in show business. "I doubt that he will give interviews," he said. "I don't think he knows how he acts. He's hard-working and instinctive . . . a lot closer to William Holden [star of Inge's *Picnic*] . . . a Holden with temperament. . . . I wouldn't be too surprised if, some time, he gave up acting. . . . Right now he wants to prove to himself that he can act. But after he makes it, I don't know what he'll do with himself. He has awfully good instincts; he's quick to like people and quick to dislike them."[62]

Inge obsessed on able-bodied and ambitious young actors who became known as "Inge's boys," but such ephemeral, fundamentally impersonal liaisons contributed to his decline into alcoholism, drug addiction, and mental illness.[63] As a lonely homosexual male in the rabidly homophobic 1950s, and despite success and wealth, he had experienced difficulty in finding a lasting relationship with another man, and he often succumbed to near-suicidal depressions. Tennessee Williams once said to actress Barbara Baxley, "Don't you think that our whole lives, yours and mine and Bill's, have been one long nervous breakdown?"[64]

According to Rona Barrett, "Warren was trying to discover his own sexuality. He was always with women [and] I'm not saying he was ever with men, but I think there was a part of Warren that wanted to be a success so badly that he may have been willing to do almost anything to get there. . . . He spent a lot of time with homosexuals; he has his whole life. . . . There was, for the longest time, maybe his own questioning of himself, which he would never discuss with anybody else."

With the besotted Inge convinced that Warren could do no wrong, the young actor virtually took control of the Broadway production of *A Loss of Roses* and drove Shirley Booth out of the play. Inge excused Warren's behavior as that of "a young colt who's out in a new green pasture,"[65] and sided with Warren against the director, Daniel Mann. It was Mann who'd guided Shirley Booth to stardom in *Come Back, Little Sheba,* and later directed her in the films *About Mrs. Leslie* and *Hot Spell*.

Shirley Booth was replaced by the able but less popular Betty Field. "The play flopped," Warren recalled, "but it was good for me in that I got good reviews."[66] The reviews, however good, did not make him a star. He was still an unknown when the play closed after three weeks. His debut had occasioned no buzz whatsoever in theatrical circles, and he would never again appear in a Broadway play. There was a slim chance, however, that he'd make it into the film version of *A Loss of Roses*, and Inge still hoped to star Warren in *Splendor in the Grass*, if the production ever got started. Recalls costume designer Donfeld, "Warren first came to my attention in 1960, when my boss at Twentieth Century-Fox, Jerry Wald, was preparing the screen version of *A Loss of Roses*, to star Marilyn Monroe. Warren was being discussed for a screen test and possibly reprising his stage role. Both Wald and Miss Monroe were dead by the time Fox got around to filming Inge's story, which went into theaters retitled *The Stripper*, in 1963, starring Joanne Woodward and Richard Beymer in the role Warren originated. Better the whole project should've been dropped over Hanoi. But I got to know Warren socially during his tenure with Joan Collins. We partied and discothequed together throughout their sixties heyday."

Though Warren and his future best friend Jack Nicholson had not yet met, both were up for the lead in the film adaptation of James T. Farrell's classic American novel *Studs Lonigan*. Writer-producer Philip Yordan thought Warren a natural choice for the role of the good-natured Irish Catholic youth who's hemmed in by poverty and vice in Chicago in 1925. Even though still obscure, Warren started asking for rewrites, annoying the director, Irving Lerner, who cavalierly told Yordan to get rid of him. The title role went to Christopher Knight, a James Dean lookalike who, after *Studs Lonigan*, was never heard of again. Jack Nicholson was given the role of Weary Reilly, a punk who rapes a woman and goes to prison. Had Warren not been yanked from the picture, he and Nicholson would have had an extra ten years to cruise the Strip together.[67]

Warren's affair with Joan Collins made him a minor media celebrity long before he ever succeeded as an actor. Making Joan happy kept him busy, and she later revealed that they had sex four or five times a day, every day—and he talked on the phone at the same time he made love to her. Unfortunately, his dexterity as a lover exceeded his sense of responsibility. Subjecting Joan, who was twenty-six at the time, to the threat of motherhood four or five times a day was bound to get her pregnant, sooner or later. In the midst of the erotic Olympics, Warren received news that Inge's *Splendor in the Grass* was at last ready to begin filming. Joan Collins estimates that Warren telephoned Inge twenty-five times a day.[68] The playwright still wanted him for the lead.

In his screen test, Warren was letter-perfect. "Kid, you got the picture," said director Elia Kazan, who became Warren's formidable ally. Having guided Marlon Brando and James Dean to stardom, in *A Streetcar Named Desire* and *East of Eden*, respectively, Kazan now told his latest male protégé, "I don't even have to see the test. I need you to help me direct this movie."[69] Jane Fonda did a screen test opposite Warren for *Splendor*, but failed to land the role. Dan Petrie, who later directed Jane in *The Dollmaker*, was present and thought Jane looked like a female impersonator doing an impression of Henry Fonda.[70]

Rumors were rife that Inge was in love with Warren, and that Warren had encouraged the playwright's obsession in order to further his career. Inge's gay friends in Manhattan were calling him "Warren's fairy godfather."[71]

As Warren packed to fly to New York to begin filming on location, Joan told him, "I think I'm pregnant." When a shocked Warren wanted to know how such a thing could have happened, Joan quipped, "The butler did it." For

Warren, it was a "terrible" situation. At twenty-two, with his career about to take flight, he wasn't eager to get married. Fortunately, Joan was not eager to have a child. A realist, she saw both herself and Warren as "selfish, careless, argumentative, combative and just plain immature," not even suited for marriage, let alone parenthood. Warren found an abortionist in Newark, but at the last minute Joan's maternal feelings surfaced. She insisted on having the baby and subsequently putting it up for adoption.

Years later, Joan remembered that Warren told her, "Butterfly, we *can't*, we can't do it. Having a baby now will wreck both of our careers—you know it will." She agreed to undergo an abortion, and Warren rented a station wagon to drive them to the quack's office. En route, Joan almost lost her nerve. Warren drove on, holding back his tears and trying to reassure her. According to Joan, Warren said, "Nothing's going to go wrong—*nothing*. He's the best around. Don't even *think* about *that*, Butterfly."

In Joan's description, the abortion was "horrifying." Afterward, they rented an apartment on Fifth Avenue to use while Warren made *Splendor in the Grass* at New York Filmways studios. Joan studied Italian at Berlitz in preparation for filming *Esther and the King* in Rome. Though she was in love with Warren, she expected little of him, having been told by her astrologer, Ben Gary, whom she trusted implicitly, that as an Aries born on March thirtieth, he was "ruled by [his] cock," and wouldn't get married "for a long time. Probably not until he's forty-five or older . . . [after] many, many women." The astrologer added, "He will need a constant inflation of his ego—one woman will not suffice to satisfy him sexually." Joan's astrologer could hardly have been more prescient had he been the Delphic oracle.

One day Warren surprised Joan by giving her a carton of chopped chicken liver. "What's it for?" she asked. "It's your engagement ring, dummy," he said. Going along with the joke, she dug into the chicken liver and extracted a diamond-and-pearl ring. "We . . . er, could get married at the end of the year," he said. She didn't exactly leap at the chance. A busy, if second-rank, star, she was off to Rome to make her biblical potboiler. Later, by long distance telephone, they planned their wedding, and Joan went to London to choose her dress. Then, taking a weekend respite from filming, she flew to New York to rendezvous with Warren. They spent the entire forty-eight hours fighting. In a fit of marriage jitters, he accused her of having an affair in Rome.

"Warren didn't see the institution of marriage back then as something that was right for him," says Rona Barrett, "because he was very old-fashioned in a different kind of way. He saw his parents staying together whether it was a brilliant marriage or not, but he saw them stay together, and underneath it all, he wanted that kind of relationship and knew in his heart of hearts he just wasn't ready to make that kind of commitment. He liked playing the field. Because Warren picked such public women to get involved with, that's why there was so much conversation that it was all for show. All yack and no shack. But the truth is that for better or worse, I have had at least a dozen friends who've had relationships with Warren and they all say pretty much the same thing: 'charming, handsome, a great lover when he starts out, and, excuse the expression, he sort of peters out after several times.' But what the girls remember is those first two or three times, when they got so hung up and thought, 'Oh, well, if he made love to me like this two or three times, why can't he do it the fourth and fifth?' I've known Warren for a very long time. If every three minutes you've got a new girlfriend, and one is more beautiful and famous than the next, everybody is going to say, 'You're the stud extraordinaire.' Sometimes, that is not the case."

Though Joan would often be on the set with Warren while he filmed *Splendor in the Grass*, her days with him were numbered. In time, she revised her opinion of Warren as a lover. She was talking with Shirley MacLaine one day in 2000 when Shirley asked, "How was my brother?" Joan replied, "Overrated."[72] But the following year, when, at sixty-eight, she told Dominick Dunne she was "madly" in love with thirty-five-year-old theater company manager Percy Gibson, she said, "Listen, I never thought I could feel this way again. You remember me and Warren. It's like that."

CHAPTER TWO

NATALIE WOOD: THE BISEXUAL BLUES

APART FROM SEX, it always was power and manipulation that most fascinated Warren Beatty. Despite youth and inexperience, his power over William Inge paved the way for his film debut in Inge's *Splendor in the Grass*, and gave him clout in the movie industry. The film's director, Elia (Gadge) Kazan, was perhaps the most powerful man in Hollywood at the time. He'd always cast his pictures himself, but in the case of *Splendor*, he was inclined to go along with anything Inge wanted. Kazan had put great effort into convincing the prestigious Broadway playwright to undertake his first Hollywood script and did not want to jeopardize its success. "Warren Beatty was introduced to me by Bill Inge," recalled Kazan. "I liked Warren right off so I took a chance on him. Warren had never been in anything before. He had been a high school football player. . . . [He was] uncertain but charming. He still is."[1] Said Pat Hingle, who'd play Warren's father in the film, "He could hardly have been more of a neophyte."[2]

Amidst rumors of Inge's crush, Warren laughed it off, quipping, "They say that I secretly like men." Inge's lust unrequited, he assuaged his disappointment in his elegant East River apartment, drinking until he blacked out. In his eyes, Warren could do no wrong. Fellow actors and director Daniel Mann scorned Warren for the favoritism Inge had shown him in *A Loss of Roses*. Inge staunchly defended the actor, rationalizing Warren's flaws. "A really sound ego has its negative side, too," he said. "There's an awful lot of negativism in Warren, but he has a real intelligence. And he has a basic self-confidence that's made of iron. Indestructible."[3]

Unfortunately Inge himself was anything but indestructible. A dozen years later, after numerous suicide attempts, he killed himself on June 10, 1973. "Near the end of Bill's life," recalls actress Barbara Baxley, "when he was in great trouble, I turned to Tennessee Williams. He gave detailed instructions on what to do. He said, 'Don't let them put Bill where they put me [in a mental lockup],' and he asked hard questions so I could try to help Bill's sister decide what to do. 'What has he taken?' Williams asked. 'How much of this and how much of that?' He advised me how to go about getting Bill the proper help."[4] One of the saddest and most talented figures in the American theater, Inge created five enduring plays and the movie script for *Splendor*. All of them lay bare the vulnerability of the human heart, and they remain among the best in the American repertory.

Though a heterosexual love story, *Splendor in the Grass* actually expressed Inge's personal agony as a gay man forbidden by society to live according to his natural instincts. It was based on a true story Inge had heard during his youth in Kansas about two troubled high-school students. The story adapted for the screen focuses on the anguished passion of Bud Stamper and Wilma Dean Loomis, whose love for each other cannot be consummated in the puritanical atmosphere of 1929 Kansas. Repressing their normal desires drives them to nervous collapses; Inge was being driven to suicide by a homophobic society. In both cases, heterosexual tyranny destroyed innocent people by denying them the right to love and consigned them to lives of shame and guilt. The power of *Splendor in the Grass* sprang from Inge's ability to channel the poignancy of homoerotic angst into a mainstream heterosexual story. The feat was often attempted by gay playwrights and novelists but never with the compassion and universality Inge achieved.

Warren's starring in *Splendor in the Grass* was full of paradoxes. Though he was becoming famous as a voracious heterosexual, his career was being built on essentially gay material. "It is oddly interesting that Beatty's acting should be at its best in milieus, and among people, of homosexual or bisexual persuasion," wrote Lawrence J. Quirk in *The Films of Warren Beatty*. "He made his initial impact in *Splendor*, a 1961 film which, to sophisticated 1990 eyes, seems more the memories of a repressed gay's childhood than a depiction of 1928 hetero doings in a stultifying small-town Kansas atmosphere."[5]

The irony was not lost on Warren, who said, as filming began, "I'm a bit scared and worried, but I'd try anything involving Bill and Gadge." In the course of filming in and around New York, Inge kept in close touch with the company, and even assumed a small role in the film, playing Reverend Whitman, at Kazan's request, because he wanted to be as close as possible to Warren. Inge relished his role of mentor, and loved interpreting Warren to the press. Originally, Carolyn Jones was to be Warren's costar. She was a promising newcomer who'd been nominated for an Oscar for *The Bachelor Party*, yet her later career faltered. After marrying producer Aaron Spelling, she made inconsequential films like *Ice Palace*, ending up in TV sitcoms, and was determined unsuitable for *Splendor*. Kazan preferred Natalie Wood, though she lacked the virginal aura he was after, or Jane Fonda, or the enchanting Lee Remick, the protégée Kazan had introduced in *A Face in the Crowd*, but Remick was unavailable. Earlier, both Remick and Carroll Baker had vied with Natalie, unsuccessfully, for the role of Judy in *Rebel Without a Cause*,[6] and when Warner Brothers lured Natalie back to the studio by promising her *Splendor*, Kazan at first demurred. Though Natalie had shot to fame as the little girl who didn't believe in Santa Claus in *Miracle on 34th Street*, costarring Edmund Gwenn and Maureen O'Hara, she had never achieved stardom on the level of such child stars as Shirley Temple, Jane Withers, Butch Jenkins, and Margaret O'Brien. As James Dean's high-school girlfriend in *Rebel Without a Cause*, she'd briefly recaptured the spotlight, but her career as an adult actress was later derailed by her lackluster performance in *Marjorie Morningstar*. "People said generally that she was finished, washed up," Kazan recalled. "We got her inexpensively," he added, explaining how she finally won the female lead in *Splendor*.[7]

Psychologically, Natalie was just as fragile as Inge, and just as susceptible to Warren's predatory wiles. She'd eventually fall under his spell, but not right away. Richard Sylbert, *Splendor*'s production designer, says, "As opposed to Hollywood mythology, Warren and Natalie had nothing to do with each other on *Splendor in the Grass*. They disliked each other intensely. I was there *all* the time. It wasn't until long after that that they got together. Warren was with Joan Collins." And Joan wouldn't let him out of her sight.[8]

In her mid-twenties, Natalie had matured into a beauty with "great big marvelous huge mothering brown eyes,"[9] wrote journalist Tom Wolfe. Adds Dick Sylbert, who created forty-six sets for *Splendor* on two soundstages at Filmways Studios in the Bronx, "She was a miniature. Five foot four. She was perfect. When photographed later in *Gypsy*, she looked five foot nine. Perfect, charming, very sweet. Spent a long time in psychoanalysis. A really wonderful girl."

Since early 1958, Natalie had been married to the dashing Robert John (R.J.) Wagner, who'd never quite made it as a major star despite scene-stealing appearances in 1952's *With a Song in My Heart*, as the wounded soldier serenaded by Susan Hayward, and in the 1953 film *Titanic*, with Barbara Stanwyck, Clifton Webb, Audrey Dalton, and Thelma Ritter. "R.J. was wonderful," says Sylbert. "That was a good marriage." The son of a rich steel executive, R.J. grew up next door to the Bel-Air Country Club, "with nothing on my mind, much, but my hair," he admitted.[10] When he decided to go into show business, he hired the gay agent Henry Willson, which automatically gave rise to rumors of bisexuality.[11] These would still persist in 2001, when Suzanne Finstad's biography of Natalie, *Natasha*, laid the blame for the failure of the Wagners' marriage on Natalie's walking in on R.J. having sex with another man. Finstad seems completely unaware of Natalie's bisexuality, which would certainly have made Natalie more accepting of R.J.'s. Mostly, Finstad seems determined at every opportunity to minimize Warren's importance in Natalie's life, which is odd, since Warren was the primary cause of the Wagners' breakup.

The marriage was already shaky, largely due to Natalie's insatiable need for emotional reinforcement. Said Kazan, "Natalie was a restless 'chick' who reminded me of the 'bad' girls in high school who looked like 'good' girls. . . . I could see that the crisis in her career was preparing her for a crisis in her personal life. Then she told me she was being psychoanalyzed. That did it. Poor R.J., I said to myself."[12]

Like many former child stars—Elizabeth Taylor comes immediately to mind—Natalie's personality had been damaged by working, as a minor, in the studio system. She emerged from the experience addicted to being catered to, and she tended to turn the men in her life into butlers, secretaries, and caregivers. At the same time, the false Hollywood values she'd acquired made her a snob. She got along fine with such adoring gay men as Mart Crowley and Tommy Thompson, who enjoyed being her males-in-waiting.[13] With heterosexual men, her expectations were unrealistic. It wasn't enough that a man loved her, he had to be a success, and in this respect she was truly a creature of her industry, sick in a very Hollywood way. When Wagner's career failed to take off, and hers soared, she became bored with him, developing a crush on Frank Sinatra, her costar in *Kings Go Forth*. Before her marriage she'd had one of the most active sex lives in Hollywood, going through a succession of lovers including Jimmy Williamson (a high-school affair); Barbara Hutton's playboy son Lance Reventlow; businessmen Bob Neal and Nicky Hilton; Elvis Presley; actors Tom Irish, Bobby Hyatt, Scott Marlowe, Raymond Burr, Robert Vaughn, Nick Adams, and Dennis Hopper; and director Nicholas Ray, who guided her to an Oscar nomination in *Rebel Without a Cause*. "We were both fucking Natalie Wood," Hopper recalled, referring to the simultaneous affairs Natalie pursued with Hopper and Ray.[14] No one—at least no male she'd yet been involved with—seemed capable of satisfying her. Natalie, future star of the open-marriage classic *Bob and Carol and Ted and Alice*, and R.J. were accompanied on their honeymoon by the equinely proportioned Nick Adams, and the three had checked into the Waldorf Towers together.[15] In the first few years of the marriage, she became dependent on Seconal, Dexedrine, Nembutal, and Dexatrim, and her life veered out of control.

When Warren first met her on the set, he was not impressed, and the feeling was mutual. "She didn't like him," recalled Robert Redford, Natalie's co-star in *Inside Daisy Clover* and *This Property Is Condemned*. According to Natalie herself, Warren was "difficult to work with," and she secretly christened him "Mental Anguish," or "M.A.," remarking to makeup artist Bob Jiras, "Here comes M.A.," when Warren arrived on the set. Assistant director Don Kranze considered Warren "a pain the the ass. . . . His emotional maturity was about thirteen." For Natalie, there was no avoiding Warren since they didn't have separate dressing rooms and had to share the same makeup area. Associate producer Charlie Maguire told Kranze, "She can't stand him, she wants him out of there." Warren's vanity seemed excessive even for an actor, and his self-adoration became such a joke that Kazan ordered the crew on *Splendor* to cover all mirrors in the makeup area, because he spent so much time gazing at his image. Kranze came upon Warren peering into a mirror and meticulously grooming his eyelashes with a straight pin, "putting that pin into each eyelash, and separating and moving them forward . . . separating every goddamn eyelash. . . . This is six feet of pure ego."[16] Eventually Kazan gave him a hand mirror with the inscription "Good God, Warren."

After their early scenes, Warren and Natalie still were not getting along; his mind was on Joan, and Natalie's was on R.J. Then Joan left for London early in the production to make *Esther and the King*,[17] and one day Warren and Natalie started filming a passionate love scene. According to Kazan—and despite what Richard Sylbert remembers—sparks flew. "It was clear to Natalie," Kazan observed, "that Warren was bound for the top; this perception was an aphrodisiac."[18] Sylbert adds, "Warren was very pretty. He had these big bee-stung lips, as Kazan used to describe them." In *Natasha*, Sylbert revealed, "The crew called him 'donkey dick.' "[19] Kazan once told a film scholar from UCLA, "All of a sudden, he and Natalie became lovers. . . . I wasn't sorry; it helped their love scenes." The filming was "spurred on by what was happening in the wings," he added. "Warren was a little 'snotty' . . . [Barbara] Loden [who later married Kazan] a little bitchy . . . I enjoyed them."[20]

Kazan was a past master at wresting, from actors like Brando, Dean, and Beatty, performances notable for a natural coiled edge. There was always a suggestion of violence, of great power barely held in check. Though Warren was not really in the league of Brando and Dean, he, along with Paul Newman, Robert Redford, and Steve McQueen, were the most interesting U.S. actors to emerge in the hiatus between the death of Dean in 1955 and the emergence over a decade later of the next era's major stars, Dustin Hoffman, Al Pacino, and Robert De Niro.

Splendor had a sixty-three-day schedule, with location shooting in West Islip, Long Island; Victory Boulevard in Staten Island; Horace Mann High School gym in the Bronx; High Falls, New York; the waterfalls of Roundout Creek near Kent, Connecticut; and Christ's Church in Riverdale. Sylbert's design of every scene, from the dance in the gym to Deanie Loomis's smotheringly respectable middle-class house, was unforgettable. In preproduction, Sylbert realized he needed a house with a grocery attached, since Deanie's father was a grocer, and he found a perfect place in Staten Island, owned by Nicholas Blanchard, a water tender for the Staten Island ferry. Blanchard rented it to Kazan, and allowed his house to be retouched, with the addition of gingerbread, a garden, and a stake fence. For interior shots of the Loomis house, Sylbert built a complete replica of the Blanchard home, so that he and Kazan could furnish it as they liked. The set for Warren's parents' house was equally inspired. Sylbert made the Stampers' huge home reflect the nouveau riche taste of the 1920s, replete with phony antiques and Elizabethan stonework which was obviously plaster made to resemble stone. In these settings, Warren forged two of his finest moments as an actor: pushing Natalie to her knees in the smoldering, sadistic love scene in the Loomis house, and trying to choke back his tears when Barbara Loden slaps his face in the vaguely incestuous confrontation in her bedroom in the Stamper home.

When a reporter from *Woman's Day* visited the set and wanted to quiz Warren about Shirley MacLaine, he made short work of the interview by saying, "Maybe it's sibling rivalry. . . . We're not that close right now."[21] Kazan cut in and said, "He'll be bigger than Jimmy Dean." One day R. J. Wagner appeared on the *Splendor* set and discovered Warren with his arm around Natalie's waist as they waited for the lighting of the next scene to be set. Warren accused R.J. of keeping tabs on him and Natalie. R.J.'s "sexual humiliation was public," wrote Kazan.[22]

Finstad states in *Natasha* that Natalie went into hysterics when she discovered R.J. in a homosexual encounter a day or so following Natalie and R.J.'s double date with Warren and Joan.[23] R.J. denied any allegation of bisexuality, despite Natalie's little sister Lana Wood's assertion about R.J.'s alleged *in flagrante delicto* episode, which was followed in quick succession by Natalie's overdosing on sleeping pills, the Wagners' separation, and Warren and Natalie's going public with their affair.[24] In failing to take into account Natalie's own bisexuality, Finstad overemphasizes the importance of the anecdotes about R.J.'s, and underestimates Warren's role in the marital crisis.

But Warren was not the only name on Natalie's dance card. No male would ever be able to claim that distinction. One of her lesbian flings was with a woman we shall call Joan Eliot, who, although she wore khaki pants and Brooks Brothers shirts, spent a great deal of time preening in front of the mirror. A close friend of hers recalls, "Joan was very butch. Lipstick lesbians loved her and were always taking her home and throwing her clothes off. Growing up in the South, her fantasy lover was Natalie Wood, and it would all come true years later when she became a successful theatrical agent in Manhattan. Joan was casting a play, and when the star dropped out, it occurred to Joan to ask Natalie Wood to replace her."

To everyone's surprise, Natalie said she was interested. Joan flew to the Coast and checked into the Chateau Marmont. The weekend was just beginning when she called Natalie, who was living with R.J. He was not at home when Joan arrived to talk with Natalie about the role. The girls immediately hit it off. Another case of a lipstick lesbian, Natalie, going after a butch, Joan. Natalie came on to her, and the two girls spent the entire weekend together. In bed, Natalie seemed to know exactly what to do. Joan later told her friend that Natalie took a lot of pills. She'd lay out the pills in lines, according to color. At one point R.J. came into the bedroom to get a shirt. During the weekend, R.J. and Natalie had a brief conversation, and he went on his way. Natalie and Joan didn't leave the house until Sunday night or Monday morning.

With this apparent latitude and freedom in the Wagner marriage, it seems obvious that Natalie wouldn't have left R.J. if R.J.'s encounter with another man had been the issue. The issue was Warren.

"I do not know which came first," said Lana Wood, who often visited the set as *Splendor* neared completion, "the end of her marriage or Warren Beatty, though I suspect—now that I know Warren—he might have precipitated the end of a deteriorating situation. Warren is nothing if not charming and insistent. He is accustomed to having his way. All I know is that one day Natalie, weeping, her hand bleeding because she had squeezed and broken one of her cherished crystal wineglasses, arrived at our house to tell us that R.J. was moving out and that the marriage was over."[25]

Natalie was now completely addicted to Warren, because he made her feel womanly and beautiful the way no other man had. Indeed, there was a glow about her in *Splendor* that she would display in only one other film, *Love with the Proper Stranger*, in which she based her performance on the pain she'd experienced as a result of Warren's fear of commitment. In the final scene of *Splendor*, where her voice-over quotes Wordsworth's lines about not regretting the past, "the splendor in the grass, the glory in the flower," but finding strength in what remains, it's as if she's seeing the beginning and the end of her relationship with Warren. As Finstad points out, she was also drawing on the heartbreak of her thwarted first love, the rebellious and wiry junior-high-school farmboy Jimmy Williams. The Wordsworth lyric also expresses the philosophy found in most of Elia Kazan's movies: the important thing is not the resolution of discord but acceptance of life on life's terms.

Rona Barrett recalls seeing Warren around this time with Joan Collins. "I was spending a weekend in Palm Springs and I was invited to dinner at Trader Vic's with Kirk and Anne Douglas. Into this restaurant there arrived Natalie Wood and Bob Wagner, Warren and Joan, Tony Curtis and Janet Leigh. We were all laughing and having a good time, hugging, kissing, telling stories, and drinking. I can't believe it, I thought, I'm here with all these people and my dreams are coming true. I wasn't really famous Rona Barrett [with her own network television show] yet. The following Monday or Tuesday, within days of this great time, the headlines come: Warren Beatty dumps Joan Collins for Natalie Wood. R. J. Wagner is in a state of shock. Shortly thereafter Tony and Janet break up. Everyone, except for Kirk and Anne, breaks up. And I thought, Here they were all together, never revealing that there was anything wrong, and they were all switching partners."

After announcing her separation, Natalie went to Florida to be with Warren while he filmed *All Fall Down*. She had given up a lot for him (she would never stop loving R.J.), but, according to Dick Sylbert, "It never entered Warren's mind to marry her or any woman." Years later, Joan Collins reflected, "Warren was the most ambitious person I'd ever met, [and] a sizzling romance with the hottest film star helped him *enormously*. Don't forget he dumped Jane Fonda for me and I introduced him to everyone I knew in Hollywood."[26]

Splendor had not yet been released, and Warren had never been seen on the screen, but Florabel Muir wrote in the *New York Daily News*, "He's so choosy he has turned down nine major pictures he felt weren't right for him. He won't retreat from his $150,000 asking price, even for a fat part in a Hemingway film. . . . Off the set, there's no doubt whatsoever that Warren is catnip for the opposite sex. The six-foot-one bachelor with brown hair and half-closed blue-green eyes is already a star, romantically, at twenty-four." Elia Kazan recalled that Warren suffered from "lower back trouble," and when Kazan asked if it hampered his lovemaking, Warren replied, "Well, it doesn't hurt them."[27]

So excited were they about their love affair that Warren and Natalie hired the same press agent and business manager and began to discuss forming a corporation to produce their own movies—all before he'd ever appeared on a screen. He had her completely in his power. At one point he was up for the role of Tony in *West Side Story*, but so, ironically, was R.J. In real life as well as reel life, Natalie wanted both men, and she was in danger of losing both. Over her bitter protests, the male lead in *West Side Story* went to Richard Beymer. Warren and Natalie's first public date was a screening of *West Side Story* on July 27, 1961, and on August 15, Natalie signed a property settlement with R.J., splitting their assets equally. On another date in 1961, Warren and Natalie went backstage to congratulate Robert Redford following his Broadway curtain call in *Barefoot in the Park*. Natalie later confided to Redford that she "couldn't be alone," and longed for a solid marriage and children to raise. "Vulnerability was part of her attractiveness," said Redford. "She had a girl-woman quality: she was a little girl, but a woman at the same time."[28]

Splendor and *West Side Story* premiered almost simultaneously in Manhattan in October 1961, and opening-night crowds were staggered by the sight of Warren and Natalie arriving together, Warren's fair, luminous complexion heightened by his dark evening clothes, and Natalie swathed in white mink and white satin. With Warren's first film, he achieved an instant stardom that eclipsed even Shirley's. Ecstatic, he celebrated by returning to California and renting a house above the Sunset Strip. *Life* crowned him "the biggest new name in American entertainment" and "the most exciting American male in movies."[29] Columnist Hedda Hopper agreed with *Life*, echoing their encomium, but chided Warren and Natalie for allegedly refusing to make a personal appearance tour for *Splendor*.[30]

As it was distributed around the nation, the film stirred enormous controversy. Natalie's bathtub breakdown scene marked the first time that the star of a feature-length American film appeared stark naked. The picture was widely praised and damned, but most of the major reviewers recognized it as a classic. *Newsweek* called it the best picture of the year, and it made the *New York Times* ten-best list. With Warren's debut, he scored a home run, and even hostile reviewers compared him with the greatest contemporary actors. Wrote *Time*, "With a facial and vocal suggestion of Montgomery Clift and mannerisms of James Dean, he is the latest incumbent in the line of arrogant, attractive, hostile, moody, sensitive, self-conscious, bright, defensive, stuttering, self-seeking and extremely talented actors who become myths before they are thirty."[31]

Much of the credit for his achievement was due to Kazan's expertise at presenting hunks on screen in the most erotic conceivable light—Brando's famous torn-T-shirt scene in *A Streetcar Named Desire* and James Dean's courtship of Julie Harris on a Salinas rooftop in *East of Eden*, for example. "If Warren Beatty couldn't act, he could make stardom on his looks, and if he was cross-eyed and bald, he could make it on his acting," said Kazan. Not every critic agreed, but even those who found his acting skills deficient were impressed.

Phillip K. Scheuer of the *Los Angeles Times* wrote of Warren's "clean-cut sincerity that more than compensates for his occasionally stumbling delivery." *Box Office* hailed this "rugged youngster whose appearance and acting are a cross between Marlon Brando and the late James Dean." No male had ever appeared quite as pretty, and at the same time as macho, on the American screen. Abroad, pretty men had always proliferated, from Jean Marais in Cocteau's classics, Horst Buchholtz in *Mon Petit*, and Alain Delon in *Rocco and His Brothers* to Laurence Harvey in *Romeo and Juliet* and Albert Finney in *Saturday Night and Sunday Morning*. In *Splendor*, which was released before androgyny became commonplace in the late 1960s, Beatty made it okay for a male to be a sex object in a way that heretofore, in films, only women were. His pouting, languorously lounging about in a series of alluring poses, teasing, making Natalie kneel before him in the Loomis house, repulsing her advances at the senior party, and finally letting Jan Norris seduce him under the waterfall, all were precedent-setting. Kazan lovingly photographed him as he might have photographed Marilyn Monroe, revealing Warren as a baby-pink but quintessentially masculine confection, one who would strike both women and men as highly edible. Arlene Dahl dubbed him "Warren Beauty."

"He has never been better since," observed Kazan in 2000. "He was new then. What is terrible with an actor is that it's hard for him to prevail over success . . . more difficult to prevail over than failure. They all use success to isolate themselves, to keep aloof from experiencing life, so that the more success an actor has, the more he acquires the look of wax fruit; he is no longer devoured by life. That is why I must always find new actors for my films, among those who do not have—not yet—success, among those who still have a passion, an anxiety, a violence that they will almost always lose later. . . . I try to catch my actors at the moment when they're still, or once again, human."

Kazan was perhaps unduly harsh on Warren, whose later performances in

Bonnie and Clyde, *Shampoo*, and *Reds* almost matched his magnificence in *Splendor*. Kazan also was tough on the film itself, saying that although he liked *Splendor*, he didn't consider it "particularly filmic,"[32] but in another interview, he defended it against its critics, stating, "Everybody says it's just a big can of corn and sentimental or some damn thing. They're full of shit. . . . It's beautiful."[33]

In any case, with *Splendor*, Warren Beatty became the sixties' first full-blown screen idol, *homme fatale*, and culture hero, one reflecting the younger generation's impatience with a sexually restrictive society. His six-foot-one physique had a natural-looking perfection to it; his broad shoulders tapering to a slender torso and lean hips betrayed no sign of artificial help from barbells, as in the later heyday of weight lifters like Sylvester Stallone and Arnold Schwarzenegger. Indeed, Warren eschewed jogging and tennis as well as weight lifting, maintaining enviable definition and tone largely by means of healthy living habits. He subsisted on a diet of health foods, avoiding drugs, tobacco, and heavy drinking. His talent was as natural as his physique; every move he made in the film was informed by the unpremeditated, genetic gracefulness that typifies many outstanding athletes.

Critics exalted him as a major new performer, Archer Winston of the *New York Post* writing, "The way he projects his personality and emotions in front of the camera is an amazing achievement for a young man so lacking in experience." "One of Kazan's best films," wrote James Powers of the *Hollywood Reporter*, who ranked *Splendor* with Kazan's best work, citing *East of Eden*. Both Beatty and the film had detractors. Bosley Crowther of the *New York Times* wryly wrote, "Except that he talks like Marlon Brando and has some small mannerisms of James Dean, Mr. Beatty is a striking individual." Years later, journalist David Thomson described the Beatty phenomenon and its impact on the post-fifties public: "He produced a heat-haze atmosphere of erotic frustration. No film had been so infused with the adolescent's urgency about sex. Beatty had a desperate smile fixed on some faraway bliss or orgasm he could not yet feel, but which accounted for the wild dark hair, the luster in his narrowed eyes and the sensual mouth. *Splendor* was like a wet dream; you came out of it in a stupor of rapture and guilt. With one film, Beatty was established as a male sex symbol." The usually more sedate critic Molly Haskell confessed, "You want to kiss him with your eyes open."

The competitive Shirley MacLaine reacted characteristically to her little brother's superior celebrity. Later on, in 1970, when she was attempting a come-back in a one-woman stage show, an audience member yelled, "Where's Warren?" "You want Warren?" she retorted. "You can have him! Practically every other woman has."[34] The outburst further underscored the brother and sister's prickly personalities. It is almost impossible to come up against either without getting punctured. For those who don't like to bleed, Warren and Shirley are best appreciated at a distance, and both are the exact opposite of their kooky (Shirley) and sensitive (Warren) screen personas. Socially, Warren can be blunt to the point of rudeness, criticizing people to their faces, and he has been known to have his representatives deny workmen their full fees. Shirley can be equally cruel and uncivil; when I met her in the 1960s at the home of *Good Housekeeping* fiction editor Leonhard Dowty, she was all business, with little taste for levity, let alone kookiness. A movie-studio executive was also present that evening in Dowty's home in Greenwich Village, and when he told Shirley he was a vice president at Paramount, she remarked, "Oh, one of Bob Evans's yes-men." On another occasion, I dined with Shirley and her date, television anchor Sandor Van Ocher, and author Angela Huth at Le Madrigal restaurant on Manhattan's Upper East Side. Although I'd introduced her to Miss Huth, whom Shirley admired and had been pursuing, Shirley snapped at me over some opinion or other I expressed, and at the end of dinner, neither she nor Mr. Van Ocher reached for the check, despite the fact that the event had been arranged to help Shirley acquire film rights to Miss Huth's novel, *Somewhere There Must Be a Brass Band* (published in the U.K. as *The Nowhere Girl*). I received no thanks for paying the hefty bill, which ran into hundreds of dollars.

Shirley's insistence on the perks of stardom sometimes backfired. Recalls a leading television and movie director, who requested anonymity, "The author Charles Higham once arrived in a city at the same time as Shirley, and it was pouring rain. 'That's the wrong car,' Shirley said, when her driver arrived. She wanted [a Cadillac or a Rolls-Royce], and told the driver, 'You'd better bring it to me.' Higham left in his car, and the last he saw of her, she was still standing in the rain."

Karen Bihari, a friend of Warren's, was appearing in a bus-and-truck tour of *Godspell* when her show followed Shirley's into a theater on the east coast in the mid-1970s. "We got into our hotel in North Carolina, and after checking in, I went outside and saw Shirley MacLaine by the pool. She was alone, and since it was a hazy day, she was fully clothed, so it seemed okay to approach her. I was about twenty years old, soft- and gentle-spoken, finding my way in the theater, and was usually treated graciously by stars I ran into, like Ginger Rogers, who talked with me for two hours and said, 'If it wasn't for fans like you, I wouldn't have a job, kiddo.' So I went over to Shirley and said, 'Excuse me, I just finished reading your book, and I know your brother, Warren. Can I have your autograph?' *'Leave me alone,'* she said. It was so mean and evil, I ripped my paperback of her book in half."

A more charitable view of Shirley was expressed by one of her peers in the movie industry, director Curtis Harrington, who said, "She's abrasive but honest and direct. You always know where you stand with her."

Warren's performance in *Splendor in the Grass* caught the eye of the glamorous young U.S. first lady, Jacqueline Kennedy, who, eager to meet him, suggested to her husband, President John F. Kennedy, that Warren should play him in the upcoming film *PT 109*, an account of the president's heroic WWII exploits in the navy. JFK had already spoken to Frank Sinatra, who was eager to assume the role. When Jackie heard this, she told the White House protocol chief, Letitia Baldrige, "Thank goodness I'm not portrayed in the movie. Sinatra would probably pick that dreary Angie Dickinson to play me." JFK, who knew that Warren was a loyal Kennedy Democrat, eventually agreed to cast him. After press secretary Pierre Salinger conferred with the producer of *PT 109*, Bryan Foy, he said, "Foy described Beatty as mixed up, and he said something about Kennedy also coming off as 'mixed up' if Beatty played him in the movie."

Flattered at the notion of being portrayed by the latest male sex symbol, JFK dismissed Foy's remarks and urged Salinger to go to L.A. and "feel Beatty out," Salinger recalls, "in terms of whether he might want to do the role, and whether or not I thought he was a mixed-up person, whatever that meant. So I went to L.A., met Beatty at Peter Lawford's home, and found him to be completely charming and likable. He wanted to do the movie, he said, and would be honored—except that he loathed Bryan Foy and felt that he couldn't work with him."

After Warren declined the role, JKF told Salinger to cast someone else, and Salinger chose thirty-six-year-old Cliff Robertson, later a Best Actor Oscar winner for *Charly*. When Jackie heard this, she complained that she didn't even know who Robertson was. Refusing to give up on Beatty, Jackie suggested that he be invited to the White House for dinner, and offered to extend her personal invitation. She felt confident that she could persuade Beatty to take the role, given a chance to sit next to him at table.

Amazingly, Warren refused to accept any more calls from the White House following his meeting with Salinger. When Jack Warner, whose studio was producing the film, told Warren that the president wanted him to come to the capital to "soak up the atmosphere," Warren said, "Let *him* come here to Los Angeles and soak up my atmosphere."[35] Not one to give up easily, Jackie had her social secretary attempt to ring Warren, but he proved unreachable. When he did not answer or even acknowledge a personal handwritten invitation from the first lady, Jackie said, "What unparalleled arrogance, just like all of those superficial Hollywood types. The better looking they are, the worse their manners."

After *PT 109* flopped in early 1963, Warren encountered JFK, who said, "you sure made the right decision on that one." Warren's personal chemistry was better with Robert F. Kennedy and, in time, he would become RFK's confidant, according to *Variety*'s Peter Bart.

Being in demand in Hollywood—and hard to get—raised Warren's salary per picture to $150,000 (the equivalent of one million dollars in 2001). At the time, his contemporaries' salaries ranged from Tony Perkins's $40,000 for *Psycho* to Steve McQueen's $300,000 for *Soldier in the Rain*. Warren's agent, Stan Kamen of the William Morris office, was one of the best, representing (then and/or later) Barbra Streisand, Chevy Chase, Goldie Hawn, and Diane Keaton. The Morris office was still, in the sixties, the bellwether of talent agencies, having handled the giants of the business, from Charlie Chaplin, Al Jolson, and Mae West to Frank Sinatra, Marilyn Monroe, and Elvis Presley. Enjoying his new affluence, Warren bought a Thunderbird. One of his first girls at this time was Cher, who had not yet hooked up with Sonny Bono. Warren had a fling with her in 1962, when she was still an unknown in show business. "I was only sixteen," Cher recalled, and added, "Maybe I can get out of it with that."[36]

Secure in his new stardom, Warren proved as brash and outspoken as his older sister, making the crucial mistake of insulting Bosley Crowther in Sardi's one night. Future decades of bad reviews in the *New York Times* were the baleful result, for hell hath no fury like a critic scorned. While the Hollywood Women's Press Club gave Warren its Sour Apple Award, citing him as the most uncooperative actor in Hollywood,[37] he was more diplomatic within the industry, taking care to cultivate such powerful allies as mogul Lew Wasserman, ruler of the then-notorious MCA show-business monopoly. When the U.S. Justice Department broke up MCA in 1962, Democrat Warren sounded like anything but a liberal champion of the working man: "I think MCA is getting a bum rap," he said.[38] But he was otherwise genuine in his enthusiasm for the Democratic Party, and he was welcomed into the circle of politicians and stars who flocked to Camelot. Hollywood moguls shrewdly sized up Warren as the rebel they could trust, and even make use of. They sensed that, under his bluster, he was really one of them. Though he wanted to shake up the Establishment (and would), he also wanted to be a functioning part of it.

In Los Angeles he wasted no time making a beeline for the A-list, currying favor with such blue-chip L.A. socialites as agent/producer Charles Feldman, who became his mentor. Sam Spiegel, producer of such megahits as *The African Queen*, *On the Waterfront*, *The Bridge on the River Kwai*, and *Lawrence of Arabia*, also took Warren under his wing, as did veteran pioneer independent producer Samuel Goldwyn, real-estate titan Robert Tisch, and literary legend Clifford Odets, author of *Waiting for Lefty*, *Golden Boy*, and *Clash by Night*. When Warren, who wanted to talk literature, came to call, Odets, who was now old and feeble, only wanted to play gin rummy.

The affable, luxury-loving Sam Spiegel, portly and balding in his early sixties, often took Warren and other friends cruising on his yacht, the *Malahne*. In addition to the crew of twenty and a *cordon bleu* chef, those on board for a typical outing in the Mediterranean might include Yul Brynner and his wife, a brace of Hollywood money men, a living legend such as Claudette Colbert or Rosalind Russell, Frank Sinatra, and a foursome of youthful starlets, each determined to give Spiegel such a good time that he'd promise to make her a star.[39] Spiegel became Warren's personal and professional role model in Hollywood. Being tremendously competitive, Warren would criticize his mentors in time, gradually discarding them as he became a mogul himself. There was something in him—a combination of insecurity and competitive drive—that made him want to invalidate other men. Friendship with members of his own sex would be difficult and rare for years.

But from the movie industry's point of view, the young star, so unlike Brando and Dean in his attitude toward the Establishment, was choosing his friends wisely, and in time, the picture business would come to regard Warren as a bridge between Hollywood and Washington. Director Stanley Kubrick knew exactly whom to call when he needed to keep the U.S. government from blocking release of *Dr. Strangelove*, which satirized the administration's aggressive Cold War policy. Warren set up a screening for high White House officials. They thought the Kubrick film hilarious; it was released without any interference from the federal government.

Warren would often demonstrate more diplomatic savvy in Washington than in Hollywood. While scripts and roles were being flung at him in L.A., he said, "The producers are governed by fear. They don't know whether I'm any good or not, but they're afraid I might be, so they want to hire me." Shirley was at the peak of her career, pulling down $250,000 for films such as *Can-Can* and *Irma La Douce,* but *Time* called her "a female Jerry Lewis," and Bosley Crowther thought her "frightening" in *Can-Can*. With the exception of her poignant portrait of a lonely, clinging, suicidal girl in *The Apartment*, she remained shrill and strident, but regularly received Oscar nominations, a darling of her industry.

Warren's turbo-charged rise as an actor eclipsed his sister's reputation for many years, until she at last developed impressive acting muscle decades later in *The Turning Point*, playing a middle-aged woman. Inevitably, Shirley began to snipe at him in the press, and Warren was too self-involved and frenetically driven to handle his relationship with her with the required degree of finesse. Fearing charges of nepotism, and loath to be referred to as Shirley's little brother, he refused to discuss her in interviews, and his abruptness and apparent absence of normal familial feeling was quite understandably interpreted by the press as evidence of a brother-sister feud.

He told reporters, "I am *not* Shirley's brother. She is *my* sister!"[40] Sadly, *Family Weekly* reported an "estrangement." It didn't look good, and Warren, attempting to repair the damage, said, "She has great talent. Let's just leave it at that." Such coldness was the worst possible tactic he could have chosen. It hurt his sister's feelings, and, being Shirley, she fired back, saying, "We haven't been close for the past seven years. I only know what I read in the papers about Warren. We rarely see each other anymore. I've tried to reach out to him, but he just doesn't seem to want to communicate with me."[41]

His reputation for being difficult was once explained by a later co-worker, the actress Estelle Parsons, who said, "It's a game out there in Hollywood. The people who make the crazy demands and do the bizarre things are the ones who don't get kicked around. Maybe that's what Warren had to do in the beginning to get ahead." It was an act that had worked for Brando and James Dean, and like those two matinee idols, Warren figured he was good looking and desirable enough to give the same act a try. It worked for him only up to a point, for he never attained the immortal status of Brando, Dean, and Clift, whose reticence and rudeness were excused as the quirk of genius. The press was less tolerant of Warren, rapping his knuckles frequently.

The young actor's hungry ego and narcissistic self-involvement could lead him into some embarrassing gaffes. According to a source who requested anonymity, Kim Novak, one of the era's biggest box-office stars, met him at a party, and he mistook her natural enthusiasm for sexual interest, asking if he could go home with her. He ended up pounding on her bedroom door even after she bolted it against him. Later, he bowed out of *Moll Flanders* after Kim replaced Sophia Loren as his co-star.[42] Kim married her new leading man, British actor Richard Johnson. Another actress who found Warren somewhat gauche was Mamie Van Doren, who observed, "He drools a lot. He has such active glands."[43]

Meanwhile, Warren and Natalie had become the most photographed and written about lovers in Hollywood. Kazan reflected, "To be in love with Warren Beatty! What girl can run that fast? And why use the word 'love'? Warren . . . wanted it all and wanted it his way. Why not? He had the energy, a very keen intelligence, and more chutzpah than any Jew I've ever known. . . . Bright as they come, intrepid, and with that thing all women secretly respect: complete confidence in his sexual powers, confidence so great that he never had to advertise himself, even by hints."[44]

Natalie's stardom benefited as much as Warren's from the publicity generated by their affair, and she won the coveted lead in the film version of the Broadway hit musical *Gypsy*. Warren helped her get a handle on playing a stripper, taking her to a burlesque club where the bump-and-grinders included Fran Sinatra and Natalie Should. Later, on the *Gypsy* set, when Natalie clashed with a competitive and resentful Roz Russell, Warren came to lend his support to Natalie on a daily basis. "She'd sit on his lap and she'd whisper in his ear and he would reassure her," said Morgan Brittany, who played Baby June in the film.[45]

"Together in public, they were something to behold: beautiful, exciting, sophisticated," observed Lana Wood. "Together, in private, they were in the midst of a tumultuous love affair. It became so intense that Warren, who had a reputation for maintaining both a separate identity as well as a separate residence, moved into Natalie's house."

After leaving R.J., she had rented a spread in Bel Air and then, restlessly, moved to a house in Benedict Canyon. "He talked often about his desire to direct and produce," recalled Lana, "and Natalie always listened patiently. I don't think either of them had any inkling of the success that awaited Warren. . . . There was no question that they were in love, though at times it seemed to me the one more stricken was Natalie. . . . Mom too was worried for her."[46]

One night, they'd made plans to attend a dinner party together. He came home too late for them to go and offered no excuses for his tardiness. "Then it started," Lana said. "Natalie and Warren fought, and when the screaming became too much, Warren slammed the door and left, and did not return that night. Natalie, weeping, went to bed."

Around the house, unless they were having sex, there was a strange lack of intimacy. Sometimes they asked friends over to dinner, but when they were alone, they lived more like roommates than lovers. He kept to himself, often playing the piano for hours at a time. "When Warren was in one room, Natalie was in another," Lana related. "Natalie would lie by the pool in the sun for an hour and then when Warren would appear in his trunks, his usual book tucked under his arm, she would get up and go into the house. It wasn't hostility, it certainly wasn't disinterest, and I have since come to think of it as two lives coming together briefly, but always at cross-purposes. There was always a distance between them."

Natalie was nominated for the Best Actress Oscar in February 1962 for *Splendor in the Grass*, but Warren wasn't nominated for Best Actor. The voters of the Academy of Motion Picture Arts and Sciences—his workaday peers as opposed to the Hollywood Establishment—completely snubbed him. Though his performance deserved at least a nomination, he wasn't even included on the preliminary ballot for nominees, partly because Warner Bros. pushed him for Best Supporting Actor for *The Roman Spring of Mrs. Stone*, in an ill-advised tactic to promote the faltering film at the box office. Angry over being consigned to the supporting category, Beatty informed the academy he would reject the nomination. It was a pathetic and arrogant threat; the selectors had no intention of putting him on the ballot. When Natalie argued with him that as a first-year movie actor, he should be grateful for any nod from the academy, he walked out on her. The next day, he returned. He was "never gone for very long," said an acquaintance, "when he had a lady who was paying the rent."[47]

The crowds nearly rioted when Warren and Natalie arrived for the April Oscar presentations at the Santa Monica Civic Auditorium, Beatty in a tuxedo and Natalie stunning in a form-fitting gown and white mink. It became painfully clear during the program that the voters had turned against her because of her extramarital affair with Beatty; almost everyone except Natalie got an Oscar for *West Side Story*, including supporting players Rita Moreno and George Chakiris. A nominee for *Splendor*, Natalie lost to Sophia Loren for *Two Women*. "Natalie Wood was robbed," wrote columnist Hedda Hopper the following day. "But at least she got the nicest consolation prize—Warren Beatty." Not only that, her earning power went from $250,000 per picture to $500,000 when *West Side Story* won the coveted Oscar for Best Picture of 1961.

On April 17, 1962, after having been Warren's mistress since the previous August, she at last filed for divorce from Wagner in Santa Monica Superior Court, charging mental cruelty. R.J. was "cold and indifferent," she told Judge Allen Lynch, adding that he preferred golf to marital pleasures. Warren's *All Fall Down* was the U.S. entry in the Cannes Film Festival, and she flew to France with him in May 1962, but the festival jury, like the academy, disdained him and the picture. Natalie attracted most of the attention at Cannes, especially after they met the Russian delegation and Natalie charmed them with her knowledge of their country. The daughter of Siberian immigrants, Natalie's real name was Natalia Nikolaevna Zakharenko, and at Cannes she conversed with the Russians in their own language and even led them in a native folk dance. Watching the hostile, standoffish Russians fall under Natalie's spell at the height of the Cold War, Warren became fascinated by their country and its history, which would result later in his movie *Reds*, an homage to John Reed, author of *Ten Days That Shook the World*. "Nine years to make *Reds* after he [discovered] Russia with Natalie," muses Dick Sylbert. "Natalie was Russian. Her father was a Russian. He was a very great carpenter. He worked for me on *Manchurian Candidate*." While on the Riviera, Warren and Natalie had such a romping good time in their suite at the Carlton that the management later complained of torn wallpaper and draperies.

Meanwhile, R.J. was in London filming *The War Lover* and dating Joan Collins, which provoked the media to remark on "Natalie and Joan's Strange Love Swap." Collins later said there was no romantic spark between her and R.J., describing him as "gentle and sweet and too nice for me." She preferred "complex, difficult men"—like Warren. On a date with R.J., she met Anthony Newley, star of the West End musical hit, *Stop the World—I Want to Get Off*, whom she later married. R.J. continued to carry a torch for Natalie.

Beatty and Natalie vacationed in Paris and Rome, inspiring columnist Sheilah Graham to dub them "the poor man's Liz and Burton," and adding, "If they're not married, they're doing an awfully good imitation." Including, unfortunately, marital battles; at the Grand Hotel in Rome, they fought almost constantly, "like people on the verge of a divorce," commented a former UPI correspondent. "Knowing Warren's reputation as a cocksman, we assumed that Natalie didn't want to spend *all* of her time in bed." In fact, she'd come to the Eternal City to discuss film projects with Françoise Sagan and Federico Fellini.

R. J. Wagner, in Rome to pursue Marion Marshall, who was in the middle of a tense divorce from director Stanley Donen, encountered Natalie and Beatty at the Hostario Del Orso nightclub. R.J. invited them to his table, introduced them to Marion, and later danced with Natalie, who subsequently told a friend, *Life* reporter Tommy Thompson, "The divorce had been a terrible mistake." Later, at the Grand, Beatty kept Natalie's phone tied up with business calls all night, causing her to miss R.J.'s calls. If R.J. had succeeded in reaching her, she told Thompson, "I would have dropped everything and gone running back to him." Only twenty-four, she was disturbed by the nature of her relationship with Beatty, which was based on lust rather than love. She was starved for genuine emotion and suicide-prone.

Returning to Hollywood in June 1962, Warren and Natalie continued to enjoy her spectacular house in Benedict Canyon, which had a stream that came rippling through the interior from a waterfall in the garden outside. Unfortunately the indoor waterway attracted swarms of mosquitoes and had to be filled with cement. Their relationship continued to deteriorate when Natalie told Beatty she expected him to become a permanent member of her on-set entourage whenever she filmed. While R.J. had not hesitated to hold her hand during the challenging and often frightening process of making a major picture, Warren balked. During *Gypsy* he'd tried to give her the help she needed, but his own career ambitions took priority.

He wasn't being offered the serious roles he wanted, and at home, he refused to be at Natalie's beck and call, or to put up with her tearful fits and sullen moods. He also refused to co-star with her in *Youngblood Hawk*, holding out for better roles. The affair was one of great sensual highs and shattering emotional lows—and "the lows came because of Warren's wandering eye," observed Lana. Eventually, that wandering eye fell on Lana herself, who, at sixteen, already had the figure she would soon display as Sean Connery's co-star in *Diamonds Are Forever*. When Lana caught Warren gazing at her seductively, she giggled and retreated to another room in Natalie's house. Lana was one of the few girls not drawn to Warren, largely because she blamed him for her sister's growing unhappiness.

About a year after they'd first become lovers, Warren and Natalie went out to Chasen's for dinner. They were seated in the pine-paneled main dining room, which was jammed with Hollywood Establishment luminaries. During the meal, Beatty went to the men's room, leaving Natalie alone at their table for over ten minutes, humiliated by the curious stares of concerned industry peers like the Alfred Hitchcocks, the Jimmy Stewarts, and the Gregory Pecks. After she dispatched the headwaiter to look for Beatty, owner Dave Chasen informed her that Warren had hit on the bosomy (38–23–34) checkroom girl[48] and sneaked out the back door with her—for what turned out to be a three-day sex orgy.[49] Apart from everything else, Natalie was stuck with the check. The news of her public abandonment hit the press the next day, exacerbating her heartbreak. Dorothy Kilgallen sarcastically suggested that Warren would next hit on R.J.'s future wife, Marion Donen; Natalie would steal Tony Newley from Joan Collins; and Joan would console Richard Burton after Elizabeth Taylor ran away with R.J.

In a rage, Natalie burned all of Beatty's clothes and belongings, refusing to let him in when he returned to Benedict Canyon a week later. The issue separating them was at last clear to her: she wanted love and marriage, he wanted sex and freedom. She began to contemplate ending the affair, realizing that he had used her for sex and for the publicity that a romance with one of America's two or three most beloved actresses would be sure to generate.[50]

The ruse had worked—their much-publicized affair had made him, by the time he deserted her, the hottest Hollywood personality since James Dean. His brutal rejection of her at Chasen's left Natalie on the verge of a nervous breakdown. Warren was too busy to be upset. He did not restrict himself to famous women like Joan Collins and Natalie, but went out with waitresses, writers, secretaries, photographers, and movieland groupies.[51] According to Rex Reed, Warren wanted "the entire world to want to go to bed with him. And what he really is unable to take more than anything else in life is rejection."[52] By no means did he succeed with every woman he pursued. He relentlessly wooed the female assistant of Steve Roberts, the Los Angeles bureau chief of the *New York Times*. "Think how many women would love to be in your position," Roberts told his assistant. "Think how many have been," she said.[53]

Perhaps the only thing that saved Natalie at this juncture of her brief, tortured life was her occasional ability to laugh at the absurdity of lust-driven relationships. Her best friend, Hope Lange, recalled, "We'd laugh at ourselves—at what asses we were."[54] Natalie had wanted a strong man, something R.J. had never been, and, according to Sheilah Graham, she mistook, in Beatty, "ruthlessness for strength. She was shattered when he dumped her."[55] Eager to restore her reputation as a desirable movie princess, she rushed into affairs with agent Sandy Whitelaw, director Henry Jaglom, David Niven Jr., Tom Courtenay, Arthur Loew Jr., Caracas shoe salesman Ladislao Blatnik, Sinatra, Michael Caine, millionaire Del Coleman, lawyer David Gorton, and actors Stuart Whitman and Richard Johnson. She also made a play for her *Love With the Proper Stranger* co-star, Steve McQueen, but at the time he was happily married to attractive, petite Neile Adams, and, besides, he was a loyal friend of R.J.'s. The picture brought Natalie another Oscar nomination. The plot of *Stranger* was virtually a recapitulation of her agonizing entanglement with Warren. It told of an emotionally vulnerable young girl who—like Natalie—had normal desires for marriage, and of her affair with a lovable but maddeningly indecisive hipster musician who lacks the courage to commit to marriage until she forces his hand, driving herself to distraction in the process. "She was able to use, obviously, her relationship with Beatty in some of the scenes with McQueen, there's no question about it," said Tom Bosley, who played a supporting role in the film.

Warren wasn't ready to give Natalie up, especially after her two Oscar nominations made her the most sought-after feminine star in the industry with the exception of Elizabeth Taylor. A reconciliation was attempted in New York, and Natalie foolishly brought along her nubile little sister, Lana. Natalie by then was having a halfhearted fling with bisexual *Life* journalist and later novelist Tommy Thompson. Tommy and Lana accompanied her one night when she went to dine with Warren in New York. It turned into a fiasco, with Natalie and Warren fighting and then sulking in hateful silence. Finally, Natalie left with Tommy, telling Lana to stay with Warren, a very big mistake, of course. No sooner had Natalie and Tommy left the table than Warren started trying to seduce Lana. Only sixteen, she felt uncomfortable as he cornered her in the restaurant and again at the hotel where she was staying with her sister. She rang Natalie on the house phone in the lobby, and then turned to Warren and said, "I can't, Warren. I'm very sorry, but I just can't."[56] Soon enough, she would become involved with Sean Connery, and subsequently Alain Delon.

Back in Los Angeles, Warren came to call on Natalie one day, and a bitter scene erupted. Her best friend and onetime secretary, the playwright Mart Crowley, who was writing *The Boys in the Band* in her guest house, heard raised voices, and then Warren abruptly stalked out. Natalie went upstairs to her boudoir. Shortly, she appeared on the staircase, screaming. Mart found her in a heap on the stairs, in a coma. She had tried to commit suicide by overdosing on barbiturates; then, overcome by terror, she'd started downstairs for help, collapsing on the way. Mart rushed her to Cedars of Lebanon Hospital in Hollywood, thoughtfully registering her under the name of Helen to keep from tipping off the press. According to her psychiatrist, John Lindon, she'd swallowed a bottle of sleeping pills, and her stomach had to be pumped. When Lana visited, Natalie's hair was stringy and hanging in her face, she was dressed in a regulation hospital smock, and her face and body were pitifully bloated. "I didn't want to live anymore," she moaned. After a few days, she left Cedars in disguise, wearing some drab clothes that Lana had brought to the hospital in an attempt to evade the paparazzi.

Though Warren's behavior was heavy-handed and needlessly cruel, he was by no means entirely responsible for Natalie's crack-up. At the time of his visit, she was guilt-ridden over an affair she was having with a married director. She knew she had to end it but didn't want to. Warren's ill-timed call had come a day or so after she'd finally broken off the affair, and she was miserable, lonely, and depressed. Her suicide attempt would remain a well-kept secret for almost a quarter of a century. When Warren's affair with Natalie finally ended, Lana claimed that it was her sister who was "the injured party."

CHAPTER THREE

THANK HEAVEN FOR LITTLE GIRLS (& BUNNIES & PLAYMATES)

ONE NIGHT when Warren was alone, he called the Bunny Room at the Playboy Club on Sunset Strip, and asked for a woman with whom he'd been sleeping. She wasn't at work that night, and he started flirting with the woman who had answered the phone, who introduced herself as "Kevin Lauritzen."[1] "They started sleeping together just like that," according to a Hollywood insider. She added that Warren was always trying to get Kevin Lauritzen into a three-way scene, but she didn't like group gropes. "He's very jaded, that's why he was into scenes," said the source. "Once you can have anything you want sexually, you start looking for new things to want." Appropriately, the logo of the Playboy Club was a rabbit—symbolizing profligate sex, inexhaustible desire, endless stamina, and loveless intercourse.

It was also an apt symbol for what happened to Warren Beatty in the 1960s after *Splendor in the Grass*. Logically, his progress as an artist should have continued after his auspicious debut, but no such thing happened. Instead, he muddled through a succession of mediocre movies, hitting both artistic and financial bottoms, because, like all sex addicts, he was very distracted, very disturbed. The women with whom he got involved were equally complex and unable to help him find stability. In the early sixties, one of his girlfriends, Barbara Harris, was generally recognized as the most original American stage actress to emerge since Kim Stanley and Geraldine Page. A leading exponent of the Second City's improvisation technique, Harris attained iconic status among theatergoers from the moment she stepped on stage in Arthur Kopit's *Oh Dad, Poor Dad, Mamma's Hung You in the Closet and I'm Feelin' So Sad*, an irreverent black comedy that helped define the revolutionary sensibility of the sixties.

Harris had a steady boyfriend, playwright Arnold Weinstein, one of the most popular and respected figures in the innovative downtown art scene dominated by poet Frank O'Hara and painter Larry Rivers, but at about that time she seems to have become involved with Warren. She was in constant demand after her debut in the Kopit piece for such major Broadway musicals as *Apple Tree* and *On a Clear Day You Can See Forever*. The former opened at a theater, not far from Sardi's. An assistant maître d' at Sardi's at the time recalled in 2001, "Being at the social center of the American theater, we at Sardi's heard about everything that happened on Broadway stages first, sometimes only moments after it occurred. One night during *Apple Tree,* in the middle of a song, Barbara Harris stopped singing and just stood there. 'I can't do this,' she said, and walked out of the theater in full costume. On the street, she hurried down Forty-fourth, jumped on a bus, and went home. The story went around Sardi's almost immediately, but we thought it was made up, it was so strange. Then Warren Beatty came in and asked, 'Have you seen Miss Harris? I'm trying to find her.' "

Barbara may have proved to be more than Warren—or Broadway—could handle. She went on to Hollywood, starring in *A Thousand Clowns* in 1965.

Warren went on to an affair with Leslie Caron. The turmoil and litigation in Leslie's marriage to Englishman Peter Hall would spill over into Warren's life, all but consuming him and extinguishing his career. He later blamed his poor choice of roles during this period on the fact that Leslie lived abroad, and therefore he "had to make [pictures] in England." Altogether, he made six films in five years—*The Roman Spring of Mrs. Stone, All Fall Down, Lilith, Mickey One, Promise Her Anything*, and *Kaleidoscope*. Although *Mickey One,* directed by

Arthur Penn, is taken seriously by many critics, the others were decided come-downs after *Splendor*.

Blaming Leslie for the impasse he'd reached was unfair. His stalled career sprang from inner chaos, not geographical happenstance. Sex obsession had blinded him to everything but nailing the next encounter, and his predicament was worsened by the friends he fell in with in the sixties—other Don Juans, like Hugh Hefner, the notorious soft-porn king who published *Playboy* and ran a string of clubs, and Roman Polanski, an actor-cum-director, who already had the brilliant *Knife in the Water* and *Repulsion* to his credit, and who'd eventually face deportation for having sex with a thirteen-year-old girl. Still another skirt-chasing friend, Jack Nicholson, would become intimately involved with Warren after the triple late-1960s New Hollywood breakthrough represented by Warren's *Bonnie and Clyde* (1967), Polanski's *Rosemary's Baby* (1968), and Nicholson's *Easy Rider* (1969)—all movies that grew out of the filmmakers' obsession with sex, violence, and drugs. The three films deeply influenced the culture of the sixties, which began in idealism and positive social change but degenerated, at least in California, into the bloodshed and horror of the Manson murders in Los Angeles and the Rolling Stones concert at Altamont. Between them, Beatty, Hefner, Polanski, and Nicholson established the era's personal style of rapacious sex and emotional dissociation. Of the four men, Warren was the best looking, Polanski the most reckless, Hefner the richest, and Nicholson the smartest.

"Roman Polanski was very attractive," recalls Nan Morris-Robinson, who had been a regular around the Sunset Strip when she first met Warren, and then went on in the sixties to experience the scenes in Beverly Hills and London. "Roman was quite short, but, unlike a lot of short guys, who compensate by being aggressive, he had no personality conflict because of his size, and was quiet, shy, and appealing." Polanski's first wife, Barbara Lass, pinpointed his appeal as "a fire burning inside him that always attracted people. He had brilliant ideas, and he was always the center of attention. . . . When he went to America, it changed. When I heard later on of Roman's deviant behavior, I couldn't believe it, and still can't."[2] His oddball interests, which included drugs, witchcraft, and sex with minors, placed him, and everyone around him, in mortal danger.

Beatty, Polanski, Nicholson, and Hefner—the Four Horsemen of the Sixties Apocalypse—became good friends, often convening at Hefner's worldwide

Playboy Clubs. In retrospect, they were the archetypal male chauvinists in the twilight days of America's male-dominated society. Ironically, though all they thought about and talked about was women, they found female companionship difficult. All of them had had countless girlfriends, but few continuing relationships. Polanski's friend Henryk Kluba, a former actor, once observed, "If one is really looking for an area in which [Polanski] might have had complexes, it was certainly women. I don't know whether he had some problem with them, whether he had failed as a man, but there was something about him. . . . He was always showing off, playing superman, yet he was curt, almost unkind, to women."

A well-known underground director of the sixties, who agreed to be interviewed off the record, recalls, "Polanski was hosting a party at the Chateau Marmont, and he was using female parking attendants. When I left the party, a girl valet, a Bunny type, went to get my car. I was waiting on a narrow street, and a guy pulls up across the way and parks. He starts flirting with one of the other girl valets, and pretty soon he spots me and says hello, calling out my name. 'It's Warren,' he says. He was trying to pick up a parking attendant in the middle of the night. I don't think he knew Polanski yet, because he hadn't been at the party, and it was late. I like Warren, he has a nice, sweet, gentlemanly quality, but I remember my surprise at seeing a star of his magnitude hitting on a parking attendant."

Hugh Hefner, the ultimate exhibitionist in the group, who shrewdly and greedily grabbed the opportunity for stardom that the timing of the sexual revolution made possible, provided men like Warren and Polanski with a convenient selection of beautiful women: his Playboy Clubs. Hefner said the clubs were designed for "urban fellows who are less concerned with hunting, fishing and climbing mountains than with good food, drink, proper dress, and the pleasure of female company."

Hefner's consigliere, confidant, and alter ego was handsome, boyish Victor Lownes III, who personified the carefree, sex-driven bachelor's existence endorsed by the magazine. Wherever Victor was, there was never a dearth of girls—or of party boys such as Beatty, Polanski, Nicholson, Bernie Cornfield, Dean Martin Jr., Berry Gordy, Jim Brown, George Burns, *New York Post* columnist Max Lerner, Barry Goldwater Jr., and Joe Namath.[3]

"Victor Lownes was a lech," says Nan Morris-Robinson. "I was in London at the time, managing P. J. Proby, and I went to the Ad Lib one night. Victor came out of nowhere and pinched my bottom. Later on, there was a party in his town house. I made a disparaging remark about *Playboy* and Victor leapt over the bar and tried to attack me. I beat it out of there."

It was at one of Victor's parties that Warren Beatty met Polanski. "I was originally introduced to Warren by John Shepritch, one of the 20th Century–Fox executives who'd proposed to cast him in an Americanized version of *Knife in the Water*," Polanski recalled. Like Beatty, Polanski would amass an impressive but highly erratic filmography. A Polish Jew whose parents had been dragged away to the concentration camps in WWII, his childhood experience of the Holocaust underlay the outstanding films he would later direct—devious examinations of the perversity of human nature. His own psyche, like Warren's, was sex-obsessed to a degree that precluded a normal life and coherent career. A worshiper of his own penis, on one occasion Polanski posed, fully erect, while his friend, producer Gene Gutowski, made a clay mold that was subsequently cast in gold by jeweler Marvin Himes ("give the head a high polish and hammer the testicles").[4] On Victor Lownes's next birthday, Polanski gave him the Golden Prick Award, and Lownes called it a "life-sized portrait."

Warren, during the early sixties, made bad pictures for big money, declining good ones that would have paid much less, all the while expending his energy on pointless relationships. Polanski also fumbled his career after *Knife in the Water*, which had been a minor masterpiece in the Polish original. Now he wanted Warren to co-star in an English-language remake with Elizabeth Taylor and Richard Burton, Warren playing the youthful drifter who disturbs their relationship. But his salary would have been ten times the total budget of the picture, and Darryl F. Zanuck, head of Fox, refused to pay it. Though the Polish-language *Knife in the Water* received an Oscar nomination, Polanski ultimately told Fox, "Why remake a perfectly good film?" The project languished, but it succeeded in cementing Beatty and Polanski's friendship.

The two playboys had more in common than their insatiable hunger for sex, but both were too self-involved for healthy human relationships. Polanski's friend Henryk Kluba once remarked, "Something was not right. I was not sure this man was able to fall in love. He was so narcissistic that he loved primarily himself. With women, it seemed to be only the physical side which attracted him—the sex." Polanski himself confirmed this when he admitted, "All I was interested in was to fuck a girl and move on . . . I just liked fucking around. I was a swinger." At their core, Beatty and Polanski were incorrigible sexists. Decades later, at a panel on the subject of women in film, Beatty betrayed politically incorrect thinking when he said, "Women's screenplays aren't as good" as men's.[5] The remark was greeted with boos and hisses.

Contempt for women, coupled with an obsession for their bodies, fed into and was an essential part of Beatty's and Polanski's film aesthetic. From early in their relationship, the two conducted long, weighty dialogues about cinema, and these continued for years, culminating in two of the signature movies of the decade, *Rosemary's Baby* and *Bonnie and Clyde*. Though the films were still in the future, their genesis was in talks Beatty and Polanski had about breaking through the barriers of modern filmmaking and frankly exploring sex and violence. The conversations took place mostly in London, and shaped both of them as auteurs. The explosive synergy of their friendship, and the brilliant but amoral movies that sprang from it, contributed heavily to the atmosphere in which Charles Manson and his gang thrived and wound up murdering Polanski's wife.

When the L.A. Playboy Club opened on the Sunset Strip in the mid-sixties, Warren wasted no time ingratiating himself with Hefner and his harem of scantily clad "Bunnies." Hef's mansions as well as his clubs were little more than high-class brothels ("if you don't swing, don't ring"), where he lavishly entertained VIPs like Warren, acting as their unofficial pimp. Hef understood how essential discretion was for celebrities, as well as for the middle-class crowd *Playboy* magazine had always catered to, and he made sure from the start that the Playboy Clubs maintained an aura of well-heeled respectability. Things were considerably wilder at Hef's L.A. residence, Playboy Mansion West, high above Sunset Boulevard, but only the elite were admitted, and they could be trusted to be discreet. "Warren would never go to a girl's apartment, because he was so paranoid," says Sarah Porterfield. "He was terrified of hidden cameras that would show them doing it. If he wanted sex with a girl, he always went to the Beverly Wilshire. The only place he ever did sex besides the Wilshire was at Hugh Hefner's. It was safe there. I remember being up at Hef's one day and Warren appeared with a Bunny on each arm, and Hef said, 'Have you been robbing the hutch again, Warren?' I think he was doing Playmates as well."

One of the architects of the sexual revolution, a mid-twentieth-century movement that swept through every level of society, Hefner was essentially a sleaze merchant who ultimately changed sexual mores and behavior. In casting his lot with Hefner, Warren was plunging a long way down the social ladder. The Chicago-born Hefner was strange and a loner as a child, and his parents, puritanical teetotalers, consulted a doctor, who told them Hugh would never grow up, because he was somehow emotionally deficient. He wasn't, however, lacking in energy or imagination. As a boy he started his own neighborhood magazine, complete with pictures he'd taken, and sold it on the sidewalk for a penny a copy. He haunted the movie theaters and developed a steamy fantasy life. As a teenager, he proved luckless in love, spurned by his girlfriend Betty, but he blossomed later at the University of Illinois, where he became the student-body president and editor of the school paper.

After proving a whiz as circulation director of a children's magazine, Hef launched his own adult girlie rag, hyping it as a publication "for city guys, a celebration of the good life—cars, martinis, hi-fi, jazz, and fashion." The original name, *Stag Party*, morphed into *Playboy*, and he sold a nude photograph of Marilyn Monroe to raise money for the first issue. It was an overnight sensation, selling fifty-four thousand copies the first time out. *Playboy* eventually published well-known writers to disguise its real role as a heterosexual masturbation "stroke book," an unofficial *Gentlemen's Home Companion*. Hefner led a workaholic life, with the exception of daily sex with his secretary, even while wife Millie was pregnant with their second child. "I want to share you with *Playboy*'s readers," he told his mistress, talking her through a nude photographic session. "Good girls not only do it, they like it."[6]

Soon, hordes of girl-next-door types were lining up to strip for Hef's photographers, hoping for a spot in *Playboy*. He subsisted on Dexedrine, working around the clock, hosting his own TV show, until he met Victor Lownes, who taught him how to relax. Lownes introduced him to hip Chicago, which was all about cool jazz, risqué comedians like Lenny Bruce, upward mobility, and the intimacy of dark, smoke-filled, romantic nightclubs like the Black Orchid, the Cloisters, and Chez Paree. The *Playboy* style was pure 1950s Chicago, part Beat, part hip, part square.

Finally, with Lownes and a few other shareholders, Hef opened Playboy Clubs offering both food and entertainment, and featuring, in the Showroom, such performers as Lainie Kazan, George Carlin, Redd Foxx, Mabel Mercer, Bill Cosby, Peter Allen, and Dick Gregory. And then there were the mansions. For lost souls in emotional free-fall, Hefner's infamous mansions in Chicago and L.A. provided an illusory home, if a bordello could be called home. He permitted his chums, Warren included, to sample the tarts. Known by his friends as the man who loved women and lost them all, Hef was no more cut out for a lasting relationship with a woman than was Warren. According to the original *Playboy Club Bunny Manual*, later amended to allow fraternization with the customers, the girls weren't supposed to date "keyholders," as the three hundred thousand members were called, but Hef always made exceptions for such VIPs as Warren and Polanski.

Recalls Bunny Kevin Lauritzen, "Warren started calling me late at night, and without even saying, 'Hi, it's Warren,' he'd tell me how much I fascinated him. 'If you could meet any woman in the world,' he asked, 'who would you pick?' I told him Jackie Kennedy, and he said, 'You should have said Bunny Kevin.' He wanted me to think he found me more interesting than Jackie Kennedy. He fucks your mind before he fucks anything else."

Kevin Lauritzen later told Sarah Porterfield that she had been having sex with Warren for about two months when he rang the Bunny Room one night and Kevin answered. "Oh, Kevin," Warren said, "can you come over?" Kevin replied, "Well, are you alone?" He answered yes, and she said, "If I get there and you've got a chick with you, I'm leaving." Warren promised, "No, baby, it's just you. Only you and me."

He was living in El Escondido (the Hideaway), the penthouse suite at the Beverly Wilshire Hotel (today the Regent Beverly Wilshire) on Rodeo Drive. The Wilshire has the unique distinction among Hollywood's prime hostelries of being smack-dab in the glamorous, bustling heart of Beverly Hills, unlike the more remote Bel-Air and Beverly Hills Hotels. The Bank of America squats at one end of North Rodeo Drive and, at the other, facing the street from the south, stands the stately, ornate Wilshire. Warren's suite had two rooms and a bath, and he kept a separate room in the hotel for his secretary. He would spurn owning a house for many years. "Elvis Presley had the penthouse suite at the Beverly Wilshire before Warren," recalls Nan Morris-Robinson. "I used to rub Elvis's neck, massage his scalp. He was so tense when he first came to Hollywood, working so hard."

Kevin Lauritzen arrived at the Wilshire for her date with Warren. After taking the elevator, she got out, climbed a flight of stairs, and proceeded to Warren's black lacquered door. He greeted her in a bathrobe and started kissing her in the doorway, finally kicking the door shut. He continued kissing her, arousing her excitement. Then he picked her up and carried her into the bedroom and sat her on the bed. There was a naked woman on the bed already, smoking a cigarette. "I was so hot by that point, I didn't even care," Kevin later told Sarah Porterfield. "He said all the right things to me, fed me mentally, like, 'Baby, you're so hot.' He's a cerebral fuck." Obviously he was different things to different women.

His rooms were cluttered with scripts, books, and dirty plates from room-service meals. Whenever he was shooting a film and wanted no disturbances, he always suspended maid service. There was a private terrace that was larger than the rest of the apartment, and Warren usually told his girlfriends to go outside and sunbathe while he watched TV, read a script, or ate lunch from a tray. In his closet, he kept only four suits and a dinner jacket. All his other possessions, including cars, he rented or placed in storage. "I can pack up and move tomorrow," he boasted. Later on, he also maintained hotel suites in London and New York, where he stayed at the St. Regis, the Carlyle, or the Delmonico. Distracted by his endless quest for kicks, he paid little attention to business, often carrying as many as thirty-five uncashed checks in his suitcase. When a friend once commented that the floorboard of Warren's car was covered with unpaid bills, the actor explained that his debtors should contact his business manager if they expected payment; he couldn't be bothered.

The night of his date with Kevin Lauritzen, Kevin told the woman Warren was already with, "You stay over there and mind your own business and don't touch me!" Warren was "not a good lover" in the conventional sense, Kevin said, adding, "It's the attention he gives, the reaffirmation. What makes him a good lover is that . . . he just really pays attention. It's not about what happens in bed with Warren. He was the most sought-after man in Hollywood, which makes you think, 'Well, I'm good enough to be hanging around Warren Beatty.' It reaffirms your femininity, your womanhood."

From the time he moved into the Wilshire, it was a virtual certainty that any female movie star stopping at the hotel would look in on Warren for servicing. Despite his reputation as a cool cocksman—the personification of "the man who reads *Playboy*," an unrepentant chauvinist glorying in his superficiality as he bounces from girl to girl—he couldn't help feeling rather foolish, for he was smart enough to know that mature people viewed his behavior as bordering on sick. As film historian David Thomson observed, "He cannot endure or dispense with this legend of Don Juan."

His notoriety as a make-out artist sometimes worked against him. "He's a good guy, but he wanted every type of woman known to man, long, tall, short, old, young—that was his goal," says singer-comedian Karen Bihari, who today owns a gift shop near the French Market in West Hollywood. "I was a blond Beverly Hills High School student and we used to hang out Friday and Saturday nights at MFK's, a classy old-fashioned fifties-style malt shop in the Beverly Wilshire with red-leather booths, beige-marble countertops, cigarettes, candy, and cosmetics. I was a sixteen- or seventeen-year-old street-wise smartass who'd been around the block with the Beatles, a wild child, a Rolling Stones maniac. I knew of Warren Beatty's reputation because he'd been horsing around with some of my girlfriends. Then one night I met him. This was years before my incident with Shirley MacLaine.

"I was going with Don Johnson. He was my first love—blond, with wild Native American eyes, and he'd acted in a couple of movies—*The Magic Garden of Stanley Sweetheart* and *The Harrad Experiment*. One night, after a Crosby, Stills, Nash and Young concert, we went to MFK's and sat down at a table and gave our order to a waitress in a beehive hairdo and a circle skirt. After a while, I told Donnie I was going to get some cigarettes, and left him at the table. As I was buying a pack, I heard a man's voice behind me:

" 'Let me buy those for you. You have beautiful hair. Would you like to have dinner with me tomorrow night at seven o'clock? What's your phone number?'

"I recognized him at once and thought, With Don Johnson, who needs Warren Beatty? I said, 'Would you just cut it out? I know who you are.'

" 'Listen,' he said, 'tell me your phone number. I'll call you at six-thirty or seven.'

" 'I live at home with my mom,' I said. 'I'm a teenager.'

" 'I know that.'

" 'Well . . . you're older.'

"Though I didn't like that kind of aggressive, unromantic, obnoxious come-on, I gave him my phone number and went back to the table to join Donnie. The next night, the phone rings, and I'm under the hair dryer. Mother comes in and says, 'There's a man on the phone—he's been grilling me for the last fifteen minutes. He wants to take you to dinner. You wanna go?'

"I looked bored, and she said, 'Is he pissing you off?'

" 'Yeah,' I said, but I took the call and told him, 'What are you bothering my mom about?'

" 'You're a feisty one.'

"Mother took the phone again, and Warren apologized to her but persisted, 'Can I take Karen to dinner?'

"She told him yes, and handed me the phone.

" 'I'll be over in five minutes,' he said.

"He took me to the Beverly Wilshire, where he has two suites. We ate in the restaurant downstairs, maybe Hernando Courtwright's.

" 'Hey, this is an old man's restaurant,' I told him. 'I think I'll order a steak.'

"It was a big steak, and it was good. 'Come on upstairs with me,' Warren said. 'I have to make a couple of phone calls.'

"He turned the lights down low and said, 'Have you seen *Ryan's Daughter*? Didn't you get excited over Christopher Jones? Weren't you hot about what Christopher Jones and Sarah Miles were doing, fucking in the forest?'

" 'Hey, hey, hey!' I said. 'Just wait a damn minute here.' Warren was cute, and Warren was famous, and Warren was rich, but, let's face it, he wasn't Don Johnson." Besides, she knew how to spot a sex addict, "the kind of man who lies to women to get them in bed and then he's out the door, without so much as leaving cab money. I was from a divorced family, looking for love, and Warren was unstable, noncommittal, phony, and patronizing.

" 'You're testing me, aren't you, buddy?' I told him. 'Let's just stop this. Do you think talk like that is sexy? It's beyond the valley of the turnoff. I may be young, but my boyfriend is just as handsome as you and half your age. I can't believe you think that kind of line still works.'

"He turned the lights back on. He was beet red and said, 'I'm so sorry. Let's be friends.'

"And that's what happened. He made a better friend than lover. As a girlfriend I wouldn't have felt that special because I knew he slept with everyone. Everybody knew it. But we had a good friendship. We'd go to his place, or call some friends of his, go out to the airport, hang out. I remember one night he called Goldie Hawn—they were making *Dollars.* I never had an affair with him.

"I was devoted to Donnie. One time, Donnie was up for a movie, and he put me up for the girl's role. I was doing *Tommy,* the rock opera, at the Aquarius Theater in L.A.—Sally Simpson's replacement. Donnie had me meet this producer, who took me to dinner at Dan Tana's restaurant. My mother dropped me off. After dinner he says, 'Let's go to my place and I'll pick up a script to give to you.' What did I know? Street-smart, yes, but still naive in many ways. We go to his apartment, one of those places like in *Melrose Place,* apartments around a courtyard and pool, second floor, on Wilshire and Westwood. Once we got inside, he went to the back room to get the script, and I stayed in the front room, but immediately sensed it didn't feel right. It was creepy, especially when he summoned me. 'Karen, come here,' he said. I walked back, and he's standing in the semi-darkness in boxer shorts next to the bed. I was livid, and later told Warren the whole thing.

" 'Warren, he pulled me in there, ripped my shirt, pulled my clothes off. I almost got raped by this disgusting little man.'

" 'I'll handle it,' Warren said.

"The film never got made, and the producer was not heard from again for many years."[7]

Despite Warren's descent into prurience with Hefner, he assiduously kept up his more prestigious social contacts as well. His post-fame life was one of spectacular diversity. Instead of settling into marriage and family or even establishing a permanent entourage, he flitted from one social scene to another, and from one bed to another, like a frenetic phantom of delight—appearing unexpectedly, being amiable or passionate as the case required, and then disappearing just as quickly, by fading into the mists of emotional drift and romantic dislocation. Like the mysterious uncle in *Shadow of a Doubt*, he showed up after long absences, seeking warmth from later, more settled friends like Dustin and Lisa Hoffman.

At Hollywood parties, where ambitious starlets proliferated, he seldom failed to score. The French director Roger Vadim recalled seeing him in Malibu in 1965, "surrounded by young actresses." Breaking away from the girls, Warren told Vadim he'd "become suddenly impotent and would be leaving for India the next day." Vadim concluded that "sometimes Warren loves to mystify people."[8]

Professionally, only one or two sound decisions stand out from the morass of bad career moves he made following *Splendor in the Grass*. It had probably been wise of him to turn down *PT 109*, for playing JFK brought neither honor nor superstardom to actor Cliff Robertson. Surprisingly, Warren chose to play the gigolo in the film version of a tepid, decadent Tennessee Williams novel. *The Roman Spring of Mrs. Stone*, one of the Pulitzer Prize–winning playwright's least distinguished pieces of writing. The story concerned a rich American widow, played by fifty-year-old Vivien Leigh, who becomes involved with an unscrupulous hustler, Paolo. Miss Leigh, who had casting approval, originally wanted Alan Bates, but after one look at Warren, she ordered director Jose Quintero to cast him. It was "speculated subsequently that Beatty may have given himself in sex to Leigh," wrote David Thomson.[9] Warren later referred to Leigh as "a terrific lady who made me feel immensely important."[10]

There is little agreement among film historians with regard to how Warren won over Tennessee Williams, who originally felt that an Italian should play the role. Warren was so determined to get the part that he flew to Puerto Rico, where the gay playwright was vacationing. According to Williams, Warren sought him out in a hotel casino, and then they went to Warren's room.[11] "He read fabulously," Williams recalled. "With an accent and without. And I said, 'Warren, you have the part.'"[12] Williams himself later stated that Warren certainly possessed all the right instincts for playing a gigolo.[13]

Warren told Hedda Hopper, "The picture was offered to me and at the time I couldn't make up my mind. When I finally decided I'd like to do it, I realized Tennessee Williams had the say on the casting. After I hadn't accepted the part, an Italian boy was cast. Then I thought maybe I would like to do it, so I got on a plane and flew to see Tennessee."[14] Elsewhere, Warren elaborated: "I walked up to him in a gambling casino and began to talk to him in an Italian accent. In fact, I brought him a glass of milk on a tray, because I had been told that he had ulcers from his reviews of *Sweet Bird of Youth*."[15]

When filming began, Warren was late to the set, Vivien Leigh later told author Roy Moseley. Angrily grabbing up a book, Lady Olivier dragged a chair to the middle of the set, and sat reading until Warren finally appeared. Then, in front of the assembled company, she stood and announced, "*This* is the star of this film. Without this star, there is no film. If you keep me waiting again, I'm out of the picture." Afterward, Warren always reported to work on time.

Lotte Lenya, who played Paolo's procuress, claimed that Warren became involved with Vivien Leigh shortly after filming began in Rome. "Vivien had a tremendous crush on Warren," said Lenya. "He kept her so preoccupied that she allowed me to steal our most important scenes together." Leigh later told columnist Radie Harris, "Warren is the most talented actor I've ever worked with. . . . He has a sort of grace, intelligence, and an instinct for timing that is surprising. He does things quite naturally that other actors take years to develop."[16]

Lady Olivier notwithstanding, Warren in the role of Paolo proved to be as vacuous as Paolo himself. He succeeded in undoing much of the progress he'd made in *Splendor*, and he didn't even look good. Too slick and too tanned, he resembled a poor man's George Hamilton. During breaks in filming, he sampled *la dolce vita*, which flourished on the Via Veneto, where young men did little all day but occupy café tables and down their cappuccinos. Rome was at this time what Paris had been in the twenties, the artistic center of the universe. Occasionally Federico Fellini or Luchino Visconti would stop by the cafés on the Via Veneto. Italy's peerless auteurs Fellini, Visconti, and Michelangelo Antonioni were making the best movies anywhere in the world. *La Strada*, *Rocco and His Brothers*, *La Dolce Vita*, and *L'Avventura* expressed a dazed, elegant postwar pessimism that was about to give way to the vitality of the counterculture, but they were profoundly cinematic, and confirmed what cultural historians had long been suspecting: that movies were the dominant art of the twentieth century.

Quintero's rather conventional treatment of the limp Tennessee Williams tale had nothing in common with the film renaissance that was going on in Rome under their noses, but Warren's gigolo characterization, based on solid research, appealed to the critics. Alexander Walker wrote, "He catches brilliantly the Via Veneto manner of a Roman parasite; the vain voice, languorous limbs, petulant temper, lazy eyelids and tremendous sensual charm." Lawrence J. Quirk, author of *The Films of Warren Beatty*, attributed the authenticity of Warren's performance to his understanding of the gay sensibility. "In the creative conceptions of homosexual writers, Beatty always seemed to shine. In oddly ambivalent, velvety, indeed lavenderish, ambiences, the artist in Beatty seemed to emerge more clearly."

In Rome, he was dating TV star Inger Stevens and Broadway actress Susan Strasberg. The latter noticed Warren's tight, revealing pants and marveled that he could even sit down in them. Later, Strasberg let him move into her

Rome apartment. "I found him charming and intelligent, with a tremendous need to please women as well as conquer them," she said. They went to a party at the home of gay director Luchino Visconti, who fancied Warren. In a roomful of beautiful young men, who were chatting as they draped themselves on Visconti's priceless antique furniture, Warren whispered to Susan that he was going to the bathroom, and asked her to follow him in a moment. When she joined him in the small toilet, she asked him to explain his strange request. He said not to worry, he'd show her. Twenty minutes later, they joined the gay throng outside. Everyone stared at them, many focusing on Susan's unbuttoned blouse. "Warren beamed, at one and all, an enchanting, ingenuous smile," she recalled. Finding himself at a gay party, had he felt a sudden need to prove his heterosexuality, or was he making love to all of them, gay and straight alike? To call him an enigma is to put it mildly.

Valerie Allen, a young actress from New York, who'd started as a chorus girl at the Sands Hotel in Las Vegas, met Warren when he got back from the Rome location. Valerie had also been abroad, playing the title role in an Italian production, *Helen of Troy*. It was the break she'd longed for after a hapless struggle in Hollywood. "I had been under contract at Paramount for four years," she recalls, "but I looked too much like Ava Gardner, and Ava was such a major star, they didn't need a second one. It was a transitional period in Hollywood, the end of the studio system. They really didn't know what to do with us. It was a very lonely time." She had been aware of Warren ever since her appearance with Shirley MacLaine in *Hot Spell*, but she'd always thought of him as Shirley's brother or Joan Collins's lover, never as an actor. During his big breakout in the early sixties, she'd been in Italy filming, and was still ignorant of his newfound fame. After returning to America, she received a call from her friend, the songwriter Sammy Cahn, who said, "I'm here with Warren Beatty. I'm coming over with him."

They arranged to meet at the Luau, a dimly lit restaurant with lots of tiny tables. "In walks Sammy and Warren, who was *drop-dead gorgeous*," says Valerie. "Warren told me he had just finished *The Roman Spring of Mrs. Stone*. And of course actors are all rather self-involved, so I said, 'Well, I don't know about *Mrs. Stone*, [but] I'm doing *Helen of Troy*.' "

She noticed that Warren was picking Sammy Cahn's brains, learning everything he could from the master songwriter, creator of Academy Award–

winning standards like "Three Coins in the Fountain," "High Hopes," "All the Way," and "Call Me Irresponsible." "In his relationship with Sammy Cahn, Warren was learning about the role of music in filmmaking," Valerie continues. "He wanted to know about each and every element of films.

"We became marvelous, flirtatious friends. He was very introspective and not actor-ish. He talked about not wanting to do film all the time, like doing film six months of the year. He really thought a lot about projects, and it led to what he later became—a multitalented person in the industry.

"My house in L.A. was right up the street from Warren's friend Charlie Feldman's. Charlie was a handsome man who could have been a more urbane brother of Clark Gable's. I heard of Charlie through Warren about six months after I came back from Italy. Warren phoned me one night and said, 'I've got a friend I'd like you to meet.' I was going with somebody, and we had a date that night, so I didn't meet Charlie until later, when I moved to New York to become a stage actress and study." Valerie and Feldman began an affair in New York.

When *The Roman Spring of Mrs. Stone* was released, Bosley Crowther of the *Times* summarily dismissed Warren as "hopelessly out of his element as a patent-leather ladies' man. . . . His manners remind one of a freshman trying airs at a college prom, his accent recalls Don Ameche's all-purpose Italian-Spanish one." In one of *Time* magazine's typical backhanded compliments, the newsweekly patronizingly allowed that "Shirley MacLaine's little brother may be able to act after all."

William Inge wanted Warren for his next film, *All Fall Down*, which the playwright adapted from gay author James Leo Herlihy's novel. Herlihy would later write *Midnight Cowboy*, a gay-inflected story with Jon Voight as the hustler and Dustin Hoffman as the gigolo; it won the Best Picture and Best Director Oscars for 1969, as well as Best Actor nominations for both Voight and Hoffman. No such honors were in store for *All Fall Down*. Warren's role was another typical product of the mid-twentieth-century gay sensibility represented by *A Streetcar Named Desire*, *Picnic*, and *Cat on a Hot Tin Roof*, rather transparent homoerotic fantasies about wayward, usually misogynistic hunks. Warren portrayed a stud who breaks the heart of an older woman, Echo, played by Eva Marie Saint, who'd been Brando's luminous co-star in *On the Waterfront*. Interviewed in 2000, the still-magical Ms. Saint said, "*All Fall Down* was a wonderful experience. Warren's a bright man, and at the time he was intensely interested in acting. Later he became interested in many things other than acting, becoming a good director. I loved working with him."

The film was an icily unengaging early effort of John Frankenheimer, who later directed the powerful *Manchurian Candidate*, but Beatty's performance rang true. The gay preoccupations of Herlihy and Inge—self-absorption, rebellion against convention, narcissism—jibed with Warren's own psyche and enabled him to summon up a passable performance. It was no fault of his that the character he was playing, Berry-Berry Willart, was thoroughly unsympathetic, and he was roundly upstaged by his co-star Brandon De Wilde, who played Berry-Berry's younger brother, Clint, with touching sincerity. De Wilde had been stealing scenes ever since his childhood tour de force with Julie Harris and Ethel Waters in *The Member of the Wedding*.

Though quickly forgotten, *All Fall Down* received good press. *Variety* lauded Warren's "star quality," and Paul V. Beckley of the *New York Herald Tribune* called Beatty's performance "the finest of his career." But it must have hurt that his old bête noire, Bosley Crowther of the *New York Times*, held Warren up to ridicule in April 1962, denouncing him for being "disgusting . . . surly, sloppy, slow-witted." Later, Beatty fumed in an interview, "I don't like him either."[17]

If he was clumsy and unprofessional with the press, Beatty was downright rude to the crews on his films.[18] As a result, his peers in the industry denied him the Best Actor Oscar throughout his career, though he deserved it five times (*Splendor in the Grass*, *Bonnie and Clyde*, *Shampoo*, *Reds*, and *Bulworth*). While making *All Fall Down* in Key West, he got in a barroom brawl with members of the crew, sustaining a laceration in his hand from a broken bottle. After shooting a scene in the Monroe County jail, the crew left him locked up in a cell, throwing the key away.[19]

Instead of apologizing and reforming, he bragged to a reporter, "All right, so I'm not buddy-buddy with the crews. I don't get paid to be friends with them."[20] He was so blinded by egotism that he boasted about his character flaws as if they were virtues instead of trying to correct them. Like Brando, he used rudeness and hostility to conceal his basic insecurity and inarticulateness.[21] To a reporter who'd asked what sort of women he liked, he replied, "Mary Baker Eddy."[22] Years later, he frankly admitted that his problem with interviews was that he didn't have anything to say.

Common courtesy would have helped, and his career would have benefited had he viewed the press as an ally rather than an adversary. His antagonistic attitude invited attacks, and he was always poised for a counterthrust. He demanded and received an apology from the powerful Curtis Publishing Company, via his legal firm, Pepper Hamilton & Sheetz, for saying that he delayed production of a film for six weeks.[23] Blaming the press for his reputation as Hollywood's enfant terrible, he finally stopped giving interviews, explaining, "You just can't win that way."[24]

His first two years in the limelight left him feeling that too much had happened in too short a time, and that he needed to regroup. In the interim, he searched for viable film properties, turning down seventy-five scripts, and he continued to search for himself in brief sexual relationships. He became a camp follower of the Bolshoi Ballet's darkly dramatic prima ballerina Maya Plisetskaya, known as Russia's "flying angel," and attended her performances in London, Toronto, and Moscow. During their affair, his fascination with the Soviet Union grew, but mostly he would remember 1962 and 1963 as "a series of very good times, good food, a lot of good-looking girls, and a lot of aimless fun. . . . I drank wine. . . . I met people like Jean Renoir, people I had only heard about before, in Paris and London. I was becoming an adult. I didn't want to pass up really tasting my early twenties in order to churn up momentum."[25]

He finally treated himself to a black Lincoln Continental with red leather upholstery, as well as three Fords. Each year thereafter, he purchased the latest models of all four cars.

His friend Valerie Allen, whom he'd fixed up with Charles K. Feldman, recalls, "One night Charlie told me, 'I'm going to a party tonight and Jack Kennedy, the president, is going to be there. I'd take you, but I'm afraid I'd lose you.' 'Fine,' I said. 'That's great. I really don't want to go.' I had heard the president did like ladies very much, and I wouldn't get near someone that attractive when I was already involved with someone else. Today, part of me really regrets not having met the incredible JFK, but part of me doesn't, because of Charlie."

When the president was assassinated on November 22, 1963, Warren was in Stanley Kubrick's apartment in New York, trying to persuade him to direct *What's New Pussycat?*, a comedy Warren described as "the plight of the compulsive Don Juan."[26] Kubrick usually appreciated Warren's sense of humor, but *What's New Pussycat?* was far below the standards of the director of *Paths of Glory*, *Dr. Strangelove*, and *Lolita*. As Warren left Kubrick's apartment building on Manhattan's Central Park West that day, he heard a voice on the radio in the lobby announcing Kennedy's death. Shocked, he nevertheless kept his appointment across Central Park with Woody Allen, whom he'd hired to rewrite *What's New Pussycat?* "We all sat there, stunned," Warren recalled.[27]

Later he joined Valerie Allen and Charlie Feldman, in whose Manhattan town house he was staying. "The night after Jack Kennedy was killed, we were all at a restaurant called Sheila Chang on Third Avenue," Valerie recalls. "Warren was dating a model named Reynada. We all talked about how much we loved Jack Kennedy, and just sat there in a booth comforting each other. We were in shock, actually. We'd try to talk about something else and then revert to, 'Isn't it just horrible,' like when a close family member dies. Charlie [who was close to JFK's father, Joseph P. Kennedy] told us that when Jack was courting Gene Tierney at Hamburger Hamlet, Joe would call Charlie and say, 'Go get him out of there.' Charlie knew all of them, Jack and the whole family, and I remember Warren just listening with rapt fascination."

Warren had first uttered the expression "What's new, Pussycat?" while staying in Feldman's house. "That's how Warren used the phrase when he'd be calling up girls," says Valerie. Eventually Beatty and Feldman, a formidable deal-maker whose real name was Charles Gould and who'd been a lawyer before becoming an agent and later a producer, went into business together. Feldman had founded the Famous Artists Agency, handling such clients as Marlene Dietrich, John Wayne, Gary Cooper, and Greta Garbo. "Charlie taught Warren a lot, like you don't put anything in writing, you don't sign contracts, you can walk out at anytime," says Richard Sylbert. "Charlie would not be denied. He was a seducer, just like Warren. Warren would always say, 'You don't have any friends; just make the best deal you can.' "[28] Adds Valerie Allen, "Warren just adored Charlie. Warren learned all about how writers work, how producers work. He always had in mind to be more than an actor, to use all his creative powers."

The sixty-year-old Feldman, who'd discovered Lauren Bacall in 1943, was still agenting such stars as William Holden, John Wayne, and Capucine. A connoisseur of fine houses in Hollywood and on the French Riviera, he knew the provenance of wines and was at home in the world's grand hotels and gambling spas.[29] After he married Jean Howard, a former Ziegfeld showgirl, their house in Coldwater Canyon became the focus of Hollywood social life until their divorce in the 1940s. When Charlie started producing movies, he teamed up with Howard Hawks, who'd directed such classics as *Bringing Up Baby, Scarface,* and *Red River,* and together they filmed Marilyn Monroe's *The Seven Year Itch.* More significantly, Feldman was responsible for one of the best films ever made—Kazan's *A Streetcar Named Desire*, starring Vivien Leigh and Marlon Brando. "Charlie and Warren were very close, very close," says Dick Sylbert. He was Hollywood royalty, as was his partner Hawks, who was married to the socialite Nancy Gross "Slim" Hawks. When the Rat Pack was formed in 1955, Feldman and his mistress, the lovely but wooden Capucine, were in the original gang that Frank Sinatra flew to Las Vegas for Noel Coward's opening at the Desert Inn. After four days of partying with Judy Garland, Sid Luft, Angie Dickinson, "Swifty" Lazar, Martha Hyer, Jimmy Van Heusen, Humphrey Bogart, and David Niven, Lauren Bacall surveyed the hungover carousers and declared, "You look like a god damn rat pack."[30]

Warren wanted Charlie to produce *What's New, Pussycat?* which he intended to star in himself, but he was afraid Charlie would foist Capucine on him as his costar. Laurence Harvey once said, "Kissing her was like kissing the side of a beer bottle," but Feldman was besotted with Capucine's undeniable physical assets. When Warren said she couldn't be in *What's New Pussycat?* Feldman objected. Dick Sylbert recalls, "Charlie did what Charlie wanted to do."

Feldman was more agreeable when Warren insisted they go down to Greenwich Village to see Woody Allen's act at the Bitter End. They decided that night to hire Allen to punch up *What's New Pussycat?* with new jokes, offering him thirty thousand dollars. Allen insisted on forty thousand dollars, but later accepted the original sum, provided he could also appear in the movie. It was a sly move, one that would not work to Warren's advantage. As the script progressed, Warren's role was virtually written out of the story, and the leading lady's role was punched up for Capucine. Finally, Feldman said, "Well, we're ready to go." Dick Sylbert was present when Warren confronted Feldman in his suite at the Dorchester in London, threatening—strictly as a bluff—to drop out of the picture. "Charlie, I'm not going to do it," Warren said. "I'm not doing the picture."

After Feldman angrily cursed him, Warren walked out, vexed but confident that everyone would eventually accede to his terms, that his part would be built up, that Woody's role would be diminished, and that Capucine would be out of the picture. Instead, Warren recalled, "They were only too happy to let me go." But his defection broke Feldman's spirit, according to Peter Bart.[31] Sylbert says, "I got really angry with Warren. He went back to Hollywood, to Universal. He was going to do a picture with some for-the-moment blond bimbo—I forget the name of the picture. I got up there and said, 'You know what's going to happen to you? You're going to end up like fucking George Hamilton before this is over.' He never answered me. He walked away." *What's New Pussycat?*—starring Woody Allen, Capucine, and Peter O'Toole—turned out to be one of the most successful films of 1965, and Tom Jones's famous recording of the theme song became a Top 10 hit. "I would have gotten rich off it," Warren mused. Tragedy loomed for poor Capucine, who lost a steady, stabilizing mentor in Feldman when she jilted him for William Holden. Soon bored with Capucine, Holden dropped her, and she began to take barbiturates. Her next lover was a handsome, high-born young Frenchman, but she eventually sent him away, advising him to marry someone his own age. The young man committed suicide, as, later, did Capucine, who jumped from a balcony to her death at the age of fifty-seven.

Though Warren was learning to burnish his style from suave operators like Feldman, who dressed in regulation dark suits and ties, he hadn't yet acquired their business acumen. By 1964, he'd spent everything he'd made and was ten thousand dollars in the hole. Broke, he went into a terrible picture, *Lilith*, directed by the estimable Robert Rossen, whose film *All the King's Men* won an Oscar. *Lilith* starred a beautiful but suicidal actress named Jean Seberg. Warren played an occupational therapist in a mental ward, which is where the entire picture and everyone connected with it belonged.

Difficult as ever to direct, he questioned every move and line of dialogue. "If I die," moaned Rossen, "it'll be Warren Beatty who killed me."[32] The actor was so unpopular with cast and crew that his dressing room was trashed, and there were rumors that Peter Fonda and other cast members intended to beat him up. Nervous Columbia executives had Warren whisked out of the wrap party early, hoping to avoid a rumble. Jean Seberg angrily accused Warren of deliberately undermining her performance by upstaging her at every turn.[33] After completing the picture, Rossen died of a litany of ills including diabetes, heart disease, alcoholism, boils—and recalcitrant actors. The best performance in *Lilith* was turned in by Gene Hackman, whose single scene so impressed Warren that he'd cast Hackman three years later in *Bonnie and Clyde*.

Critics hated Warren, *New York* magazine's Judith Crist accusing him of "nonacting," and ridiculing "his apparent inability to deliver a line without counting to ten." That the young performer was "deeply confused,"[34] as Arthur Penn, the bespectacled, philosophical, cigar-smoking director of *The Miracle Worker*, had always known, was now apparent to Hollywood insiders. But Penn admired Warren for having chosen, in his early pictures, to associate himself with gifted directors—Kazan, Quintero, Frankenheimer, and Rossen—which set him apart from pretty-boy peers like Troy Donahue, Tom Tryon, John Gavin, George Hamilton, and Tab Hunter. Said Penn, "He has designed a career for himself based on working for directors he admires rather than deciding that he was going to become a leading movie star and that material would be tailored for him, which is inevitably what happens with a certain kind of star whose own character remains consistent and perpetual. He's going to be the biggest male star since Clark Gable." What Penn didn't yet realize, but would learn soon enough, was that Warren was studying his directors carefully, with the intention of replacing them and running the whole show himself.

With Penn, Warren formed Tatira Productions, hoping to provide a haven for writers to develop their scripts without interference from the studios. Beatty and Penn started talks with Elaine May and Budd Schulberg about writing properties for Tatira, and they acquired Alan Sergal's *Mickey One,* a surrealistic story of a small-time stand-up comic and lounge pianist, to be played by Warren. The film was shot over a period of six weeks in Chicago at Niles Studio, later moving to the Marina Towers apartment building, where twelve hundred Chicago actors were recruited. Warren lived on the twenty-seventh floor of the swank Astor Tower, next door to the Ambassador East, and enjoyed a splendid view of Chicago. His co-star, Alexandra Stewart, was dating bandleader Ray Anthony,[35] so Warren spent his nights playing the piano. Stewart later became the girlfriend of French New Wave director François Truffaut, who would eventually engineer a crucial move in Warren's career.

Warren was still making an effort to be respectful of his directors, and said of Penn, "He is the one who tells me what to do." But Penn found him "difficult . . . impossible."[36] Their bright hopes for Tatira were pretty much dashed by the ill-conceived *Mickey One*, an attempt to make a French New Wave film.

Bosley Crowther of the *New York Times* called Warren "affected and oddly ama-teurish . . . shapeless and superficial." Though Archer Winsten of the *New York Post* applauded the actor for trying to make an art film with no concessions to commercial considerations, he felt Warren lacked the requisite wit to play a comedian. "This is all a surface act, surface and sweat," wrote Winsten.

Two box-office bombs in a row did not bode well for Warren's career, and he confided his disappointment to William Inge. "He's been so intent on his career that he's devoted his entire self to it," Inge later reported. "He's just sit-ting around now, waiting for the rest of his life to come back to him." Had Warren not been the handsomest male face in Hollywood and the industry's favorite cocksman, he'd have been washed up. "He's the greatest roll in the hay," one of his girlfriends told Sheilah Graham. "It was the best I ever had in my life."[37] This sort of talk was raising him to mythic status, and Warren-watching became a favorite Hollywood pastime.

He was getting an enviable reputation for treating all women the same, from movie queens to extras. Many later revealed that he'd made them feel like the most beautiful and desirable woman in the world. Of course, there were excep-tions. Jennie Golden, who was nineteen when she worked as an extra in *Mickey One*, said that Warren approached her one day and asked, "Are you wearing Arnel?" She told him yes, and he said, "I just love Arnel. But I just love what's in it better." Thinking, He doesn't even know me, she said, "That's nice, too. You can look—but don't touch." He walked off. "I'm glad he did," Golden reflected. "He didn't have to talk that way."[38]

Another extra, a twenty-one-year-old girl identified only as Miss Koch, was dozing on a mattress when Warren emerged from his trailer and jabbed her in the ribs. "Waiting for something?" he asked. "Baby, I don't have to wait for *any-thing*!" Koch snapped. Warren shuffled off, and Koch went back to sleep.[39]

Meaningful relationships with men were largely precluded by his compul-sive one-upmanship, which extended even to his mentors, all of whom he'd even-tually undercut, driven by an inner demon that could not accept instruction or guidance. Said one acquaintance, "He likes and can get on with every woman, any woman. But every man is a competitor."[40] His stand-in in *Mickey One*, John Gibson, recalled, "I spent about ten weeks with Beatty and we exchanged about twenty words. The rest of the time he tried to give me orders—'Get my water!' 'Get my yogurt!' 'Get my orange juice!' After a few days, I told ol' buddy

Warren to 'Get lost!' "[41] Of true friendship, he knew little, but he continued to court the affection of older men he thought could help him. The supplicatory gleam in his eyes seemed to tell prospective advisors like William Inge, Elia Kazan, Robert Rossen, Clifford Odets, and Arthur Penn that he was looking for a father figure, but when they accepted the role, he immediately began looking for some flaw in their character or talent that he could magnify in order to repudiate them. Such toxic competitiveness, which demands a feeling of superiority even over one's friends and teachers, virtually assures that one will end up with no continuing relationships. Even in a game of gin rummy with the dying Clifford Odets, Warren had to prove he was a better player.

Both Warren and Arthur Penn keenly felt the need to have a best friend, and for a while they were able to convince themselves they had found one in each other. Penn invited Warren to move in with him and his family in New York so they could savor every minute of their newfound intimacy. They expected to become bosom buddies who'd talk late into the night, every night, for the rest of their lives. The relationship suffered the usual setback, however, when their roles were reversed by the imperatives of Warren's ego. Penn was his guru when they filmed *Mickey One*, but later, when the dynamic Penn tried to direct him in *Bonnie and Clyde*, Warren seized control. Penn the leader suddenly became Penn the follower. If Warren's need for a hero was voracious, so was the insecurity that made him nullify his teachers. Though rather sad, the process was by no means entirely negative or exploitive. Many would benefit from their association with Warren Beatty. Sammy Glick he wasn't, because his motives weren't as calculated, clear, or selfish as those of Budd Schulberg's classic Hollywood hustler in *What Makes Sammy Run*. Warren was an idealist who wanted to improve the world.

One of Warren's girlfriends in the sixties, Claudine Albuquerque, who today lives in Monte Carlo, recalls, "When I went up to his place at the Beverly Wilshire Hotel he was always working on scripts. I was under contract at Columbia Pictures at the time. Warren always called me Claudia. If he wanted to flirt or have you do something, he did it in such a nice, tender way that you'd melt and you'd just go for it. He knew very well how to speak to young ladies and women. I can say he really liked women, was full of charm in a very elegant, sensitive way. I'd first met him at a party in Beverly Hills, one of those garden parties everyone from the studios used to go to. I had some fabulous experiences with Warren, and he's probably the first person I ever had those types of experiences with. I think he sincerely likes women and knows them. He's not afraid of the opposite sex.

"I did it with him, and he was the first one I did it with. I was with another actress, who could have been a very big star but, afterward, she got into drugs. She was beautiful. Warren was curious about how two women go about making love. We had a little something, some grass or something, and all of it was done with love and beauty, there was no ugliness in the sex. It was more like a beautiful statue. I think Warren really knows the tenderness a woman needs, the delicacy, the femininity. He didn't force anything. 'Oh, come,' he'd say. 'It would make us so happy.' If he's attracted to someone, he wants to savor it like a wonderful meal. He definitely is, and was, a Lothario."[42]

As Warren's fame as a footloose Don Juan began to overtake his accomplishments as an actor, he reinforced his ban on interviews, hoping the Romeo image would wither if starved of publicity. Frustrated reporters descended on Shirley MacLaine, relentlessly quizzing her about her secretive younger brother. She flatly told journalist Hollis Alpert, "I don't want to talk about him." When Alpert asked her if there were bad feelings between them, she replied, "Yes, there is some feeling. But I don't want to discuss it. Listen, I felt all that jazz years ago. Why rehash old things? It's my life now and I want to forget the past." Occasionally she used the press to goad and embarrass Warren, telling one reporter, "I keep my daughter as far away from Warren as possible." To another she revealed her disapproval of his profligate lifestyle, remarking, "Warren seems to be quite enthusiastic about sex, to put it mildly. To me, there are other things with higher priority. . . . What appeals to me sexually is always someone's mind, imagination, sense of humor. Whereas with Warren, evidently the sex act itself is what is sexy."

That did it. Suddenly available to the press, Warren got even with her, telling a reporter, "There have been times when Shirley and I have had a lot of very strong differences of opinion on things, very strong differences. And at a certain point I realized that it's best not to try to convince each other and not even get into certain subjects. We have different approaches to almost everything, but I don't disrespect hers in the least."[43]

When Warren and Leslie Caron first met in early 1963 at Le Bistro restaurant in Beverly Hills, the occasion was a dinner party hosted by Leslie's agent,

Freddie Fields, head of Creative Management Associates (CMA). Warren already, like most of the rest of the world, had a crush on the pixyish star of the last great Metro musicals, *Gigi, Lili*, and *An American in Paris*. In 1963 she had just been nominated for the Best Actress Oscar for *The L-Shaped Room*, and Fields's Bistro party was being thrown to woo academy members like Warren to vote for her. After Warren and Leslie chatted, he asked her to let him take her home. The answer, although she was married to director Peter Hall, founder of the Royal Shakespeare Company, was *oui*. And the answer to everything else he asked her to do for the next three years was *oui, oui, oui*.

"Warren liked Leslie, and he thought she was just the most extraordinary person on film," says Dick Sylbert. "They went off the first night they met at a dinner party." At thirty-two, Leslie was six years older than Warren, and fell rather naturally into the role of mentor. Because she believed in him and inspired him, she would come to wield great power in their relationship. He liked hearing her tell him that his future lay in being an independent force in films, a Hollywood outlaw, forging his own destiny outside the artistically restrictive system. When he ultimately proved unfaithful to her, she changed her tune, describing him as a power-mad lecher, which casts some doubt on the sincerity of her original estimation. Empty flattery, skillfully applied to Warren's ego, was perhaps Leslie's strategy in hooking her young lover.

Born July 1, 1931, in Paris, the daughter of a French pharmacist and an American ballerina, Leslie only appeared fragile. An exquisite, atypical beauty who, like many beauties, missed plainness by only a fraction, she was five foot three-and-one-half inches, weighed 112 pounds, and, in her teens, had been a dancer with the Ballets des Champs Élysées. When Cyd Charisse became pregnant with Tony Martin Jr. and had to drop out of *An American in Paris*, Leslie replaced her and became Metro's last musical star. Intelligent and chic, she was not one to suffer fools gladly, having ended her first marriage to meat-packing tycoon George Hormel with the remark, "When love is over, it should be broken off at once."[44]

In her marriage to Peter Hall, she had borne two children, a son and a daughter, by 1964, the year that Warren insinuated himself into her life, telling her how much he admired her films. After they became lovers, he accompanied her to Jamaica, where she was filming *Father Goose* with Cary Grant. Though adultery was common in Hollywood, people were still secretive about it, and

Warren had to hide out in Leslie's house as she worked, to prevent reporters from discovering him. During long hours of self-confinement, he reflected on his career and confided to Leslie that he was disappointed that critics didn't take him as seriously as Brando and Clift, whose stature he would never attain. "He was considered just a playboy," Leslie recalled. "He had spent too much time wooing women in the public eye. Of course it bothered him that he wasn't taken seriously. . . . He was in despair about it."[45] He had only himself to blame. Tail-chasing and partying had consumed the lion's share of his energy, and he was making horrendously poor career choices by appearing in arty fluff like *Mickey One* and *Lilith*, a far cry from Brando's triple-threat film debut—*The Men*, *A Streetcar Named Desire*, and *Viva Zapata*—and Clift's string of early hits, *The Search*, *Red River*, *The Heiress*, and *From Here to Eternity*. Not to mention the incredible concentration of James Dean, who hit nothing but homers, *East of Eden*, *Rebel Without a Cause*, and *Giant*, in two years.

During an interlude in New York, Warren encountered the fabled Italian director Federico Fellini. Costume designer Donfeld recalls: "While I was working on a film in New York in 1965, socialite Dorothy Strelsin invited me to a dinner party honoring Fellini, who was in town for the premiere of *Juliet of the Spirits*. Dorothy chose a noisy trattoria in the lobby area of Grand Central Station, and Burt Bacharach, Angie Dickinson, and I pulled our chairs close to Fellini, surrounding him with laughter and conversation throughout the night. As I left, I asked maestro Fellini, 'Is there anything at all I can do for you during your stay in New York?' He thought for a very long moment, and then replied, 'Do you know Warren Beatty? I would like very much to meet with him, or speak to him, while I am in America.' By coincidence, as I started toward the exit door, I glanced out the front windows and saw Warren and screenwriter Robert Towne hurrying from a train platform to the taxi rank. I banged on the window and begged them to come inside."

Donfeld delivered Beatty and Towne to Fellini, who, understandably startled, said to the other guests, "How'd Donfeld do this?" The kindly Fellini was delighted to learn that Warren admired him as much as he admired Warren. On another occasion, Donfeld was in New York working on a series of Hollywood specials for NBC-TV. "Warren and I were roaming around the East Side one night, and decided to have a nightcap at P. J. Clarke's. As we walked down Third Avenue from Fifty-seventh Street, every hustler in the doorways stepped out of the shadows to offer themselves to Warren, gratis. His reaction to the tight-jeaned, adoring young men was rather comical. 'This is really spooky,' he whispered to me, and we made our way through the crowd that had collected and went into P.J.'s. Over drinks, I told him that an attractive girl at NBC, a production assistant I was working with, had said she was 'nuts' about him. 'Wanna meet a nifty?' I asked."

Warren followed Donfeld to the girl's apartment, which was within walking distance of Clarke's. Though she was already in bed, she came downstairs to the lobby and fell into Warren's arms. "I didn't see either of them again for several weeks. Finally, I ran into the young girl onstage during filming, and asked how Warren was. 'We broke off this morning,' she said. 'He woke me up really early, saying his electric typewriter was on the fritz. He asked me if I could come by his hotel, pick it up, and take it across town to some repair shop. I hung up on him. That's *that*.' "

Back in Los Angeles, Leslie Caron moved into the Beverly Wilshire to be near Warren, and she made arrangements to bring her children, seven-year-old Christopher John and five-year-old Jennifer, to Hollywood. All this was perhaps more than Warren had bargained for. While one woman was not enough, two children were definitely too many. At one point he was seeing socialite Alicia Corning Clark, whose previous husbands were Singer sewing machine heir Alfred Corning Clark and actor Edmund Purdom. "He had many girlfriends," said Alicia during an interview in September 2000. Today Alicia divides her time between homes in New York and the Bahamas, Alfred Corning Clark having left her the bulk of his ten-million-dollar estate. "Warren was gorgeous, glamorous, very well dressed and polite and a very good dancer," she continues. "Every girl wanted him if it was for a night or for a day or for an hour. We knew a lot of the same people. At the time, however, I was in love with the French actor Alain Delon. Girls were very happy to be with Warren because he was a gentleman and treated them like ladies. But as far as sex is concerned—not a big deal. A girl I know in Monte Carlo told me it was not a big deal. He would have more than one girl. I said, 'If he's not that good, then why would he want *two* girls?' She said, 'Well, he just wanted to see, it turned him on to see what two girls were doing.' "

Alicia's own personal history could hardly be more varied or colorful. According to FBI files made public in 1977, she was engaged to marry

Congressman John F. Kennedy in 1951, but his father, Joseph P. Kennedy, objected to her being half Jewish and ended the romance. There were other reasons
for the patriarch's disapproval. As Edmund Purdom once put it, she was "a very
dangerous woman," and FBI reports reveal that she once had a reputation with
both U.S. authorities and the NYPD as a onetime high-priced New York pros-
titute and operator of "a call-girl service" in mid-Manhattan. In an interview for
investigative reporter Seymour Hersch's book *The Dark Side of Camelot*, Alicia,
whom Hersch described as "blond and beautiful," confirmed that JFK wooed
her in the 1950s. "He told me he'd like to buy me diamonds, but he had trouble with his father, who was telling him he was spending too much money. . . .
I preferred to be married to a movie star [Purdom]. . . . [JFK] wanted to run away
from it all with me—to Europe, just to skip town. But I'd say, 'Jack, you don't
have enough money.' " Later, during the Kennedy administration, Alicia and
the president ran into each other at a ball at the British embassy in Washington.
Delighted to see her again, JFK "whisked her off," said Maxwell Rabb, who was
secretary of the cabinet during the Eisenhower administration and was present
that night.[46]

"I knew Warren very well for a very long time," says Alicia. "The last time
I saw him was in Beverly Hills, when he came to see me with Leslie Caron. It
was a very cold night, and I was wearing a beautiful long chinchilla coat. I was
with James Fox, the British actor, and he looked gorgeous. Warren invited me
to go to the hotel, but since I'd heard what I'd heard, I didn't want to. Leslie was
inviting me to come with them too, you know."

With Leslie to take care of—and now two children on his hands—Warren
was not exactly flush with money. A source who has known Alicia Corning
Clark for twenty years, and who requested anonymity, said, "Warren wasn't nice
to Alicia, who is at least twenty years older than he. She bought him a car, a
Spyder or an Alfa Romeo, to trap him, and had it delivered to him at the Beverly
Wilshire. He took the car and wouldn't lay her. He refused to. She told me she
had the car repossessed."[47] When asked about this, Alicia denies it, saying, "No.
Although I wouldn't have minded if he asked me, as we were very good friends.
I would have said to him, 'If that helps your career,' you know? I would have
bought him . . . I could afford it, but I didn't. That's a lie. I am not that type of a
person that goes around and buys things for men. Especially my lovers. My lovers
have to do things for *me*. I mean, I would buy something for a friend. I didn't

have that kind of relationship with Warren. I just knew Warren very well for a very long time."[48]

As Warren was shooting *Mickey One* in Chicago, Leslie's husband, Peter Hall, hired a private detective to document his wife's assignations with Warren. He also had them under surveillance in Beverly Hills and during their stay in Jamaica. He filed for divorce, naming Warren as corespondent, charging Leslie with adultery, and petitioning the British government to make his children wards of the court in order to keep them in England. "He was not living up to his marital vows either," says Jack Larson, who played Jimmy Olson in the original TV *Superman* and has been friendly with Leslie for years. "He was a hypocrite." Rushing back to England with Christopher and Jennifer, Leslie told reporters, "I cannot give up my children. I was going to live with Warren in Hollywood. But now I'll live in England to be near them, and Warren has agreed to live here. When I have my divorce, we will be married." In London, they settled into her five-story Knightsbridge Georgian town house overlooking leafy, elegant Montpelier Square, where her cat Gigi loved to crouch in a tree near her doorway. Warren was a shy prospective stepdad.

Without hesitation, he confirmed that he'd marry Leslie any time she told him to. During the custody battle, he remained in England by her side for the next year and a half. The judge condemned Warren for having stolen Hall's wife. In London filming *Cul-de-Sac* at Shepperton Studios, Roman Polanski sympathized with Warren. Like Polanski, Warren and Leslie began filming at Shepperton, co-starring in a slapstick sex comedy, a genre for which neither had the slightest flair. Many scripts had been offered to Warren, and his way of testing them was to read them twice before arriving at a decision. "If I find I don't want to read it the third time, then we've had it with that one," he explained.[49] Because of his determination to be with Leslie, he was restricted to selecting whatever trivia was available to him abroad. *Promise Her Anything* would become known as "Warren Beatty's turkey." He played a Greenwich Village producer of porn flicks, and Leslie was his neighbor, a young widow whose infant son somehow ends up in one of Warren's girly movies. The director, Arthur Hiller, was known as "a hack of all genres, master of none."[50] Sadly, Warren made *Promise Her Anything* during an otherwise exciting period in cinema that saw Albert Finney's *Tom Jones*, Steve McQueen's *Love with the Proper Stranger*, Paul Newman's *Hud*, and Marcello Mastroianni's *Yesterday, Today and Tomorrow*.

Columnist Sheilah Graham wrote, "*Promise Her Anything* was unsuccessful, and apparently 'anything' did not include a promise of marriage. Not for Leslie; not for Joan Collins, who flew to New York from Israel, where she was making *Esther and the King*, just for a weekend with Warren; or for Natalie Wood, who was sure they would marry when she left Robert Wagner. . . . Warren seems quite happy in his bachelor state."[51]

He escorted Leslie, a leading contender for the Best Actress Oscar for *The L-Shaped Room*, to the academy's thirty-sixth awards ceremony, held February 24, 1964, at the Santa Monica Civic Auditorium, with Jack Lemmon emcee-ing, but many wondered whom Warren would be rooting for. Leslie's competi-tion included his sister Shirley for *Irma La Douce* and Natalie for *Love with the Proper Stranger*. The other two nominees were the dark horses of the race: Patricia Neal for *Hud* and Rachel Roberts for *This Sporting Life*. Natalie was feeling particularly vulnerable that night; though never at a loss for men, no grand passion had replaced Warren in her life. When she'd taken his picture out of the frame in her bedroom, she'd scrawled a question mark in the empty space, as if asking, Who's next? None of the candidates, including William Peter Blatty, author of the bestselling *Exorcist*, managed to fill Warren's shoes. On Oscar night, Natalie lost the prize to Pat Neal, and the pain of her disappointment was dou-bled when she saw Warren with Leslie. Though Natalie was the current reign-ing queen of Hollywood—named "Star of the Year" by the United Theater Owners—she was so desolate over having lost both Warren and R.J., who'd by now married Marion Marshall and fathered a baby daughter, Katie, that Tony Curtis, Natalie's *Sex and the Single Girl* co-star, observed, "Natalie would have been much happier as a nun or a hooker."[52]

In London, one of Warren and Leslie's neighbors was Roman Polanski, who lived nearby, just off Eaton Square. A frequent dinner guest at Montpelier Square, Polanski was as distraught as Warren that both their careers had derailed and, again like Warren, he was filming potboilers to pay the bills. One was *The Fearless Vampire Slayers*, featuring a lovely blond starlet from Texas named Sharon Tate. Back in Hollywood, she'd had an affair with Jay Sebring, a hair-dresser, but the magnetic Polanski easily won her. Despite his "fear of possessive women," he let Sharon move in with him, after she promised, "I won't swallow you up like some ladies do."[53] The compliant Sharon allowed Polanski to sleep around to his heart's content, but he always came back to her. "We took to spending more evenings at home," recalled Polanski, "and entertaining more people, some of them Hollywood friends like Warren Beatty, Dick Sylbert, and Yul Brynner, others 'locals' like Victor Lownes, Andy Braunsberg [later producer of Polanski's *Macbeth*], Larry Harvey [star of *Room at the Top* and *Butterfield 8*], and Michael Sarne, who had just finished directing his first feature, *Joanna*. Jay Sebring, Sharon's former boyfriend, also showed up in London. . . . We developed an immediate rapport, almost as if we'd known each other for years, and Sebring quickly became a regular member of our circle."

It could only have happened in the so-called swinging London of the sixties. Jay Sebring, Sharon's former lover, became the best friend of her current lover, Polanski. Around the same time, Sebring became Warren's barber. A good-looking, kinky man, given to group sex and bondage, Sebring counted among his star clients Steve McQueen, Paul Newman, Peter Lawford, and George Peppard. According to Polanski, Sebring "liked to whip-tie girls. Sharon told me he tied her to the bed once."[54] Sharon and Jay did cocaine and LSD together, until she freaked out and had to ease up on drugs.

Nan Morris-Robinson gave a contrasting view of Sebring, and also offered insights into another rising hairdresser/style setter of the time, Gene Shacove, both of whom would later figure significantly in the genesis of Warren's seventies movie *Shampoo*. Shacove trimmed Hugh Hefner's locks for three decades. Recalls Nan, "Gene Shacove and I double dated in 1964 with Jay and Sharon Tate, who were going together. Gene and Jay, who were both hairdressers, were the best of friends, and Jay and Sharon were going steady. Jay was a little guy, sassy and fiery. He could do karate. Sharon had been brought into our circle by Richard Beymer, who spotted her when he was at the Tropicana one night. She was Richard's discovery; he got her an agent and introduced her around. I thought she was the sweetest, most angelic creature, one who radiated gentility."

After Sharon's affair with Sebring, she married Polanski, who cast her in *Vampire Killers*, a film that contained elements of all his fixations: voyeurism, nudity, homosexuality, sadomasochism, and vampirism. She found Polanski sexy in his cute, diminutive way. He resembled Christian Slater, star of a later Hollywood era. Muscular and athletic, Polanski was a daring skier, a man who lunged at life head-on, obsessed with the question "Who shall I gratify tonight?"[55] He was one of the very first of the sixties directors to get leading ladies to do nude scenes. Even the remote, classic French beauty Catherine Deneuve stripped for him in *Repulsion*. Sharon also obliged Polanski in *Vampire Killers*, finding it sensual and irresistible just to be asked by Polanski to take her clothes off. Increasingly, Polanski would become involved, both personally and professionally, with such figures in Warren's circle as production designer Richard Sylbert and Sylbert's sister-in-law, Anthea Sylbert, who'd capture the sixties look "to a T," Polanski said, in her costumes for *Rosemary's Baby*.[56]

In London, Warren started filming another of his potboilers, *Kaleidoscope*, costarring Susannah York, one of Britain's attractive sixties superstars. Warren played a rich adventurer who tries to foul up Europe's great gambling casinos. "There was a certain amount of turmoil in my private life then," he said. "I had to make some pictures [abroad]."[57] Caron was on the set when Warren tried to pinch York's bum. York slapped his hand, and Caron, according to York, was "quite jealous." York discovered that if a girl didn't submit to Warren's advances, "it precluded you from being friends."[58] On location in Monte Carlo, he had better luck when he spent three days playing baccarat and chemin de fer, for total winnings of $150,000.

Time thought *Kaleidoscope*, which was released in 1966, a routine crime caper, writing, "Beatty tries so hard to act like Sean Connery that once or twice he almost develops a line in his face." With four artistic and commercial failures in a row, he was more or less a Hollywood has-been.

During the child-custody battle that followed Peter Hall's filing for divorce, Leslie's children had to remain in London temporarily. They were placed in boarding schools, a resolution that was satisfactory to neither parent. After Warren finished his picture and returned to the U.S., Leslie found herself commuting between London and Los Angeles, trying to be with Warren but needing to be in England for regular visits with Christopher and Jennifer. "I want to live while I'm alive," she said.[59] Warren paid all her court costs during the long legal battle with Hall. Eventually she won custody, and Warren rented Peter Lawford's thirty-five-hundred-dollar-a-month beachfront house for them in Santa Monica. The place boasted three swimming pools and two tennis courts for the children. President Kennedy, Lawford's brother-in-law, had once stayed there, but later Lawford was forced to rent it out just to meet the mortgage payments.[60] Leslie Caron loved to entertain guests at dinner, and Warren came out of his shell and tried to enjoy her gracious evenings at home. "I love him madly," she said, "and he is a great actor."[61] One night she went to a party without him, and someone remarked to Natalie Wood, who was also in attendance, "Leslie is looking so beautiful." Poignantly, Natalie uttered one word: "Warren."

Like Natalie, Leslie wouldn't have him for long. While in London he was introduced to the quintessential girl of the sixties, Julie Christie, Oscar-winning star of *Darling*, described by one journalist as "the mod, the rocker, the cool beatnik, the new face of the sixties, the strong, sphinxlike, stainless steel little soldier." Warren later recalled, "When I met her, I thought she had the most wonderful face." Indeed, it was one of the greatest faces since Garbo—intense, soulful, and with a golden glow of soft eyes and straw-colored hair. Amazed by the stir she was kicking up on both sides of the Atlantic, Julie once said, "For men, I don't think it's sexiness in me that appeals to them, but an air of abandonment. Men don't want responsibilities and neither do I."

She sounded like the perfect match for Warren, but both stars at the time were deeply involved with others, Warren with Leslie and Julie with British artist Don Bessant. "I cannot imagine not being in love with Don," Julie said. "I also can't imagine a time when I wouldn't be with him. But marriage—it's like signing your life away."[62] On a subsequent trip to New York, Warren was walking along Fifty-eighth Street with Donfeld when they passed a movie theater showing Julie's film *Petulia*. Recalls Donfeld, "Knowing I'd seen a rough cut of the picture at Warner in Hollywood, Warren asked my opinion. 'Oh, I dunno,' I said. 'It's one of those love-me-or-I'll-hit-you movies.' Warren said, 'That's a great phrase, Donfeld. I warn you, I'm gonna use it some day in my writing.' As he spoke, he was gazing intently at a full color, larger-than-life photograph of Julie."

Though intrigued by Julie, Warren continued to search for projects that he and Leslie could share, but Leslie was more interested in doing a biopic of Edith Piaf. Warren followed her to Paris when she filmed *Is Paris Burning?* and then went on to Venice for a *Mickey One* screening. Sheilah Graham asked him if he was marrying Leslie, and his answer was a typical cop-out. "Whenever she wants to," he said, passing the buck. It was time for him to get back to his neglected career. He was itching to sink his teeth into a juicy, challenging role, like Dick Diver, the psychiatrist, in F. Scott Fitzgerald's *Tender Is the Night*. Unfortunately, at twenty-seven he was considered too young for the role, which was played by forty-one-year-old Jason Robards Jr. in an unsuccessful film starring Jennifer Jones.

He turned his attention to *Natural State*, a political story he was developing, set in the U.S. and Russia, with key roles for two men and two women—obviously a precursor to *Reds*. In another venture, he and James Baldwin discussed collaborating on a script about a white man and a black girl, but nothing came of it. Nor did something called *Promiscuous Bound* take flight. A more durable project was *Keith's My Name, Hair's My Game*, which Warren started co-writing with scenarist Bob Towne. At one time it was known as *Hair*, before the title was co-opted by a hit Broadway musical. Eventually it would be known as *Shampoo*.

All these projects lost steam, and with a string of bad films haunting him, Warren's career seemed headed for oblivion. Then one evening, when he and Leslie were dining with Roman Polanski, the director told them that François Truffaut, creator of *Shoot the Piano Player* and *Jules and Jim*, who'd suggested Alexandra Stewart for *Mickey One*, was casting a new picture, *Fahrenheit 451*, adding that it would be a perfect costarring vehicle for Warren and Leslie. Coincidentally, Leslie was already in touch with Truffaut regarding her Edith Piaf project. Thanks to the critics' deification of France's nouvelle vague cinema, Truffaut was currently one of the world's most fashionable directors, along with such other New Wave auteurs as Jean-Luc Godard, Louis Malle, and Alain Resnais.

At Warren's suggestion, he and Leslie flew to Paris to meet with Truffaut. Warren spoke no French, so Leslie lunched with Truffaut, and Warren joined them for dessert. "It turned out that Truffaut had already cast Oskar Werner and Julie Christie for his film," recalls Caron, "but he had another script that he thought might interest Warren and me . . . *Bonnie and Clyde*. Warren read it and went like an arrow to New York to buy the rights." The authors were two young *Esquire* writers, David Newman and Robert Benton. *Bonnie and Clyde* was the rip-roaring gangster tale of Clyde Barrow and his moll Bonnie Parker, who cut a swath of robbery and terror through the American South during the Depression. "Being an outlaw was a great thing to want to be [in the counterculture sixties], whether it was Clyde Barrow or Abbie Hoffman," said Benton. "All the stuff we wrote had to do with *épater le bourgeois*, shaking society up, saying to all the squares, 'We don't do that, man, we do our thing.' " Truffaut had originally sent the authors to Jean-Luc Godard, whose *Breathless* was about gangsters, but Godard couldn't put a deal together, and Truffaut finally agreed to direct it for $80,000, provided Alexandra Stewart played Bonnie Parker. The American producers wanted Paul Newman for Clyde Barrow, but Truffaut preferred Scooter Teague or Robert Walker. Insisting on a star, the producers then suggested Beatty, but Truffaut raised strenuous objections. He was no admirer of Warren, he said, and added that he found the actor to be "unpleasant." Beatty and Brando were two of Truffaut's least favorite human beings, and he'd prefer never to make another film than work with either of them. Truffaut needn't have worried. Warren was already in the process of buying the rights out from under him.

Back in the U.S., he rang Benton on a frigid February morning in 1966, saying, "This is Warren Beatty." Unable to believe his ears, Benton said, "Who is this, really?" Warren replied, "This is really Warren Beatty," adding that he was on his way over to the young journalist's Manhattan apartment to pick up a copy of the script. Twenty minutes later Benton's wife, Sally, opened the door; Warren came in, took the script, and left. Thirty minutes later he called and told Benton, "I want to do it." Benton asked him what page he was on, and Warren told him, "Page twenty-five." Benton warned him to read on, at least to page 40. By then Warren would discover that the screenplay was about a homosexual—a love story about Clyde Barrow and his sidekick C. W. Moss. He didn't care.

An hour later, Warren called and said, "I've finished the script. I understand what you mean, but I still want to do it." He acquired the rights for seventy-five hundred dollars for his company Tatira (named after his mother, who was called "Tat" in childhood, and his father, Ira), and later paid Benton and Newman seventy-five thousand dollars to write the final screenplay. Since Clyde Barrow was described as a runt, Warren at first envisaged Bob Dylan in the title role.

Knowing that gangster films were passé, Warren had serious second thoughts and went around asking his friends whether he should stick with the picture or write off his investment. The very determined Leslie Caron, despite her pronounced and trademark French accent, convinced herself that she could tailor the role of Bonnie Parker to her talents. In the film, Bonnie's mother could be a French woman from New Orleans. *Bon!* Confident that she was part of the package, Leslie urged Warren to proceed. The realization that, as the owner of the property, he could be completely in control made him decide to produce as well as star in the picture—another inspired career move. He wanted to direct it as well but wisely decided his plate was full enough and engaged Arthur Penn, his old *Mickey One* colleague. "I knew that I could collaborate with Arthur," he said.[63]

Benton and Newman came out to Hollywood to work with Penn, whose first task was to expunge the homosexuality from the script. Like many criminals, Clyde Barrow had blossomed into a practicing bisexual while serving time in jail, but Penn convinced Benton and Newman that *Bonnie and Clyde* should be a heterosexual love story, which would be more appealing, he thought, to the general public. Beatty decided to play Clyde as impotent, perhaps as a slap at a world that had stereotyped him as a playboy. In the final picture, though Bonnie and Clyde can't consummate their love, they have a deep yearning to connect emotionally with each other as human beings, which became one of the picture's themes.

Penn tried to withdraw when he read the final script, but the canny Warren knew how to hold his package together, bringing in a friend, writer Robert Towne, who'd earlier helped him find his way around the studios as a fledgling producer in search of financial backing, a new and unfamiliar undertaking for the actor. Although Towne had not yet done a major screenplay, he'd doctored so many scripts that he knew the ins and outs of the movie business, and was viewed as a precocious master at manipulating the system. Amusing, soft-spoken, discreet, self-assured, and persuasive, he called himself "a relief pitcher who could come in for an inning, not pitch the whole game." Jack Nicholson trusted him so much that, on Towne's advice, he turned down the heavy-handed *Great Gatsby*, on which Robert Redford later tripped and fell.

Warren managed to string Penn along by signing Towne to turn out a quick rewrite, fully aware that Towne always worked slowly. Towne had to revise certain scenes as many as fifty times before they were deemed acceptable to both Warren and Penn.[64]

Meanwhile, Beatty and Penn's Tatira company bought Bob Towne's *Keith's My Name, Hair's My Game*, ultimately filmed under the title *Shampoo*, and also purchased James B. Harris's *Hot Time in the Old Town Tonight*, which was planned as a co-starring vehicle for Warren and Sidney Poitier, but never came to fruition. (Harris produced Kubrick's *Lolita*.) *Shampoo* was first written in 1968, with Warren providing the story and Towne the structure and dialogue. Warren developed the main character while working with Mike Nichols and Groucho Marx on an ill-fated project in the early 1960s.[65]

Bonnie and Clyde continued to encounter obstacles; Columbia and United Artists both turned it down. Warren next went to Warner Bros., and David Newman accompanied him when he met with Jack L. Warner to raise money. Warner didn't see *Bonnie and Clyde* as a bankable package, complaining that Beatty's track record hardly inspired confidence, that Benton and Newman were unknowns, and that Arthur Penn had done nothing of note since *The Miracle Worker*. Determined to win at any cost, Warren got down on his knees and begged for the money. According to Hollywood columnist Joe Hyams, who was present, Beatty actually kissed Warner's feet.[66] "Come on, kid," Warner said, "you're embarrassing me." To get rid of him, Warner offered him a modest budget, two million dollars. Then, assuming that the picture was a dog and would never break even, he gave Warren 40 percent of the gross (thirty million dollars, as it turned out).

"Warren's a great wheeler-dealer," said Newman, but others at Warner Bros. didn't think so. One executive joked that Beatty had a huge cut of nothing, certain that the film would never break even.

"With this film," wrote Warren's eventual co-star Faye Dunaway, "Warren really became the first in a new wave of producer/director/actor power combinations. . . . That was the only way the studio could get the project, and Warren was a big star, so they agreed. I once asked Warren if he was the first actor/producer, momentarily forgetting those early people like Charlie Chaplin and Mary Pickford, who were indeed actor/producers. He said, 'No I wasn't the first one, but I was the best one.' That's Warren for you. Snappy, very capable."[67]

Leslie Caron was tremendously excited that she and Warren would be starring together in what had always struck her as a major motion picture, despite the fact that everyone else put it down. She was heartbroken when he coolly informed her that her French accent and delicate Audrey Hepburn–type personality made her all wrong for the tough gun moll Bonnie Parker. His reasoning seemed sensible on the surface but was actually quite arbitrary in the context of movie history—Marlene Dietrich's thick German accent hadn't hindered one of the most popular American westerns of all time, *Destry Rides Again*, nor had Vivien Leigh's British origins wrecked *Gone With the Wind*, nor had Garbo's thick Swedish accent hurt *Camille,* though Camille was one of the most classically French of all heroines. Another Swede, Ingrid Bergman, had seemed as American as apple pie to the U.S. public in blockbusters like *The Bells of St.*

Mary's. No doubt the audience that adored Caron in *Gigi* would have embraced her in any role she chose to play. But most likely, Beatty was beginning to back away from the prospect of marrying Leslie and raising her children. Understandably, she felt utterly betrayed and abused, remarking, "The way he discarded me after I got him to buy *Bonnie and Clyde* was rather ruthless. . . . Anyone who has come close to Warren has shed quite a few feathers. He tends to maul you."[68]

Although Warren insisted he was still in love with her, she terminated their affair after he showed his true colors. "I am not sure about marriage any more," he said. "Most people I know seem to have been married twice. Sometimes it all seems like a bit of a farce." Some years later, Warren confessed, "I look back at that particular period with a deep and profound sadness."

According to Sheilah Graham, everyone had assumed that marriage was imminent. It certainly hadn't been as far as Warren was concerned. He'd kept his suite at the Beverly Wilshire, consigning Leslie and her brood to the rented house. He'd continued to use his bachelor's quarters at the hotel whenever he wished—hardly an inducement to marital fidelity. "Warren's conquests of women are not totally successful," his later co-star Lee Grant once explained. "His percentage is about fifty-fifty. Those he can't conquer don't want to be part of a crowd—one of Warren's girls. But the Peter Pan quality in Warren is very attractive to some. He teaches them to fly, and they have extraordinary experiences with him. Then they grow up and go on, and he keeps flying. Like Peter Pan, he always comes back to another little girl who's ready to fly off with him to Never-Never Land."[69]

After Warren and Leslie broke up, she went on to marry Michael Laughlin, producer of *Joanna*, in 1969, though the union was short-lived. Summing up her impressions of Warren, she said, "He never made any secret of the fact that he wanted the world. He loved power and went for it . . . a very passionate man in every respect."

One day, Warren was being interviewed by *Los Angeles* magazine writer Thomas Thompson in London when they were joined by a twenty-six-year-old German journalist. She was lean, fetchingly modish in her boots and miniskirt, and Warren took her upstairs to bed. He also ran into old flames like Joan Collins, who gushed over him when she spotted him dining in a restaurant. Joan left her escort and dashed to Warren for a hug. Leslie Caron visibly flinched when she saw him at a screening. In Paris one night, he found himself wedged between Julie Christie and Natalie Wood, both obviously intent on monopolizing him. Thomas Thompson recalled, "The two women threw verbal poison darts at one another from the crudités to the crème caramel. Warren sat uneasily in the middle."[70]

When it was reported that Shirley MacLaine was going to co-star with Warren in *Bonnie and Clyde*, Shirley quipped, "That would be adding incest to injury." There was a modicum of Freudian truth in her reference to incest. On another occasion, discussing her brother's love life, she shocked the movie industry and the public by offering this confession to a reporter, "Warren's looking for a woman like me. Everybody in our circle knows that. Sure, we laugh about it. It's cute. Look at all those women he dates. They're all actresses, talented, intelligent, usually either a dancer . . . or a person who won't agree with him. It's too bad we're related."[71]

She later claimed she was only kidding, but she'd already gone on record as saying that in every joke, there was a kernel of truth. Pamela Des Barres's experience with Warren seems to bear out MacLaine's contention. Years later, he considered filming Pamela's book about a groupie sleeping around in Hollywood, *I'm with the Band*. During one of their meetings "in his spotless chrome kitchen," Pamela got the distinct impression that he was coming on to her, and suspected it was because she resembled Shirley MacLaine. She was right; Warren told their mutual friend Joyce Hyser, "Pammie looks just like my sister, doesn't she?"[72]

Shirley obviously enjoyed speculating what it would be like to act with Warren. "All that stuff in the cornfields," she mused. "I guess he couldn't do it with his sister. But come to think of it—maybe he could."[73] Just as likely, Warren sought Shirley for *Bonnie and Clyde* to secure the package by capitalizing on her fame and bankability. Though her films were often critical and financial disasters, she was highly paid and in constant demand in the mid to late 1960s, starring in *Gambit*, *Woman Times Seven*, and *Sweet Charity*, while Warren had been wasting himself with Leslie Caron in rubbish like *Promise Her Anything*. Though Warren was on the brink of launching a new era in picture making that would come to be called the New Hollywood, Shirley was not particularly supportive, explaining, "I hear he's a very strong—and good—producer, but it's all gotta be *his* way. . . . I don't think Warren and I are ever going to co-star. Warren works by instinct—I don't like his chaos." No doubt she was still smarting over his social rebuffs. "He has a hard time deciding where to have dinner," she said, adding, "which, of course, leaves his options open for a better offer."

Later, she seemed to reconsider, perhaps as talk spread that Bonnie Parker was a strong role. "He hasn't made me any real offers yet," she complained to a reporter. "You know, all talk and no action. Of course, that's the opposite of what his girlfriends say about him." She added that "it would be hard to do a love story" with her own brother,[74] but she later claimed that she'd have taken the role if Warren had made a firm offer. He later told *Daily Variety*'s Army Archerd, "It was my idea to direct it, have my sister play Bonnie, and have some guy play opposite her."[75]

Instead, he offered the role to Tuesday Weld, but she had wed screenwriter Claude Harz and now had daughter Natasha to raise.[76] Warren next attempted to cast Natalie Wood. By now, she'd become a much bigger star than Warren. She permitted him come to her house and make his pitch, but she kept taking telephone calls as he attempted to synopsize the plot. "I guess I wasn't too persuasive," Warren recalled. "At that point I wasn't getting a lot of offers and Natalie was riding the crest of her career. Well, it didn't take long to see she wasn't interested in doing a picture with me. Besides, she figured the idea didn't have a chance." On the contrary, Natalie "loved the script and loved the part," she later said, but she was afraid that Warren would drive her to another nervous breakdown. "Working with him had been difficult before," she recalled.[77]

At one point, Carol Lynley almost won the role. Jane Fonda turned it down.[78] Warren was on the verge of signing Sue Lyon, the saucy nymphet in *Lolita*, when Penn brought a relative newcomer named Faye Dunaway to his attention. A protégée of Warren's friend and mentor, producer Sam Spiegel, Dunaway already had *Hurry Sundown* and *The Happening* to her credit, but neither film had yet been released. "With Sam in charge," Dunaway recalled, "I entered the star machine at warp speed," but no one knew what the public's verdict on her would be when her films were seen.

After Penn screened some scenes from *The Happening*, a fast-moving caper story, he called Dunaway's agent, CMA's David Begelman, and said, "Tell me about Faye." Begelman was Judy Garland's agent, and he knew how to hype his clients. He arranged for Penn and Dunaway to meet at the Plaza in New York. The director and actress hit it off, and Dunaway then flew to the Coast to meet Warren. "This is a game," she later wrote, "this is moviemaking, this is deal-making." Though still an unknown, she was going to demand star billing. When her manager, Simon Maslow, warned her she'd blow the deal, she lost faith in him. "I realized then that Si was a little out of his depth," she said. He wouldn't be her manager for long.

One evening, just after twilight, Dunaway and Penn arrived at Warren's penthouse suite in the Beverly Wilshire, which struck Dunaway as "plush but cozy." Warren and Faye read through the first scene in the movie: Bonnie stands in a hotel room, wearing no clothes, and looks out the window to see Clyde Barrow hot-wiring her mother's automobile. Instead of objecting to the theft, she sees a chance for a more exciting life and flees with him. "I played that moment like a house on fire and never looked back," she said.

Of all the careers Warren helped launch as a producer, Dunaway's would prove to be perhaps the most brilliant. His treatment of this sensitive, very special talent was impeccable from the start, later culminating in her bravura performances in *Chinatown, Network*, and *Mommie Dearest*. Hollywood's most coveted prize, the Best Actress Oscar, went to her for *Network*.

Dunaway's poor southern background made her ideal for the role of Bonnie Parker. Born January 14, 1941, to a Florida panhandle farmhand and his high-school dropout wife, Dorothy Faye Dunaway "could stand in the middle of the dirt road that ran in front of the house I was born in and look hard either way and see nothing but the long rows of peanuts snaking their way up to a stand of trees in the distance." From her mother, Grace, she got the "backbone" that gave her roles steely strength and elegance. But when her parents' marriage broke up, Faye blamed Grace. Later, when she saw the Lana Turner–Susan Kohner remake of *Imitation of Life*, she related to Kohner's portrayal of Sarah Jane, a girl at war with her mother. Like Sarah Jane, Faye left the South to escape poverty.

Making her way north, she studied acting at Boston University, appeared in several productions with the Harvard Summer Players, and debuted on Broadway in 1962 as Lady Margaret in *A Man for All Seasons*. At 115 pounds and five-foot-seven, she was a statuesque head-turner, part Bacall, part Dietrich. Late one night that fall she dropped into the Village Vanguard near Sheridan Square, where comic Lenny Bruce was playing. Struck by the magnitude of his comic genius, she asked the bartender to introduce her after the show, and a romance began between the forty-year-old Bruce and the twenty-one-year-old ingenue.

"Years later, on the set of *Bonnie and Clyde*, Michael J. Pollard and I would pass the time doing Lenny Bruce bits," she remembered. "I wanted to be like him, at least in attitude. I wanted to challenge it all, too—conventions, the establishment, the status quo."

When Faye read for Warren in his suite at the Beverly Wilshire that day, he liked her back-country toughness. Her reading of the line "Boy, what you doing with my mama's car" was perfect. He had qualms, however, about appearing with an unknown whose films hadn't even been released. Though sexually attracted to her, he respected her so much that, for once, he didn't try to bed down one of his aspiring leading ladies, or perhaps he was already in character as an impotent bank robber. Dunaway wasn't drawn to him sexually, but she liked him at once, even though he didn't want to give her star billing. She overheard Beatty and Penn talking about her, and at one point Penn said, "Either she does it or I don't do it."

Not until months after the movie was shot did Warren grant Dunaway star billing. "That's because he's got a lot of class," she said. "Warren was smart enough to know that this movie would make me a star, and he may as well beat the town to the punch."[79]

Character actor Michael J. Pollard, an old friend of Warren's and one of Janis Joplin's lovers, was signed to play C. W. Moss. Warren knew Pollard from their days together in New York in *A Loss of Roses*. Jennifer Lee, a subsequent Beatty girlfriend, had an affair with Pollard and revealed, "The only antidote for Michael's morose insanity is making love. This need has resulted in an intense sexuality, making him one of the best lovers I've ever had."[80] Pollard's oddball looks, though verging on grotesque, gave him an impish, boyish quality that enamored many, including Joplin and Edie Sedgwick.

Rounding out the brilliant cast were Gene Hackman, Estelle Parsons, and Gene Wilder—all significant but as-yet-unproved talents. So far, as a producer, Warren was batting a thousand. "I wanted to see if I could play with the big boys," he said, revealing his determination to be taken seriously.[81] In the independent-producer tradition of David O. Selznick, he supervised every aspect of the picture. Casting the actors, hiring the technical personnel, and scouting for locations intrigued him as much as his own starring role. In postproduction, he would go into hiding until he'd cut and mixed the picture, emerging only to take over the advertising and publicity. Wrote screen historian David Thomson,

"Nothing else in life seems to have fulfilled his obsessive energies as much as pro-ducing a film. He stakes his life and his fortune on it."

Beatty claims that he was abstinent throughout the making of *Bonnie and Clyde*. "You should not have sex at all," he advised James Toback, who was writ-ing a script for Warren. "You should be totally abstinent from the start of pre-production. The film will be better if you never come. On *Bonnie and Clyde*, I never fucked once. It was important."[82]

On August 10, 1966, he left on a ten-day location-hunting trip, later decid-ing to shoot the film around Dallas. The movie was made on a tight budget. When the company arrived in Dallas, they stayed not in the fabled Adolphus Hotel but at the modest North Park Motor Inn. Each day they drove from the motel to various small towns in the area for shooting, and Warren set up house-keeping in a Winnebago. "Girls clambered in and out at all hours of the day and night," New Hollywood historian Peter Biskind later reported. "The cast and crew watched it rock back and forth like a ship upon the sea."[83] So much for Warren's claims of abstinence.

The first scenes were filmed in Midlothian, Texas, after which Warren and his cast repaired to a battered old theater in downtown Dallas to view the rush-es. The auditorium stank of stale popcorn and rancid butter, and the tattered carpet was spotted with melted chocolate and spilled Cokes. He was pleased with the rushes, but noticed that Dunaway seemed to be in shock.

In fact, she was on the verge of throwing up. She'd never before seen her vis-age on a screen this big, and she thought, "I look ugly, I feel ugly. . . . I couldn't stand how I was—my manners, my gestures. It was the first time I really got a sense of how I must look to other people. . . . I just thought I was sadly lacking." Chatting and comparing notes with Arthur Penn, Warren ignored Dunaway's crisis, but Michael J. Pollard tried to cheer her up by imitating Lenny Bruce and Mel Brooks, and saying, "Fer-git-it, Faye." All she could think was, God, do I really look like that? Though attractive, she, like Warren, had escaped ugli-ness by a hairbreadth, with her Jane Wyman puglike face.

Suddenly she stood up and walked out of the theater, climbed in her car, and drove out of town. After a while, she stopped, got out, and walked to the center of a field of new-mown hay. "The bales, which are scattered around the field, are drying to a golden brown in the Texas sun," she recalled. "My arms are hugging my knees up close against me. If I could disappear, make myself somehow smaller, I would." For the next three days, she returned periodically to the field, refusing to speak to Penn. Finally, she submitted to his direction, and he helped her overcome her anxieties. At last, she could look at herself on screen and say, "Hey, it's not that bad." Dunaway realized that Penn was "one of those really smart, intellectually gifted directors, very much in the Kazan school of directing. He knows writers. He knows about screenplays. He knows how to deal with actors, how to let the talent breathe and develop a role."

Warren's portrayal of Clyde also inspired her. As the sexually recessive outlaw, Warren eschewed stereotypical gangster bravado. "He often had the look of a shy boy, vulnerable, unsure of himself, even awkward," Dunaway said. "It was a remarkable performance." He was stretching his talent well beyond anything he'd done before.

They filmed a bank-robbery scene in a one-horse town called Point Blank, which was not much more than a wide place in the road. As planned with the local people, Warren, Gene Hackman, and Faye drew their guns and stormed the town's one bank. A poor Depression family looked on, and Warren, introducing his gang, explained, "We rob banks." After the sequence, Dunaway strolled over to the "honey wagon" for a Coke, and an extra from the town told her that she'd seen the real Barrow gang hold up the bank years ago, and Warren was staging it exactly as it had happened. Despite some liberties the writers took in depicting the relationship between Bonnie and Clyde, the movie's authentic look was the result of Warren's Selznick-like research and attention to detail. In one scene, he had to jump on the running board of the getaway car just as Dunaway gunned the motor and raced away from the bank. The stunt "took a lot of guts on Warren's part," Dunaway recalled. Naturally, Warren required many retakes before he was happy. Dunaway's driving was perfect in every take, and at one point he stuck his head in the car window and told her, "You've got a lot of class."

Dunaway was giving the performance of her lifetime. "Never have I felt so close to a character as I felt to Bonnie," she said in 1995. "She was a yearning, edgy, ambitious southern girl who wanted to get out of wherever she was. . . . She was heading nowhere. . . . The end was death." Warren too was at the peak of his form, oozing kamikaze daring and boyish charisma.

On weekends during the Texas location, the cast rehearsed the new pages that Robert Towne had written while they filmed during the week. At some point, Towne had taken over from Benton and Newman, and he would remain an important force in Beatty's career. Towne's dialogue was some of the best in Hollywood, and for years he would work undercover as "*the* script doctor," said veteran screenwriter William Goldman. "He was this mysterious figure and he seemed to have fixed *everything*."[84] Not until 1972 would the world beyond Hollywood hear of Towne, when Francis Ford Coppola, accepting the screenplay Oscar, acknowledged Towne's contributions to *The Godfather*. Above all, Towne understood the secrets of dialogue. "Good screen dialogue is shorthand," Dunaway observed, "but it's poignant and poetic." It was Towne who gave Gene Hackman, playing Buck, Clyde's brother, his touching death line, "Clyde, Clyde, the dog got my shoes." Warren considered Hackman's performance the most authentic in the picture. Neither young nor particularly handsome, Hackman went on to become one of the biggest stars in Hollywood. As a producer, Warren was proving himself to be a formidable starmaker, and, in harnessing Bob Towne, he demonstrated that he could control inspired below-the-title work horses. Towne started writing *Shampoo* while working on *Bonnie and Clyde* in 1967.

The final scene, the killing of Bonnie and Clyde, was one of the most violent ever filmed. Warren and Faye were in makeup for hours, as a black center was placed at each spot where they'd take the lawmen's barrage of shotgun bullets. Wax was put on top of the black spot, and then the wax was covered with makeup. A squib and a hair-fine wire were attached to the wax, and during the scene, the squibs were exploded, including the ones on the actors' faces. They felt to Warren and Faye like small dynamite explosions, and the actors' realistic twitchings and writhings as bullets supposedly hit them were totally convincing, leaving audiences in shock as they watched it in slow motion.

Dunaway pretended she suffered from St. Vitus' dance as a means of simulating death by multiple gunshot wounds. The resourceful actress also tied her leg to the gearshift, so she wouldn't fall all the way out of the car, but dangle helplessly from the seat in an eerie dance of death. "It released, as the Greeks put it, the pity and fear of the audience," wrote Dunaway, "because they see this girl they've come to know shot to ribbons."

The only conflict between Warren and his leading lady concerned working methods. He required thirty takes, even in dangerous shoot-out and chase sequences or in a freezing stream, and he got better with each take. Dunaway, however, was at her best on the third or fourth take and went stale after the fifth or sixth. In one scene, Warren was so eager to escape her kisses that he bumped his head getting out of the car. They did thirty-eight takes, and he audibly smacked his brow every time. Though in obvious pain, "Warren thrived on going the limit," Dunaway said. Like Warren, she did her own stunt work, including wading for hours in a filthy, cold river, as the Barrow gang attempted to escape from the law.

Though the completed film was enormously entertaining, *Bonnie and Clyde* was a shamelessly amoral glamorization of crime. Under attack, Warren tried to rationalize the film's social irresponsibility, saying he'd intended to mirror the violence of the sixties, a decade torn by social upheaval and war.[85] More likely, as would increasingly be the case, he went overboard in his earnest effort to understand the character he was playing, completely losing perspective and showering inappropriate sympathy on a criminal who murdered twelve innocent persons, including police officers. Decades later, he'd make the same mistake playing Bugsy Siegel, a sadistic killer whom Beatty saw as a visionary American dreamer sacrificing himself in the (dubious) cause of inventing Las Vegas. Penn, who at least pretended to be morally responsible, tried to justify *Bonnie and Clyde*'s prurient nature, pointing out that Clyde Barrow was a kind of Robin Hood, who "preferred to rob the rich to help the poor. He only held up banks that foreclosed on poor people." On the contrary, the Barrow gang had more in common with what was going on in the rest of the world—the rise of Hitler and lawlessness in Europe. Benton was equally specious when he compared Clyde Barrow, a thug, to Abbie Hoffman, an altruistic revolutionary and counterculture leader.

In a further distortion of reality, the film ignored the fascinating sexual dynamics of the Barrow gang. In real life, Bonnie and Clyde enjoyed a ménage à trois with Roy Hamilton before he was replaced in the gang by W. D. Jones. (Roy later returned to the gang.) Arthur Penn was so bent on creating representative folk heroes that he missed the real story, which was far more intriguing than fiction, and would have pushed the boundaries of film subject matter even further.[86]

Though morally suspect and historically inaccurate, the film was a genuine original, right down to the costumes, which introduced a delightfully retro look into the fashion of the late 1960s. Costume designer Donfeld, who'd been Oscar-nominated for his splendid work in *Days of Wine and Roses,* recalls, "Arthur Penn and Warren offered me *Bonnie and Clyde,* but I was tied up on another film." Penn and Beatty next sought out veteran designer Dorothy Jeakins, but when contacted, she said she was on her way to Italy to do *Reflections in a Golden Eye.* Jeakins, impulsively deciding to do a favor for a complete unknown, rang a woman with the odd name of Theodora Van Runkle, taking mercy on her because Theodora didn't even have a decent car to drive, which consigned her to the absolute bottom of the heap in L.A., where a good car is as de rigueur as a good table at Morton's. "I have been asked to do a little cowboy movie at Warner Brothers," Jeakins told Van Runkle. "It's for Arthur Penn and Warren Beatty, and no one can stand them. I think with your particular valor you can do it."

Van Runkle took the job. More than thirty years later, during a telephone interview in L.A., she says, "Warren is only interested in women he can have sex with, except for Pauline Kael and Elaine May. He never calls you unless he wants something."

At a 1999 costume-design seminar at the Academy of Motion Picture Arts and Sciences, Van Runkle was anything but modest as she described working with Beatty and Penn. While other designers on the panel said they depended on the director to determine a film's costume designs, Van Runkle boasted, "I can't tell you how opposite it is. It never once occurred to me to ask the director what he thought about anything. I would just do whatever I wanted to do." The moderator, somewhat taken aback, said, "You tell me when you were doing *Bonnie and Clyde* you made it all up? You read the script?"

"I read the script, I knew on the first page that it was going to be an immense hit. I knew I'd get a nomination. It was my first film, and it was my first design job, but I knew everything, how it was going to be. I just showed [Arthur Penn] my drawings. I didn't know Warren, who was living at the Beverly Wilshire Hotel in a penthouse. After looking at my designs, Arthur just threw my portfolio down and grabbed me and danced me around the roof and said, 'If our movie is as good as the drawings, then we'll have a hit.' But I never asked anybody what they thought.

"Warren wanted Faye to appear much shorter than he, so I had to . . . cut [her] heels down. Six foot four is not enough [for him]." Estelle Parsons turned down the vintage clothes Theodora made for her. "She was the only person in the film that wasn't accurate, because she didn't want to wear old clothes," the designer said. "She was insulted. So she went through a hamper. I wasn't taken to Texas, because they were saving money, and Estelle went through a hamper of stuff that was sixties, forties, and fifties and selected what she wanted. If you look closely at the scene on the highway where she stamps her foot, her clothes are highly incorrect. Warren wanted everybody to go to the bathroom in the bushes. He didn't even want to have honeywagons. I got paid three grand for doing [the film]. I was so naïve I didn't know how to break down a script [continuity]. And Warren came in one day and raged at me. I was fitting Faye, the off-white dress that she's wearing when Warren first sees her at her mother's house. I thought that's the thing that came up first in the script, so that was the first dress I had made. I knew nothing, and no one would help me."

Van Runkle was right about at least one thing. The picture was going to be a hit. In the anti-Establishment mood of the late 1960s, *Bonnie and Clyde* came at exactly the right moment to catch the public imagination. Clyde Barrow was raised by Warren's cool, sixties-laid-back portrayal to the summit of iconicity. Ironically, Beatty, an ambitious, driven, egocentric, new-style Hollywood wheeler-dealer, became the personification of revolution, with the social vision and flawed morality that America brought to its brief era as motherland of the counterculture. To film historian and biographer David Thomson, who considers *Bonnie and Clyde* to be "the crucial American movie about love and death," the moral ambivalence of the picture is transformed by its beauty as a work of art. Whatever one's view of it, surely no one who has ever seen it can deny being helplessly and joyously caught up in Warren's sense of fun, in the sheer excitement he felt in making the film. Just as his friend Roman Polanski's fear and insecurity were the legacy of having come of age as a Jew in Nazi-occupied Europe, Warren, in *Bonnie and Clyde,* was reliving the rebellious glee he and Shirley had felt as troubled children blocking traffic, dumping garbage, and ringing neighbors' bells. He was still reacting to the pain of growing up in a restrictive Baptist household.

Being boss during the making of *Bonnie and Clyde* brought about a measure of professional growth in Warren Beatty—not exactly humility, and certainly not a more stable personal life, but, in relation to his film colleagues, more of a collegial attitude. Now that he was in charge of the whole show, he took a

genuine interest in those who worked for him and depended on his good judgment. There were no more clashes with the crew. He saw them anew as people
who could make or break his picture, and he tried to absorb everything they
knew like a sponge. "I learned so much from the men on the set—cameramen,
the grips, prop men," he said. "They'd tell me, 'Why don't you do it this way'—
and explain. *They* should be producers." The *Bonnie and Clyde* cast loved him
too. "He ran everything himself, made all the decisions, contributed very important comments, and we all got paid on time," said Estelle Parsons.[87] Warren
brought the negative in for $1.9 million, delivering enormous bang for the buck
with every inch of footage.[88]

When Jack Warner screened *Bonnie and Clyde,* he wrote it off as a complete
loss. Since no one at the studio dared disagree with the mogul, Warner Bros.
made no plans to release the picture. Warren lay down in the middle of the floor
of Warner's office and said, "Sell me the picture." He was bluffing. The picture's
cost would increase during postproduction, and it already had some of Warren's
money in it. To buy the print he'd need to come up with another two million
dollars. Jack Warner didn't believe Warren could raise the money. Continuing
to bluff, Warren promised, "I'll be in your office six o'clock tonight with a check.
Sell it to me." He stood up and walked out, risking everything, but in doing so
he took control of his destiny in a way few men ever have the nerve to do.

One of Jack Warner's executives said to him, "Who's shown it to Fox? They
must want it. What're we gonna do?"[89] Warren's ruse had worked.

"I learned from Warren," said Dunaway, "that if you have a vision, the only
way to protect it is to fight body and soul, to go to the mat time and again."
William Goldman concurs, writing, "I have worked with [Robert] Redford. I
have been in a room with Beatty. They are brilliant men, passionate about what
they produce, and boy are they not dumb."

At first it was a Pyrrhic victory. Though Warren succeeded in forcing
Warner Bros. to release the film, the studio figuratively tossed the picture in the
trash can, releasing it in second-class theaters with no fanfare. The release
date, August 13, 1967, was box-office suicide. During this era of moviemaking,
the summer was notoriously slack, the worst time to release a film. All that
would change toward the end of the twentieth century, when studios targeted
summer and Christmas for their major releases, but in the 1960s, critics and
the public alike knew that Hollywood displayed its best products during the fall
and winter holiday cycle—not in the dog days of summer. To make matters

worse, instead of opening in New York at a movie palace like the Radio City Music Hall or the Paramount, *Bonnie and Clyde* was consigned to the B-circuit, playing the Forum and the Murray Hill. In Los Angeles it played a single theater, the Vogue, far from the glitter of Grauman's Chinese, the Pantages, or even Westwood's Bruin. Each week another city or two was added, and Warren flew to the site of every venue to promote it. On the strength of these appearances and word-of-mouth alone, it became, by the eighth week, the number-three grosser in the U.S. Still, Warner refused to advertise it. And the review press was no help.

Warren paid for the millionth time for having insulted Bosley Crowther, who trashed it in the *Times,* objecting to Beatty's comedic use of "the hideous deprivations of that sleazy, moronic pair." Joseph Morgenstern of *Newsweek* called the picture "a squalid shoot-'em-up for the moron trade."

Even Shirley MacLaine joined in the chorus of denunciation, saying, "I thought I'd known Warren, but I did not know what he was capable of. . . . I couldn't make a picture about that kind of violence. Warren *feels* it with his magnificent hostility. . . . It assaulted me. I turned away."[90]

He had a few defenders, and one of them was the prestigious cineaste Pauline Kael of *The New Yorker.* "How do you make a good movie in this country and not get jumped on?" she began. "*Bonnie and Clyde* is the most exciting American movie since *The Manchurian Candidate.* The audience is alive to it. . . . *Bonnie and Clyde,* by making us care more about the robber lovers, has put the sting back into death." Still, Warner Bros. was content to let the film survive on its own momentum, with no advertising program to propel it to number one.

Frustrated, Warren fell into a depression. Roman Polanski offered him the male lead, opposite Mia Farrow, in *Rosemary's Baby.* He read the script, but, caught up in his battles to get *Bonnie and Clyde* properly distributed, he turned down just about everything submitted to him. "I'll play Rosemary," he told Polanski, joking. He didn't consider the role or the movie deserving of his talent, but he was wrong; later, John Cassavetes was chosen for the male lead and was memorable, managing to be both romantic and sinister, and the movie itself was a startling original, as good as vintage Hitchcock. Robert Redford had been considered for the role, but he was in litigation with Paramount, the studio that owned the film, and therefore automatically out. Jack Nicholson, still an unknown, was auditioned, but Polanski deemed him too scary.

What finally brought Warren out of his funk, and reactivated his old varsity-football Mad Dog Beatty instincts, was his stubborn determination. Though he detested interviews and found them "demeaning," he granted them now, courting the press to resell *Bonnie and Clyde*.[91] He was helped by a strong "thought piece" from reviewer Judith Crist, who saw a parallel between the rebelliousness portrayed in the movie and the terrorist temper of the 1960s. That was enough to get young people flooding into the theaters, and by the following year, 1968, they were storming the streets, creating their own revolution, energized and emboldened, in part, by Warren Beatty's endorsement of gratuitous violence. The movie became such a favorite of the hippie generation that both *Time* and *Newsweek,* embarrassed by their earlier denunciations of the film, sent their critics back to see it. Both magazines recanted their original pans, an all-but-unprecedented event in newsweekly journalism. "I am sorry to say I consider [*Newsweek*'s] review grossly unfair and regrettably inaccurate," wrote Joseph Morgenstern. "I am sorrier to say I wrote it." Altogether the turnaround in *Bonnie and Clyde*'s fortunes took about six months. In September 1967, it grossed two thousand six hundred dollars for a week in one Cleveland theater; in February 1968, it grossed twenty-six thousand dollars in the same theater. At the end of 1967 it had only netted $2.5 million, but in the following year it netted $16.5 million, making it one of the twenty top-grossing movies of all time.

The extraordinary critical reassessments, by no means coincidentally, had come after the film's triumphant September 15, 1967, London opening, which put the American review press to shame.[92] Five magazines, including *Time,* devoted cover stories to *Bonnie and Clyde,* which came to be regarded as a watershed moment in movie history. The *New York Times* was so appalled by Crowther's negative review that they fired him for being so out of touch with the Zeitgeist. The *Village Voice* sent star reporter Blair Sobol to interview Warren, and Blair brought along freelance photographer Linda Eastman, the future Mrs. Paul McCartney. "Linda squatted in front of Warren to take his picture," Blair recalled in 2000, "and I noticed that she wasn't wearing any panties. Warren must have noticed too, because I didn't see Linda again for two weeks."

The epic of *Bonnie and Clyde*'s critical and commercial resurrection had come in several stages. At one point, despite the astonishing flip-flop in the press, the film had begun to wind down at the box office. Beatty threatened to sue if Warner Bros. didn't re-release the film in top-flight venues and promote it in a manner commensurate with its critical reevaluation. In the end Warner capitulated, re-releasing it with a major ad campaign for which Warren supplied the advertising copy. He made personal calls on theater managers around the nation, urging them to take out their own individual ads. He checked their sound and projection systems and helped them make improvements. "I got out and sold the picture," he said. "It's demanding to an actor and it's taken a big chunk out of my life and I didn't know a thing about it, but I learned." Box-office receipts in many theaters increased eightfold, partly due to Beatty's skill as a spin doctor. Morally, he defended his film as a depiction of folk heroes staging a bloody battle against the Establishment, parroting Penn's rationalization of simple greed. With some justification, Beatty was proud of *Bonnie and Clyde*'s impact on the evolving revolutionary ethos of the late 1960s. "Violence is a part of social change," he said, and history bears him out.

The picture earned him a personal fortune and a secure place in the Hollywood Establishment. "*Bonnie and Clyde* would also turn me into a star," wrote Dunaway. Box-office receipts came to thirty-six million dollars, but over the long haul Warren's risky venture would gross a then-whopping $125 million. The film was widely imitated for the rest of the twentieth century and beyond, in genres ranging from "buddy" films to *Pulp Fiction*. The Academy of Motion Picture Arts and Sciences accorded *Bonnie and Clyde* ten nominations, including Best Actor, Best Actress, Best Supporting Actor (both Pollard and Hackman were named), Best Supporting Actress, and Best Cinematography. In the final balloting, the only actual winners were Estelle Parsons and cinematographer Burnett Guffey.

Beating out Dunaway, Katherine Hepburn won the Best Actress Oscar for *Guess Who's Coming to Dinner.* Philosophical about her loss, Dunaway was grateful that *Bonnie and Clyde* turned her into Hollywood's "golden girl . . . one of those women who was going to be nominated year after year for an Oscar and would win at least one. The movie established the quality of my work." But Warren was already the golden boy, and his loss, as both actor and producer, cut deeper. According to author Anthony Holden, there was a "Beatty jinx. . . . It was the beginning of the Oscars' love-hate relationship with Beatty, still simmering almost a quarter of a century later, when his disappointing *Dick Tracy* received the Academy's thumbs down, again . . . when *The Silence of the Lambs* shattered his high hopes for *Bugsy*."[93]

By the time Dunaway scored an exciting new role opposite Steve McQueen in *The Thomas Crown Affair,* Warren decided he had to have her. Late one night, while she was still filming with McQueen, she received a call from Warren, who said, "Everybody wants you, and so do I."[94] Later, discussing his technique as a Casanova, she said, "He has a very direct approach. He plays it for shock with a girl, telling her in front what he wants. What he wants is to go to bed with her. He's tenacious and audacious—totally unconventional. He's also one of the most charming men I've ever met. I wouldn't have anything to do with him if my life depended on it. I consider him dangerous."[95]

During his telephone call that night, Faye found Warren to be "pretty alluring," but decided she'd "never fool around with any of these above-the-title guys because . . . they were often womanizers of the first order . . . and I knew that meant inevitable parting. No way would I ever think of a long relationship where I would remake the pain of my past and my parents' divorcing with a man like Warren or, later, Jack Nicholson. Though I adored their friendship, I never wanted it to progress beyond that, because I knew it would have been a relationship doomed to failure. . . . I wasn't about to let myself in for that kind of heartbreak."

Even without womanizers, there would be heartbreak enough for Faye. After Lenny Bruce died of a drug overdose, she went on to an affair with actor Michael O'Brien. Next came photographer Jerry Schatsberg, a hip New Yorker who invested in the disco Ondine, where the Doors and the Rolling Stones entertained nightly for café society. "He was the first in a long line of men after Michael O'Brien that I would hope could fix my life for me," she related. Schatsberg later opened the disco Salvation in Greenwich Village and booked Jimi Hendrix and other trailblazing sixties rockers. Her affair with Schatsberg was "filled with tense silences and hollow laughter." Like Warren, Dunaway knew that she "couldn't commit to a lifetime any longer." They parted, and she fell in love with Marcello Mastroianni, her costar in *A Place for Lovers*, but he didn't leave his wife for her. Another lover was Peter Wolf, the J. Geils Band's lead singer, who struck Dunaway as "half rock 'n' roller, half mystic . . . velvet eyes that you can drift in forever." They got married in 1974, and her Best Actress Oscar for *Network* came in 1977. A famous *People* picture of Faye and her Oscar by photographer Terry O'Neill makes her look very jaded and lonely. Years later, she explained, "Success is a solitary place to be." She and O'Neill, who was married, began a serious affair. Though Wolf was "the one true love" of her life, their marriage ended in divorce. So did her subsequent marriage to Terry O'Neill, after the birth of a son, Liam O'Neill. At one of her lowest emotional points, in the 1980s, she was flying to the West Coast and Warren happened to be on the same airplane. He spent the entire flight sitting next to her as she poured out her heart to him. "He's a gentleman," she said, "a cunning businessman, a great film star, and a very worthwhile person."[96]

Beatty jinx or not, *Bonnie and Clyde* changed Hollywood. In its wake came other important independent, anti-Establishment films, principally *Easy Rider*, the tale of two drug-dealing hippies riding their motorcycles across America. Released in 1969, two years after Beatty's film, *Easy Rider* marked the emergence of one of Hollywood's most colorful and popular male stars, Jack Nicholson, who'd become one of Beatty's closest friends. In a piece describing Los Angeles's favorite eateries, Sheilah Graham mentioned the Bistro Garden on North Cañon Drive and added, "I saw Warren Beatty and Jack Nicholson dining there together: two of the most eligible girl-loving actors in Hollywood, without a woman."[97] A girl they once shared later said, "They were like the blind leading the blind, Jack and Warren. Lust is always blind, because all you see in the eyes of the seduced is your own reflection. Lust is nothing but obstacles and misery that keep you from ever finding out what life and love are all about. Love is where all the real fun is—the generosity people can have with each other. Lust, ultimately, is always tragic."

Nicholson would try marriage only once, to actress Sandra Knight. "Marriage in Hollywood is like a nice hot bath," he said. "It cools off after a short while." But Nicholson's libido didn't cool off, and producer Bob Evans, among others, kept him supplied with "wind-up dolls"—mindless, vacant-eyed milk-maids fresh in from the Midwest, hoping to crash the big time.[98] Altogether Nicholson would father four children by three women.[99] Warren seemed no more likely than Jack to settle down, and a friend of his at the time explained, "Warren wants the entire world to go to bed with him. And what he really is unable to take more than anything else in life is rejection."[100]

Warren's generosity and genius were expressed far more in his work of this period than in his life. Only thirty years old, he had smashed the suffocating mold of American movies and opened a thousand doors for other filmmakers. *Time*'s Stefan Kanfer rated *Bonnie and Clyde* as a groundbreaker on a par with

The Birth of a Nation and *Citizen Kane*, pointing out Beatty had introduced European innovation into mainstream American filmmaking. The hallmarks of the new cinema were disdain for moral judgments; indifference to traditional storytelling techniques, including chronology and character motivation; sexual honesty; and an obscuring of the line separating comedy and tragedy, protagonists and antagonists. In the wake of *Bonnie and Clyde*, other anti-Establishment films continued to herald a new golden age for Hollywood, including Bob Rafelson's *Five Easy Pieces*; Peter Bogdanovich's *The Last Picture Show* and *Paper Moon*; Francis Ford Coppola's *The Godfather* and *Apocalypse Now*; Martin Scorsese's *Mean Streets*, *Taxi Driver*, and *Raging Bull*; George Lucas's *American Graffiti* and *Star Wars*, and Roman Polanski's *Chinatown*. Warren also set another important new style, that of the actor/producer, which was later emulated by Robert Redford, Clint Eastwood, Burt Reynolds, Kevin Costner, Mel Gibson, and Winona Ryder. When the American Film Institute drew up its list of the top one hundred films of all time, *Bonnie and Clyde* came in at a respectable number twenty-seven (*Citizen Kane* was number one).

In terms of Warren's own career, *Bonnie and Clyde* was not so much a comeback as it was an extraordinary second chance, since he'd been working fairly steadily ever since his debut. He had started at the top in *Splendor*, fallen from eminence through bad judgment of material and a demoralizing personal life, but now found himself back on top, not only as an actor but as a force in the industry. "How do you spell fashionable? W-A-R-R-E-N B-E-A-T-T-Y," said former studio chief Robert Evans in 1994. "From his first film till today, Warren remains the quintessential Hollywood movie star. He defies the bottom line, in an industry where the bottom line is the only line. He has remained for more than thirty years without missing one, front and center on every studio's A-list."[101] The savvy Robert Towne said, "You'd have to be crazy if you were a studio executive, and Warren Beatty was producing, not to do it."

In time he would come to love making deals almost more than making movies, not unlike Paramount owner Charles Bluhdorn, about whom *Vanity Fair* wrote, "Making a deal to him was one orgasm after another."[102] Sometimes it was more like coitus interruptus, as when Beatty and Bluhdorn clashed one day during the former's phone call from London. "He began to scream at me about the money that actors were getting," said Warren, who realized during the conversation that Bluhdorn was showing off in front of an officeful of studio executives and decided to outshout him. "I nearly lost my voice. The person who was three floors above came downstairs thinking that there had been a burglary. I said, 'No, it's just Bluhdorn.' "

At the height of Warren's power and popularity, gonzo journalist Rex Reed decided to deconstruct him in *Esquire*, exposing Warren's insecurities, his "desperation to be liked, approved of, the fear (the greatest terror of his life, to be exact) of being considered unintelligent." But Warren's perch atop the Hollywood pecking order was unshakable, and in explaining why he was able to turn down the best roles being offered in the industry, he reached for a sexual metaphor. "It's like I've been all night in the whorehouse," he said, "and I stagger out in the morning and I see Marilyn Monroe waiting."[103]

The allusions to whores and Monroe were indicative. Evidently too much of a good thing, even sex, palled. Early burnout was looming, and it had already overwhelmed Monroe, a suicide at thirty-six. When Warren and Natalie were still seeing each other in the early sixties, they'd encountered Marilyn at a party. *"Thirty-six, thirty-six, thirty-six,"* she'd said. *"It's all over."*[104]

CHAPTER FOUR

INDESCRIBABLY INDULGENT

WARREN, whose swinging-sixties crowd now included Roman Polanski, Sharon Tate, Peter Sellers, Jay Sebring, scriptwriter James Poe, and Peter Lawford,¹ dropped by the *Rosemary's Baby* set at Paramount Pictures one day to visit Polanski. The director was licking his chops over a satanic episode he'd just directed in the occult thriller, in which Mia Farrow's character is raped in front of a coven of witches and conceives the devil's child. The scene was prophetic. It would shortly help spawn a hideous real-life sequel in Polanski's own household.

That day at Paramount, Warren persuaded Polanski to take a break, and hosted a dinner at his favorite Italian restaurant, also inviting Peter Sellers and his wife, Britt Ekland. It was a lighthearted evening, but ominous clouds were gathering, and shortly the lives of Polanski, Tate, Sebring, and, by association, Warren himself would turn into a nightmare.

Sharon Tate had recently told an interviewer that Polanski was the only man for her. Despite the growing popularity of women's lib, she was an old-fashioned girl who lived only to please her husband. A typical male chauvinist, Polanski condescendingly described Sharon as "a born housewife. Aside from cooking like a dream, she used to cut my hair—a skill acquired from Jay Sebring." Despite their basic incompatibility—Sharon was a monogamist, Roman a polygamist—they got married on January 20, 1968. Trouble started when Sharon objected to the groom's plans for his stag party, which was to be held at Victor Lownes's townhouse in London. Despite Sharon's disapproval, each of Polanski's male friends, including Michael Caine and Terence Stamp, was supplied with a young woman for the evening.[2] Women's lib had not yet made any appreciable impact on the way the men talked and behaved. Women were still objects to be exploited for pleasure and quickly discarded. As Jack Nicholson put it in a *Playboy* interview, "Three days in a new town and you're thinking, 'Why can't I find a beaver in a bar?' It's not that sex is the primary element of the universe, but when it's unfulfilled, it will affect you."[3]

Hundreds of photographers and reporters flocked to the Polanskis' wedding ceremony at the Chelsea Registry Office, in King's Road. Sharon's *Valley of the Dolls* costar, Barbara Parkins, was her sole bridesmaid, and Roman's friend and business partner Gene Gutowski was best man. Warren attended the reception at the Playboy Club in Park Lane. There were some awkward moments— former Beatty flames Joan Collins and Leslie Caron were among a glittering throng of wedding guests that included Jacqueline Susann and her husband Irving Mansfield, Prince and Princess Radziwill, Peter Sellers, Rudolf Nureyev, Sean Connery, Keith Richards, Brian Jones, Vidal Sassoon, Kenneth Tynan, Candice Bergen, John Mills, Laurence Harvey, Anthony Newley, James Fox, David Bailey, Mia Farrow, and Michael Sarne. Afterward, the newlyweds attended The Supremes' show at The Talk of the Town before jetting off to the Swiss Alps for a skiing honeymoon, followed by a Parisian holiday at the chic Left Bank hotel where Oscar Wilde had died, L'Hotel, now a favorite stopover for rockers.

Before they'd been married a full year, the Polanski union was in trouble, Roman having involved himself in several extramarital affairs after their return to L.A.[4] When Sharon confronted him, he reminded her that she'd promised not to change him, and thereafter he arrogantly referred to his infidelity as "Sharon's big hangup."

By this point in the sixties, faithfulness was getting a bad name. In Warren's life, the primacy of the pleasure principle superseded everything else, and became a rapacious creditor, severely curtailing his range and power as a performer when he failed, following the success of *Bonnie and Clyde,* to spend more time on his career, particularly to develop as an actor. *The Godfather*, one of the best products of the New Hollywood, was in development. Director Francis Ford Coppola wanted the relatively untried thirty-year-old actor Al Pacino for the role of the youngest son, Michael Corleone, but Paramount was plugging for an established box-office star, preferably Warren or Jack Nicholson. Producer Al Ruddy wanted Robert Redford, and Frank Langella also was briefly considered before author Mario Puzo cast the decisive vote. "Above all," said Puzo, "*Pacino* has to be in the film."[5] Warren's future girlfriend Diane Keaton got the role of Michael's fiancée. "They were mainly concerned about Al," she recalled, "and I think they finally got so tired of seeing me they said, 'Oh, for God's sake, give her the part.' " In the title role, Marlon Brando was the star of the picture, and when Diane met him, she was speechless, sputtering, "Yeah, right, *sure*." Later she said, "I was *so* high school, so totally into self-loathing." The movie became the stuff of cinematic legend. Pacino rose to instant stardom, and Brando was reestablished as the premier actor in American film. "Pacino's Michael Corleone may be the most shocking study of deteriorating character in all of American cinema," David Thomson wrote. "*The Godfather* is a masterpiece, and Michael is without doubt its central character, the most resonant metaphor of America." Pacino had worked for thirty-five thousand dollars, Diane Keaton for six thousand dollars.[6] They became lovers.

Having pulled no strings, Warren had lost a role that would have given him the opportunity to use what he'd learned as Clyde Barrow, and, more importantly, to acquire some essential and badly needed acting experience as part of the *Godfather* ensemble of Brando, Keaton, Robert Duvall, John Cazale, and James Caan. When offered Nabokov's *Laughter in the Dark*, he again declined because he thought the role had a suggestion of homosexuality. Most actors at the time declined gay parts, some out of their own insecure masculinity, and some because they feared future typecasting or worse, blackballing. With the public's gradual acceptance of gays in the decades following Stonewall, Hollywood's best actors, including Al Pacino, Richard Gere, Keanu Reeves, River Phoenix, Tom Hanks, Antonio Banderas, Robin Williams, Jude Law, Leonardo DiCaprio, William Hurt, Robert Downey Jr., Paul Reubens, and

James Gandolfini, eagerly embraced gay roles, which harmed none, and brought prizes to some, including an Oscar for Hanks, star of the AIDS drama *Philadelphia*.

Warren also had other motives for passing up work. A millionaire at thirty, he was feeling a need to stop and smell the flowers. He "sort of relaxed and thought, well, what am I really running after?"[7] Running *from* was more like it. A few years later he'd be fighting the Internal Revenue Service, which claimed he owed them $916,000 due to having underpaid in 1968 and 1969.[8]

His primary occupation, conquest of the world's most beautiful women, led him, inevitably, to the boudoir of Brigitte Bardot, who despite the cult of Marilyn Monroe became the world's No. 1 "sex kitten" in 1956 with her sensational international hit *And God Created Woman*. Her hairstyles, attitudes, postures, and movements were copied by Jane Fonda and the other emerging love goddesses of the 1960s. The daughter of well-to-do parents living in the shadow of the Eiffel Tower in the Parisian equivalent of Manhattan's Upper East Side, she grew up rebelling against middle-class values. Spoiled and selfish, she was one of the first of the pre-hippie, so-called "Silent Generation" to expose the hypocrisy and smug self-righteousness of the generation that had fought WWII.

At the age of sixteen, she became the mistress of an aspiring twenty-two-year-old journalist and filmmaker, Roger Vadim, who joined the staff of *Paris-Match* expressly to promote her as a cover girl. Strangely attractive with his long thin face and Dostoyevskian air, Vadim had lost his virginity at sixteen in a Normandy barn that was under bombardment on D-Day. He had the savvy to recognize in Bardot's unbridled animal sexuality the look and attitude that would dominate movies and fashion for decades to come. At five-foot-seven, she was a barefoot vixen who seemed to have just risen from an unmade bed that still smelled of a night of messy sex. With her ripe, full figure (34–20–34), brunette hair (soon to become a tawny mane), fawn's eyes that ranged in color from brown to hazel to green, and a retrousse upper lip eternally poised for a kiss, she'd been trained as a dancer, and she walked with athletic grace, arching her back and thrusting her breasts forward.

Thanks to Vadim's efforts, she graced the May 1952 cover of *Paris-Match*, captioned "the new Leslie Caron." Her movie debut followed later that year, in producer Jean Boyer's forgettable *Le Trou Normand*. The next year, at eighteen, she married Vadim. After they settled in a two-room love nest in the rue

Chardon-Legache, he set about turning her into an international star. As teacher, master, lover, husband, and father figure rolled into one, Vadim showed her how to be more brazen than Monroe, insisting that she walk around their flat nude, urging her to draw attention to her crotch. Stimulated by these lessons, she required sex three times a day and turned to others when her husband grew tired. He didn't mind her dalliances; indeed, he encouraged her to develop as a separate person, and to explore every facet of her talent. In time he'd play Svengali to other women as well, including Jane Fonda, Annette Stroyberg, and Catherine Deneuve.

By the mid-1950s Vadim was sufficiently established as a director to showcase Bardot in his second feature, *And God Created Woman*, which made her a national treasure in France and an instant celebrity throughout the world. Here was a true original: a new woman who scorned makeup and manners and who sinned without suffering retribution. On the set of *And God Created Woman*, Bardot's sensual costar Jean-Louis Trintignant made love to her in front of Vadim, who raised no objection. Nor was he jealous when she left him to move in with Trintignant in a flat at 71 avenue Paul Doumer after Trintignant abandoned his breathtaking wife, Stephane Audran.

Americans flipped over Bardot, finding her part ingenue and part courtesan and coining the term "Bardolatry." In attempting to define her appeal, Simone de Beauvoir, doyenne of the Left Bank existential literary set, wrote, "The male is an object to her." Author of the early feminist opus *The Second Sex*, de Beauvoir, mistress to Jean-Paul Sartre and Nelson Algren, had always wanted women to be as free as men, and regarded Bardot as a feminist heroine.

Though she would continue to make films after her big breakthrough, Bardot had little interest in developing her minuscule talent. She grew rich, pulling down $350,000 per film (in inflation-adjusted dollars) in a string of undistinguished pictures, but she would never again score a success like *And God Created Woman*, nor would she ever become a major star in Hollywood films. Rather like a female version of Warren Beatty, she went from lover to lover, soon shedding both Vadim and Trintignant. She frankly cared nothing for love, even less for art. Sex was her only real interest.

The guitarist whose strumming was heard on the soundtrack of *And God Created Woman* was a darkly exotic youth named Sacha Distel. He became her next lover. Bardot popularized the bikini while lolling beside Sacha on the

Riviera's beaches, transforming Saint-Tropez from a sleepy fishing village to a chi-chi resort that soon attracted the international set. After Sacha—soon disposed of as too macho and possessive for a free woman—she sampled the masculine charms of Spanish actor Gustavo Rojo, tennis pro Jean-Noel Grinda, singer Gilbert Becaud, and her male secretary Allain Carre. Promiscuity had the same effect on her as it later would on Warren's character George Roundy, in *Shampoo*, reducing her to despair over the emptiness of her life and causing her to attempt suicide. Later, she tried to reinvent herself as a wife, marrying actor Jacques Charrier in June 1959. After settling down in La Tour Margot, their home in Haut-de-Cagnes near Nice, Jacques got Brigitte pregnant and patiently waited for her to change into something resembling an expectant mother, with maternal instincts. Instead, Bardot felt undermined by pregnancy, and even after the birth of a healthy boy named Nicholas, she refused to adjust to motherhood. When Nicholas was two, she divorced Jacques and gladly let the father keep the baby. Her statement to a stunned journalist, "I am no mother and won't be one," more or less turned the world against her, irreparably damaging her movie career.

She resumed her pattern of serial love affairs, always choosing the same physical type: such full-lipped, boyish buckos with tousled dark hair as Gerard Blain, Charles Belmont, Jean-Pierre Cassel, Marc Michel, Jean-Marc Bory, and Hugues Aufrey, or sinewy, mournful Sami Frey, star of Jean-Luc Godard's innovative 1964 gangster film *Band of Outsiders*. "I love to love and I hate to leave, but I love freely and I leave freely," Brigitte boasted. With that attitude, she inevitably ended up alone and helpless. Only twenty-five but already "tired and worn out,"[9] she again attempted suicide, slashing her wrists and overdosing on barbiturates. Ex-husband Vadim, who romanced Catherine Deneuve and, in 1965, married Jane Fonda, patched the broken Bardot back together. She quickly went on to more lovers—photographer Jicky Dussart, South American businessman Bob Zaguri, and finally thirty-two-year-old Opel automobile-and-bicycle heir and playboy Gunther Sachs, whom she married in 1966.

Neither wealth nor luxury assuaged her boredom, and she again became a sexual gadfly. A new round of lovers included actor Mike Sarne; rich Italian Luigi Rizzi; Patrick Gilles, a garage-owner's son from St.-Etienne; and finally Beatty, who met her while he was in Paris in the late 1960s. By that time Bardot hadn't made a movie since *Masculin/Féminin* in 1966 and had virtually become a recluse, taking a dozen stray dogs and cats into her home and appearing at animal benefits. She was still looking "for a man who could make me vibrate fully as a woman." She found him in Warren.

In her early thirties, she used the same seduction techniques on Warren, no doubt, that she'd been perfecting ever since Vadim taught her how to vamp. Her custom was to telephone whomever she desired and date him up: "I am Brigitte Bardot. I want to meet you." So far as is known, no one ever refused her—certainly not Warren, who, as the king of Hollywood, was eager to conquer the queen of the Riviera. She always met her prey on equal ground—always in public and usually for lunch. Sex was never discussed. She scrupulously refrained from flirting, and the man often came away confused and crestfallen. Despite her reputation, she was, in fact, a *fleur bleue* (shrinking violet). The challenge was for the man to make her fall in love with him. He was required to take her dining and dancing. She was good company. Though not an intellectual, she was funny, and she always kept her dates laughing. She drew them out, creating an impression of genuine interest in their work and dreams. Shrewdly concealing her own predatory wiles, she manipulated the target male into thinking he was seducing her, rather than the reverse, which was decidedly the case. Finally, one evening, she'd let herself be led into the bedroom.[10]

Most men found sex with her to be oddly cerebral. Even during orgasm, her partners remained detached, thinking, I'm having the definitive fuck. And they also sensed menace—the unspoken possibility that at any minute she'd lose interest and walk out—as well as a momentous feeling of being inducted into the secret, ultimate sex game. Though supremely sexual, uninhibited in body and feelings, Brigitte seemed to exist at the edge of ennui. In bed, the man's job, it soon became clear, was to hold her back from slipping into the doldrums. Evidently Warren was equal to the task, and set about it manfully. Bardot's appeal endured, though her body had become somewhat coarse from the Saint-Tropez sun. The famous figure was intact, but the ropy mane that whirled about her head was now far from silky.

In Warren, the heartless sex machine met her match. Whether or not she found him to be the best lover in the world—Britt Ekland's estimation of him—Bardot came back for more. They became occasional sex partners, neither of them desiring a more serious attachment.

During a 1967 stay in Paris, Warren received a telephone call from Jane

Fonda, who had spent most of year in France with her husband, Vadim. She invited Warren to come out to their old farmhouse at St. Ouen, which lay about twenty-five miles from Paris. She then called Bardot and invited her for the same evening. Neither Fonda nor Vadim was aware that Beatty and Bardot already were sex partners, and Jane wanted to play matchmaker by introducing them at a dinner party.

Bardot wasn't jealous over Jane's marriage to Vadim because it was so obvious that Jane was no happier with him than she had been. Just as in Bardot's marriage to Vadim, Jane and Roger had wed with illusory ideas of each other that bore little relation to reality. If there had been undying love in Vadim's marriage to Jane, Bardot would have felt threatened. As it was, Bardot had gotten into the habit of fleeing to St. Ouen every time her husband Gunther Sachs was out of town, and Jane found it amusing to round up playmates for her.

Jane's old friend Sandy Whitelaw was working for United Artists in Paris, and Jane asked him to drive Warren out to St. Ouen, making no mention that Bardot would also be present. She wanted to spring Bardot on Warren as a surprise, then sit back and enjoy the fireworks. During dinner, Warren complimented the gourmet meal that Jane had spent all day preparing, but then he looked pointedly at Brigitte and said he knew of something that tasted even better. "In that area," interjected Vadim, who was intoxicated, "Jane is not quite in Brigitte's class." Bardot was pleased, but Jane was understandably offended. Sandy Whitelaw tried to mollify her, saying, "This will all come out all right in the end." Jane told the hapless Sandy to shut up, and added, "I always thought you were a creep. Now I know it."[11]

Back in Paris, Warren and Brigitte continued to see each other. He was sitting with her, in a corner of the Cafetière restaurant, when news of her divorce from Gunther Sachs was announced, ending her third marriage. Bardot, who was about to turn thirty-five, was wearing eyeshades and had a bandanna around her head. "I am a woman who has undoubtedly made a success of her career but certainly not of her private life," she once remarked. "Let's say that because of that I am someone who is incomplete. That is why I don't want to work anymore." She and Warren continued to date occasionally in the 1970s, often accompanied by Jane Fonda and Donald Sutherland, whom Jane fell in love with following the dissolution of her marriage to Vadim and the birth of their daughter, Vanessa, whom she named after her idol, Vanessa Redgrave.

Bardot also enjoyed brief flings with a number of boys half her age, ones who were capable of dancing through the night at Chez Castel. Often, however, the young men found their suitcases in the street, outside her door, after spending a night or two with her. She made a few more films, all of them disappointing, before escaping to her home in Saint-Tropez and the company of abandoned animals, including a lamb virtually snatched from the hands of the butcher. In her curious world, animals were treated as human beings, and human beings were treated as animals. But by the end of the twentieth century, the aging but still arresting star would succeed in making people take animals' rights seriously, throwing herself between Arctic seal clubbers and their prey and saving the lives of a hundred thousand abandoned dogs in Bucharest, Romania.[12]

Warren's unavailing lifestyle placed him in danger of the same kind of demoralization that afflicted Bardot in the 1960s, but he tried to adopt the positive attitudes and healthy styles that California brought to the forefront of national consciousness at the end of the sixties and the beginning of the seventies. There had always been something profoundly wholesome and sane about his personal habits. He'd never abused tobacco or alcohol but had grown fond of junk food in his early days as a starving actor in New York. "I find myself turning more and more to organically grown foods," he said. "Some people think that's silly, but only a few years ago they called Rachel Carson a crazy lady for writing a book about the balance of nature. And only a few years ago, they said everyone was crazy for worrying about DDT. Now even the Republicans fear it."

Though half of America seemed stoned in the seventies, drugs held little appeal for him. "It hasn't been proved to me yet," he said, "that marijuana does not cause chromosomal or brain damage." He called the drug problem "one of the most serious we're facing today." To help him navigate the emotional land mines that lay in wait for him as a compulsive sex addict, he enlisted the services of a therapist, Dr. Martin Grotjahn, to whom he occasionally referred celebrity friends.[13]

A new compassionate streak was noticed in Warren by costume designer Donfeld, who was nominated for an Oscar for *They Shoot Horses, Don't They?* "I was in New York on location with *The April Fools* in 1968, and Warren, Robert Towne, and I were walking along Central Park South one balmy night," he recalled. They were struck by the strange sounds of someone who was trying to sing opera, and at the same time imitate every instrument in the orchestra. The racket seemed to be emanating from bushes in the park. "Warren stopped in his tracks," Donfeld said, "then, almost in a hypnotic trance, wandered into the wooded area north of Fifty-ninth Street. We followed, and found a disheveled fellow who seemed to have memorized every famous love aria. Warren was mesmerized by his performance, and wanted to know all about him. He'd been a stagehand at the old Metropolitan Opera House in its glory days, when it was located just below Times Square, before the move to Lincoln Center. He'd never got over his shock when the old auditorium was torn down, and this was his way of mourning. Warren said, 'Oh, my God.' Somehow he identified strongly with that wretched soul. We had a hard time coaxing him away. It was a tender side of Warren that I'd never seen before."

Being a Hollywood power clearly was not Warren's ultimate ambition. Politics and finance were beginning to exert a strong appeal. "Why don't I just have some fun and do some studying and some living?" he said. "I really picked up more interest in politics and economics." He engaged a business manager, but he also took a keen interest "in what the market is doing in general—what over-all changes are coming—[not just] what happens to a particular stock."[14] Politics soon became a consuming passion, one that would occupy him for months and sometimes years at a time, severely curtailing his movie output, but also giving his life a new sense of meaning, of purpose beyond personal gain, of contributing to society and not just taking.

"Politics has always been important in Hollywood," wrote Sheilah Graham. "I mean the right-wingers in Hollywood on the stump for the Republican Party, such as Charlton Heston and John Wayne. For the Democrats, Shirley MacLaine, Angie Dickinson, and Lauren Bacall, and, more recently, Warren Beatty and Robert Redford. In many ways Washington, like Hollywood, has always been full of the pursuit of power mixed with the same kind of gossip and scandals."

Warren was further politicized when he realized that President Lyndon Johnson's towering achievement, the Great Society, was being undermined by the Vietnam War. How strange, some thought, that Warren Beatty, a social snob and philanderer, professed a liberal's compassion for the common man, but couldn't remain loyal to a single woman in his own life. His sympathy was too often abstract and theoretical; where was it—indeed, where was even common decency—in his callous insensitivity to Natalie Wood's vulnerabilities? Ironically, Warren, who over the next decade would become the best-known liberal in Hollywood, was anything but liberal, in the large-hearted, chivalrous sense of the word, in his dealings with those closest to him. With women, his pattern had been to conquer them when they were either married or engaged or living with other men. After they fell in love with him, he ultimately disappeared, and they found themselves out in the cold, with no one. In the most intimate and meaningful area of life he had betrayed everyone. "I'm really a bum of sorts," he said in a rare moment of total honesty.[15]

His compassion, such as it was, would be acted out in the political rather than the personal arena. When Robert F. Kennedy denounced the war in 1968 and campaigned for the Democratic nomination for the U.S. presidency, Warren rushed to his support. From that moment on he would immerse himself in the machinery of the Democratic Party, becoming known and respected as one of its hardest workers.

A feeling had always gnawed at Warren that the profession of acting did not utilize his potential. "I didn't want, as Cary Grant put it, to spend my life just tripping over cables on soundstages," he said. "Bobby [Kennedy] was one of those few people who was completely accepted by the Establishment who still wanted to rattle the Establishment."[16] When Warren turned his attention to politics in 1968, he became a perfectionist. As Pierre Salinger later attested, he read every speech RFK had ever delivered in the Senate, quoting them when he addressed hostile students on university campuses. "He won them over as skillfully as Bob [Kennedy] himself did," Salinger said. "Warren was a 'guts' worker, not a movie star."[17]

RFK spent an intimate evening with Warren and a few other friends when he came to California in 1968. John Frankenheimer hosted the party at his Malibu home, inviting Warren, Shirley, Warren's *Lilith* co-star Jean Seberg, and her husband, novelist Romain Gary, author of *The Roots of Heaven*. For someone in his early forties, RFK seemed like an old man, showing the strain and emotional wear and tear of all he'd been through—WWII; raising a family of ten children (soon to be eleven; Ethel was pregnant again); the battle for civil rights; fighting Castro and the mob; losing his brother to an assassin's bullet; running for the U.S. Senate; and at last, vying for the U.S. presidency. That night at the Frankenheimers' (the director was married to actress Evans Evans, who'd appeared in the original Broadway production of Inge's *The Dark at the Top of the Stairs*), Kennedy seemed strangely resigned. He was concerned about his rebellious son David, a troubled twelve-year-old who'd recently been caught throwing rocks at strangers. Romain Gary, in the cool guerrilla style of French intellectuals, asked Kennedy why he wanted to run for president, since it would only get him killed. RFK's attitude was that it all went with the territory. He'd often enough said, "If anyone wants to kill me it won't be difficult," and quoted Edith Hamilton's observation, "Men are not made for safe havens." Though his campaign for the Democratic nomination had met with raucous adulation at huge rallies, he seemed to have little enthusiasm for the presidency, and commented that he probably wouldn't be able to get much done if elected.[18]

On June 14, 1968, RFK's last day of primary campaigning in California went well, and he returned to Malibu to relax on the beach with Ethel and six of their children. As usual, David was a problem. Romping in the surf, the boy was swept out to sea by a powerful undertow, and his dad had to swim out to rescue him. Later, they went to the Ambassador Hotel in downtown L.A. to wait for the primary election result. When the vote count came in, Kennedy won over Eugene McCarthy, and now held 198 precious delegate votes. He seemed a shoo-in to become the Democratic candidate for the White House. From the podium he told his supporters, "I think we can end the divisions within the United States, the violence." But then, as Kennedy headed through the hotel kitchen to the press room, came the crackle of gunfire. "It sounded like dry wood snapping," said one witness. Robert Kennedy fell to the floor, a .22-caliber "long rifle," hollow-nose slug in his brain. It took eight men, including author George Plimpton and athletes Rafer Johnson and Roosevelt Grier, to overpower the slight, five-foot-three, 120-pound assassin, Sirhan Sirhan, an anti-American Jordanian nationalist. In the melee, Sirhan managed to shoot five other people. Ethel Kennedy, struggling to get to her husband, knelt long enough to kiss one of Sirhan's victims, seventeen-year-old campaign worker Erwin Stroll, who'd been shot in the left shin. Then she accompanied her husband to the hospital, where, for the next twenty-five hours, surgeons tried in vain to save his life. Just as Romain Gary had predicted that night at the Frankenheimers', Robert Kennedy had not survived his presidential aspirations. Nor would Gary and Jean Seberg long survive. Within a decade both committed suicide.

Following the assassination, a grieving Warren poured all his energy into working on the Emergency Gun Controls Committee. On July 6, 1968, he spoke to the crowd at Candlestick Park, just before the San Francisco Giants–St. Louis Cardinals game. Julie Christie, who was shooting her film *Petulia* in San Francisco, was in the stands as the crowd warily regarded Warren, who was standing in the middle of the field, conservatively dressed in a dark pin-stripe suit and dark turtleneck, but, unwisely, sporting movie-star shades, which stood out like a badge of debonair superficiality. "A sound and reasonable gun-control law will only help curb violence in our society," he said. "Now is the time to act, and Americans should wire or write their congressmen to approve a law that will impose reason and good sense on possession of firearms."

The crowd of 28,233 turned on him, booing and hissing. He struck them as a clown and interloper on the sacred all-American turf of baseball and politics. Recalled a former Castro Street hippie who'd been in the stands that day, "Sure we booed. Here was Clyde Barrow himself, blathering on about gun control, when only recently we'd watched Faye Dunaway caressing his rod."

Bruised but unbowed, Warren went on to speak that night at the Sonny Liston–Henry Clark fight at the Cow Palace. This time, he was challenged about his propensity for on-screen violence. Wasn't there an obvious conflict between his position on gun control and all the fun Bonnie and Clyde had shooting up half of Texas in his film? "I see no conflict," he said. "The movie tried to show a historical situation as it was. . . . To my mind, the movies that are most dangerous are those that show violence but show it as not being dangerous—the type where all the shooting goes on but nobody gets hurt." Such graceless public statements rarely convinced, and for a while he chose to remain in the background, leaving the political limelight to others. Obviously the public did not trust playboys, and resented pretty faces in the political arena. His best role, he decided, would be as a behind-the-scenes organizer.

In his quiet way, he continued to fight for gun control, and contributed significantly to the eventual passage of the Tydings Bill. "It was later watered down," Warren said, "but it was better than nothing."[19] Eventually his retreat from the podium won the respect of politicos. They saw him as different from the usual show-business types, who were motivated by self-interest and a desire to bask in attention. Warren's personal style of reticence and anonymity made him welcome in the Democratic Party's power elite.

While in San Francisco, he at first resumed his affair with Maya Plisetskaya, who had a dancing engagement in the city, and then he went after the gray-eyed, blond Julie Christie, visiting her *Petulia* set and trying to seduce her. She was still involved with Don Bessant, but when Plisetskaya left for other engagements on her tour, Warren begged Julie to reconsider and go out with him. By now Don Besant had returned to Britain, but Julie refused Warren's invitation to accompany him to the premiere of *Camelot*, and, insultingly, conveyed her regrets through a smart-alecky studio executive. Congenitally incapable of taking no for an answer, Warren later asked her to dinner. She accepted this time, and they had a romantic evening at a seaside restaurant in Sausalito, just over the Golden Gate Bridge, with a breathtaking view of the shimmering city across the bay. He assured Julie that he wanted "to do something less selfish" with his life, his single-minded pursuit of sex and fame having left him somewhat deflated. Julie believed him and accompanied him when he gave his talks on gun control.

As soon as *Petulia* wrapped, they ran off to Mexico. They discovered they had many tastes in common, principally modern jazz and pop music. He found her to be "almost pathologically honest," and he loved her candor though sometimes he was hurt by it. "She'll always tell you what she thinks, with clarity and the directness of an arrow," he said. "The pain, too. But it's valuable."[20] Their chief difference, and it was a very large one, was that Warren's life represented what Julie called a "flash, switched-on existence," the kind of Hollywood glamour that the earthy, practical Julie abhorred.

Born in Assam, India, where her father was a tea planter, she and her brother Clive had been sent to England for boarding-school educations. She got kicked out for telling dirty jokes, and her parents then put her up with friends of her mother's in France, hoping she'd learn the language. After returning to England, she attended Brighton Technical College and studied speech training and dramatic art before she appeared in a science-fiction play and landed parts in two minor movies. Finally, John Schlesinger assigned her a small role in *Billy Liar*, and American critics singled her out as one of the freshest talents of 1963. She was twenty-two when Schlesinger cast her in his jet-set opus, *Darling*, for which she received an Academy Award nomination as Best Actress. On Oscar night, she defied the academy's ban on miniskirts, striding onto the Santa Monica Civic Auditorium's stage in daring sixties gear after being announced the winner. Clutching her Oscar, she stammered, "This is the most wonderful thing on earth." The following day, international headlines predicted that the statuette would bring her one million dollars a year for the next ten years, but the advent of Warren Beatty in the actress's life did not bode well for her career.

Though brief, Julie Christie's stardom had a uniquely gorgeous glow. Truly, there had never been anyone like her. Her beauty, her intensity, her honesty, her talent—and, above all, her Oscar—made her irresistible to Warren, an incorrigible status seeker. He also loved her spontaneity, her ability to live in the present moment, and to relish all experience. "I can enjoy almost any sensation," she said. "When a toothache or a chilblain is gone, I miss it. I live as though I'm going to die tomorrow. All the time, I see how short life is. It is today—now—that counts for me."[21] Warren said he'd "always loved her on the screen, beginning with *Darling*. I like her even when she's in a bad movie. *Demon Seed* was bad, and I still loved her." When they got back to L.A., he rented a house to share with her, but as usual kept his suite at the Beverly Wilshire. "Any need for possessions or 'roots' is unnecessary," he said.

Julie returned to Don Bessant but couldn't forget Warren, whose unconventional, rebellious spirit and proud rootlessness appealed to her. A left-wing activist, she'd later lead a walkout from *The Deer Hunter* at the Berlin Film Festival (though the film was antiwar, it seemed to her to exult in violence).[22] After *Petulia*, she went to Geneva to film *In Search of Gregory*, and Warren followed her, patiently loafing around her set until she completed the day's scenes. Later, when she shot *The Go-Between* in the English countryside, he flew to London, not far from where she was filming her takes with co-stars Edward Fox and Alan Bates. By then, Don Bessant was history.

At times she could resemble an unkempt hipster—a softer, British version of Shirley MacLaine—but when she chose to, she could outshine any star in the industry, as she'd proved in 1965's *Doctor Zhivago*. As Lara, Zhivago's beloved, her combination of inner strength and romantic vulnerability were definitively captured, and afterward there were few in the Western world who weren't humming the haunting "Lara's Theme." Even in the harsher role of Bathsheba Everdene in 1967's *Far from the Madding Crowd*, she was indisputably the world's reigning beauty, and in fashion magazines she became the epitome of sixties chic. Even as one of the biggest stars in the world, she preferred to remain on a farm she'd bought in Wales. Anthea Sylbert, who'd later costume her in *Shampoo*, said that Julie would prefer to "live in a log cabin, drive a truck and wear overalls if she could."

She resisted the dehumanizing process of stardom, scoffing at reporters who called her a myth or a legend, and she found it "tortuous and agonizing" to have to talk about herself to the press, still preferring "to live a private life when I'm not working. I couldn't care less about publicity."[23] Warren made the same claims, but it was only Julie who meant it. He wanted wealth and fame, and only pretended to disdain publicity. Robert Altman, who'd later direct Beatty and Christie in *McCabe and Mrs. Miller*, observed, "Julie doesn't *like* being a movie star. All she wants is to act. . . . This is very genuine with her. Warren, on the other hand, is so many things in addition to the superstar that he is and feels [he is]. He is also the businessman, extremely astute. The director. The writer. He is very strong and cares about what he does."

At first, Warren found that his and Julie's differences and similarities dove-tailed nicely. "This is *it*," he said. Though it was the dawn of women's lib, in some respects she was surprisingly conventional, looking for a man who'd take charge of her. Beginning in late 1967, Warren and Julie became inseparable, at least whenever she was filming in L.A. She lived with him in the Beverly Wilshire, appearing in the lobby in a see-through white cotton sari. After she returned to England, Warren hit on other girlfriends. When they said they thought he was in love with Julie Christie, he admitted it. "You get slapped a lot, but you get fucked a lot, too," he said.[24]

Inevitably he told his agent, Stan Kamen, "Let's find a picture I can do with Julie." The idea was bad from the start, because Beatty and Christie were anti-thetical performers—he was an analytic control freak who didn't even warm up until the fourth or fifth take, and she was a spontaneous, instinctive charmer who was at her best the first time around. Like Gary Cooper and Spencer Tracy, Garbo and Dietrich, she was a natural-born movie star. "I feel no difference between me acting and not acting," she said. "There's only one Christie. But I know I'm never more myself than when acting, because I put all of myself into it."[25]

Warren, who still hadn't grasped that one should never mix business and pleasure, kept searching for a project they could share. Christie remained skep-tical, both personally and professionally. Sheilah Graham wrote after interview-ing her, "Would they marry? I did not think so. Neither did she. 'But whether I marry nor not,' she said, 'I want to have a child by the time I am thirty.' "[26]

In 1968, at the height of the sexual revolution, Beatty became convinced that his promiscuity would ultimately leave him desolate and unfulfilled. He decided to make a movie about sleeping around as a sort of wake-up call to himself and a cautionary tale for others. He gave his good friend Robert Towne, a neighbor of Sharon Tate and Roman Polanski in Benedict Canyon, a story idea about a heterosexual hairdresser (an oxymoron if ever there was one, since most male hairdressers are gay) who finds that bedding down every client who offers herself to him is ultimately unsatisfying. Towne had already been drawn to the subject of compulsive womanizing, having contributed an episode to the TV show *Breaking Point*, entitled "So Many Pretty Girls, So Little Time," and also having started his own version of *Shampoo* after rewriting *Bonnie and Clyde*. When Warren went to London and leased a town house in South Audley Street, Towne moved in and became his roommate. Julie Christie, whose London home was in Selwood Terrace, contributed to the genesis of *Shampoo* by sending Warren and Bob to see Maggie Smith's revival of William Wycherley's 1676 Restoration comedy, *The Country Wife*, in which a rake deflects a jealous husband's suspicions by pretending to be gay. The savage cynicism of Wycherley's play and its coarse, mordant wit further galvanized their hairdresser project.

Finally Towne showed Warren the script, and although Warren liked the way the story demonstrated that "even the promiscuous feel pain,"[27] he pointed out that the women characters should be stronger. Towne disagreed. "Warren was very angry about it, and I don't know anybody who's a bigger prick, but there's no one I love or admire more," Towne recalls. The two friends fought so bitterly that the project was canceled, and they refused to communicate with each other for a year. Though Towne loved him like a brother, he did not hesitate to say that Beatty could "be a genuine bastard."[28]

In 1968, though still shaken by RFK's death, Warren resumed his involvement in presidential campaign politics, supporting Hubert Horatio Humphrey in his bid for the presidency. A son of the Midwest, Humphrey was a native of South Dakota who had served as mayor of Minneapolis and sponsored a historic civil rights plank at the 1948 Democratic National Convention. Humphrey served four years as the thirty-eighth vice president of the U.S., during the troubled administration of Lyndon Johnson. A tireless leader of the pro-labor and civil rights factions of the Democratic Party, Humphrey was a talkative, high-spirited man who espoused the "politics of joy." He got along very well with

Warren Beatty. He had enjoyed *Bonnie and Clyde* and was aware it had radical-ized millions of potential Democratic voters. Warren threw his considerable weight behind Humphrey's presidential campaign, seeing the likable liberal hero as the nation's only hope to stop the reactionary Richard Nixon's assault on the White House.

In Chicago for the 1968 Democratic National Convention, Warren was asked by Humphrey to appear in a campaign documentary. He agreed on one condition, saying, "Hubert, you need to break with the administration on Vietnam, which I assume you're going to do." "Don't worry," Humphrey told him, "that'll be happening within the next week and a half." Antiwar protests were regarded as riots by Chicago mayor Richard Daley, who unleashed his bru-tal police force in the park across the street from the Hilton Hotel, where the Humphrey team was encamped. During one demonstration, Warren glanced at his watch and realized it was 10:45. "I really must be going," he said, "because I have a meeting with Hubert."[29] As he crossed the street and tried to enter the hotel lobby, he was teargassed.

Worse was yet to come: Humphrey reneged on his vow to defy President Johnson on Vietnam, and remained a hawk in order to get the presidential nom-ination. His defense of the war cost him the support of the antiwar movement, and Richard Nixon was elected president. Humphrey remained in politics, returning to the Senate and twice again seeking the presidential nomination, but Warren refused to support him.

When he returned to Beverly Hills after the convention, "an assemblage of girls larger than a Broadway chorus call" was waiting "outside his door" at the Beverly Wilshire Hotel, according to *Los Angeles* magazine.[30] A woman who occupied the suite below Warren's lay awake many nights listening to the bump-ing upstairs and finally asked the manager, "What goes on up in that penthouse apartment? I hear the strangest noises at all hours of the night."[31] Jennifer Lee could have told her. Jennifer was a sultry, engaging, clever Finch College dropout who later married Richard Pryor. She met Warren through actress Nancy Allen, star of *Dressed to Kill* and later Mrs. Brian De Palma. During one of Warren's visits to New York, Nancy took Jennifer to meet Warren at the Carlyle Hotel.

Greeting them at the door in a terry-cloth robe, Warren explained that he'd just stepped out of the shower. He was about thirty-three at the time, and

Jennifer later described him as being "warm and sweet and adorable . . . with a strong, tight body and lots of energy." He took the girls out to eat, and then Nancy left them alone. While making love to Jennifer, Warren took calls from Julie Christie. Nevertheless, Jennifer found him to be "a good lover, strong, passionate, and sensual, but . . . not a particularly great lover. He's not *that* well endowed, no matter what Madonna [much later on] said in her *Advocate* interview. . . . He likes to give directions, not only about positions, but about how you should feel and react. The pressure to have the biggest, most earth-shattering orgasms can get a little relentless. I've definitely had to fake a few."

She found it easier to connect with him emotionally during threesomes, which he appeared to prefer. The third party was usually a model or a rich married woman, who became the object of Warren and Jennifer's joint desire, providing a focus that somehow took the pressure off and allowed a deeper intimacy.[32]

When Drew Barrymore's future mother, twenty-one-year-old Jaid Mako, hit L.A. in the late sixties, she acquired a job waitressing at the Troubadour, a popular live-music venue favored by the Doors, Jackson Browne, Elton John, and James Taylor. "The first guy to hit on me in Hollywood was Warren Beatty," Jaid recalled. "He walked into the club with girlfriend Julie Christie on his arm and he came over to me and started flirting. I couldn't believe it. Here he was, so handsome and with this beautiful girl . . . and he's coming on to me. I got the impression that he did this with every girl."[33] What Jaid didn't understand about Warren's sex addiction was that one lay was always too many, and one thousand were never enough. In compulsive sexuality, as the Rolling Stones put it in their sixties anthem "Satisfaction," there is no such thing as contentment, no matter how hard—or often—one tries.

Though Warren's relationships with women were frail and destined for early extinction, his relations with men were improving. Perhaps because of his growing involvement in politics—a game in which he, for once, was not competing, but devoting his mind and energy to helping the candidate—friends noticed that he was beginning to be able to bond with men. Goldie Hawn, for one, felt that this ability to form close ties within one's own gender made a man a better lover. As Goldie put it, "I don't think you can love the other sex unless you love your own, and you sense this in Warren by the number of men friends he has and how loyal they are."[34] Like many males in the 1960s, Warren was yielding some of his macho poses. This was the decade of long hair and androgyny. Ironically, the unisex styles didn't always become him. Though still in his thirties and as solid in build as he'd been at eighteen, his new touches of Edwardian elegance—especially the ladylike scarves he affected and his long, flowing locks—were not what his already almost feminine, pretty face needed. Sometimes, especially in profile, his eyeglasses, dimples, and cascading curls turned him into a dead ringer for lesbian tennis champ Billie Jean King. As a rule, the peacock look came off better on rock stars than movie stars.

To Goldie, Warren seemed to be trying to seduce the whole world. "It was just his nature," she said. "He does it with everybody—women, women of all ages, men, children."[35]

Shampoo was a long time a-borning, and in the interim, Warren made a horrendous miscalculation, going into the ill-fated Elizabeth Taylor picture *The Only Game in Town*. He thought it would be a quick shoot for an easy $1.25 million. He had been in the movie business long enough to know there was no such thing as a quick shoot when Elizabeth Taylor was involved. Amazingly, he turned down *Butch Cassidy and the Sundance Kid*, for which he'd have been paid $3 to 3.5 million, explaining that he wanted to work with George Stevens, who was directing *The Only Game in Town*, and, besides, he "didn't feel much like getting on a horse and riding around."[36] That wasn't precisely the way it happened, according to Peter Bart, editor of *Daily Variety*, who wrote, "Director George Roy Hill became so frustrated with Beatty's demands and procrastination that he told him to take a walk and went with Redford, instead."[37]

Nor was Warren George Stevens's first choice for the gritty role of Joe Grady, a compulsive gambler. Frank Sinatra originally had the part. Stevens's production notes and correspondence, housed today in his archive at the Academy of Motion Picture Arts and Sciences in Beverly Hills, indicate that there was great turmoil on the set: "Bad news all around me," Stevens wrote on July 30, 1968. "Start of picture—Taylor's health. Sinatra's disposition. Fred [Kohlmar, producer] worried, might go to England tomorrow to see Liz' agent." Stevens drank two martinis and went to bed loaded.[38] Matters had scarcely improved by August 9, when Stevens wrote, "Kohlmar, Dick Zanuck, and Hugh French desperately trying to figure out how and when we can start this picture with Liz Taylor after recuperation and keep Frank Sinatra in it."

On the same day, Stevens received, out of the blue, a call from Warren, who said that he would like to see the director about "a script that Warren wanted me to read." Stevens started thinking about replacing Sinatra with Warren, and he also thought about replacing Elizabeth Taylor. On August 12, Warren called Stevens again and said he was flying to Paris to see him the next day, but never showed up. Stevens was frantically working with Stanley Donen (Richard Burton's director in *Staircase*), Taylor's agents Hugh French and Robin French, and Sinatra's pal Mickey Rudin, to juggle the shooting schedule and keep both Sinatra and Taylor in the picture.

On the nineteenth, Stevens succeeded in finding Warren's telephone number and called him in London. "He said he would not need to read the script but would go on my say and commit to do it if asked," Stevens wrote in his diary. Warren agreed to a salary of $750,000 (Taylor received $1,250,000), and a memo from Twentieth Century-Fox in the Stevens archive spells out Warren's requested credit as "100% same size, style, prominence, and color as name of Elizabeth Taylor; must also be on same line as name of Elizabeth Taylor."[39]

Stevens prepared for directing Beatty by viewing all his movies, ordering numerous cans of film to be sent to his suite in the George V in Paris. On August 22 and 30, 1968, he screened *Bonnie and Clyde*, *Kaleidoscope*, and *Promise Her Anything*. Throughout late August he was also screening Julie Christie's *Dr. Zhivago*, *Darling*, and *Petulia*, and Mia Farrow's *Rosemary's Baby* and *A Dandy in Aspic*, obviously thinking about replacing Taylor, who fell ill on September 9, delaying the film.[40]

On September 16, Warren came to a studio meeting with Stevens and Fred Kohlmar, and on the eighteenth, viewed part of *All Fall Down* with Stevens in the cutting room. By September 20, Stevens's notebook indicates he lunched with Warren at the George V and at 5 P.M. met with Elizabeth Taylor at the Plaza Athenee. Shooting started on September 26, and Stevens was on the set from 12 noon until about 6:45. On the same day, Stevens jokingly wrote his friend Al Horwitz in Beverly Hills, "Detached Sinatra from this enterprise so that he could help you on the Humphrey campaign . . . We have brought Warren Beatty over here carefully disguised as a star to appear with Liz Taylor in a film. Of course you were aware that this is part of the plan to oust [Governor Ronald] Reagan and Jane Wyman [*sic*; he meant Nancy Reagan] from the State House and replace them with Warren Beatty and Julie Christie."[41]

The film supposedly was a light romantic comedy about a Las Vegas show-girl and a lounge piano player with a gambling addiction, but was unrelievedly leaden. Taylor was too old for her leading man—and looked it. Stevens, one of Hollywood's greatest directors, was in decline. His papers at the Margaret Herrick Library are full of receipts for medication and exercise equipment that was sent to him in Paris, where he was drinking far too much. The Paris location shoot was ludicrous—Las Vegas was of course the logical setting, but it had to be made in Paris so Elizabeth could be close to her husband, Richard Burton, who was making a dismal movie there called *Staircase*. Stevens and his crew tried to make the French interiors look like Vegas, and the results were bizarre.

When Warren first encountered Elizabeth, who was then known as the most beautiful woman in the world, he laughed in her face. She demanded an explanation, and he told her, "I laughed because nobody can be that beautiful." She was used to such behavior from her leading men. When she'd earlier filmed Stevens's *Giant*, both of her co-stars, Rock Hudson and James Dean, were so stunned by her beauty that they couldn't perform. She relaxed Hudson by dressing up as Minnie Mouse, which made him laugh. It was harder to thaw out Dean, who held Elizabeth upside down, by her ankles, and eventually exposed his penis in front of two thousand five hundred spectators on location in Marfa, Texas, before he could loosen up enough to enact his first scene with her.

Burton was naturally jealous when Elizabeth told a reporter, "I'm absolutely crazy about Warren."[42] On a scale of one to ten, he rated a fifteen for Liz. Burton remained civil enough to have drinks with Warren when he came to collect his wife after work. The Welsh actor needn't have worried unduly. As critics of the film later pointed out, Liz had been helping herself to French cuisine and consequently was suffering from "avoirdupois." *The New Yorker* noted that "Beatty is obviously younger than [ET] is." *Women's Wear Daily*'s Richard Cohen scolded Elizabeth for "letting herself go to fat. . . . You cannot accept her as a Las Vegas dancer and you cannot accept her as the girlfriend of a sexpot like Beatty . . . [who] often looked more like her son than her lover."

Warren got sick with a cold in late October 1968, and this, together with Elizabeth's usual medical problems and the leisurely French way of filmmaking, caused *The Only Game in Town* to stretch into months. Every Friday at the close of the work week, a cocktail party was held on the set, with a different VIP hosting, beginning with Stevens. Elizabeth had to cancel a future commitment, *Two Mules for Sister Sarah*; the role went to Patricia Neal, who also had to cancel, and the part finally devolved to Shirley MacLaine. Shirley and her husband, Steve Parker, visited Warren on the set during a visit to Paris. Sheilah Graham dropped by and later called Warren "the hottest property in pictures." He had landed the coveted lead in *The Arrangement*, which had been vacated by Brando, but ultimately it went to Kirk Douglas.

On October 31, Elizabeth hosted a luncheon, and the guests included HRH the Duke and Duchess of Windsor, longtime friends of the Burtons. On November 5, Mia Farrow and Roger Vadim visited Warren and Elizabeth on the set, and on the nineteenth, Elizabeth had a cocktail party. Her father died the following day, and she took time off to attend his funeral, flying to Los Angeles. She was back in time to co-host with Burton a Thanksgiving dinner for all the Americans in the company, on November 28. The next day, there was a Thanksgiving party on the set.

While in Paris, Warren dated Maria Callas, who'd just been dumped by Aristotle Onassis. He also saw Princess Elizabeth of Yugoslavia, one of the leaders of European society, and had various flings in London. For Warren, playing around on Julie Christie became a way of life. Fear of exposure is part of the strange joy being unfaithful. In London, he met with Michelle Phillips, the exquisite singer from the rock group the Mamas and the Papas. At the time she looked like a combination of Julie Christie and Leslie Caron, and it was almost as if Warren chose her because she was a composite of his favorite physical features in a woman. The *Los Angeles Herald Examiner* reported that he and Michelle were dating, and quipped, "She will be the next Miss Michelle Phillips."[43] The daughter of a seaman, Michelle had lost her mother at a young age, growing up to become one of the most elegant women in show business. Slim and aristocratic looking, with finely chiseled bone structure and honey-blond hair, she would later dress in stylish designer clothes, but in the sixties she was the archetypal hippie chick, with long, ironed hair and often wearing striped stovepipe pants, boots, and a man's white shirt. As a member of the Mamas and the Papas, she contributed to the haunting harmonies of "Go Where You Wanna Go," "California Dreamin'," "Creeque Alley," and "Monday, Monday." While still in her teens, she married the group's leader, John Phillips.

The marriage ended in divorce, but John remained a possessive ex-husband, later revealing that he "phoned Warren once and, like the [Sinatra] thugs in the elevator warning me about Mia [Farrow], I warned him, in a drunken, stoned stupor, to lay off other guys' wives or he'd get himself seriously injured." Earlier, there'd been trouble with John during Michelle's affair with Roman Polanski. In John's rather chilling memoir, *Papa John*, he confessed that Polanski "might have concluded that I could have been enraged and unstable enough to seek revenge by committing—or orchestrating—a mass murder."[44]

Even Mad Dog Beatty wouldn't take on a nut case like John Phillips. He went crawling back to Julie, with whom he was about to film *McCabe and Mrs. Miller* in Canada. Michelle went on to have an affair with David Giler. Producer Julia Phillips (no relation to either John or Michelle Phillips) "was amazed that this unprepossessing fellow with the sharp nose and the glasses was such a cocksman. . . . He had a deep voice and looked from his tight pants to be fairly well hung."[45]

After Warren returned to L.A., as Nan Morris-Robinson recalled in a recent interview, he "was off asleep in another room" when Nan, Roman Polanski, and a group of friends, who'd been partying at the Candy Store, descended on Polanski's house in Beverly Hills. "This was before Roman and Sharon moved to Benedict Canyon," Nan said. "It was an English brick two-story house, and I remember Roman had two giant wolfhounds. They were very gentle, but he explained that when they were told to attack, they could break your back. They'd jump up and land on you and crack your spine. One of them could fight off eight men."

Women were invariably taken with Polanski. In a summer 2001 interview, novelist/memoirist Elaine Dundy, author of *The Dud Avocado* and *Life Itself!*, and the first wife of theater critic Kenneth Tynan, recalled meeting Polanski just after *Knife in the Water*. "Ava Gardner called it a 'real Hollywood movie,' with Hollywood production values. We were on the street, and Roman started leaping over fireplugs—a sweet, gay thing to do, I thought. Gay in the old sense, that is. He was like an elf." Ruth Gordon called him "such a charming youth," though he was thirty-four when he directed the actress in *Rosemary's Baby*.

The house the Polanskis were renting on Summit Ridge Drive was owned by Patty Duke, and according to Leslie Caron, a good friend of Sharon's, it was getting a bad reputation. "Sharon and Roman were lax in a way, and their house was very available. They invited an awful lot of people there, and I always thought that there was something really dangerous about the way they lived." Inevitably, among the night people along the Strip, the Summit Ridge house became infamous as a place to score drugs. Sharon didn't object when she saw unknown people in her living room, telling a reporter that her philosophy was "live and let live."[46]

Eventually Patty Duke told the Polanskis she was reclaiming Summit Ridge for her own use, and they had to move out. With the help of real estate agent Elaine Young, they found a Normandy-style farmhouse in Benedict Canyon in Beverly Hills, at 10050 Cielo Drive, not far from Bob Towne's place on Hutton Drive, and took a one-year lease, paying $1,200 a month in rent. Built by French actress Michele Morgan in the late 1940s, the house's previous tenants included Henry Fonda, Cary Grant, and, most recently, Candice Bergen and her record-executive boyfriend, Terry Melcher, who was Doris Day's son as well as the producer of the Byrds' classic "Mr. Tambourine Man." Moving in on February 12, 1969, the Polanskis invited Warren to a housewarming on the fifteenth, which was also attended by John Phillips, Peter Fonda, Tony Curtis, Danny Kaye, Roger Vadim, Jane Fonda, and Roman's business manager William Tennant. The party turned rowdy when a drunken uninvited guest, Billy Doyle, stepped on Bill Tennant's foot, and a shoving match ensued. Polanski threw Doyle and two other party crashers out of the house, but the atmosphere remained tense. Taking their leave, Vadim and Jane Fonda invited Warren and John and Michelle Phillips to their Malibu beach house, where they all partied until daybreak.[47]

At Cielo Drive, between overseas film commitments, the Polanskis became popular hosts, entertaining such counterculture figures as Janis Joplin, rock star Jim Morrison, Dennis Hopper, Peter Fonda, Steve McQueen, and all four of the Mamas and the Papas (John Phillips, Michelle Phillips, Cass Eliott, and Denny Doherty), as well as A-list notables like Warren, Mike Nichols, the Kirk Douglases, the Yul Brynners, and Peter Sellers. Cielo Drive was also home base for the Polanskis' growing entourage, which included Roman's fellow Polish émigré, Wojtek (pronounced *Voytek*) Frykowski, a penniless would-be producer; "Fryko"'s mistress, Abigail (Gibby) Folger, a coffee-fortune heiress; and hairdresser Jay Sebring. "It was the crowd from the Daisy that went in and out of the house on Cielo Drive," Warren recalled, referring to the L.A. disco.

According to novelist and L.A. social observer Dominick Dunne, the hardcore Daisy set included "Joan Collins, Michael Caine, Ryan O'Neal, Mia Farrow, Jane Fonda, Warren Beatty, the Sinatra sisters, and maybe a Vegas figure or two."[48]

Polanski commuted to London for his films, Sharon Tate to Rome for hers, and when she was away, Polanski and Warren continued to play, hitting the Daisy or the Factory, cruising the streets, or frequenting topless bars along the Sunset Strip.[49] Warren was enjoying the lifestyle he'd helped launch in *Bonnie and Clyde.* It cheered amorality, reveled in blood and guts, and its finger-flipping attitude toward the Establishment had long since seeped into the culture. Though the film's influence in such areas as art, fashion, and politics was salubrious, launching the New Hollywood and delightful retro clothes and, more important, lending support to the antiwar movement and to the counterculture in general, it resonated with an ominous strain that fostered violence and sadism. In describing the late 1960s in L.A., novelist Joan Didion wrote, "I recall a time when the dogs barked every night and the moon was always full." Those who had espoused chaos and lawlessness were about to pay for it, from Altamont in Northern California to Polanski's menagerie in Beverly Hills. The heartwrenching tragedy that was about to consume Sharon Tate would be played out against the violent backdrop of an entire nation ripped apart by war and devastated by riots.

For a long time, Polanski's life had been a catastrophe waiting to happen. Faye Dunaway, who'd spent some time in Rome with the Polanskis during her romance with producer Andy Braunsberg,[50] recalled that Polanski "had a complicated connection to women for much of his career, with taste that ran to young, malleable girls." Dunaway would feel "strange vibes" emanating from him when he directed her, rather autocratically, in *Chinatown.* "What he did to me throughout the film bordered on sexual harassment," she says. "He always hung out with young girls. Young girls are not threatening, young girls don't have ideas, they're not independent, and I was all of those."[51] Another woman, who requested anonymity, remembered being in a car with Polanski and her fourteen-year-old daughter. "He was all over her," she said. Sharon Tate could have passed for an adolescent, according to novelist Jerzy Kosinski, part of Polanski's old circle from Lodz, Poland, who mistook Sharon for a teenager when he first met her. Polanski had heightened her "little girl" impression when he directed her in *The Fearless Vampire Killers,* assigning the English actor Alfie

Bass, who played her father, the task of spanking her."[52] Sharon also went along with Polanski's desire to film her nude, despite Filmways memos objecting to the actress being "unduly exposed."

Excessive compliance to her husband's wishes would prove to be Sharon's undoing. A cozy marriage would have satisfied her; she wanted to pamper her beloved "Ro," serve him tasty dinners of Virginia ham, upside-down cake, and other soul-food specialties she'd learned from her Texas mother, but with the motley entourage ensconced in their Benedict Canyon home, the Polanskis' domestic life degenerated into an increasingly lethal situation. When Ro and Sharon were away on their jet-setting trips abroad, both Fryko and Sebring treated their house as a social club, throwing noisy parties that had to be broken up by the police. Gibby Folger, who was by now a drug addict, was on the verge of ending her affair with Fryko, weary of supporting him, bored with his marathon nine-day mescaline trips, and terrified by his dope-peddling in Los Angeles's subterranean drug culture. Fed up with listening to their fights, Sharon told Roman that she wanted both Fryko and Gibby out of the house. Roman tolerated Fryko because, back in Poland, Fryko had raised the money for Roman's first film, *Mammals*. In L.A., Roman found Fryko a job as a construction worker at one of the studios, but it only lasted a day or two before Fryko complained of "knocking nails in the fucking floor," and quit. Jerzy Kosinski had introduced Fryko to Gibby Folger. After emigrating to America, Kosinski struck it rich at the altar, marrying a steel tycoon's widow, Mary Hayward Weir.[53] In fixing Fryko up with Gibby, Kosinski assumed all his friend's financial needs would be met, as his own had been.

Though Sharon accepted her marriage to Polanski as a typical sixties "open" union, she became nervous when her husband's appetite for promiscuous sex began to rival Warren's. By 1969, the year following their marriage, she felt embarrassed and emotionally adrift. The Polanskis embarked on a ménage à trois with Jay Sebring, but the situation between Ro and Sharon did not improve. By the time Sharon got pregnant, the marriage was wobbly. Their friend Kirk Douglas later speculated, "The baby might have been Jay's."[54] Polanski abused Sharon in public, calling her a "dumb hag," and made little effort to adjust to her pregnancy. "We'd made love almost every night since starting to live together," he explained. "Now that we'd ceased to do so, she was afraid that my feelings toward her might be changing, that my lack of desire might become ingrained. For my part, I longed for the time when her body would return to normal; I failed to understand how men could have sex with their wives till the very last moment." Struggling to rationalize her husband's coolness, Sharon tried to excuse it, finally accepting it as "a subconscious fear of harming the baby."[55] The restless Polanski asked Warren to take over the lease at 10050 Cielo Drive.

At the time, unbeknownst to Warren and the Polanskis, the house was being cased by Charles Manson and his gang of thrill-killers, who were holed up at the Spahn Movie Ranch, a fake western town on the northern fringe of the San Fernando Valley, where *Duel in the Sun* and television's *The Lone Ranger* had been filmed. They made occasional forays into L.A. for "garbage runs" in rich neighborhoods, or to crash for a while in empty houses. An ex-convict who'd attempted to reinvent himself as a hippie messiah during San Francisco's 1967 Summer of Love, Manson preached the same kind of insanity that would later be espoused by the Muslim terrorists of the millennium: Bring down the Establishment at any cost, or, as Manson put it, "Now it's the pigs' turn to go up on the Cross." In time, he surrounded himself with the dropouts and runaways he picked up in the Haight Ashbury and other druggy counterculture pit stops, and they became known as the Family. Moving on to L.A., he was determined to become a recording artist, and by 1968 had assembled a surprising number of contacts.

These included Angela Lansbury's beautiful, intelligent daughter Deirdre Shaw, who, in typical sixties fashion, was experimenting with people and lifestyles, but would later find herself and become a superb chef. At the time I knew Deirdre, she was living with a brilliant fashion photographer named René Volpe, and Angela Lansbury would occasionally appear, like a guardian angel, and put their duplex apartment in order. It was Deirdre who introduced Manson to one of his future Family members, Nancy Pitman, soon rechristened "Brenda." The Beach Boys' drummer Dennis Wilson, who liked to pick up hitchhikers and take them home for sex, met Manson after giving rides to Manson groupies Patricia Krenwinkel and Ella Bailey. Wilson ended up turning over his lavish three-acre estate at 14400 Sunset Boulevard, a former hunting lodge owned by Will Rogers, to the Family when he realized he could have all the sex he wanted with Manson's harem of "great-looking chicks." "Come over and just fuck any of them you want," Wilson told John Phillips. Terry

Melcher, a producer at Columbia Records who'd worked with Paul Revere and the Raiders, met Manson at Wilson's house and promised to give him a studio session.

Dennis Wilson and the Beach Boys recorded Manson's "Never Learn Not to Love," but it stalled at sixty-one on the *Billboard* charts. After contracting gonorrhea from Manson's girls, Wilson fled his own home and hid in a small apartment while his business manager ejected the Family from 14400 Sunset Boulevard. Manson then focused on Terry Melcher, expecting him to pull the necessary strings at Columbia. In the summer of 1968, Family members Charles Denton "Tex" Watson and Dean Morehouse attended parties given by Melcher and Candice Bergen when they were still living at 10050 Cielo Drive, and on a later occasion, Watson, covered in grime after hitchhiking across L.A., invaded the house and demanded that Candice fork over bail money for Gregg Jakobson, Melcher's liaison man with the Manson Family, who'd been busted on drug charges. Fortunately for Candice, Melcher appeared and got rid of Watson.[56]

Terry and Candice moved out of Cielo Drive and into Doris Day's Malibu beach house over Christmas 1968, temporarily leaving their twenty-six cats in the care of the owner of Cielo Drive, Rudolph Altobelli, a showbusiness agent who resided in a guest house on the property. In the six weeks before the Polanskis took possession of Cielo Drive, Melcher's assistant Gregg Jakobson arranged for Manson disciple Dean Morehouse to crash there, and Family members Tex Watson, Susan Atkins, and Catherine Share were often around, splashing in the pool.

The following spring, Warren was unaware of the house's sinister history when he arrived to inspect Cielo Drive with a view to leasing it. Various cronies of the Polanskis were roaming the rooms as he took his tour of the premises that day. "Yeah, I'll stay here for a while," Warren thought, "because I wanted to get out of the hotel." Suddenly, Gibby Folger and Fryko sauntered in from another room, and one of them said to Warren, "Roman told us to take the house. There's plenty of room for everybody." Warren declined, observing, "I don't want to be in a house with other people."[57] Particularly, no doubt, with Fryko and Gibby, whose Folger fortune had brought a huge supply of marijuana, LSD, cocaine, hashish, and mescaline into the house.

Not long after Warren inspected the property that day, Charles Manson appeared suddenly on the front porch, demanding to see Melcher. Sharon Tate was at home at the time, dining with Jay, Fryko, Gibby, and her Iranian friend and personal photographer, Shahrokh Hatami. The latter went outside and told Manson that Melcher no longer lived there. As Hatami was advising him to go round to the guesthouse and check with the landlord, Rudi Altobelli, Sharon came out onto the porch and inquired, "Who is it, Hatami?" For some reason, Manson fled to the parking area as soon as he saw her. Then, as Sharon watched from the porch, Manson retraced his steps across the lawn and took the dirt path to the guest house. Altobelli, who was taking a shower, resented Manson's walking in without knocking, as if he owned the place, and he refused to tell Manson anything about Melcher's whereabouts. When Manson tried to pick Altobelli's brains about show business, Altobelli, a major agent in the city, shut the door in his face.[58] Shortly thereafter, Sharon and Altobelli flew to Europe on the same airplane. Sharon was to film *Thirteen Chairs* with Vittorio Gassman in London and Rome, and Altobelli was also traveling on business, after turning over the guesthouse to a hitchhiker he'd picked up, eighteen-year-old William Garretson, whom he hired as caretaker. At one point in their flight, Sharon asked Altobelli, "Did that creepy-looking guy come back there yesterday?" So far as is known, it was the only reference Sharon Tate ever made to Charles Manson.

In April 1969, Melcher at last agreed to record Manson, perhaps yielding to unrelenting pressure from Dennis Wilson. They all gathered in a Santa Monica studio, and Wilson sang along as Manson chanted his latest lyric, "Die today, die today, die today." Melcher's blood ran cold, and he suddenly lost all interest in Manson's recording career. When Melcher later blew off a planned documentary about Manson's hippie commune, Manson decided to kill him, and even tried to hire a hit man for $5,000. In July 1969, Manson went to see Dennis Wilson, who was away from his office, and when he attempted to extract money from Wilson's agent, he was thrown out and warned that the police would be called if he ever came back. Increasingly desperate as he saw his dreams of stardom go up in smoke, he again sought out Terry Melcher, and they had their final falling out when Melcher said, "Look, Charlie, there's mixed emotions about promoting you. You're unpredictable. You amaze me at times, and at other times, disappoint the hell out of me."

Manson told a friend, "How are you going to get to the Establishment? You can't sing to them. I tried that. I tried to save them, but they wouldn't listen. Now we've got to destroy them." By the summer of 1969, not only was Manson plotting to murder Melcher, he intended to wreak havoc among the rich of Beverly Hills and Bel Air, inspired by the Beatles' *White Album,* which he completely misinterpreted and twisted into a blueprint for race war. "Helter Skelter," one of the cuts on the album, takes its title from the British term meaning a giant slide, but Manson, using the U.S. definition, assumed the Beatles were promoting chaos and confusion. He adopted Helter Skelter as the name for the blitzkrieg of terror he was about to unleash on L.A., sending Family members out to maim and kill for him as he remained in hiding.

Meanwhile, Warren continued to show up at Cielo Drive as a guest. Sharon and Ro were both filming abroad in the early summer of 1969 when Jay Sebring decided he wanted to use the house to entertain prospective investors in a new business venture. He'd kept his original salon at 725 North Fairfax but also opened numerous franchise shops under the name Sebring International, in which Abigail Folger had already invested $3,500. Both Warren and John Phillips were present when Sebring's party was crashed by two drunken men. Fryko, who was tall and strong, kicked them out. "You fucking son of a bitch," one of them screamed. "We'll be back and we'll kill you."[59]

On Tuesday, August 5, Sharon, who'd returned to Cielo Drive in July, hosted a party for Roger Vadim, Jane Fonda, and approximately thirty-five other friends. On August 7, Steve McQueen, her former lover, made plans with Jay Sebring, while Jay was cutting Steve's hair, to have dinner with Sharon on August 8. Instead, McQueen, who'd been getting girls and drugs from Sebring for some time, picked up a woman and spent the night with her.[60] McQueen and Sebring were both under surveillance by Charles Manson and his spies. In fact, Manson placed both McQueen and Elizabeth Taylor on his hit list. A few days before Manson's gang arrived at Cielo Drive with instructions to kill everyone in the house, Sharon, Gibby, Fryko, and Sebring staged a scene that could have come straight out of *Rosemary's Baby.* According to Sebring, they invited twenty-five people to view the mass whipping of Cass Eliott's drug dealer, who'd burned Sebring for $2,000 worth of cocaine. Fryko and Jay allegedly bound the drug dealer to a chair and sodomized him before beating him, although LAPD officer Mike McGann later said that the event took place at Cass Eliott's house "and didn't involve either Sharon Tate or Jay Sebring."[61] In any case, there was a significant link between the Polanski household and that of the Mamas and the Papas' lovable, heavyset alto, Mama Cass, who lived nearby, just across

Woodstock Road: Cass knew members of the Manson Family. There was also a drug connection; Fryko was dealing the first big shipment to L.A. of the new synthetic, euphoria-inducing drug, MDA (methlenedioxyl-amphetamine), and he'd acquired it through one of the pushers feeding off Mama Cass. Perpetually stoned, both Fryko and Cass Eliott were sinking fast in L.A.'s seedy drug world. "Wojtak had a kind of weird vibe about him, a hustler-like feeling," said Michelle Phillips. "No one really wanted to be around him that much." As Dominick Dunne would later write in *Vanity Fair,* some Hollywood insiders believed "the murders were the result of a drug deal gone bad between Frykowski and Charles Manson."[62]

On Friday, August 8, 1969, Warren was in London with Dick Sylbert and Polanski, who was directing *Day of the Dolphin,* and had left Sharon behind in Los Angeles. Warren had been in and out of London throughout the Paris shoot of *The Only Game in Town,* due to interruptions occasioned by Elizabeth Taylor's back problems. He was staying with Julie Christie, but mostly partying with Polanski. In L.A., in the last few weeks of her pregnancy, Sharon Tate kept calling Polanski long distance, pointedly asking him when he was returning. He promised he'd be at her side within four days. That night, he dined with Victor Lownes and later went to the Revolution in Bruton Place, where, according to Lownes, Roman picked up "a bimbo" and had sex with her.[63]

In Benedict Canyon, it was hot and muggy as Sharon entertained her friends Joanna Pettet and Barbara Lewis. "That's why the little rat is still in London—he can't stand the sight of me fat and bloated," Sharon complained, "and he can't abide having me and my nerves around while he's working."[64] After Pettet and Lewis left at 3:30 P.M., Sharon went for a swim, and later was joined in the house by Sebring, Gibby, and Fryko. They dined at a Mexican restaurant on Beverly Boulevard, El Coyote, where Gibby and Fryko, both on speed, kept up a hectic argument. After dinner, they returned to the house on Cielo Drive. Sharon went into her bedroom with Sebring. She stripped to her bra and panties. He sat on the side of the bed in his blue shirt and black and white striped pants, smoking a joint and sipping a Heineken. Police would later discover both marijuana and cocaine in his Porsche. Elsewhere in the house, Gibby and Fryko took some MDA. She went to her bedroom, and he listened to the stereo before falling asleep on the living room couch.

Around midnight, four Manson groupies pulled up at Cielo Drive in a battered '59 yellow-and-white Ford. In a car outside was Steven Parent, an eighteen-year-old with no connection to the Polanskis, who had just visited the caretak-er of the estate, William Garretson. Manson gang member Charles (Tex) Watson rushed up to Parent's car and slashed him with a knife, then shot him in the arm, twice in the chest, and once in the head. Parent slumped in his seat, dead.

Entering the house, Tex found Fryko on the couch, kicked him in the head, and told Susan Atkins, known in the gang as Sadie May Glutz, to tie him up. When she finished, Atkins went around the house, rounding up the others and herding them into the living room. Tex brutally grabbed Sharon's arm, and Jay protested, demanding, "What are you doing here?" He was warned that if he said "one more word," he'd be shot. "Jay fought back," recalls Nan Morris-Robinson. "Jay knew his karate, knew how to run up the wall. He penned Tex, who grabbed onto something and left a thumb print, which would later be useful in nailing the Manson gang. In the struggle, Jay broke Tex's glasses." But Tex was a former varsity football player, and he prevailed, subduing Sebring and placing his neck in a noose suspended from a ceiling beam. Then he forced Jay to sit in an armchair next to the couch.

Still wearing only her bra and panties, Sharon, too, was strung up to the rafter and then forced to lie down on her stomach, the rope tightening around her neck. Jay tried to struggle toward her, yelling, "Can't you see she's pregnant? Let her sit down!"

"I told you, 'One more word and you're dead,'" Tex said, firing a .22 cal-iber Buntline revolver. The bullet pierced Jay's left lung, and he fell to the floor, fatally wounded. Tex walked over and kicked in the bridge of his nose. Sharon and Gibby were both screaming. Gibby was strung up to the beam, and they were ordered to reveal the whereabouts of their money. Then the ropes around Jay, Sharon, and Gibby were pulled taut, and the women had to stand on their toes to keep from being strangled.

Dying, too weak to defend Sharon any longer, Sebring heroically asked his assailants to spare the pregnant woman's life. Lunging at him, Tex stabbed him in the chest six times, then kicked him in the face repeatedly. Later, a defen-sive stab wound to his left hand was discovered by the coroner, indicating that Sebring had gone down fighting. With his final breath, the fashionable hair styl-ist invoked the name of Jesus Christ.

Putting up a fierce fight, Fryko broke free from the killers, but he was stabbed fifty-seven times, battered on the head with a blunt object thirteen times, and shot twice before finally dying, outside, on the lawn. Gibby also attempted to flee but was stabbed twenty-eight times, begging her assailants just before she died, "Stop! Stop! I'm already dead." Screaming as she watched the massacre, Sharon, now seated on the couch but with the rope still around her neck, endured taunts from Tex Watson, who called her "Piggy." "Please don't kill me," Sharon said, Susan Atkins later recalled. "I don't want to die. I want to live. I want to have my baby." Atkins said, "Look, bitch, I don't care if you're going to have a baby. You had better be ready. You're going to die, and I don't feel anything about it."[65] Sharon then asked that the baby be cut from her womb, so it could survive, and when that was denied, she begged to be taken into the gang until she could give birth, after which they could kill her. Suddenly, Tex slashed her across the left cheek, and Atkins joined in, stabbing Sharon until she stopped screaming. They hung her before she died, murmuring, "Mother, mother." Altogether, her body sustained sixteen stab wounds, many of them four inches deep, piercing her heart, lungs, and liver. "The breast was in the bread box," Buck Henry later told Jack Nicholson, Bert Schneider, and Dennis Hopper. "The cock was in the glove compartment of Sebring's car."[66] Using a towel saturated with Sharon's still-warm blood, Atkins wrote "Pig" on the front door.

When the maid, Mrs. Winifred (Winny) Chapman, came to work the following morning, she stumbled on the grisly scene and ran for help, screaming, "Murder! Death! Bodies! Blood!" Neighbors rushed from their houses, and soon an officer, Jerry De Rosa, arrived in a LAPD squad car. He approached the house with his rifle held aloft, discovering Parent's body first, then the two on the lawn, and finally Jay and Sharon. She was lying in a fetal position, her hands clutching the noose around her neck, an incongruously wistful smile on her face. Other policemen arrived, and when they found Garretson, the sole survivor of the massacre, in the guesthouse, they at first assumed he was the killer. Polanski's business manager, William Tennant, a handsome young man who later became production VP at Columbia, arrived at the house around noon and identified the bodies, breaking down, sobbing, and vomiting. In London, Polanski was with friends in his mews house, preparing to go to dinner with Victor Lownes, when the phone rang at about 7 P.M. It was Bill Tennant, who said, "[It's] bad. . . . There's been a disaster at the house. Sharon's dead. Wojtek's dead, too, and Gibby and Jay. They're all dead. Come over here right away. Just get over here."

Yelling "No, no, no," Polanski started banging his head against the wall. "Roman, they were murdered," Tennant said. Dropping the phone, Polanski began pacing the room in circles, unable to comprehend the horror. His friends summoned a doctor, who sedated him. Polanski later recalled, "I have a recollection of Warren Beatty and Victor Lownes arriving, as well as Dick Sylbert. . . . Gene [Gutowski, producer of Polanski's earliest films], Victor, and Warren accompanied me on the flight."[67] Warren and Lownes reserved first-class seats on a Pan Am jet, and arranged, by long-distance phone, for an immigration official to board the plane in New York and give Polanski clearance, so that he'd be able to avoid the expected mob of reporters and photographers.

"Roman was sitting on my lap on the way there, crying," Sylbert recalls in a 2000 interview. "He suspected a lot of his friends. He had either fucked their girlfriends or their wives."[68] The prime suspect, in Polanski's estimation, was John Phillips,[69] who was seeking revenge on Polanski for having had a one-night stand with his then-wife Michelle while Sharon was filming in Rome. John Phillips later laughed off the charge, insisting that it was Polanski, not he, who was the criminal psychopath, having once threatened him with a meat cleaver. "We were all running around with guns in our purses," recalled Michelle Phillips. "We all suspected *each other.* . . . 'Would your husband have any reason to have any animosity toward anyone in that house?' [the police] asked me. I told them I had had a night in London with Roman. I felt bad about that, because of Sharon."[70] The evening after the murders, Michelle started waving a gun around the bar at the Daisy. "Darling, put the gun away," said Daisy co-owner Sally Hansen.

Polanski even suspected action star Bruce Lee, his workout buddy at the Paramount gym.[71] Long before his acting career took off, Bruce Lee had been Sharon's martial-arts coach during the filming of *The Wrecking Crew*, in which she played a kung fu expert. Polanski also suspected his friend Jerzy Kosinski after Victor Lownes pointed out that the novelist had precisely the right profile to commit murder, basing this charge on something he'd read in one of Kosinski's books.[72]

In Hollywood, Polanski was taken to Paramount Studios and secluded there in Julie Andrews's old dressing room (the studio would later charge him three days' rent). "Various friends took turns keeping me company—Warren . . . Dick Sylbert, and Bob Evans," Polanski said. For a while he stayed at Michael Sarne's house in Malibu Colony, until neighbors circulated a petition stating, "The presence in your home of Mr. Polanski endangers our lives."[73] Dick Sylbert put him up at his place on Old Malibu Road. Warren attended Sharon's memorial service, which was held at the Holy Cross Memorial Cemetery chapel in Culver City on Wednesday, August 13, and was attended by 150 mourners including Lee Marvin, Kirk Douglas, Michelle Phillips, John Phillips, Yul Brynner, James Coburn, Peter Sellers, and the Tate family—Sharon's mother Doris, her father Paul, and her sisters Deborah and Patti. According to Joan Collins, the celebrity mourners "were weeping uncontrollably." For Michelle Phillips, the sadness was overwhelming, and she stood up and left the chapel, went outside, lay down on the grass, and gazed up at the sky. Steve McQueen, one of Sharon's oldest friends, was afraid to come, as the killers were still at large. "I never forgave him for that," Roman said. "I sat next to Sharon's mother, hugging her and crying. . . . All I could think of was the scar on Sharon's left knee . . . a little white scar— the result of a cartilage operation after a skiing accident—the scar I would never see again." Victor Lownes had selected Sharon's burial dress, a blue and yellow Emilio Pucci print mini. Placed beside her in the satin-lined silver coffin, which was covered with white and pink tea roses, was her unborn baby, Paul Richard Polanski, wrapped in a shroud. Mother and son were interred near Bela Lugosi's grave. "Goodbye, Sharon," said her priest, Father Peter O'Reilly, "and may the angels welcome you to heaven, and the martyrs guide your way."

Afterward, Warren hosted a modest wake at El Escondido, and then proceeded to Forest Lawn Memorial Park in Glendale for Jay Sebring's funeral. By now Steve McQueen, action hero, had collected himself sufficiently to venture out of his house. Armed with a gun, he delivered one of the eulogies before a crowd that included Paul Newman, George Hamilton, James Garner, John and Michelle Phillips, and Henry and Peter Fonda. Michelle was fortifying herself with regular hits from a bottle of Crown Royal. "I think I was probably drunk," she remembered. Sebring's casket was open, and despite the gruesome beating his face had taken, "the morticians had done a masterful job," recalled Neile McQueen. The funeral was disrupted by a strange man who charged the casket and began chanting. "Warren Beatty was sitting next to me," Neile said, "and he was ready to throw me onto the floor, fearful that some sort of altercation was about to occur. He was aware Steven had a gun and was concerned what might happen if anybody opened fire. But somebody removed the man who was chanting in front of Jay's body and order resumed."[74]

Gibby Folger was buried in Portola, California; young Steven Parent was interred in El Monte, an L.A. suburb; and Fryko, whose feckless life was transformed by his bravery at the end, was cremated, his ashes flown to his native Poland.

Almost immediately after the funerals, Polanski was subjected to intense police grilling as well as a polygraph test. He passed the test and was cleared of any suspicion of having staged the murders, telling the police that he felt that he or Sebring had been the target of the killers, not Sharon. "I am the bad one," he said. "I always screw around." The motive for killing him, Polanski felt, would have been "jealousy," and for Sebring, it would have been "some money thing [or] drug deliveries. . . . He must have been in serious financial trouble."[75] Nan Morris-Robinson recalls that Polanski visited the crime scene with psychic Peter Hurkos, whom Polanski hoped could help them identify and find the killers. "Hurkos found the thumbprint of Tex Watson, at the spot where Jay Sebring had tried to fight him off. They tracked him back to Texas." Extradited and tried in California, Tex was sentenced to die in the gas chamber, as was the rest of the gang. When California subsequently outlawed the death penalty, the Manson sentences were commuted to life in prison.

"I started having sex again quite soon," Polanski admits, "perhaps a month after Sharon's death. My friends did their best to entertain and amuse me. Warren Beatty, in particular, kept up a stream of improbable stories, mostly relating to his hyperactive sex life and containing details I'm sure were invented just to make me laugh."[76]

Nan Morris-Robinson received a visit from Polanski at the Chateau Marmont, where she was living. "I had Troy Donahue's blond wolfhound when I met Roman in the elevator—the same kind of gigantic dog that Roman owned a brace of. 'Can I talk to you?' he asked, and he came to my apartment. He looked at Gaylord [the Irish wolfhound] and wept. 'If only I had these dogs at the other place [Cielo Drive], the dogs would have chased off [the killers].'" Recalling that moment, Nan says she was touched by Roman's "little-boy quality." She attended a special memorial service for the baby boy that had perished in Sharon's womb. According to L.A. coroner Dr. Thomas Noguchi, the infant survived his mother by fifteen to twenty minutes.

With the exception of Beatty, Jack Nicholson, Nan Morris-Robinson, and a few others, Hollywood proved to be a town without pity, blackballing Polanski rather than rallying round when he needed sympathy and employment. "His situation was a very interesting case of what notoriety can do to you," Nicholson reflected. "He would be excommunicated by Hollywood because his wife had the very bad taste to be murdered in the newspapers." But it was more than that, according to such insiders as Dennis Hopper, who said, "The people at the Tate house were victims of themselves because they had fallen into sado-masochism and recorded it on videotape. . . . What goes around comes around."[77] The LAPD discovered a tape of Roman and Sharon having sex, but Roman later characterized their on-camera lovemaking as "frivolous rather than lewd and exhibitionistic," though he also confessed that Sharon had asked him, "What characters shall we play?"[78]

Striking at the heart of the Hollywood Establishment, the Manson killings unleashed an understandable paranoia among L.A. celebrities. Years later, Candice Bergen said, "I could have been killed. It terrified me then. I'm still scared."[79] Virtually everyone felt that it could have been them. "It was the defining event of our time," commented Buck Henry. "It affected everybody's work, it affected the way people thought about other people."[80] Manson represented the dark side of the New Hollywood, the Jekyll-Hyde monster that had been created by *Bonnie and Clyde*, *Rosemary's Baby*, Sam Peckinpah's *The Wild Bunch*, William Goldman's *Butch Cassidy and the Sundance Kid*, and the Dennis Hopper–Peter Fonda–Jack Nicholson hippie drug-dealer epic, *Easy Rider*. The latter was the big hit of the summer and fall of 1969. Wrote Joan Didion after the Manson murders, "No one was surprised." Joseph Morgenstern's original description of *Bonnie and Clyde* in *Newsweek*, later recanted, bore an eerie resemblance to the crime scene at Cielo Drive: "The most gruesome carnage since Verdun, and for those who find killing less than hilarious, the effect is stomach-turning."[81]

In time, members of the New Hollywood elite came to view Manson, a drugged-out hippie, as one of their own. Manson later asked Dennis Hopper to play him in the film version of his life. Ironically, many celebrities lost no time in trying to associate their names with the massacre, turning it into a ghoulish Hollywood status symbol. Everyone from Steve McQueen and Jerzy Kosinski to Jackie Susann and Bob Evans (who served hot dogs at a reception held at his home following the funerals) claimed to have been invited to Cielo Drive that night, "for some dark purpose of their own," noted Buck Henry. To the rest of a shocked nation, Manson was not a counterculture hero but a rock-star wanna-be who'd turned on his heroes.

For Warren, as for so many others, it had been a close call; had he been in L.A. rather than London, he'd probably have been among Manson's victims, or, conversely, he might have been able, with Fryko's help, to beat them off. But the odds would have been against him. "People who were close to Roman had a tendency to die," said Paramount executive (*Goodbye Columbus*) and later Hollywood *Daily Variety* columnist Peter Bart, who worked with Polanski on *Rosemary's Baby*. Sixties superagent Sue Mengers attempted to reassure her client Barbra Streisand, saying, "Don't worry, honey, they're not murdering stars, only featured players."[82]

In the end, apart from a flurry of new security gates, bodyguards, and sudden defections from Benedict Canyon, like Bob Towne's flight from Hutton Drive, the massacre brought about no substantial change in the way most people lived and died in L.A. Despite the wake-up call, Warren continued to live at the edge of the flame, but Sharon's execution did make him reflect on the role he'd played in breaking the rules of what could and could not be shown on the screen. In the future, he would make no more violent films, at least until the nineties, when he reverted to his fascination with thugs, in *Dick Tracy* and *Bugsy*.[83] He suggested that Dominick Dunne write a book on the Manson murders.[84] Instead, the deputy district attorney who co-prosecuted the trial, Vincent Bugliosi, wrote *Helter Skelter*, and it was a classic of the crime genre, comparable to Truman Capote's *In Cold Blood*. In an extraordinary postscript to the trial, Sharon's mother and youngest sister Patti emerged as heroines in the ongoing battle for victims' rights. For decades, every time one of the Manson murderers came up for parole, Doris Tate—and, after her death in 1992, Patti—prevented it from happening. To this day, not one of Sharon's tormentors is on the loose, despite dramatic and increasingly desperate pleas.

As soon as Roman Polanski pulled himself together and got back to work, he offered Warren the lead in the prison-escape epic *Papillon*, for which Warren had, according to Polanski, "just the right combination of good looks, toughness, and charm. Like Papillon, he could con anyone into anything."[85] Flying to Paris to meet with Polanski at the Hilton Hotel and read the English translation of the manuscript, Warren got seriously sidetracked. "All our good resolutions were knocked on the head," Polanski recalled, "when Simon Hessera, who happened to be in Paris, joined us for dinner the first night. [Hessera, a French Moroccan Jew, was Polanski's screenwriter.]"[86] Seduced by his entertaining company, we embarked on a whirlwind round of parties, discos, and girls. The second day was a repetition of the first. So was the third. And the fourth. By this time, Simon had dropped out and moved to another hotel. Knowing Warren, I grew uneasy. 'Okay,' I said, 'that's it.' He grinned. 'You're absolutely right, we've had our fun.' But over dinner that evening, after a couple of glasses of wine, he said innocently, 'Let's just see what Simon's up to.' The result: we dragged him out of bed and painted the town for the fifth consecutive night. I was so frazzled for lack of sleep I couldn't take anymore. We'd been in Paris almost a week, and Warren still hadn't read a page of the book. 'Shit,' I told him, 'I've had enough.' "

Leaving Warren in Paris, Polanski flew to London, where he immediately had a call from Warren, who'd at last read the manuscript. "I'm not going to appear bare-ass," he said. "It's a hang-up I have. What did you say the budget was?"[87] Polanski took that to mean "yes" and flew back to Paris, where, at a meeting with the author, Henri Charrière, on the crowded, lively first floor of the Café Flor, Warren said he loved the book and wanted to star in the film. The project folded when Polanski, still persona non grata in Hollywood, proved unable to finance the picture. Later *Papillon* would reach the screen under other auspices, with Steve McQueen and Dustin Hoffman in the starring roles.

Warren's loyalty to Polanski sprang from mixed motives, not all of them noble. Lillian Hellman once called Warren "her foul-weather friend, the first person to call when you were in trouble." Dick Sylbert adds, "He was great with wounded birds," someone who liked to be kept abreast of friends' marital crises, separations, and divorces.[88] Polanski moved to Rome, carrying a pair of Sharon's panties with him in his bag.[89] He was put back in business by Hugh Hefner, whose *Playboy* empire was hitting its all-time high, with clubs sprouting up around the world, not to mention casinos, hotels, and even a film division. Hef agreed to finance Polanski's production of *Macbeth*. "The deal was clinched at Marbella by Hefner himself," recalls Polanski. "He flew there in his black *Bunny* DC-9, with a retinue of girls and courtiers, played a lot of backgammon, and gave the go-ahead. Playboy Productions advanced $1.5 million." The producer was Faye Dunaway's ex-beau Andy Braunsberg, who acted more British than the British despite his German-Jewish bloodline. Andy and Polanski formed Caliban Films, and Polanski asked critic Kenneth Tynan to explain Shakespeare to him. "Ken helped him put it together," recalls Elaine Dundy. "They gave Lady Macbeth a nude sleepwalking scene." Despite such attempts to jazz up the Bard,

Playboy's investment in *Macbeth* was never recouped. Unfortunately, Polanski blew what was left of his relationship with *Playboy* when he was asked, during an interview, why he'd associated himself with Hefner. "*Pecunia non olet*, money doesn't smell," said Polanski. Breaking off all relations with Polanski, *Playboy's* Victor Lownes promptly told him to go and shove his Golden Prick Award up some other "friend."[90]

Julie Christie remained the focus of Warren's emotional life, and they spent Christmases together at Lillian Hellman's place. Warren lived in Julie's Malibu home, but as usual kept El Escondido available. When she went to England for *The Go-Between*, she leased a cottage near the sea in Norfolk, riding a bicycle to work. To relax, she made small glass figurines, wrapping them herself and posting them to friends. Her peace was shattered when Warren joined her in Norfolk, trailing hordes of reporters and photographers brandishing telephoto lenses. She refused to cooperate, explaining, "It's a waste of time and energy to feed curious minds. . . . Curiosity is never satisfied. I know how I'd like to be thought of: scintillating, witty, intellectual and gracious, which I am not. I haven't got control over what people think so there is not much point caring."[91] Her negative attitude toward the press, coupled with Warren's ban on interviews, made the media pursue them all the more, soon turning them into another Taylor and Burton. Julie's and Warren's lifestyles were fundamentally opposed, and although their arguments became almost as famous as those of the Burtons, the resemblance ended there. Liz and Dick made it to the altar twice while Christie and Beatty were still debating the pros and cons of matrimony. They were the Hamlets of lovers, the prince and princess of indecision.

In the summer of 1970, Warren encountered Britt Ekland, the former Mrs. Peter Sellers, at a London party for Polanski, and they began a torrid affair. Britt had tired of her lover, Patrick, Lord Lichfield, and was ripe for ravishing. Still in love with Julie Christie, Warren nevertheless took advantage of her absences due to filming and trysted with Britt at secluded restaurants in London's West End, or at Tramp's, a trendy nightclub. "Then he would drive me back to my studio," Britt recalled, "where we would make love until sleep came from sheer exhaustion."[92] When Britt flew from England to California to appear on *The Dean Martin Show,* Warren moved her into El Escondido. "We would sprawl about naked for most of the day or sunbathe on the terrace. . . . Warren was the most divine lover of all. His libido was as lethal as high octane gas. I had never known such pleasure and passion in my life. Warren could handle women as smoothly as operating an elevator. He knew exactly where to locate the top button. One flick and we were on the way."[93] Britt found him to be as affectionate as he was passionate, and for the two-month course of their affair, she tried to wean him away from his other girlfriends. When they went out in L.A., he tried to dodge photographers, fearful that Julie, back in England, would see their pictures in the London papers. One night, he and Britt slipped into a shabby porn theater, then returned to El Escondido to work off their excitement.[94] Nonetheless, he seemed relieved when Britt returned to London to film a television show.

Whatever sexual chemistry existed between Warren and Julie Christie did not transfer to celluloid, at least not in 1971's *McCabe and Mrs. Miller,* a Western. Julie already had been cast as Constance Miller, a frontier whorehouse madam, circa 1902, when Warren, who was abroad, being courted by Bernardo Bertolucci for the lead in *Last Tango in Paris*, read the script. In a fateful moment for his career, he chose to do a mannered but basically vacuous Western rather than the Bertolucci classic, a huge acting challenge that later went to Marlon Brando (Pauline Kael would proclaim *Last Tango* a turning point in Western art comparable to the 1913 premiere of Stravinsky's *Sacre du Printemps*).[95] Warren returned to L.A., eager to land the role of John McCabe, a compulsive gambler with pretensions to a past as a gunslinger.

Elliott Gould was still up for the part when Warren made a dramatic entrance at Warner Bros., standing in the doorway of a conference room where screenwriter Brian McKay was meeting with a group of production executives. "Your words brought me seven thousand miles," Warren told McKay. Since Warren's name assured the financing, he immediately won the role. Despite his reverence for Brian McKay's words, Warren concocted some of his lines, and Julie wrote or rewrote most of hers, according to script girl Joan Tewkesbury."[96] Bob Towne contributed "quips and snappy aphorisms" by phone. Evidently, none of them had ever heard the truism, "A camel is a horse made by committee." After rehearsals, Tewkesbury would write down the mishmash of new material. Thus, *McCabe* became a classic example Hollywood's abuse of writers, and perhaps as a result of this mauling of the script, the movie has always struck me as having no story line, intelligible theme, or recognizably human characters.

It never would have been made by the old Warner studio that had turned out *Dark Victory, Casablanca, Mildred Pierce*, or even *Bonnie and Clyde*. The old order, led by mogul Jack L. Warner, had been replaced by New Hollywood's thirty-nine-year-old John Calley, who loved the macabre sense of humor director Robert Altman had introduced in *M*A*S*H* in 1969. Altman brought *McCabe* to Calley, but once Warren came on board, Warren took control. "This picture is about me as a movie star and Julie second, and then all the rest of the people in this picture, who don't count," he said, according to Altman.[97]

Even in retrospect, it is difficult to see what appealed to Warren about *The Presbyterian Church Wager*, as *McCabe* was originally called, beyond providing yet another opportunity for genre deconstruction. *Bonnie and Clyde* had reinvented the gangster film, and perhaps *McCabe* could refashion another Hollywood standby, the Western, or so he must have reasoned. After throwing out Brian McKay's work, Warren boasted, "I had to write a script." In his scribblings for *McCabe*, he borrowed liberally from *Bonnie and Clyde*—and from his own complex nature—to patch together a supposedly likable, helpless protagonist. For Warren, Clyde Barrow and John McCabe "shared a sort of foolishness. They were not heroes. I found that to be funny, and Altman found it to be funny; we really agreed on that."

They agreed on little else. The star and his director were on a collision course from the moment location shooting commenced in West Vancouver, British Columbia. Altman was a "fun guy," according to his biographer, Patrick McGilligan, but Warren, flashing a "Big Star" attitude, made the director feel uptight. One day, Altman told everyone on the set he wanted to go to Houston, Texas, for the premiere of his film *Brewster McCloud*, which, like his classic *Nashville*, displayed an impressive command of pungent peculiarities. Mindful that Altman's proposed Houston junket would include a lot of drinking, hoopla, and parties at the Astrodome, Warren feared the director wouldn't be alert for the Monday morning shooting and refused to let him go. "It was Beatty's way of letting Altman know who was boss," said one source.

Altman got even, making sure that Warren received no writing credit for the movie. He also wanted to exclude the writer himself, Brian McKay. "Bob didn't want to split the credit with McKay," revealed Altman's first assistant director, Tommy Thompson. "He wanted to be the auteur." In the end, Altman and McKay shared script credit, and Warren's contributions remained uncredited. In his own way Altman was just as intimidating as Warren, especially after a few glasses of Cutty Sark. "Bob had a black side when he drank," said Thompson. "All of a sudden the booze'd hit him, and he'd go after you—he could just say, 'Let me tell you something about yourself. . . . Your fucking personality is just . . .' and you'd be in tears and leave." According to former *American Film* editor in chief Peter Biskind, Warren "felt he had been screwed out of [co-screenwriting credit] by Altman on *McCabe*."[98]

The fracas over the writing perpetuated Hollywood's sorry practice of bashing authors of screenplays. Decades later, in 2001, writers at last initiated in an industry-wide strike to gain the respect they'd long been denied. Movie executives have always maintained that high production costs require one person, usually the director, to exercise total authority over everything, including script changes. The specious argument has been disproved in the New York publishing industry and the Broadway theater, where writers retain editorial control.

The script wasn't the only problem with *McCabe and Mrs. Miller*. Beatty and Altman had totally different ways of making a film. In one scene, Warren is talking to himself alone in his room with a bottle that falls, then he catches it and pours himself another stiff one; it was shot twenty times and Warren still wanted another. Tired, Altman left, saying, "Print seven and eleven—I'll see you guys tomorrow." Tommy Thompson remained behind with Warren, and they did another twenty takes before Warren was satisfied. On that particular evening Julie was patient and seemed better with each take; usually her performance went down the drain after the first take. "I had one actor who was getting better, and another who was getting worse," Altman complained. "Warren is basically a control freak. He wants to run the show."[99]

The off-set social scene was lively, recalls Judy Feiffer, who at the time was married to Jules Feiffer, author of *Carnal Knowledge,* a coruscating portrait of the war between the sexes, which was also filming in the Vancouver area, directed by Mike Nichols and starring Jack Nicholson, Art Garfunkel, Ann Margret, and Candice Bergen. "We came up from New York on weekends," says Judy. Warren and Julie lived in a modern timber-and-glass cottage atop a cliff with a view of the Pacific Ocean. Like newlyweds, they turned it into a center of warmth and conviviality, frequently entertaining friends at leisurely dinners, no more than six at a time. "Julie was very good with the wine and cheeses," recalls a member of the crew. "The two of them divided guests between them. . . . She would come over to him suddenly, sit on his lap, and hug him." At larger gatherings, the differences between Warren and Julie became more apparent. He circulated among the guests, talking to everybody, while Julie sat in a corner, shy and retiring, and ready to leave at the first opportunity. The only time she came alive was if the conversation turned to politics, and then she did not hesitate to express her opinions, which were so far to the left that few could relate to them.

One night Jules Feiffer introduced Warren to Jack Nicholson, who was to become Warren's closest friend for years. Complimenting Warren on his good looks and taller stature, Nicholson remarked, "Now, *that's* what a movie star looks like." According to Jules Feiffer, from that point on, Beatty and Nicholson began a duet of adoration. Feiffer, in a later conversation with Lillian Hellman, allegedly said *Carnal Knowledge* was "a picture about men's hatred of women. All heterosexual men hate women." Disagreeing violently, Hellman retorted, "You're talking about homosexuals." "No," Feiffer said. "Homosexuals love women. And heterosexuals hate women." Reflecting on their argument later, Hellman mused, "He means a man who thinks he's an unattractive small fellow has a tough time." According to Hellman, Mike Nichols, Buck Henry, and John Calley "were so upset about [*Carnal Knowledge*], they all decided to get married."[100]

Warren and Julie made the same decision, said some observers, and others claimed they'd already tied the knot. In Vancouver, they continued to behave like honeymooners, and when a reporter asked Julie if they were married, she replied, "If we are, we are. If we are not, we are not."[101] There is little doubt that she would have married Warren had she been able to trust him. But Julie was faithful to the man she loved, and Warren was notorious for his wandering eye. Their artistic differences went even deeper. Although Warren sometimes seemed casual in his attitude toward his career, denigrating acting as a profession, he remained deadly serious about preserving the stardom he'd recaptured in *Bonnie and Clyde*. Julie's priority was to remain grounded in the real world, to be an authentic person rather than a lonely icon. To Warren, the real world was less important than absolute fidelity to his muse. Though his megalomania could be trying and wasteful, it helps explain why his best work (*Splendor, Bonnie and Clyde, Shampoo, Reds, Bulworth*) stands up today; it is a testament to unreserved, maniacal passion for art. Inevitably, he and Julie began to fight late into the night,

Julie objecting that being a movie star was unreal, just another form of class distinction that alienated one from the human race. The next morning, Altman
could tell on the set if they'd been fighting, because their moods poisoned the
atmosphere. "There was nothing to do but wait it out," he recalls. Though
Altman criticized Beatty for his "nit-picking, the way he pushed and bugged me,"
the perceptive director acknowledged that without the irreverence of *Bonnie and
Clyde*, *M*A*S*H* might never have surfaced in Hollywood.[102]

If Warren had stuck to acting and let Altman do the directing, the picture
might not have been such a turkey. "Bob would wonder why I was working so
hard," Warren reflected. "When you go to all that trouble to set up a movie . . .
I don't see any harm in doing a number of takes."[103] But in not heeding Altman,
Warren missed the opportunity to grow as a performer. Altman made a star of
Donald Sutherland in *M*A*S*H* because the actor did what he was told to do.
Warren, in browbeating the same director into submission, won the battle but
lost the war. In *McCabe*'s final cut, Warren lacks even basic screen presence. His
lighting certainly didn't help—a dingy yellow hue favored by Altman and his
cameraman, Vilmos Zsigmond. The muddy sound track would have been
unthinkable in the immaculately professional Old Hollywood of Louis B. Mayer,
Darryl F. Zanuck, and Harry Cohn. The picture finally wrapped, to everyone's relief, in late January 1971.

The previews on June 22, 1971, at the Broadway Criterion in Manhattan
and the Academy of Motion Picture Arts and Sciences theater in L.A., were
awful. Predictably, people complained that the color was off and the sound ama-
teurish. In reaction, Altman got stinking drunk. Later, Beatty and Altman
blamed each other for the fiasco. "Had I been the producer I would have killed
Robert Altman," Warren said. Beatty "was really a bit of an asshole," Altman
said.[104]

Indeed, *McCabe* was the most pretentious film Warren had involved himself in since *Mickey One*, and it was panned by Vincent Canby in the *New York
Times* for having "intentions [that are] not only serious, they are also meddle-
some, imposed on the film by tired symbolism." *Films in Review* scorned it as an
"immature farrago of ignorantly conceived characters and symbolic situations.'"
When a corrected release print was screened for Pauline Kael and the weekly
reviewers, Kael wrote in *The New Yorker* that the film was "a testimony to the
power of stars. Warren Beatty and Julie Christie have never been better. . . .

There's a gleefulness in Beatty, a light that comes on when he is on screen that says, 'Watch this—it's fun!' . . . A fresh, ingenious performance." Charles Champlin of the *Los Angeles Times* was not fooled, writing, "There is less [about the film] than meets the eye."

After months of battling with Warren, Julie finally said, "Marriage sort of frightens me." Nor was he eager to take the leap, knowing he'd tire of monogamy.[105] They went to New York together to promote *McCabe* when it opened at selected theaters that summer. Leaving the U.S., Julie bought a cottage in Dorset, England, and Warren promised to join her there after completing his next film, *$ (Dollars)*, a bank-heist caper with Goldie Hawn. Most serious artists are not above doing the occasional potboiler, but with Warren it was becoming a habit.

Goldie loved making the film, later recalling, "When you act with Warren, it's almost like a marriage, and he leads you through the dark and shaky areas."[106] Goldie's husband was a man named Gus Trikonis, and she managed to get him a deal to film the making of *$*. According to Goldie's next husband, Bill Hudson, a singer with the group the Hudson Brothers, "While he's filming the making of the movie, she's making Warren Beatty. The movie lasted about three months. I asked her later where they would have their meetings and she said sometimes Gus wasn't there and they'd use his trailer. Gus and Goldie had an open marriage. That was Gus's idea."[107] Despite Goldie's well-known charms, Warren was preoccupied with Julie Christie, and he longed for her so much that he flew from his Hamburg location to London to see her every weekend. "He's very complicated," mused Goldie. "Beneath the playboy exterior is a very conservative side. That's the side you'd like to spend the rest of your life with, curled up in front of the fire. It's only one little corner of Warren, but it's probably the corner that keeps him on the ground."[108]

He almost killed himself while filming a train sequence in a railyard, stumbling and falling on the tracks before an onrushing locomotive. Director Richard Brooks and the crew were too far away to help. Injured and half unconscious, he looked up and saw the train approaching at twenty miles an hour and finally managed to summon the strength to lurch out of harm's way. At St. George's Hospital, he was treated for a torn ligament in his ankle and multiple bruises, but mostly for "a bad case of nerves." When an attendant in admissions asked if he was married, he smiled, despite severe pain, and said, "No. But I'm in love"—

a reference to Julie. He was confined to bed for two days. When he returned to work, the cast jokingly referred to him as a "track star."

When *$* was released, Gary Arnold wrote in the *Washington Post*, "Didn't it occur to Beatty that *$* was *Kaleidoscope* all over again, only worse?" As for Warren's leading Goldie through those dark and shaky areas, critics said she was caught in a "tart rut." The film was more popular abroad than in the U.S. Well-meaning critics reminded Warren that he should search out more "worth-while fare." His answer was: "I have no apologies to tender anyone, anywhere, any time."[109] In fact, he owed apologies all over town, not least to himself.

With his choice of poor material, he was trashing his career. Said one studio executive, "While Redford's career took off in the 1970s, Beatty, after a couple of impressive star vehicles, found himself struggling through turkeys like *$* and *The Fortune*.[110] Added *Daily Variety*'s Peter Bart, "He's been an elusive creature of Hollywood who's made a way of life out of promising more than he delivers. . . . He agonized endlessly about his deal, his script, his costars, and supporting players. . . . [He] systematically let it be known that he had read and rejected every script to which Robert Redford had committed."[111] But Redford was a more discerning judge of material; he ended up with a legendary hit, *The Sting*, after it was declined by Warren, who couldn't read the script without dozing off. Not until he viewed the finished film did he realize that the terrific ending justified the plot's tiresome obfuscations. He passed on *The Way We Were* because he considered Hubbell Gardiner "apathetic." Explaining how he declined "to produce and act in" *The Godfather*, he said, "I couldn't get interested. I'm interested in original movie scripts . . . not usually in making books, plays, or musicals into movies, or in remakes of movies."[112] Fortunately, David O. Selznick had felt no such compunction when he came across Margaret Mitchell's novel *Gone with the Wind*, nor had John Ford when he filmed John Steinbeck's *The Grapes of Wrath*, Richard Llewellyn's *How Green Was My Valley*, and Erskine Caldwell's *Tobacco Road*. The movies of Hollywood's Golden Age did not suffer from having been adaptations.

The scripts Warren chose to film often performed as poorly at the box office as his sister's. After *Two Mules for Sister Sara* in 1971, Shirley's movie career was stalled, and she undertook a TV series, *Shirley's World*. The money was good—fifteen million dollars—but the scripts were terrible, and the show folded after five weeks and some of the lowest ratings in television history.[113] Her next movie, *The Possession of Joel Delaney*, did nothing to revive her moribund career, and she would not make another movie until 1977. Good scripts and studio financing were no longer available to her.

Warren was seeing Carly Simon, and when her scornful song "You're So Vain," came out in 1972, many assumed it was a jab at his well-known narcissism. Carly, who was also dating Mick Jagger, chose to let the song's origins remain a mystery.[114]

The current queen of Hollywood was Barbra Streisand, who had risen, like Shirley MacLaine, from the ranks of Broadway musical comedy. But after her film debut, *Funny Girl*, for which she received an Oscar, her tyrannical behavior on movie sets annoyed the Hollywood Establishment, and she went into a career slump. Eager to rebound, she asked Warren, who was so popular that he could afford to turn down seventy-five scripts a year, to co-star with her in *The Way We Were*. He had little enthusiasm for the picture, but she refused to take no for an answer. A biographer later wrote, "She indulged in 'one of my flings' with the sensuously handsome actor, whom she had known since they met in summer stock when she was sixteen."[115] Their affair was a typical case of two Hollywood users exploiting each other.

After they met one day in El Escondido, Barbra started negotiating for Warren to appear in *The Way We Were*. He strung her along, hoping to get her to sing at a fund-raiser he was organizing for George McGovern, who was seeking the 1972 Democratic presidential nomination. A former history teacher at Dakota Wesleyan University, who later served in the U.S. House of Representatives and the U.S. Senate, McGovern commanded the support of younger delegates and opponents of the Vietnam War. He was extremely grateful for Warren's endorsement. "[Warren] took a year out of his life to do it," McGovern recalled. "He traveled around the country making speeches, debating issues, interpreting me to the public, and he personally was responsible for raising more than a million dollars."

In two years of working for McGovern, the first big name in Hollywood to do so, Warren recruited such surefire vote-getters as Streisand, Julie Christie, Goldie Hawn, James Taylor, Carly Simon, Paul Newman, Gene Hackman, Jon Voight, Carole King, Joni Mitchell, and Jack Nicholson. By the time he was through, names like George, Teddy, and Sarge (McGovern, Kennedy, and Shriver) were dropping from his lips. His most visible contribution was producing a series of political rock concerts. According to Gary Hart, McGovern's national campaign director, Warren "invented the political concert," staging musical extravaganzas in Los Angeles, New York, Cleveland, San Francisco, and Lincoln, Nebraska.

In his efforts to enlist Streisand for the fund-raiser, Warren "was relentless," wrote journalist Shaun Considine. "He worked on her head. And on her hands, feet, and shoulders. Barbra matched him stroke for stroke. He'd turn on the famous Beatty charm and he'd slip in a plug for the concert. He'd whisper, 'Barbra, you *should* do it. You *have* to do it. It's your civic duty. For me, baby, come on, come on.' And Barbra would moan and sigh and say, 'Oh, I know, Warren, I know. I *am* considering it. Now let's read some more of the script.' And he'd say, 'Okay, Barbra. You want to take it from the top or the bottom this time?' "

Streisand finally agreed to sing at the fund-raiser, though Warren brought Julie Christie as his date. Still sporting a prissy-looking, swinging-sixties scarf, he didn't look his best that night, but at least his full beard for *McCabe* kept him from resembling an old pioneer woman, the fate of many men with long hair after age twenty. The event was held on Saturday, April 15, in Inglewood, at the eighteen-thousand-seat Forum.

As showtime approached, Streisand grew nervous, fearing that the rock fans would boo her off the stage as an antiquated pop warbler. She was basically doing her Vegas act, using old song charts. "They're coming to hear James Taylor and Carole King," she told Warren. "They won't stay and listen to me." At first she tried to appropriate the closing spot from Carole King, and then, when King backed down, Barbra maddeningly said, "Maybe I should just go on first, and then get outta there." She monopolized all the onstage rehearsal time, leaving only thirty minutes each for the other singers' run-throughs.

Following King and Taylor's duet, "You've Got a Friend," Barbra performed her set at 11 P.M., wearing a black pants outfit, her long hair streaming down her back. The crowd loved her from the moment she launched into "Sing" from *Sesame Street,* combining it with "Make Your Own Kind of Music." Throughout the concert, the air was thick with pot smoke. Fittingly, Streisand sang "Stoney End," and then finished her forty-five-minute set with "People." McGovern joined her on stage, and King, Taylor, and orchestra leader Quincy Jones came back out as McGovern made a brief speech.

A huge critical success, the fund-raiser was hailed by the press as "the most

glamorous pop concert in recent history." But Warren's efforts netted just eighteen thousand dollars for the campaign, despite a box-office gross of $320,000.
Apart from being hellishly exorbitant to stage, the benefit apparently wasn't very
well managed. But he was learning.

Though Streisand had kept up her end of the bargain, Warren wiggled out
of *The Way We Were*. He kept telling her that the role—stuffy WASP Hubbell
Gardiner—wasn't big enough, and she kept promising that it would be enlarged,
hand tailored to suit him. When he continued to waffle, she approached Robert
Redford, but he also complained that Hubbell was a two-dimensional character. However, after accepting a $1.2 million fee, two hundred thousand dollars
more than Streisand made, Redford stopped complaining about Hubbell and
started complaining about Streisand. According to director Sydney Pollack, the
actor said, "Making the movie was like 'doing overtime at Dachau.' "[116]
Nevertheless, it was a runaway hit, grossing fifty-six million dollars in 1973.

Warren's orchestrating of the 1972 McGovern rally in the Fullerton Junior
College gym showed how far he'd come from the Cow Palace. Now, calling on
all his persuasive powers as an actor, he warmed up the audience and had it
cheering by the time the candidate appeared. Obviously he'd blossomed into
an organizer and fund raiser par excellence.

Next, he turned a one-hundred-dollar-per-ticket Madison Square Garden
"Together With McGovern" rally into an extravaganza worthy of a hip Mike
Todd or a political Flo Ziegfeld. Dressed in stovepipe velvet trousers, an
Eisenhower jacket, and an open-neck white shirt, Warren arrived at the Garden
in a cloud of elation, flanked by publicist John Springer and Julie Christie, whose
flaxen bangs grazed her eyebrows, her shiny locks cascading below her shoulders in thick, luscious coils. Her dark, delightfully skimpy, proto-hippie gown
had a floral pattern and a plunging neckline: Lara reincarnated as a sixties flower
child.

The show began. Without an introduction from Warren, or from anyone
else, Peter, Paul, and Mary plunged into a rousing set, carrying the banner of sixties liberation with "If I Had a Hammer." Nichols and May performed one of
their black comedy skits, followed by Dionne Warwick, who managed to
enthrall the crowd, despite the absence of her usual partner, Burt Bacharach, by
belting John Lennon's "Imagine." Simon and Garfunkel mesmerized everyone with "Mrs. Robinson" and the gravely beautiful "Bridge Over Troubled

Waters," so relevant in the antiwar context of the campaign. Finally, McGovern spoke. Though reporter Chris Chase and others yelled for Warren from the stands, he avoided the spotlight all evening, running his rock concert with a competence that would have put Bill Graham to shame.[117]

But his personal stamp was all over the event; only a superstar of his wattage could have assembled such a cast. The Garden concert attracted 19,500 and brought in gross estimates of $450,000 to $554,000, of which $250,000 went into McGovern's campaign.[118] Reported the fashion magazine *W*, "Big-time celebrities were put right to work by party planner Warren Beatty, who convinced stars like Julie Christie, Paul Newman, Ryan O'Neal, and Dustin Hoffman to serve as ushers at the event." A group of women burst into tears and shrieks when they saw Dustin Hoffman, who found himself being swept up and carried down a flight of stairs before managing to extricate himself from unwanted hugs and kisses. Resplendent in his white suit, Jack Nicholson shrank from the crowd, neglecting his commitment as an usher. Later, he surfaced at a dinner at the Four Seasons with Goldie Hawn, Jon Voight, and Shirley MacLaine, and cuddled with supermodel Verushka.[119]

Bette Davis also disappointed Warren, failing to show up after promising to usher, pleading a case of poison ivy, but the stellar battalion of celebrities who fearlessly went into the crowd at the Garden included Marlo Thomas, Candice Bergen, Ben Gazzara, Lee Grant, Tammy Grimes, Gene Hackman, Barbara Harris, Robert Dean Hooks (star of off-Broadway's *Dutchman* and Hollywood's *Hurry Sundown*), James Earl Jones, Stacy Keach, Raquel Welch, Robert Preston, Polly Bergen, and two fine Broadway actresses, Janice Rule and Diana Sands. With their help, Warren elicited outpourings of cash from the audience long after it had paid the hefty price of admission.

As McGovern was the first to point out, Warren's contribution went far beyond being an impresario and fund-raiser. "His ideas were shrewd and his advice valuable," said McGovern. "He has a political maturity astounding in someone so inexperienced—the instincts of a man who spent a lifetime in politics." Warren's belief in McGovern was blind and uncritical; more than merely supporting a candidate, he was looking for a hero to believe in, someone to save the world—and perhaps rescue Warren from Hollywood in the process. "McGovern is eight to ten years ahead of everyone else," Warren said, investing his candidate with the vision of a prophet. When more experienced politicos told him, before the Florida and Wisconsin primaries, that his candidate didn't have a chance, Warren replied, "What difference does it make? Do you want to be for someone who has a chance, or someone you think is right?"

He never regretted the sacrifices he'd had to make—roles lost, $1.5 million in movie fees down the drain, career momentum in ashes. Worst of all, he neglected Julie Christie, who was increasingly fed up with his absences and disloyalty. He was often on the road with McGovern, who later said, "What startled me most about Warren was learning that he is so deeply human." Perhaps the most human thing about him, apart from screwing around, was his tendency to expect too much of McGovern, to put him on a pedestal and lose sight of his inevitable fallibility. Warren was such a passionate advocate that he sometimes seemed, to observers, to be taking over the management of the campaign from the less driven Gary Hart. In out-arguing Hart on the central matter of how McGovern should be presented to the public, Warren may not have been doing his candidate, or the American people, a favor.

Everyone in McGovern's brain trust made the critical mistake of failing to capitalize on his heroic record in WWII. Volunteering for the Air Corps, McGovern, at age twenty-two, became the pilot and commander of a four-engined B-24 bomber based in Italy. In a plane carrying five thousand pounds of bombs and two thousand gallons of gasoline, he flew thirty-five missions, surviving the flak of German antiaircraft artillery. "It was just solid black except for flashes of red where shells were exploding," he recalled. On three missions he landed severely damaged bombers safely, for which he received the Distinguished Flying Cross. Navigator Lt. C.W. Cooper praised McGovern as "a cool-headed and superior pilot," and radio operator Ken Higgins said, "George brought me home," even when their B-24, the *Dakota Queen*, was riddled with 110 shrapnel holes. "What McGovern did, what the 741st Squadron did," wrote WWII historian Stephen Ambrose, "especially in their attacks against oil refineries and marshaling yards, was critical to the victory.... His career in the Army Air Forces ... could have [been] used to more effect in his 1972 presidential campaign." Patriotism and heroism were not popular subjects with baby boomers during the antiwar frenzy of the late sixties and seventies, but if McGovern had revealed his war record as a genuine combat hero, he might have attracted enough older voters to win the White House. It had worked for Ike and JFK, both of whom ran for the presidency on traditional American values. In this respect, McGovern was ill-served by short-sighted showbiz cronies who were more attuned to the youthquake than to the majority of older voters.[120]

Shirley MacLaine was also prominent in the McGovern camp, and, in politics as in acting, Warren was competitive with his sister. Despite the fact that she was floor boss of California's delegation to the Democratic National Convention in July 1972, he felt he was the better campaigner. During an interview with the *New York Times* as he sunbathed on the terrace of El Escondido, reporter Judy Klemsrud asked him if Shirley had raised his political consciousness. He slowly rubbed some cream on his lips and then informed the reporter, "There *are* other women. *I* was involved in the McGovern campaign before she was."[121]

At the convention, Shirley had the hands-on job of controlling delegates and issues. The sometimes ruthless way she carried out her duties demonstrated how wrong Warren was in saying, "I tend to be more of a hack than Shirley; I try to be practical in politics."[122] It is difficult to imagine how Shirley could have been more hacklike in her position on abortion, which changed with every puff of the political wind. Though she volubly supported free choice, she tried to block a pro-abortion campaign plank, feeling it would jeopardize McGovern's chances against Nixon, and she browbeat others into acquiescence. The indomitable Representative Bella Abzug screamed at her for betraying one of the basic tenets of feminism. Shirley nevertheless prevailed, and the abortion plank was defeated. Women's libbers would hold it against her, though she tried to justify her dishonest and unscrupulous behavior as political expediency. Warren was as deluded in regarding her as an idealist as he was in considering himself a backroom pro.

Despite both their efforts, their candidate went down in defeat in the presidential election. McGovern carried only Massachusetts, losing in a landslide to the incumbent, President Richard M. Nixon. "The most desperate feeling in the world," Warren said, "is to hope people will vote for you." When McGovern's vision failed to convince the American public, Warren laid the blame on McGovern rather than on the advice he had given him, or on the voters who mistakenly elected Nixon. Streisand was more philosophical, remarking, "I thought me and my friends were for the right things, and it's very disappointing that we turned out to be such a small bunch. In terms of lower- and middle-class groups, McGovern would have been much better for them. But I guess they just couldn't see he was really their man." Maybe he needed new advisers.

Some of Julie Christie's intimates maintained that she would happily have married Warren. He reportedly proposed to her more than once, but she sensibly demurred, still suspecting that he could never be faithful.[123] That was an issue in more ways than one. With the momentum of the sexual revolution unleashing more and more cases of gonorrhea, 1973 became the Year of the Clap. Warren, who had been seen with someone known as Willow, telephoned Jennifer Lee (later Mrs. Richard Pryor), and said, "Willow gave us the clap." Lee immediately got her penicillin shots, but fell into a deep depression, partly caused by anxiety. "Warren's a bit too flip and doesn't even offer to pay the bill," she complained.[124]

According to another woman, a documentary filmmaker named Joanne Parrent, Warren called her one day, without any introduction, shortly after she'd had an unpleasant encounter with James Toback, who'd later write Warren's 1991 movie *Bugsy*. In Parrent's opinion, Toback, in giving her number out to Warren, had subjected her to blatant sexual harassment. Warren denied it, insisting that he obtained Parrent's telephone number from Ed Asner, with whom Parrent had recently worked. "Toback was probably pimping for Beatty," Parrent later alleged, "finding women for him in return for favors from Beatty."[125] She went to Warren's house a few times, later stating that "hundreds, perhaps thousands of young women in Hollywood during that period had encounters with this master womanizer." Warren enjoyed Joanne's ability to "make fun of him and call him on his act," she later averred. On one occasion, she found Barbara Hershey at his house, and Hershey subsequently told Joanne she was surprised by "the way you stand up to him."

While working together on the unsuccessful McGovern campaign, Warren and Gary Hart had discovered they had a mutual love of sleeping around. In January of 1973, Jennifer Lee wrote in her journal, "Meet Warren at the Beverly Wilshire, who introduces me to Gary Hart from Colorado. Warren says he's a political hopeful, but he seems more like a poor man's version of Warren. He flirts, and not well. He's too eager and too goofy, and what an ego. . . . He laughs and laughs at everything Warren says. Good ol' Warren. He looks like the big brother here who knows his way around the block and is going to show this country boy! Gary calls me a few times later on, but I'm busy." In February she noted, "Gary Hart calls, again; I'm busy. Waylon [Jennings] calls; I'm free! Visit him at the Universal Sheraton and emerge two days later . . . crazy 'bout that man."[126] Warren and Gary Hart remained friends, and Warren eventually became one of Hart's key political advisers in his bid for the presidency. His association with Warren was reckless on Hart's part, considering that he was a married man in pursuit of an office that demands moral rectitude.

Warren was no fonder of marriage than ever, and Julie Christie could not have appreciated some of his remarks to the press. "Marriage requires a special talent, like acting—like writing," he told a reporter. "I haven't got that talent, so I don't marry. And monogamy requires *genius*." He could be equally insufferable to the people who worked for him. One L.A. businessman recalls being insulted when Warren pointed to his jacket on their first meeting and said, "I'm very conservative. I would never wear a jacket like you're wearing." The odd thing was that the businessman's tailoring was impeccable. "I was wearing Chip from New York at the time, the same conservative style as J. Press and Brooks Brothers," he said, adding, "I will say this for Warren, however, and it's very impressive: He has a photographic memory. He can tell you the number of '21' or any well-known restaurant or hotel where he's been without looking them up." Warren was also able to recite the phone numbers of most of the good-looking women in Beverly Hills. *Daily Variety* editor Peter Bart tested him, and recalls, "Of perhaps two hundred names, Beatty faltered only five or six times while smiling smugly."[127] A photographic memory, according to Nobel laureate and Columbia University physiology and neurobiology professor Eric Kandel, is nothing to be envied, and perhaps indicates a deficiency of essential memory suppressor genes. "It's quite shallow," said Kandel, "like having your head filled with garbage. If memory is too good, you can't utilize the information."

Though Julie Christie might always love him, she must have finally realized that Warren could never be a partner. In 1973 she flew without him to Venice to film *Don't Look Now,* co-starring Donald Sutherland. Then, eager for new artistic challenges, she appeared on the New York stage in Mike Nichols's production of Chekhov's *Uncle Vanya,* with a first-rate ensemble that included some of the best actors of the time—George C. Scott, Lillian Gish, Nicol Williamson, and Cathleen Nesbitt. "I had no intention of doing it," Christie recalls. "It seemed impossible. I would not have done it if it wasn't for Mike."[128]

As an actress, Julie was disappointed she'd been unsuccessful in urging Warren to take on more demanding roles. Personally, her disenchantment went even further, as was evident in her observation, "Infidelity destroys love. If you love someone and it's good, you've got to have the sense to stick with it. This doesn't mean you will never be attracted to another living soul. But if you give in to that attraction, then you risk losing the person you're with. You can't just go swanning off with everyone who attracts you. It's greedy and selfish. It sounds great to do whatever you want at a given time. But it never works out in real life—only in the movies." She began dating a businessman.[129]

Warren's political involvement and resulting absence from Hollywood also cost him some of the best movie roles he'd ever been offered, including a remake of *The Great Gatsby*, the Fitzgerald novel that had previously been filmed, with stark power, in a 1949 Paramount version starring Alan Ladd, Betty Field, and Shelley Winters. Warren temporized, saying he wanted to renegotiate the contract, but Redford was signed in his stead. Directed by Jack Clayton and opulently produced by Bob Evans, Redford's *Gatsby* was bland; Beatty's might have clicked. He passed on another remake, *A Star Is Born*, which was being resuscitated by scenarists John Gregory Dunne and Joan Didion. Rockers Elvis Presley and James Taylor also spurned the role, which finally went to Kris Kristofferson. Elvis had wanted the part, but his manager, Colonel Tom Parker, refused to let him take second billing to Streisand, who won the female lead after Cybill Shepherd, Diana Ross, Liza Minnelli, and Cher were considered.[130] The movie was a hit. Writing off his losses, Warren said, "Had I accepted [the role], I couldn't have concentrated on what I was doing around the country for the campaign. I wouldn't have had that experience in my life."

People were beginning to think of him as a politician, which was exactly what he wanted. In 1973, a California poll ranked him as the public's favorite to replace Governor Ronald Reagan in the California state house, and he was reportedly contemplating running in 1974.[131] Many people also urged him to run for the U.S. Senate. When asked why he chose not to, he said he wasn't sure if he could "mature into an unselfish enough person to give that amount of time and energy and libido to public service. I'm not sure I'd be willing to do that." Nonetheless, he felt a sense of obligation to the public. "I want to give something back in appreciation," he said. "Perhaps when I'm older, I'll run."[132]

He was depressed by the McGovern defeat, remarking, "It was the end of a lot of dreams of the early sixties, and the morning after that election, for me the prospects were pretty grim."[133] Most of his friends began to find him boring on the subject of politics, perhaps sensing the absence of true concern. Recalled one intimate, "He would talk and talk . . . and you'd feel your eyelids uncontrollably snapping shut."[134] Nicholson, always lavish in his praise of Warren, once added, "He can also, however, bore the shit out of me."[135]

During one of Julie Christie's absences, Warren asked Jennifer Lee, who was modeling for Diane von Furstenberg in New York, to accompany him to the Essex House, where Roman Polanski had a suite. Several years had passed since the Manson murders, but Jennifer noted, "Roman [was] still on the mend. There [was] a strange kind of party atmosphere." Warren and Jennifer went to the bedroom and had sex on a queen-size bed. Roman came in and introduced them to a dark-haired woman, an Iranian who was somehow connected to Adnan Khashoggi. Warren told Jennifer, "She is a fascinating woman," but Jennifer was uncomfortable, and she left them. Later, however, she participated in threesomes with Roman and this lady. "She g[ave] Roman a blow job," Jennifer revealed. "I help[ed] her out."[136]

Warren, Roman, and Jennifer started attending screenings together, later dining at Elaine's, an Upper East Side hangout for the literary set. Jennifer sensed that both men preferred a woman who could be one of the guys, and Jennifer filled the bill. She was content to be included among Warren's numerous girlfriends, "the last stop before the ball-and-chain main squeeze, which is what Julie is." Warren offered to pay for Jennifer's tuition at the Stella Adler Studio, but Jennifer, who was young, free, and exploring other options, declined. When Warren took her to a party at Sam Spiegel's duplex on Park Avenue, they saw Roman talking to Spiegel, who'd recently produced *Nicholas and Alexandra*. Later Roman suggested she accompany the seventyish mogul on a trip to London, and Jennifer realized "that Roman and Warren ha[d] 'pimped' before for old Sam."[137] She made the trip with Spiegel, but spent all her time at Roman's two-story carriage house in Eaton Place Mews, having sex with Roman and his current girl.

Back in L.A., Warren and Jennifer had just made love in her suite at the Beverly Hills Hotel when the Iranian woman appeared. "A threesome [was] suggested," Jennifer recalls, "but for some reason she seem[ed] nervous, so we abandon[ed] the idea." It was just as well, for later, at the Daisy discotheque, Jennifer ran into Khashoggi, the notorious arms dealer and oil baron, who told her, "I've had your rooms bugged, you know. You certainly speak to Mr. Polanski and Mr. Beatty a lot." Khashoggi then swept the freewheeling Jennifer off to Acapulco, later paying her five thousand dollars for a conventional one-night stand.

Jennifer settled into a life that was part jet set, part Barney's Beanery and "the S & M [Sunset Marquis Hotel]" in L.A., and part Max's Kansas City in New York, enjoying occasional affairs with rock 'n' roll muse Bobby Neuwirth ("cheap, fast love . . . with his cowboy boots on"); Art Garfunkel (whom she told, "I think you probably prefer men"); International Famous (IFA) agent and future Tri-Star CEO Mike Medavoy ("supportive and fun"); Ryan O'Neal ("poses a lot . . . knows how he looks during every move of our love-making"); and Waylon Jennings ("one of the best lovers").[138]

Sometimes both Warren and Art Garfunkel stayed at the Carlyle at the same time, and Jennifer would sleep with both, spending the first part of the evening with Art, and then going upstairs to Warren's suite. Knocking on his door, she'd say, "Just happened to be in the neighborhood," and Warren would show her to the bedroom.[139]

Julie Christie again ended her romance with Warren, if not their friendship, when she rang him one night at the Beverly Wilshire and informed him it was over. Warren thought, She's with somebody, I can tell. After she rang off, he spoke four desolate words out loud in the solitary penthouse: "They've all dumped me." With the loss of Julie, it began to dawn on him that instant gratification as a way of life was cheating him out of his maturity. He woke up in a Paris hotel room one morning at 4 A.M., "scared for a minute because I wonder[ed] where the hell I [was]."[140] Worshiped by anonymous millions but no longer loved by anyone in particular, he was like the Beatles' "nowhere man," lacking vision, direction, and purpose. Though he continued to see Julie, she kept it strictly platonic.[141]

By the mid-1970s Warren was beginning to recognize some of the shortcomings of his way of life. For one thing, he decided to buy a house. Without Julie, hotel rooms were now a cold reminder of his rootlessness. And, besides, the Beverly Wilshire Hotel was changing. "They built a new addition to the hotel so that people now can look down onto my balcony," he complained. He found that he couldn't entirely give up El Escondido, and held onto his lease. He threw his energy into remodeling the house he'd bought, putting in a swimming pool, tennis courts, gym, sauna, and screening room. Once the excitement of renovation was over, the challenge of actually settling down and enjoying the place proved too much for him, for he was dragging into it the same old self-indulgent life that had long since begun to pall. After a while in his splendid new home, he said, "I still like living in the hotel. It's easier. Everyone likes to make a big deal out of my buying a house. They think it shows some kind of maturity. I see [needing roots] as immaturity. . . . I'm already bored with the house." Boredom is nature's way of punishing the selfish. Warren's house wasn't to blame for his ennui; what had caught up with him was the pointlessness of a self-absorbed life.

He was still emotionally demolished by the end of his affair with Julie. Their attachment, like his earlier relationship with Leslie, had represented a resurrection of his hope for a continuing relationship. Later, co-starring in *Shampoo*, Warren and Julie would re-create their breakup on screen, and it would literally bring him to his knees.

Whenever Polanski was unavailable, Warren turned to his new cruising buddy, Jack Nicholson. Though the two were among the most attractive men in Hollywood, not everyone was susceptible to their blandishments. "I was wary . . . of hanging out with Nicholson or Warren Beatty," Dunaway said. "It was one of those things Jack and I talked about in our trailer tête-à-têtes [during filming of *Chinatown*]. He was bemused that he and Warren, at different points in their lives, often ended up with the same woman. It didn't make him happy."[142]

On at least one occasion, their relationships with the same women were at the same time. A dark, exotic, rich Bianca Jagger type met Warren as a sort of payback. Her girlfriend knew Warren, and the girlfriend wanted to meet Jack Nicholson. The two women went to Warren's place at 11 P.M., and Warren was in his swimming pool in the nude, swimming around. They jumped in with him. Afterward, they toweled off and then sat around in robes. Warren had an Asian valet, but he wasn't there, so Warren brought out a little hot dog maker, and they snacked on hot dogs and drinks. The girls made small talk, while Warren came on like a phony intellectual. After half an hour, Nicholson arrived, explaining that he'd been on a set, making a movie. He and Warren had a very chummy, almost sophomoric relationship, like two college guys—American leering humor—treating these women very much like objects. The girls thought it was expected that they would have to sleep with Warren and Jack whether they wanted to or not. They felt there was no getting out of there. "I'm hot, and I'm going swimming," Nicholson announced, and Warren jumped in with him. The women went swimming with them because they were eager to get closer to Jack.

They were swimming nude. Then Warren sat on the side in a robe with one

WARREN BEATTY

Varsity Football 2,3,4; Homeroom President 2; Junior Varsity Basketball 2; Officials Club 2; W-L Club 3,4; Senior Class President 4.

In high school, Warren was president of the senior class of 1955. "I liked him as a person," says classmate Jo Ann Ratterree, "but I didn't want to date him." (1955 Blue and Gray, *Washington-Lee High School, courtesy Jo Ann Ratterree*)

Cheerleader Ann Read, Warren's girlfriend, was described by a classmate as "very sweet," a dark-haired, dark-eyed Jackie Kennedy type. "He was a flirt," says Ann. "When we got to high school, he immediately started dating senior girls." (1955 Blue and Gray, *Washington-Lee High School, courtesy Jo Ann Ratterree*)

By no means the star of the team—that distinction belonged to stubby John Meroney, who crossed the goal line nine times in the fall of 1954—Warren was nonetheless one of the six most honored gridders, singled out as a "bulwark of strength behind the lines." *(1955 Blue and Gray, Washington-Lee High School, courtesy Jo Ann Ratterree)*

Warren Beaty
Center

John Phillips, later of the Mamas and the Papas, attended a nearby school, and said Warren was a gridiron hero known as "Mad Dog Beaty." (Warren added the second "T" to his surname after becoming an actor.) *(1955 Blue and Gray, Washington-Lee High School, courtesy Jo Ann Ratterree)*

(Opposite) His classmates chose Warren and Jo Schilling "Best All Around." As the Washington-Lee Generals' center, Warren's body was much beefier than his later, sleek movie-star physique. *(1955 Blue and Gray, Washington-Lee High School, courtesy Jo Ann Ratterree)*

In the 1950s, Warren tried his luck in television (*Dobie Gillis*) and the theater (1959's *A Loss of Roses*), but nothing clicked until his discovery by powerful gay mentors who adored him—William Inge, Tennessee Williams, and Joshua Logan. Warren's New York girlfriend was Diane Ladd, whose roommate, Rona Barrett, recalls that he burst in one night and told Rona, "I'm gonna rape you. This is it, baby. You're finally gonna lose that fuckin' cherry." (*© Bettmann/CORBIS*)

He went west in the late 1950s, riding a wave of young Adonises—Tony Perkins, Troy Donahue, Richard Beymer, George Nader, Rod Taylor, Ray Danton, Tab Hunter, and Elvis Presley— who hoped to fill the void left by the death of James Dean. Jane Fonda and Joan Collins both flipped over Warren. "In a few years, I'll be worn out," said Collins (shown with Warren) after their first night of lovemaking. Though exhausted by his incredible stamina, she came back for more, got pregnant, and aborted the baby. A later sex partner, Britt Ekland, said Warren "could handle women as smoothly as operating an elevator, knowing exactly where to locate the top button. One flick and we were on the way." (*© Bettmann/CORBIS*)

Big sister Shirley MacLaine, who'd fought bullies off Warren in childhood, achieved stardom in 1955, in Hitchcock's *The Trouble with Harry,* a full six years before Warren did. Their sibling rivalry extends into politics as well as movies. *(© Bettmann/CORBIS)*

Warren and his *Splendor in the Grass* director, Elia (Gadge) Kazan, who guided
Marlon Brando to matinee-idol immortality in *A Streetcar Named Desire*. Opening at
Manhattan's Victoria Theater on October 10, 1961, *Splendor* showcased Warren's
alternating sensitivity and ferocity in a role tailor-made for him, that of high school
jock Bud Stamper. He shot to stardom at age twenty-three. (© *Underwood &
Underwood/CORBIS*)

Though sleeping with
Warren while married
to Robert Wagner,
Natalie Wood,
Warren's *Splendor*
leading lady, also had
relationships with
women. Her husband,
Robert Wagner, could
not accept the public
humiliation after her
affair with Warren. In
the end, Natalie was
left with nothing: her
marriage was in tatters,
and Warren was off to
greener pastures.
(© *Bettmann/CORBIS*)

Homewrecker Warren with Mrs. Peter Hall (Leslie Caron). Leaving marriages in ruins ultimately did not bring joy to Warren or his married mistresses. Mrs. Wagner (Natalie Wood) refused to work with him again, though he sought her box-office luster at a particularly dim point in his career. And Leslie Caron snapped, "The way he discarded me after I got him to buy *Bonnie and Clyde* was rather ruthless." (© *Bettmann/CORBIS*)

A fool for love, Warren worked in mediocre overseas productions like 1966's *Kaleidoscope* (with Susannah York) in order to be with Leslie Caron, who lived in London. Wrote critic Judith Crist, "Beatty proves again, as he did in *Promise Her Anything*, that fey comedy is not his forte." (© *Bettmann/CORBIS*)

Beatty's genius as a cinematic innovator galvanized 1967's *Bonnie and Clyde*. The old studio system was crumbling, and Warren stepped in as a trailblazing actor-producer, launching the New Hollywood—an era of visionary films by Robert Altman, Hal Ashby, Peter Bogdanovich, Francis Ford Coppola, William Friedkin, Dennis Hopper, George Lucas, Tony Bill, Terry Malick, Martin Scorsese, Bob Rafelson, Paul Schrader, Steven Spielberg, and Robert Towne. *Bonnie and Clyde*'s brilliant cast members, Gene Hackman, Estelle Parsons, Warren, Faye Dunaway (whose 1930s costumes were widely copied), and Michael J. Pollard, were all nominated for Oscars, but only Parsons won. *(© Bettmann/CORBIS)*

Politics became his consuming passion in 1968, but the crowd of 28,233 at Candlestick Park booed Warren when he got up to speak against gun control. With his movie-star shades and pin-striped suit, he seemed the epitome of debonair superficiality to Castro Street hippies, one of whom scoffed, "Only recently we'd watched Faye Dunaway caressing his rod." (© *Bettmann/CORBIS*)

While doing such early seventies trash as *McCabe and Mrs. Miller, The Only Game in Town,* and *Dollars,* he inexplicably rejected classics like *The Godfather,* perhaps because he was prejudiced against movies based on novels. The same bias would have prevented David O. Selznick from filming *Gone With the Wind.* (© *Douglas Kirkland/ CORBIS)*

At his most alluring in the mid-1970s, Warren rebounded in intelligent films like Alan J. Pakula's *The Parallax View,* playing a reporter tracking down political assassins. In his personal life, he'd become the world's No. 1 Don Juan, and Arlene Dahl dubbed him "Warren Beauty." After a dinner date with Warren, seventy-nine-year-old playwright Lillian Hellman remarked, "I think I've come to interest Warren." Brigitte Bardot, Princess Margaret, and Jackie Kennedy Onassis also pursued him, though the latter decided he was insolent and indiscreet.

(© *Douglas Kirkland/CORBIS)*

Mixing business with pleasure, Warren and Julie Christie contemplated marriage while collaborating on *McCabe and Mrs. Miller, Heaven Can Wait,* and the 1975 classic *Shampoo,* in which Julie gives Warren oral sex under a restaurant table. (© *Douglas Kirkland/CORBIS*)

When Sharon Tate was slaughtered by the Manson gang in Benedict Canyon in 1969, her husband, Roman Polanski, who directed *Rosemary's Baby*, was comforted by Warren in London. (© *Photo B.D.V./CORBIS*)

Although Jimmy Carter was uncomfortable in Warren's Beverly Wilshire penthouse, he was one of the few winners Warren ever backed. For George McGovern and Gary Hart, Beatty was more like the kiss of death. But as a Democratic Party fund-raiser, he had few peers, inventing the political concert and nabbing Barbra Streisand, James Taylor, and Carole King for one of his benefits. (© *Bettmann/CORBIS*)

Old enough to know better, Warren and Dustin Hoffman hatched one of Hollywood's all-time turkeys, *Ishtar,* a $40-million flop in 1987. Known as *"Ishtar*/disaster," it became the Hollywood code word for subsequent big-budgeted flops, including Kevin Costner's 1990 bomb, *Waterworld,* dubbed *"Fishtar"* by the media. (© *Reuters New Media Inc./CORBIS*)

(Opposite, top) Diane Keaton, Warren's girlfriend and *Reds* costar, launched a fashion fad with her delightfully daffy *Annie Hall* mix-and-mismatch getups. She couldn't take Warren seriously as a lover after he tried to sandwich dates with her between dates with Mary Tyler Moore, Hope Lange, and model Janice Dickinson. *(© Bettmann/CORBIS)*

Bulworth was the best political satire since Chaplin's *The Great Dictator*, but Warren's own forays into politics were lamentable, including his support of George McGovern and Gary Hart for the U.S. presidency and his own ill-advised bid for the White House in 2000. In a fatal miscalculation, McGovern's record as a war hero was not exploited in the campaign, and Hart's sex scandal was allegedly prompted by Beatty's womanizing. In the photo, David Geffen, the richest man in Hollywood, stands between Warren and Senator Hart. *(© CORBIS)*

(Opposite, bottom) Warren and wife Annette Bening hang on every word of Hollywood's reigning mogul, Steven Spielberg, director of *E.T.* and *Saving Private Ryan*. With Annette's marriage to Warren in March 1992, and the advent of four offspring, her acting career lost precious momentum, but her place in moviedom's power elite was secured. *(© Reuters NewMedia Inc./CORBIS)*

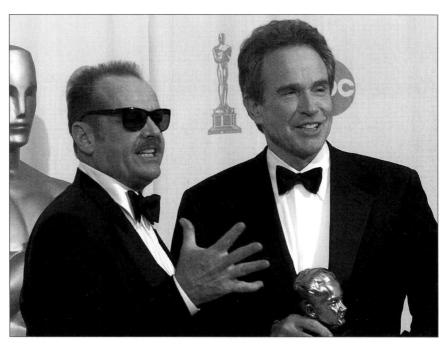

At the 2000 Oscar ceremony, Jack Nicholson presented Warren with the Irving G. Thalberg Memorial Award, Hollywood's highest honor. According to Bruce Dern, Nicholson "brags about a lot more pussy than he's ever gotten. I'd say if you cut half of his pussy in half, you'd have it about right, and still he probably gets more than anybody around. He and Beatty have contests about it." (© *AFP/CORBIS*)

Plus ça change, plus c'est la meme chose: As Mrs. Michael Douglas (Catherine Zeta-Jones) enters Warren's magnetic field, Mike wisely reaches out to retrieve her. (© *AFP/CORBIS*)

of the women. He started to put the make on her, while the other woman swam with Jack. Everyone was drinking, and Jack was in and out of the pool, running out to get another drink and another frankfurter.

Nicholson wanted to continue swimming, but his girl had had enough of the pool, said she wanted to freshen up. The two women went to one of the bedrooms to change clothes. They were in there twenty minutes, talking, and decided they really didn't want to go through with it. So, they took off and left the two Lotharios by themselves at the pool.[143]

Ever the King of Kink, Nicholson would take obvious pleasure in the scene in *The Two Jakes* in which he forces hunky actor David Keith to suck on a loaded pistol. According to author Jeremy Larner, whose *Drive, He Said* was directed by Nicholson in 1970, "Most guys in Hollywood are more turned on by each other than they are by the women they fuck."[144] Added bisexual producer Gerald Ayres, who produced Nicholson's *The Last Detail* and was a close friend of Bob Towne's, "[Bob] and Warren were so intimate, they were twisted together like a knot." When Towne warned Ayres that he'd lose his reputation in Hollywood if he came out of the closet and lived openly with his companion Nick Kudla, Ayres told Towne, "Listen, you and Warren squabble on the phone every day like a couple of lovers, go all over the world fucking the same women in the same room. If you two guys aren't lovers, you're the next thing to it." Towne refused to speak to Ayres for years.[145]

All Warren knew was that his hedonistic existence had landed him in moral bankruptcy. "I have led a very indulgent life," he admitted. "Almost indescribably indulgent. . . . One way to describe maturity is to say it could be the capacity to postpone gratification. And when someone with my particular history has not been asked to postpone certain gratifications—and I'm not speaking just of sexual gratifications—it's impossible not to sense that you might be cheated out of maturity. And I try not to get cheated out of that."

And try he would, but maturity, of course, is not a matter of trying. It's, among other things, a matter of doing, doing for others, giving rather than taking, giving as a way of life. Maturity is not just postponing gratification—which would be hard enough for this man for whom instant gratification had never been quick enough—but of actually gratifying others. What were the odds that he could improve his character, this man who'd been described as "confused, venal, money-mad, satyriacal, insensitive to others, opportunistic, and self-absorbed," and who himself had said, "How can I understand anyone else when I don't yet understand myself?"[146]

To be fair, at this point in his life Warren Beatty didn't have much opportunity for the kind of selfless action that promotes personal growth, not in the insular, elitist kingdom of fame he inhabited, isolated and protected from the world of hard knocks. The only tool he possessed for changing his behavior was an analytical mind, and no one yet has been known to attain maturity by merely thinking about it. But this was Mad Dog Beatty, and he was going to grow up if it killed him.

CHAPTER FIVE

LA RONDE, L.A. STYLE

DESPITE HIS NEW PASSION for personal growth, Beatty's sex life remained so ravenous, it was inevitable that alleged Beatty bastards would start turning up by the 1970s. "He got one girl pregnant who was married at the time," recalls Sarah Porterfield. "Her husband was in the service, stationed overseas. She had the baby and passed it off as her husband's child. The baby was named Duke. One time she called Warren and said, 'I'm coming in to town, I'd like to see you.' She'd been living in Florida, and she told Warren she had his son with her. She chickened out at the last minute.

"There's another girl whom Warren had a baby with, and at one point in the seventies, she was supposed to show up in the lobby of the Beverly Wilshire Hotel—but she didn't.

"It's a myth that Warren is a good fuck. Every guy you're with is the best fuck you've ever had while you're with him. But in retrospect they aren't shit.

With Warren, women are always excited by who he is, or what he had, or what he could do for them. You get all these girls who think, If I fuck Warren Beatty, he'll put me in his next movie."

Perpetually dissatisfied and not knowing where else to turn, Warren went back to work in films after a two-and-a-half-year sabbatical, first making a political thriller, *The Parallax View*, which dealt with a presidential assassination and reflected the anxiety and paranoia that followed the Warren Commission's failure to dispel the suspicion that JFK had been the victim of a conspiracy. In Warren's film, he and co-star Paula Prentiss play reporters who uncover a sinister plot to wipe out moderate political candidates who interfere with the greedy ambitions of a huge conglomerate. Director Alan Pakula saw it as his most visually stylized movie, a Kafkaesque evocation of the post-Vietnam world. "It was made during the Watergate hearings," said Pakula. "It's a world that has become almost surreal. . . . You never know who the Parallax people are, some fascist organization of some kind that seems to be assassinating people."[1] At the end of the film, Warren's character is killed while trying to infiltrate the band of killers. A sometimes gripping if not entirely involving picture, *Parallax* was part of Pakula's so-called "paranoid trilogy"—three movies he made about unmasking conspiracies, beginning with the psychological thriller *Klute*. In *Parallax* and *All the President's Men*, the director used reporters the way movies of the thirties and forties used private eyes.

One day while shooting *Parallax*, Warren sustained a lacerated scalp when he jumped up while watching his double, Craig Baxley, drive through a supermarket entrance. Ironically, the double was unhurt, but the star had to be rushed to a medic for stitching.

Released in 1974, the film didn't perform well at the box office, but *Newsweek* noted Beatty's "fine, low-keyed and bemused performance." Warren blamed the movie's failure on his friend Bob Evans, who had a production deal at Paramount, and thus was in a position, according to Evans's rival at Paramount, Frank Yablans, to get preferential treatment for his own projects. *Parallax* was not one of Evans's projects. Warren complained to Gulf + Western's Charles Bluhdorn, who owned Paramount and to whom both Evans and Yablans reported. "Charlie *really* loved Warren," said the late producer Don Simpson. "He was such a starfucker."[2] Bluhdorn demoted Evans, who naturally felt that Warren had stabbed him in the back. "My closest friend," Evans moaned, "he tried to kill me on it." Barry Diller was brought in over both Evans and Yablans, and Warren's friend Dick Sylbert was later named head of production. People saw Warren's hand in it, because never before had a mere production designer become a studio chief. Sylbert, whose taste proved too literary for Paramount, fell out of grace with studio powers Barry Diller and Michael Eisner, and was soon replaced by his own protégé, Don Simpson.[3]

Unscathed by the bloodletting he'd touched off at Paramount, and planning his next project, Warren dusted off an old property he owned, *Keith's My Name, Hair's My Game*, the story of a randy hairdresser who discovers that promiscuity is a loser's game. This had evolved into *Shampoo*, the project that would disrupt his friendship with screenwriter Robert Towne, one of the gifted architects of the New Hollywood. "When I first came to L.A.," recalled Valerie Allen, "in my acting class were Bob Towne, Jack Nicholson, James Coburn, and Sally Kellerman. Bob Towne was a very good actor. He had sort of a marvelous Jimmy Stewart quality. He later went on to write *Shampoo* with Warren Beatty. Bob had written the [basic] story, and I think all writers take from life and fictionalize. *Shampoo* was in part really all of our lives, Hollywood pop culture in the seventies. The story was part my life, Warren's life, Bob's life, and Jay Sebring's life. Jay was a very attractive hairdresser who all the ladies adored."[4]

Around Hollywood, people are still speculating about the identity of the hairdresser in *Shampoo*, but it appears to have been a composite portrait of Sebring, the first celebrity barber, and Hollywood's pioneering hairstylist Gene Shacove, the West Coast beautician responsible for the cult of the "in" hairdresser. In the East Coast haut monde, Mr. Kenneth reigned supreme with his scissors and hair dryer; in Paris, it was Alexandre. Together, they stormed, in the 1960s, the social bastions that had always separated the fashionable rich (variously known as the beautiful people, the jet set, café society, and celebriciety) from their servants and tradesmen. Afterward, socialites freely mingled with hairdressers, clothing designers, and interior decorators, and it was no longer surprising to see Halston, a dressmaker, and Babe Paley, a jet-setter, lunching together at La Grenouille, or hairdresser José Eber squiring Elizabeth Taylor around L.A.

Bob Towne interviewed Shacove for *Shampoo* in 1968, exhaustively picking his brains. At forty-six, Shacove had been married three times; he wore jeans, a body shirt open to the waist, gold jewelry, and a chamois jacket. He certainly sounded like the blueprint for *Shampoo*'s George Roundy. "Trust me, it was Gene," says Nan Morris-Robinson. "I went with him in '64, and he'd take me on his motorcycle, eighty miles an hour, up Sunset Boulevard, ignoring the stoplights. Warren was at Gene's shop every day; it was half a block from the Beverly Wilshire on Rodeo. Warren would pick whatever he wanted. Gene opened a private club downstairs—the Candy Store—and put in a dress shop. He and Jay Sebring were so close. Jay drove a Cobra, Gene a Corvette. I drove the 'vette when I helped Gene move to Bel Air. He was ahead of me on his motorcycle, and I saw him spin around backward on a curve on Sunset. Later he went over the hood of a car on Mulholland, and that was it for the motorcycle.

"Jay Sebring had a shop on Fairfax and did the men. Gene did the women. Larry Geller, a Russian Jew, worked for Gene and got into Elvis's circle after Elvis's studio called for a barber. At the time, I was seeing Elvis, who used to love for me to rub his hair and his hands. Larry Geller was so eager to get to the studio that he broke his wrist tripping over his attache case. He got a book on psychic phenomena from Paula Andrea, and Elvis was fascinated with that."

Discussing *Shampoo,* Shacove himself once said, "It was my character but not my story. They've cleaned it up. . . . I used to ride a Triumph motorcycle to go see clients like Janet Leigh, Liz Taylor, and Claudia Cardinale. . . . They did use my ex-wife's house for Goldie Hawn's in the film." As Hugh Hefner's barber, Shacove described the scene at Hef's mansion as "wild. I'd come over and there were twelve girls sitting around the pool naked. Who wouldn't want to watch that? I love women. That's why I got into the business of doing everybody's hair."[5]

Some insisted the model for George Roundy was the charismatic, straight hairdresser Richard Alcala, father of four, who owned his own Beverly Hills shop and ran it with his hairstylist wife, Carrie White. For a while, Carrie was Warren's hairstylist. Bob Towne haunted Alcala's shop for five months, taking notes for *Shampoo*. Alcala was a Mexican-American from San Francisco whose client list read like a who's who of Hollywood, including Rona Barrett, Rita Hayworth, Natalie Wood, Mrs. Kirk Douglas, Louis Jourdan, Jennifer Jones, Ann-Margret, Tina and Nancy Sinatra, Anthony Quinn, Lee Marvin, Ali MacGraw, Raquel Welch, and Katherine Ross. "Richard had eight girls going at the same time," said his wife, "and not one of them knew the other."[6] Dissolute Beverly Hills wives would slip sleeping pills into their husbands' nightcaps so they could rush to Alcala's shop and gossip until 5 A.M. According to Bob Towne, Alcala was "so talented but somehow couldn't get it together."

Other insiders say the character of George Roundy was inspired by Jon Peters, a half-Cherokee, half-Italian hairdresser who'd done time in reform school before getting a job with Gene Shacove and later making millions as Southern California's purveyor of the blow-dry look. Though Bob Towne did not interview Peters for *Shampoo*, there were striking similarities between Peters and George Roundy. Peters was known to have seduced his female clientele. With such male clients as Jack Nicholson and, occasionally, Warren, Peters saw to it that they were titillated during their trims by getting his assistants to describe their latest sexual acts.[7] Peters endeared himself to Barbra Streisand by telling her, when she interviewed him for the job of hairstylist on her film *For Pete's Sake*, "You've got a great ass."[8] In 1973, he dumped his wife of eight years, actress Lesley Ann Warren, who later said, "It was the best thing that ever happened to me. I was afraid of Jon because he had a quick temper."[9]

The bearded, black-haired Peters, described in *People* as "a predator, sharp, imaginative, and vulgar,"[10] was so adored by Streisand that she turned him into her lover, manager, and producer (*A Star Is Born* and *The Main Event*). Ultimately, Barbra resented her growing dependency on Peters, and cut loose from the relationship. He went on to become a successful producer in his own right (*Flashdance* and *Batman*), and briefly, as co-head of production at Sony-owned Columbia, a full-fledged Hollywood mogul.

When Peters was asked to comment on *Shampoo* after the film was released, he said, "I identified with the side of Warren that was unable to communicate with a woman on a one-to-one level, so he tried to communicate indirectly with ten instead. He was lonely. That's why there aren't many old hairdressers around. They end up as gospel preachers in the Midwest. I was like that before I met Barbra but now I've left that kind of life—that perpetuation of a game played on both sides of the chair—behind me."

It would never be entirely behind Warren, who spent a lot of his energy trying to defend his sexual frenzy and his insensitive treatment of women. He also wasted a lot of words attempting to convince people that he wasn't gay. In discussing *Shampoo*, he said, "I wanted to challenge the Victorian and Freudian theory that a hypersexual man always has to be seen deep down as a woman hater or a latent homosexual. Freud basically disapproved of promiscuity. We

tend to forget that he was a Victorian. This film does away with the double standards of society. George causes trouble in a Puritan-based society where the male
does what he wants and says that women like meaningful relationships. The idea
of the film began by my wanting to make a movie about contemporary sexuality. And the contemporary hypocrisy that comes out of a generation educated
one way about sex and living another way and the ambivalences that produces."[11]

Bob Towne had become one of the hottest writers in Hollywood with the
success of *Chinatown*. Filmed in 1974 by Roman Polanski, it starred Faye
Dunaway and Jack Nicholson, and won an Oscar for Towne's script. Conceived
as detective story, *Chinatown* was based on the conflict between farmers and land
speculators in Orange County in the early years of the twentieth century. Towne
added a plot with tangled sexual relationships and incest, paving the way for a
box-office hit. Nicholson's relationship with Towne, like Warren's, had a long
history, reaching back to Jeff Corey's acting class in 1956.

While directing *Chinatown*, Polanski moved in with Nicholson, who
referred to him as the "Fucking Polack."[12] Their collaboration in *Chinatown*—
in which Polanski played a punk who slashes Nicholson's nostril with a knife—
was awesome. Just as *Blow-Up* exposed the dark underside of swinging London,
Chinatown was a metaphor of America in the Watergate era, a country where
all was artifice, deceit, and spin, where corporate avarice ruled the national
psyche, and political corruption and blackmail were commonplace. The film
became a cult classic, and was later rated the nineteenth-best picture ever made
on the American Film Institute's "Top 100" list. Compiled by one thousand five
hundred industry leaders, the controversial list included *Unforgiven* and *Dances
with Wolves*, but ignored much better films, including *Camille*, *Rebecca*, *The
Women*, *Spellbound*, *Barry Lyndon*, and, for that matter, *Splendor in the Grass*.[13]

In the glow of critical praise for *Chinatown*, Bob Towne went back to work
with Warren on *Shampoo*. Both men were somewhat distracted. Warren was
already thinking ahead to *Reds*, a project that would occupy him, off and on, for
the next half dozen years. At the moment, he was trying to purchase the rights
to Barbara Gelb's *So Short a Time*, a biography of the lovers of *Reds*, John Reed
and Louise Bryant.[14] As for Towne, while many around Hollywood believed that
the screenwriter was Warren's slave, their relationship was far more complex.
"He was more in love with Beatty," said novelist and screenwriter Jeremy
Larner.[15] Writer Buck Henry called Towne a "shadow image of Warren, some-

one the girls just got away from."[16] Despite, or perhaps because of, this symbiotic relationship, Warren and Bob started feuding over the plot of *Shampoo*. Warren wanted a political subtext, while Bob, recalling his work on the picture in an interview in the *Los Angeles Times* in August 2000, revealed that *his* "model for the film was Jean Renoir's masterful *Rules of the Game*, which explores a forgotten time and place where everyone is compelling and complex."[17] Beatty and Towne scarcely spoke for six months. "Although I don't know anyone who's a bigger prick," said Towne, "there's no one I love and admire more."[18]

Warren was so confident of the project that, despite an incomplete script, he went ahead and put together a first-rate package, assembling some of the actresses with whom he'd been emotionally involved, including Julie Christie and Goldie Hawn, to play the women nailed by hairdresser George Roundy. The autobiographical overtones were becoming clear, and Warren said he didn't "mind the suggestion of parallels too much." The main difference between him and the fictional character was that George lied about his cheating, and Warren never bothered to. "I've never lied to any of my girlfriends . . . ever!" he said.[19] There were also obvious parallels to Fellini's 1963 classic *8½*, in which the filmmaker reviews his love life, woman by woman, fully a dozen years before *Shampoo*.

There were widespread rumors that Warren and Julie would get married as soon as they refurbished Warren's "Viking Castle" atop Mulholland Drive, the house he acquired from the Lauritz Melchior estate and was filling up with art deco.[20] Though they'd broken up, they were inextricably involved. Years later, in an interview with Norman Mailer, Warren said, "I felt Julie, and Goldie also, made the picture work for me, and particularly the ending of *Shampoo* with Julie—that was after our relationship. The integrity on that face. That person. It's never faltered." Though bigger stars were considered for the role of Jill, Warren gave it to Goldie, despite a recent career setback in *The Sugarland Express* that consigned her to the B-list of Hollywood actresses. *Shampoo* would restore her to star status.

"It's funny, because *Shampoo* was about this guy who's cheating on one girl with the other," said a crew member. "He'll never be honest with any woman because it's like, 'What does she want from me?' No one will ever know him, because Warren doesn't know himself. He did an interview with Barbara Walters, who told him how happy she was to interview him because no one else had. He dissed her, and said, 'Still no one has.' Every question he answers with a question. He will never be properly interviewed. He plays games."

Shampoo, Warren told a reporter, was his attempt to "close out that promiscuous phase in [my] li[fe]."[21] George Roundy was "dumb," he said. "He cannot sublimate his libido in any other way. . . . George can't get the energy to get his life together. The energy goes on the women. He wants to run his own shop but he'll never do it. He's always in debt, badly organized. He's not prepared to face middle age with the protections people organize efficiently."

He intended to produce as well as star in the picture, and he'd already spent a million of his own money before he sought studio backing, hiring, in addition to Christie and Hawn, two superb Broadway stars, Lee Grant and Jack Warden, and establishing a top-notch below-the-line staff: Dick Sylbert (production design), Anthea Sylbert (costumes), and Laszlo Kovacs (cinematography). He hired seventeen-year-old Carrie Fisher, whom he met through her mother Debbie Reynolds's friend George Perth, without even having her read. She was so obviously like the role she was to play in *Shampoo*, a neglected but caustic Beverly Hills kid. She had some of the movie's most famous lines, including, "Are you queer?" and "Wanna fuck?"

Confident that he had a blockbuster, Warren shopped the project around the studios before committing it to anyone, talking with Bob Evans at Paramount and Frank Wells at Warner. Wells topped Evans's offer, but the latter couldn't have made good on it anyway, since his archrival at Paramount, Frank Yablans, didn't want *Shampoo* and overruled him. Nevertheless, Warren told Evans, "Look, Bob, I'm bringing it to David [Begelman, at Columbia], and I want to tell him that you want it. He offered me three million four. I want to tell him that you offered four million." Evans replied, "I can't do that Warren, because we have a deal among the guys that we can't lie." Warren said, "Hey, come on, Bob, it's me. Begelman calls you, I want you to tell him you're offering four million for it." Ultimately, Evans, who'd always been starry-eyed about Warren—and who, as the producer of Bob Towne's immortal *Chinatown*, desperately wanted anything Bob and Warren were up to—caved in, backing up Warren's bluff. As a result, Begelman doubled his offer. His studio, Columbia, had fallen on hard times, and was hungry for a hit, though Columbia could ill afford to pay competitive prices. Once the volatile, suicidal Begelman owned *Shampoo*, he hated it, and reneged on the deal. Warren went back to Warner, but the well-posted Frank Wells cut his offer in half.

Obviously, Warren had been overconfident. Now he had nothing. Furious, he confronted Begelman at a political fund-raiser, but Begelman insisted, "I never made you any promises." Warren jabbed him in the chest and—shoving him toward the wall—practically shouted, "You're a liar. I know you're a liar and you know I know you're a liar, but we're gonna forget that, and we're gonna do this deal. You have nothing, you need this picture. Just match my original deal with Warner." Customarily unflappable, this time a shaken Begelman reinstated the deal. But he was aware, through the grapevine, of Warren's troubles at Warner. In the end, Begelman succeeded in acquiring *Shampoo* for half his original offer.

To make matters worse, at the last moment Begelman forced Warren to accept a rolling-gross deal, as opposed to a cut of first-dollar gross. According to ICM agent Ed Limato, "The best deal that you can make for any actor is what we call a first-dollar gross deal. That is when an actor gets a percentage, usually starting at ten percent, of every dollar that goes into the studio's coffers. That simply means that there is no way the studio can lie to you (about the movie's receipts) or tack on this expense or that expense. When you make that kind of deal for an artist, you know that he's home." Elaborating on rolling gross in *Easy Riders, Raging Bulls*, Peter Biskind wrote, "Rolling gross or rolling break-even was a novel idea that rendered gross profits—not to mention net profits—worthless. Essentially, it meant that distribution and other costs would be added on to the negative cost even while a film was in release, so that the break-even point kept rolling, or increasing. As some wag put it, 'the break always rolled away from the filmmakers.' " Though Warren did okay for himself, collecting 40 percent after *Shampoo* earned a certain amount of money, others who owned a piece of the picture, such as Towne, suffered severe losses due to the rolling-gross deal.[22]

Warren was itching to direct, but lacked the confidence to do so. In the past, he'd hired top directors and then undercut them, giving unsolicited advice on the set and generally interfering with their job. For *Shampoo*, he approached one of the best-loved directors in Hollywood, Hal Ashby, who had directed *Harold and Maude*, a love story about a septuagenarian, played by Ruth Gordon, and a teenager, played by Bud Cort. Subsequently he directed *The Last Detail*, an early Jack Nicholson film written by Bob Towne. Ashby was an oddball who could only have risen in the Hollywood of the 1960s and 1970s, when studios were open to innovative ideas. A sensitive and gentle man, he was much sought after by actors and actresses, who recognized his intuitive genius and saw how he could help them understand their characters. He was famous for never letting an actor say a word that wasn't genuine.

Born in 1929, too old to be a part of the hippie phenomenon but too rebellious to fit into his own, largely conservative generation, Ashby had a foot in both camps, the counterculture and the Establishment. An aging flower child, he smoked pot, sported a beard, and demonstrated for civil rights and peace. He was seeing Dyan Cannon, star of Hollywood's hip wife-swapping saga, *Bob and Carol and Ted and Alice*, but dropped her during *Shampoo* for a former Nicholson girlfriend, Mimi Machu. He was very ambitious, which was why he agreed to direct *Shampoo*. Recalled Jerome Hellman, the producer who later hired Ashby to direct *Coming Home*, "Warren was a giant star, and Hal looked up to and cherished his friendship with Warren. I think for him to do *Shampoo* was like a validation, because as complicated as Hal was, and as quixotic as he was, he didn't want to fail, he wanted to be on the A-list."[23]

In December 1973 Warren, Ashby, and Towne worked on the script for a week, starting at nine in the morning and working until eleven at night. Holed up in El Escondido, they talked over each scene. When he was ready to write, Bob would go into another room. Eventually Towne resented incorporating changes that hadn't originated with him, and later said, "Both Warren and Jack [Nicholson] in differing ways used their political power to control creative situations." While Towne still envisaged *Shampoo* as a Renoir or Bergman film, Warren was determined to forge a definitive political statement of his time. As their discussions grew more heated, Towne said to Warren, "You cunt. . . . You're just being a cunt. . . . That's more cunt stuff."[24]

In Warren's estimation, Bob's work would never address the current political scene to the extent he desired. "The story had no political context with Robert, no Nixon, no nothing," said Beatty. "All of that is ninety-nine percent me, my work." Towne continued to resist Warren's ideas, and Warren later complained, "We used to meet every fucking day, and I'd have to tell him the goddamn story. . . . Both party sequences were written by me, none of those were in Towne's original draft at all. That's half the movie."

Bob Towne disagreed: "Naa, ya know, what he did was cross out a lot of stuff that I wrote, and he told me to do this and that, and we usually fought about it, and sometimes he really fucked things up." Why, then, did Towne let Beatty get away with a co-screenwriting credit? "Oh, you know Warren," said Towne. "Unless you do things like that, you're not going to get the other stuff you can get from Warren."[25]

Conflict, in this case, produced a work of art. With Ashby's help, Towne's and Beatty's mangled scripts were melded together, and *Shampoo* was the happy result—the ultimate Hogarthian epic of America's seventies excess. Towne contributed good material on relationships, and Warren, by changing the setting to Nixon's election night, gave the film its social relevance. George Roundy's life, one of promiscuity and selfishness, became a metaphor for Nixon's hypocrisy and betrayal of the nation. Like *Bonnie and Clyde*, the *Shampoo* scenario had a freshly minted sound. At last, Warren was back in his original and innovative groove.

The versatile and bright Tony Bill was added to the cast. "My agent at ICM, Bill Robinson, introduced me to Warren," Tony recalls. Previously he'd been a light leading man, appearing with Frank Sinatra in *Come Blow Your Horn* and with Geraldine Page, Julie Harris, and newcomer Karen Black in the early Francis Ford Coppola picture *You're a Big Boy Now*. Then he became a producer, and received the 1973 Best Picture Oscar for *The Sting*. Asked in 2000 to comment on *Shampoo*, Tony said, "What I liked about the New Hollywood was its emphasis on writers. *Shampoo* was an original screenplay. You have to remember that original screenplays were pretty rare before the seventies, almost a handicap. You needed a pedigree, something from another medium. Since movies like *The Sting* and *Shampoo*, the opposite has been true. Those of us who were trying to make movies in the sixties and getting them made in the seventies brought about the era of the original screenplay. All of the movies I've directed or produced have been original screenplays, by people like David S. Ward [*Steelyard Blues* and *The Sting*] and Paul Shrader [*Taxi Driver*]."

Principal photography on *Shampoo* started in January 1974. Still railing about Bob Towne, Warren said, "Half the fuckin' time the guy didn't show up on the set, he'd be at the doctor."[26] Evarts Ziegler, Towne's agent, pinpointed the irony of his client's career when he said that Towne was quick, and acutely deadline-conscious, when working on other people's scripts, "but on his own stuff, death. Paint dried more quickly."[27]

Warren was also at war with Hal Ashby. Both power wielders, the actor and the director were on a collision course from day one. Fortunately for Warren,

Ashby couldn't stand confrontation, and stuffed his anger and frustration when Warren regularly wrested the directorial reins from him. The company was loaded with Warren's people—the Sylberts, Bob Towne, Julie Christie, and Goldie Hawn. Warren and his cronies would have meetings and then tell Ashby, "All right, Hal, this is what we're gonna do." One day Warren asked Anthea Sylbert to tell Hal that Warren's ideas for a scene they were about to shoot were exactly right. Anthea refused. "I'm not telling Hal anything," she said. "You go tell Hal." According to Haskell Wexler, the cinematographer who'd later work with Ashby on *Coming Home*, "Warren chewed Hal up and spit him out. He was like an office boy on that [set]." Film editor Bob Jones agreed, and added, "I'd go on the set, and Warren and Towne would be off whispering in the corner. Hal would be sitting in the other corner." Eventually, Ashby went to Dick Sylbert in despair and admitted, "I can't take it anymore."[28]

Despite everything, Warren was good for Ashby, who, as if by osmosis, acquired from working with Warren a cocky confidence and authority that he'd not previously shown. Ashby went from *Shampoo* to the Woody Guthrie biopic *Bound for Glory*, and then the distinguished Vietnam-vet movie *Coming Home*. After the bullying he endured on *Shampoo*, Ashby would not hesitate, on future productions, to tell his colleagues on the set, "Fuck you, this is what I'm gonna do, if you don't like it, stick it in your ear."

On one occasion, Warren put Julie Christie through thirty-eight takes, after having kept her waiting to shoot until the middle of the night. Was he punishing her for not marrying him? In another scene, he had her give him a blow job under a table at the Bistro. Julie is sitting next to a fat cat at a Republican fundraiser who informs her, "I can get you anything you'd like. What would you like?" "Well, first of all," she says, looking at Warren, "I'd like to suck his cock."

She was still hung up on him, according to reporter Marvene Jones, who asked, "Julie, did you do *Shampoo* because of Warren, because of your friendship with Warren?" "Yes," she replied, explaining that he was "a very good promoter."[29] Robin Adams Sloan of the *Los Angeles Herald-Examiner* wrote that Warren and Julie enjoyed an "open" relationship, living on different floors of the Beverly Wilshire, but that Warren was trying to hit on the twenty-year-old Miss World, Marjorie Wallace, whose late boyfriend, Peter Revson, had been killed in a racing crash.[30]

Julie now looked to Warren for advice on her career, which had not yet fulfilled the early promise of *Darling, Dr. Zhivago*, and *Far From the Madding Crowd*. Warren had been "masterminding" her affairs ever since they'd broken up, and she'd turned down numerous roles.[31] "Julie never wanted to do anything," he said. "She was the most selective actress I've ever met."[32] *Shampoo* did nothing to restore her reputation, either as a movie star or a serious actress. In fact, her career had hit the skids, though Warren would later employ her again, in *Heaven Can Wait*. Even that did not bring her out of an irreversible professional nose dive. Recalls Sarah Porterfield, "Julie Christie stayed at my friend's house after she moved out of the hotel. It was just never right. He was afraid of commitment. This is a man who can only have an intimate relationship in a horizontal position. He thinks a hard-on makes for personal growth. . . . He just wasn't ready with Julie. While she stayed at my friend's house, she talked a lot about how she thought they might get back together, but it just never happened. There's not anything about Julie that's not to be liked."

As producer, Warren worked on *Shampoo* around the clock, filming at the Bistro and in a Holmby Hills mansion. "I'm living in my dressing room," he said, "because why take the time to drive home, read the *New York Times*, and return? When I'm acting in a movie, I go out at night, but producing is a whole other thing. I'd miss the nightlife if the film lasted for seven or eight months. We've only got sixty days." He thrived on pressure and demonically created it when it was lacking. Buck Henry thought him "psychotic," adding, "His attention to detail is maniacal."[33]

Warren attended a party at Goldie's house that was thrown largely for the *Shampoo* company, including Bob Towne, Julie Christie, Lee Grant, Hal Ashby, and Jack Warden. Hollywood power broker David Geffen, a friend of Warren's, was also present. He wasn't out of the closet yet, like the character Warren was playing in *Shampoo*, whose sexual profile had become more androgynous since Warren first started talking about him. "I think if George wanted to have sex with a man, he would," Warren said. "As for comparisons between me and George, I'm not offended."[34]

According to *People* reporter Barbara Wilkins, Warren allegedly unzipped a female photographer's pants on the *Shampoo* set, and then demanded her dismissal when she discouraged his advances. He promptly called *People* editor Richard Stolley and demanded a retraction. "We had several screaming conversations," recalled the editor. "I tried to calm him down, tried to do damage control." *People*, which had the powerful Luce organization behind it, refused to run the retraction, and Warren backed down. Stolley feared that Warren would succeed in getting the entire entertainment industry to blackball the magazine, which had only recently begun publication, but *People*'s circulation soared, and Hollywood stars clamored to appear on the cover. "I think Warren was more isolated than we thought at this point," said Stolley. "No one in Hollywood would believe his story, and I think we worried unnecessarily." Warren was cordial to Stolley when they encountered each other at a party.[35]

By the time of Goldie Hawn's soiree, Warren and Bob Towne were openly fighting over screenwriting credit. Towne claimed that Warren was trying to usurp a by-line without having earned it.[36] Warren, who joined the Screen Writers Guild in 1974, insisted, "It was Towne that offered *me* the screen credit. I would have been happy to go to arbitration. . . . It's absolutely not true that every line of dialogue is his. It's an outrageous lie."[37] At Goldie's bash, David Geffen, whose keen negotiating skills were well known, attempted to settle the conflict. "You know, Warren, I really think that you're out of line," Geffen said. Warren demanded to know who'd told Geffen that Warren was making undue authorship claims. When Geffen admitted Towne had told him, Warren retorted, "I want him to tell you this in front of me." Grabbing Geffen, he dragged him over to Bob Towne. "Okay, he's telling me that you said all this shit, say it in front of me," Warren demanded. Recalled Geffen, "With me standing there, Bob said he didn't do it. And the reason he didn't have the guts was because it wasn't so. Warren called me up that night, and said, 'Don't ever do that again.' . . . It was one of the most embarrassing things that ever happened to me."[38]

Towne, like most writers in the New Hollywood, was fighting for his life, trying to survive in an industry full of egomaniacal auteurs who usurped credit for everything, especially the basic act of creation—writing—from which all movies spring. After making some changes in Carole Eastman's staggeringly original script for *Five Easy Pieces*, director Bob Rafelson took co-story credit on the same card as the writer. "If he wrote ten words," said Walton Green, who later adapted Peter Matthiessen's *At Play in the Fields of the Lord* for Rafelson, "he'd say he wrote the whole thing."[39] An old joke in the industry illustrates the low esteem in which Tinseltown holds writers: How can you tell a dumb starlet from a smart starlet? Answer: The dumb one goes to bed with the writer to advance her career, but the smart one sleeps with the director or producer.[40] The *Shampoo* screenwriting brawl subsided when Warren tossed Towne a crumb, giving him a cameo role in the picture. (Another cameo role, in a party scene, went to Jack Nicholson's girlfriend Michelle Phillips, who later lived with Warren for a time.) As the film approached its release date, Beatty and Towne joined forces again, using their press contacts to assure a strong critical reception.

Turning thirty-seven during the shoot, Warren brought the film in for a reasonable four million dollars, with $1.5 million of the total going to the cast and $2.5 million to below-the-line (production costs). When Columbia's Begelman attended a screening, he was appalled by Julie's oral-sex scene and demanded that it be cut. Warren refused. "It wasn't just a dirty moment where she says a dirty line," he insisted. "The subject of *Shampoo* is hypocrisy, the commingling of sexual hypocrisy and political hypocrisy. The reason Julie's line made for such an explosive moment was because it shredded that hypocrisy." In another controversial scene, Goldie asks Warren, "Were there other women?" and he answers, "Well, there were a few times at the shop—let's face it, I fucked them all."[41]

Ringing up his old friend Valerie Allen, Warren invited her to a preview. "I was in total shock," she recalled. "They filmed [much of it] in my [former] house. Bob Evans had been there many times, because when we were in acting class, we would rehearse at each other's homes. And of course Warren had been there. At the preview, I'm watching my living room, my kitchen, my wonderful dressing room with all the plants—the room in the film where the hairdresser [George Roundy] is talking to [Julie Christie]. In the final scene, when he's asking Julie to marry him, there's a shot of her getting in her car, and they used my driveway. There's even a little dog in the scene, like my poodle, Jezebel, that all my friends at that time knew."

Geffen gave a party after the preview at the Screen Directors Guild, and one guest was overheard saying, "They should have got Jon Peters to play himself." For the Guild screening, Chasen's catered, and around the buffet table, half the hairdressers in West Hollywood and Beverly Hills claimed they were the models for George. "Sure, it's me," said Gene Shacove. "Me and Jay Sebring . . . but more me than him."[42] In another room, Richard Alcala stood in line for chili, accompanied by his wife, Carrie. "Yeah, it's me," said Alcala, "no doubt about it." George Masters said he saw a touch of himself in Roundy, and Ara Gallant,

Faye Dunaway's old beau, also recognized some of his traits. The only denial—but not exactly a flat one—came from Vidal Sassoon, who said he never indulged in kiss-and-tell games.

After a screening for critics, Warren, Julie Christie, Bob Towne, and Julie Payne took Pauline Kael out to dinner. Predictably, her review was a rave, liberally sprinkled with references to Bergman's *Smiles of a Summer Night*. Bob Towne, not Warren, came in for the lion's share of Kael's praise. "Towne had Kael wrapped around his finger," says Buck Henry.[43] Warren's contribution was more appreciated in liberal Washington, which was delighted with *Shampoo*'s political savvy. When Warren visited the capital to promote the film, a luncheon was given for him in the Senate dining room by California senators John Tunney and Alan Cranston. "Vietnam polarized the town," Warren recalled. "*Shampoo*'s audience was the audience that didn't want to go to war, that used every means to end the war." Guests at the luncheon included Hubert Humphrey, Edward (Ted) Kennedy, Birch Bayh, Jacob Javits, Walter Mondale, Daniel Inouye, and George McGovern. Following the meal, Warren and McGovern conferred in private. Later Warren observed, "Politicians today are the real stars, aren't they? They are the fascinating people."

In a headline in her influential syndicated *Los Angeles Times* column, Joyce Haber speculated, "McGovern-Beatty in '76?" At the time, Haber, founder of L.A. society's infamous A-list, was cited by *Women's Wear Daily* as "one of the ten most powerful women in media." She was certainly one of the best informed, talking with people like Henry Kissinger almost daily. Her report of a possible McGovern-Beatty ticket probably came from reliable sources. This was still the seventies, before Ronald Reagan and Sonny Bono made their breakthroughs into national politics. Warren was their forerunner, and, moreover, he had some pretty good ideas. As long ago as 1974, he was talking about campaign finance reform. "Until that issue is solved, the right people can't be elected," he said. "Money talks." Had he been able to focus his energies, to live a day of his life without surrendering to the imperious urge of sex and the distraction of fractured romances, he could have become vice president, and then, perhaps, president. His popularity and behind-the-scenes fund-raising made him very attractive to the Democratic Party, and the American voting public often favors mavericks. But he held back, lacking the confidence and dedication that later propelled Ronald Reagan into the White House.

Warren's main achievement would be on the screen rather than in politics, and, with the release of *Shampoo*, one of his consummations as a New Hollywood auteur was upon him. Like *Bonnie and Clyde*, *Shampoo* was a watershed movie, demonstrating that the experimentations of Fellini and Resnais could be brought to bear on contemporary American experience. "The *La Dolce Vita* for the 1970s," wrote Judith Crist in *New York* magazine, adding that the film also marked Warren's "best comedy performance to date." Charles Champlin of the *Los Angeles Times* said that "*Shampoo* will be worth studying a century from now to know what a part of our times was like." And Richard Cuskelly of the *Los Angeles Herald Examiner* called it "the first unblinking, unblushing, unembarrassed sorting of the social confusions in which we all found ourselves floundering in the late 1960s."

Its well-deserved success brought in thirty million dollars in the first three months, and the already-rich Warren was suddenly six million dollars richer. Bob Towne felt Warren's production company owed him approximately one million dollars, since he had been promised 5 percent of the gross from the point where the film earned four times the cost of the negative, which was sixteen million dollars. Confronting Warren at the Beverly Wilshire, Towne complained that he hadn't received anything near his fair share. "Begelman fucked us," Warren said, explaining Columbia's rolling-gross deal. "He fucked you," Towne replied, "he didn't fuck me. My deal was with you, and you neglected to tell me that this deal was worth less than half of what I thought it was."[44] Shrugging, Warren said, "You know what they say about Hollywood. You don't get rich on your last picture, you get rich on your next picture." "That may have been true when I worked on *Bonnie and Clyde* for eight thousand dollars," Towne said, "but the future is now, as far as I'm concerned. I'm not gonna sue, and I'll still be your friend, but I'm never gonna work with you again. This is absolutely chickenshit."

A millionaire many times over—*Shampoo* eventually made thirty-five million dollars at home and fifteen million dollars overseas—Warren could have afforded to give Towne a bonus, even though Towne's deal had already been doubled on two occasions, and he received more than Goldie Hawn, Julie Christie, or Hal Ashby.[45] Still, Towne was not a friend Warren could afford to lose. In stonewalling the writer who'd helped him create *Bonnie and Clyde* and *Shampoo*, Warren would be the ultimate loser, for the star's work would rarely again be as interesting. In this case at least, a tight fist was his undoing.

The breach with his intimate friend was not entirely his fault. A success in business, art, and love, Warren was often resented by less fortunate men. According to Towne's ex-wife, Julie Payne, "Robert became very jealous of other people's work or success. It wasn't just Warren that Robert wanted to be. It was Francis [Ford Coppola], Jack [Nicholson]." Adds Robert Evans, "Bob claims to have done a lot more writing for Warren than Warren says he did. If I had to bet, I'd bet on Warren. He has a clearer head." But if that were the case, why did Beatty's work go into an immediate decline without Towne? The second half of the seventies was a wash—Warren's "clearer head" did nothing to redeem Adrien Joyce's silly script for *The Fortune* in 1975 or Elaine May's criminally lame dialogue for *Heaven Can Wait* in 1978. Adrien Joyce (a pseudonym for Carole Eastman) had served Jack Nicholson much better in 1970's *Five Easy Pieces*.

The artistic conflict between Beatty and Towne during the writing of *Shampoo* was perhaps responsible for the curious schism in the film's critical reception. Though the press was generally favorable, Jay Cocks of *Time* wrote, perceptively, "*Shampoo* is a problem . . . crafty, funny and high-spirited, but sometimes—even simultaneously—it is wormy and disingenous. . . . The reason, presumably, for setting the movie in 1968 is to groom George, the last shabby survivor of the age of grooviness, into a sardonic metaphor. There are many references to the Nixon election, and at times the movie appears to be attempting a delineation of the moral neutrality that could produce a Nixon and a Watergate. . . . The ending is a betrayal of all that is best in the film, revealing that the filmmakers have been interested in apologizing for George, not satirizing him. . . . *Shampoo* wants it both ways: wants a few laughs off George and wants, too, to bare his sensitive, desperate soul. It turns out that he is a figure looking for pity, and it hardly seems worth it." Film historian Leonard Maltin, reassessing *Shampoo* a quarter of a century later, found its satire "muddy" and its few "bright moments lost in [this] dreary comedy-drama by Beatty and Robert Towne."[46] But *Shampoo*'s reputation seems secure. The American Film Institute's millennial "Top 100 Comedies" list ranked it at number forty-seven, between *Manhattan* and *A Shot in the Dark*. The institute's number-one favorite was *Some Like It Hot*, followed by *Tootsie* at number two, and *Dr. Strangelove* at number three.

The Oscar awards ceremony in 1975 marked an unusual instance of a brother and sister both being nominated for Academy Awards—Warren in the writing category, for the screenplay of *Shampoo*, and Shirley as producer of the documentary *The Other Half of the Sky: A China Memoir*. The '75 Oscars were presented on March 29, 1976, at the Dorothy Chandler Pavilion in Los Angeles, with Goldie Hawn acting as one of the emcees. Jack Nicholson took home the Best Actor Oscar for *One Flew Over the Cuckoo's Nest*. Though Warren and Bob Towne lost in the Best Original Screenplay category to Frank Pierson for *Dog Day Afternoon*, Lee Grant won the Best Supporting Actress award for her performance in *Shampoo*. Jack Warden was also nominated in the supporting category, but he lost to George Burns for *The Sunshine Boys*. Nominated for Best Art Direction–Set Decoration, *Shampoo*'s Richard Sylbert and Stewart Campbell lost to Ken Adam, Roy Walker, and Vernon Dixon for Kubrick's sumptuous *Barry Lyndon*.

Though devoid of an Oscar, Warren was—according to the National Association of Theater Owners, an organization representing eight hundred movie theaters across the U.S.—Male Star of the Year. He asked the association not to publicize its choice but agreed to appear with Ann-Margret, who won Female Star of the Year, at the October 2 awards banquet in New Orleans's Fairmount Hotel. Another prize came from Harvard University, whose Hasty Pudding Club named him Man of the Year, citing his work as an actor as well as filmmaker and political activist. Previous honorees included Bob Hope, James Stewart, Paul Newman—and Shirley MacLaine, who'd been Hasty Pudding's Woman of the Year in 1963.

Julie was reportedly involved with a U.S. industrialist while Warren pursued Russian actress Viktoria Fyodorova, but no one was surprised to see Julie and Warren together again at the London opening of *Shampoo* and later dining at Leith's restaurant in Notting Hill. Warren found it hard to give her up, especially after he'd taken her to visit his parents. "Of all his girlfriends Julie was our favorite," said Ira Beaty. "She was a real lady, with those lovely English manners. But Warren's a real nomad, like Shirley."[47]

Shampoo received an adoring reevaluation on the occasion of the release of a sparkling new print in August 2000. "*Shampoo*, which could be thought of as the original *Sex and the City*, returns for its twenty-fifth anniversary at a most opportune time, as we grapple with who we are and where we're going in the new millennium," wrote Bill Desowitz in the *Los Angeles Times*. The critic added that the film was "one of the most incisive of the decade, capturing a tumultuous era with poignant accuracy. *Shampoo* has lost none of its edge or heart. In fact, there's an overriding sense of melancholy about the empty lives and wasted opportunities that may touch us more profoundly today now that we have greater distance and perspective on the tragic ramifications." All the performances held up, especially Julie's ("never sexier or more beguiling"), Goldie's ("never more endearing or fragile"), and Warren's: his "libidinous hairdresser has trouble gathering thoughts or finishing sentences, much like the actor in real life," wrote Desowitz. "Yet he's gentle, naive, intuitive, and physical, a real dreamer, like all the characters Beatty has played throughout his career. But this character seems the most personal."

When Warren's old friend and mentor Charlie Feldman fell seriously ill in the late sixties, Warren rushed to his bedside. "In 1968 Charlie Feldman, who I once dated, was in the hospital," recalls Valerie Allen. "Warren phoned me to go see Charlie. By this time, I was already married to Troy Donahue. Troy did not want me to go to Charlie's hospital room. I've always been sorry I didn't.

"After I married Troy—after three years of that relationship—I lost everything, the house, even my passion for the business. I was not in good shape. I was still in love with Troy when I came home one night and my mother said, 'Warren Beatty called.' I went up to my bedroom, and he called again about an hour later. I just said, 'Oh, hi, Warren.' He asked, 'Didn't your mother tell you I called?' 'I don't want to have coffee,' I said. 'I don't want to eat. I don't want to do anything.' He kept insisting, 'Come on. Come on. We'll go for a drive. We'll talk.' He was just incredible. We went out, driving down to Malibu in the night. Warren is a great listener, and I was going on and on about Troy. 'You know,' he said, 'you should have been a star.' I know he was trying to pick my spirits up, but on that particular night, when I had nothing left to give, it didn't have the effect on me it should have. But I'll always appreciate how sweet he was. He was really a good friend that night, very comforting."[48]

He often put himself out for women friends when they were in various kinds of trouble. Elaine May, whom he'd known since 1964, got embroiled in litigation with Barry Diller of Paramount when the studio refused to give her $180,000 to complete a film she'd directed there entitled *Mikey and Nicky*. Rather than hand over the unfinished film to Paramount and relinquish her right to the final cut, she ran off with it, and Paramount sued for breach of contract. Telephoning Barry Diller on her behalf, Warren urged the studio to give her the

$180,000 just to get her off its back, since Paramount's legal bill was approaching five million dollars. But Diller said Elaine May could "go to jail or the madhouse for ten years before I submit to blackmail."[49] Eventually she surrendered the cut to Diller, but her work in Hollywood thereafter was somewhat sporadic.

Despite protestations of having closed out his old life, Warren cruised Sunset Boulevard with Roman Polanski and Jack Nicholson, picking up girls, the younger the better. To the degree that anyone can be judged by the company he keeps, Warren was bordering on sleaze, particularly in his involvement with Hugh Hefner, whose magazine was increasingly pornographic. Said Bob Towne, "In the ten years I've known Warren, I haven't seen him lose his interest in women and doubt if I *ever* will. When you are excessively handsome *and* charming *and* witty *and* intelligent, the opportunities are vast. In Warren's case, they are greater than any other man's times ten! And he takes advantage of them"[50]

By the 1970s, at Hef's mansions, celebrities like Warren, George Plimpton, and Paddy Chayefsky were often in evidence. The Bel Air mansion on Charing Cross Road boasted a revolving bed, pinball machines, and twenty-four-hour sex. An impressive road led to the house, bordered by tennis courts, gardens stocked with peacocks, a pool, and a cave-enclosed Jacuzzi. Buck Henry, in foggy glasses and little else, favored the Jacuzzi, where he often had a girl under each arm.[51] Bikini-clad soubrettes Barbi Benton and Dorothy Stratton romped in the garden.

At the massive stone house, a valet was on duty to park guests' cars. Inside, a long dinner table was always well stocked with snacks. Two impressive staircases led to the upper floor, where the various rooms bore the names of colors—the Red Room, the Green Room. There was a screening room and a library. Liv Ullmann recalled a night in the screening room, where "the Playboy king is wearing terry-cloth pajamas. . . . We look at films: A dog makes love to a girl. . . . Afterward we sit in small groups, not knowing what to talk about because our host is asleep on the sofa. . . . I walk through the grounds. Inside a subterranean grotto with swirling warmed waves two people are doing things in the water under red and blue spotlights."[52] Near the grotto was the sunroom, complete with tanning machines. Throughout the estate, there were convenient nooks and crannies for guests to have sex any time they scored.

A girl who identified herself to a reporter only as Liza, a blond high-school dropout and Jerry Hall look-alike, who claimed to have had sex with Warren, George Harrison, Rod Stewart, David Crosby, Jack Wagner, Timothy Hutton, Adnan Khashoggi, and Don Henley, described a typical night at the mansion. When she arrived, she was invited into Hef's bedroom. A voyeur, he asked if he could watch Liza and her friend Marcia make out. He was content just watching. Thereafter the two girls became regulars at the mansion. Later, Liza became a Bunny at the Century City Playboy Club.[53]

"We lived in the same neighborhood as Don Henley and Warren Beatty," Liza recalled. One day, Warren dropped by, and he started flirting with her. Liza was intrigued. As Warren's next-door neighbor, she'd long beheld "sexy, hard bodies parade in and out of his home, one after the other." When Warren later called and told her, "Come over right away, Liza. I'm waiting for you," she went next door and rang his bell, taking care not to wear panties under her skirt. She was surprised to find Warren with Sean Penn. "I don't know if Warren had thoughts about a threesome, but I wasn't interested," she said.[54] A few days later, Warren called again, telling her he couldn't get any sleep from thinking about her, and his desire was driving him nuts. She decided to have sex with him, and they arranged to meet at her mother's house near Beverly Hills.

When he arrived, he virtually tackled her, pushing her across the room, knocking the breath out of her, and pinning her to a couch. His hands groped at her roughly, hurting her. He ripped her clothes off. In the next minute or so, he had an orgasm, then got dressed, combed his hair, and departed. In his earlier telephone calls, he had tricked her into thinking he really cared for her. Understandably, she felt she'd been duped. "He's a pretty good actor, after all," she mused.[55]

Not long afterward, Liza became a ten-thousand-dollar-a-night call girl. "After Warren Beatty, if any of the next ten men in my life talked about love, I thought to myself, 'Yeah, sure.' " She didn't have to worry about love talk from the Eagles' Don Henley, with whom she went shopping for sex toys at a porn store, browsing among the "potions, paddles, shackles, handcuffs, and pussy-puffs." With other hookers, she participated in orgies with Henley but later said, "I hated how he smelled. It wasn't that he didn't bathe, it was just that he had done so many drugs and had drunk so much alcohol in his life that the smell came out through his skin."[56]

With the advent of women's lib, the sex scene at the Playboy mansion started winding down. Attacking Hef, one feminist pointed out that the *Playboy* idea was based on the stupid assumption that only young women can be sexually alluring. Bolder magazines like *Penthouse*, spawned by sexists who followed in Hef's footsteps, cut into *Playboy*'s circulation, and soon the magazine as well as the clubs and hotels were losing money.

Jack Nicholson called Warren "Master Beatty," whether in reference to auto-eroticism, superior cocksmanship, or fabled negotiating ability, only Nicholson knows. Sometimes Jack frequented Hollywood madam Heidi Fleiss's nefarious blasts at her house at 1270 Tower Road in Beverly Hills. At a birthday blowout Fleiss threw for Mick Jagger, Nicholson met a five-foot-eleven-inch, ash-blond call girl named Tiffany. Charlie Sheen, one of Fleiss's regular clients, was present that day, though he disappeared with a girl who later told Tiffany that he always added a generous tip to her two-thousand-dollar fee. Fleiss brought Jack over to Tiffany, introduced them, and then rounded up another girl and told Nicholson he could have both of them for free. Instead, Nicholson took Tiffany home with him, to his Oriental-seraglio-type house. With geisha-like finesse, Tiffany massaged his entire body as they lay in bed, then straddled him and brushed her long hair from his toes to his nose. Later Tiffany said, "I've never known any really big star to pay for sex. They know they can get it for free." On their second date, she held and caressed his Academy Award as he made love to her. Their relationship consisted of six months of "Sunday visits [when the servants were off] and hot sex." On one occasion, he playfully chased her around the house brandishing a Ping-Pong paddle. Tiffany noted that Jack usually had at least one male friend around whenever sex was in the offing, "eager to share whatever Jack felt like sharing." And there was usually another girl present, as well as plenty of cocaine. Heidi Fleiss eventually ran afoul of the law, and was convicted of money laundering and tax evasion. Later, while dating burly *Saving Private Ryan* star Tom Sizemore, she was sentenced to six months' house arrest for testing positive for methamphetamines, a violation of her federal probation.[57]

By 1975, Beatty and Nicholson were so close that they co-starred in a property Beatty owned, *The Fortune*. Warren went to Warner Bros. and sweet-talked the executives into giving Nicholson his first $1.5 million fee, collecting the same amount for himself. "I don't wish on my worst enemy negotiations with that man," said a Warner executive. A thirty-two-year-old, pre-*Rose* Bette Midler was approached for the feminine lead, a runaway heiress. Mike Nichols, who already had *The Graduate* and *Who's Afraid of Virginia Woolf?* to his credit, was to direct *The Fortune*. Midler and her manager, Aaron Russo, met with Nichols, who offered her equal salary and billing with Beatty and Nicholson. The brassy Miss M looked the director in the eye and said, "What other movies have you done?" Newcomer Stockard Channing got the part. Said Midler's agent, "I smelled something rotten about it from the start."[58]

In this instance, Russo could hardly have been more clairvoyant. *The Fortune* was a stillborn mess. Enraged by Nichols's demand for cuts, screenwriter Carole Eastman refused to finish the script, and the director finally informed the actors, "We're never going to have a complete script, we're going to start anyway."[59] Warren and Jack played two con men who lure a sanitary-napkin heiress into marrying one of them so they can cheat her out of her money. Recalls designer Donfeld, "The dreaded Sylberts—twins Richard and Paul and Paul's then-wife Anthea—all served Beatty's *The Fortune*. They didn't have enough money to make the picture, but Anthea Sylbert somehow managed to squeeze *mink-lined* Levi-Strauss blue-denim jackets for Beatty, Jack Nicholson, and Mike Nichols from the budget. Ah, Hollywood."

On and off the set, Nicholson looked up to Warren, regarding him as the ultimate smoothie. "I got from Warren a trick he learned in English theater," he recalled. "If you're going to be lit for a photograph, you put dark powder here [at the hairline] because it keeps the light from making the hair you do have disappear." Off-hours, he watched Warren operate at parties. One of Jack's biographers later wrote that Warren "eyeballed his catch, smooth-talked the lady, escorted her home, and ended up having a fabulous time. No hard feelings. Whereas Jack was still lost where women were concerned. He perpetually fell in love, even for the one-night stand, and always seemed to be crying in his beer. ... Warren, even wind-tousled, was impeccably handsome. Nicholson remained self-conscious about his physical imperfections: his receding hairline, the acne scars on his back, his shortness."[60] According to Robin Williams, Nicholson referred to an erection as "a *major* chubby."[61]

Warren loved Jack as a friend and actor, and years later, in 1984, would say, "Let me describe him in sports terms; with Wayne Gretsky you have a hockey team, with Kareem Abdul-Jabbar you have a basketball team, with Babe Ruth you have a baseball team. With Jack you have a movie."[62] Not always, you don't. Not even Nicholson, his Best Actor Oscar notwithstanding, could save *The*

Fortune. Jerry Oster of the *New York Daily News* called the film "a painful illustration of the limits of the star system. . . . Cast for their box-office clout, without consideration of whether they're really a good team, Warren Beatty as Nicky, and Jack Nicholson as Oscar, get all knotted up in their idiosyncrasies. Each is a subtle scene-stealer, and the intensity with which they work at it keeps them from playing off each other with anything like the effectiveness that Paul Newman and Robert Redford had in *The Sting*."

Nicholson was in the midst of his affair with Michelle Phillips. "Where my head is at now," he told *Playboy*, "expanding sexuality is not most satisfied through promiscuity but through continuously communicating with someone specifically." In Michelle's estimation, the only areas Nicholson's sexuality was expanding in were jealousy and possessiveness. "The idea of living with [Jack] was just horrible," she said, "because he's set in his ways. . . . Jack was always peering in the windows to see what I was up to."[63] She also objected to his sleeping around on her and hanging out in nightclubs until all hours, coming home stoned and loaded.[64]

Despite the joys of supposedly "continuously communicating" with Michelle, Jack dropped her the minute Anjelica Huston made herself available to him. Anjelica was *très chic* at the time, thanks to her stark, angular beauty and impressive lineage as the daughter of one of Hollywood's favorite living legends, director John Huston. Although Nicholson was a star, he was still impressionable enough to leap at the chance to bed down the fashion magazines' girl of the year. According to Ron Bernstein, who left Paramount to produce *Killer Bees* for Robert Stigwood, "Anjelica Huston's heart was broken. They had a long affair, and she was so sure that he would marry her. It's 2002, and he hasn't married yet."

Nicholson relished having lots of sex with women, but basically didn't like them. During the early part of a relationship, he would spend most of his time pulling away from them. When the girl got fed up—usually while he was on location—he'd go ballistic, frantic over losing control. According to Nicholson's friend Harry Gittes, after whom Nicholson named the character Jake Gittes in *Chinatown*, "Jack always has the same dynamic with women—tremendous push-pull. . . . Who can have a relationship with an actor who goes on location with beautiful women, wanna fuck 'im?"[65] As Ingmar Bergman, who, like Vadim, made stars of his mistresses, once put it, "Film work is a powerfully erotic business."[66]

Sarah Porterfield recalls, "After Jack Nicholson, Michelle Phillips was doing Warren." Jack's feelings were hurt when he found out, and for a while Warren's relationship with Jack underwent some strain. The rather baroque and Machiavellian method by which Michelle was transferred from Jack to Warren was explained in *Jack's Life* by Patrick McGilligan: "The New Age Rat Pack passed the same scripts and drugs and women around. Not only did Nicholson have a romantic relationship with Michelle Phillips, but he also notched reported affairs with two of Dennis Hopper's other ex-wives—Brooke Hayward and former avant-garde dancer Daria Halprin, the leading lady of Michelangelo Antonioni's only motion picture made in America, *Zabriskie Point*. By late spring of 1973, Michelle Phillips had left Nicholson, vacating the extra house. Shortly thereafter, the ex-Mama took up with Warren Beatty, whom Mike Nichols had brought together with Nicholson to promote their friendship. Especially because it was the dapper Beatty who bested him, friends say, Nicholson found himself depressed."[67]

Part of Nicholson's insecurity harked back to his tangled and bizarre parentage. He did not realize until *Time* devoted a cover story to him in 1974 that his sister June was really his mother. Ethel May, the woman he'd thought was his mother, was actually his grandmother. She'd taken over Jack's rearing after chasing off the irresponsible bigamist who'd got June pregnant with Jack.[68]

Warren knew that Jack wouldn't stay mad at him very long over Michelle. Indeed, some of their friends suggest that the scene in *The Fortune* in which Warren and Jack pass Stockard Channing back and forth between them like a football reflects their attitude toward Michelle.[69] Warren and Jack were really more interested in each other than in any woman. They took brief trips together, and had weekly sleepovers.[70] They attended parties in Beverly Hills and Bel Air, and took in boxing matches. *Time* reported that "an occasional recreation of [Nicholson's] and Warren Beatty's is riding around town, skunk spotting on the street." The *New York Times* added that Jack "still sophomorically goes on random girl-hunts in a car with his friend Warren Beatty."

Nicholson's onetime acting rival Bruce Dern, husband of Diane Ladd and father of Laura Dern, attributed much of Warren and Jack's reputation as cocksmen to pure hype, pointing out that Jack "brags about a lot more pussy than he's ever gotten. I'd say if you cut half of his pussy in half, you'd have it about right, and still he probably gets more than anybody around. He and Beatty have contests about it. They talk in those terms. Jack'll say, 'Hey, I left Hefner's—' Well, anybody gets laid at Hefner's, come on, you know what I mean."[71] Behind all the sexist talk was a lot of hostility and insecure masculinity, according to Jack's uncle, George (Shorty) Smith, whom Jack once described as his "surrogate father-hero." "I think Jack hates women," Shorty told *Time*.[72]

Warren was far more serious about Michelle than Jack had ever been. He had dallied with her in the past but was now ready to have a full-fledged affair and perhaps even marriage. John Phillips had remarried and was no longer a threat; his new wife was Genevieve (Gen) Waite, a Cape Town, South Africa, beauty who starred in the popular and controversial sixties film *Joanna*, in which she bore a child by a black lover. *Joanna* was produced by Leslie Caron's husband Michael Laughlin, bearing out the fact that Hollywood is, after all, a small company town, where everybody, eventually, is connected with everybody else.

Michelle still harbored acting ambitions, even after her hapless debut in Dennis Hopper's *Last Movie*. She subsequently married Hopper, but the union lasted only a week and became known around Hollywood as the Six-day War. Hopper fired guns in their honeymoon house in Taos, New Mexico, and handcuffed Michelle to keep her from fleeing. Stoned and crazed, he thought she was a witch. Finally she managed to escape while he was asleep, but he chased her to the airport and drove his car onto the runway, attempting to block the plane.[73] She and daughter Chynna Gilliam Phillips sought refuge in the Bel Air home of ex-husband John Phillips, Chynna's father.[74]

Emotionally, Michelle was a mirror image of Warren. She'd had many lovers, including fellow Mamas-and-Papas singer Denny Doherty; record mogul Lou Adler; French actor Christian Marquand; and blond, blue-eyed Scott McKenzie, the singer of "San Francisco," anthem of the Summer of Love.[75] Then, in quick succession, came Jack and Warren. "I knew Michelle from the start when she was with Jack Nicholson and then Warren," says Dick Sylbert. "She didn't know whose lap to sit on when we did *The Fortune*." Some time after the film opened on May 25, 1975, at the Coronet in Manhattan, Michelle opted for Warren's lap. She accompanied him when he went to Colorado to spend Christmas 1975 in Nicholson's Aspen lodge. Like a scene out of *Bob and Carol and Ted and Alice*, the three of them celebrated the Yuletide together. After the holidays, Michelle still preferred Warren, who by now was alternating between El Escondido and his Mulholland Drive hilltop home. Michelle moved in with him on Mulholland, bringing Chynna, who'd been born in 1968, just as Michelle's marriage to John Phillips had begun to crumble.

"Warren was over at Michelle Phillips's all the time," recalls Tricia Pelham Clinton Hope, who later married into the British nobility but at the time was acting in Hollywood, "and he'd be flirting with another woman there, and, you know, hoping she wouldn't catch him, but Michelle was always walking up behind him.[76] A reporter from *Los Angeles* magazine overheard Michelle trying to "drag" Warren off for a weekend in Palm Springs. He was more interested in attending the Democratic Party's 1975 mini-convention in Kansas City as a delegate-at-large from California—"to watch and listen," he said.

The following winter he ran into his old girlfriend Jennifer Lee, who was now studying acting with Milton Katselas. He told Jennifer he was in love with Michelle, and added, "Michelle knows me the way you knew me. She's seen me all ways." But he couldn't resist hitting on Jennifer. "You look better than I've ever seen you," he said. Later, he rang and suggested a threesome with Michelle. Irritably, Jennifer snapped, "*I'm* not the object." After affairs with Gordon Lightfoot, who made "drunken, fumbly love," and Don Johnson ("drugs and drinks until he passes out, but he's a lot of fun until he gets there . . . lots of energy"), Jennifer met the love of her life, comedian Richard Pryor, and settled down. Unfortunately Richard was addicted to freebase cocaine, and was so self-destructive that he set himself afire with the 151-proof rum that he used for smoking base.[77] The loyal Jennifer would eventually end up as his caregiver after he developed multiple sclerosis.

Meanwhile, Warren and Michelle appeared to be making a go of their relationship, although Warren stayed mostly at his digs at the Beverly Wilshire. Nevertheless, each morning, like a good suburban father, he drove Chynna to school, at the wheel of his tobacco-brown Mercedes Benz 450 SL sedan. Marriage no longer seemed so threatening to him as he approached his fortieth year, and he tentatively broached the subject with Michelle, whose beauty, with its rare Dresden-china quality, always moved him. She took him at his word, but soon he started flirting with a female journalist. Catching them at it, Michelle told the woman, "He likes monogamy just fine."[78]

His behavior in the 1970s hardly bore her out. Michelle made the mistake of letting him go alone to England for the *Shampoo* opening. In no time, he was dating other women. The seventies saw the rise of brilliant singer-songwriters, and he romanced two of the best, Carly Simon and Joni Mitchell. He tried to concentrate on one girl at a time, but he remained cynical enough to quip, "The best time to get married is noon. That way, if things don't work out, you haven't blown the whole day." Despite his frequent protestations of wanting to mature, he sounded like a man who'd relapsed into incorrigible satyriasis. Marriage, he said, had "fallen on hard times. That has nothing to do with romance or love, though. They exist without it. I like to think that I picked up on living with people ten years before it happened."[79] Though suffering from a behavioral disorder, he was so mired in denial that he regarded himself as a sexual pioneer.

Michelle finally realized she couldn't let him out of her sight if she expected to keep him away from other women. This proved difficult, since she was still a working woman, with numerous professional obligations. In order to accompany him to Rome for another *Shampoo* premiere, she had to cancel a long-scheduled recording date and pay off the session musicians.[80]

Warren's house in L.A. had rarely been used, but now he and Michelle at last took possession of it, engaging decorators and resurfacing the tennis court. A prime L.A. location, one that commands a breathtaking view of the city, Mulholland Drive is a winding mountain road dividing Hollywood from the the San Fernando Valley, and it connects the Valley's several canyons—Beverly Glen, Coldwater, Benedict, and Laurel. Open and airy, Warren's house was situated on several acres of manufactured knoll, behind a stand of fruit trees and plants. When he'd first acquired the house, there were stuffed African animals all over the place. In redecorating, he chose a minimal look—distinctly modern, spare, no pictures, white walls, wood floors, and curving windows—with the sad result that his home would never achieve a lived-in feeling. "It's a house where you know there's nothing to look at but whose house it is," says an acquaintance. When an unfortunate man named Steve Wolf was murdered nearby, a terrified Warren spent two hundred thousand dollars to build a kidnap-proof vault, replete with half-inch-thick steel-plated walls and closed-circuit TV. "As soon as the kidnappers knock on the door, Beatty simply locks himself inside," wrote *Los Angeles* magazine.[81]

Perhaps unsurprisingly, Warren still couldn't bring himself to give up his suite at the Beverly Wilshire, and Michelle also maintained a separate apartment. When Warren was in his Mulholland residence, he spent much of his time by the large swimming pool or in the lagoon or jacuzzi. There was also a gym, a theater (where Margaux Hemingway liked to screen *Rebel Without a Cause*),[82] a cook, and a secretary.

When Warren and Michelle flew to New York, they visited John Phillips, whose musical *Man on the Moon* was opening on Broadway, starring his wife Gen Waite. The two couples often dined together, although John was sleeping with an ex-model friend of Gen's. On opening night Gen unsuccessfully tried to kill herself, and then had to go onstage and sing, though she was still hoarse from the tube that had been inserted in her throat at Lenox Hill Hospital. Predictably, the show was an unmitigated disaster and closed immediately. Despite Julia Phillips's documentation of John Phillips's impressive sexual endowment, Gen confessed that the first person to satisfy her sexually was a stunning young actress named Julia Robinson, a Jack Nicholson protégé who briefly appeared in *The King of Marvin Gardens*.[83]

Michelle sailed to England on the *QEII* to co-star with Rudolf Nureyev in Ken Russell's *Valentino*, as Natasha Rambova, the Latin lover's mistress, and Warren stayed behind in America. In London, Mick Jagger developed a crush on Michelle, while John Phillips, who followed her to London, ended up in bed with Mick's wife, Bianca, in the Jaggers' Glebe Place home. One day, Gen Waite burst in on John and Bianca in Mick's bed, and stormed out. She cooled off in Paris with Jack Nicholson and his girlfriend Ann Marshall. Mick, who raised no objection to John's dalliance with Bianca, took John to Wimbledon and sought his advice on how to woo Michelle. "I love that woman," Mick said. "I want to be with her. How can I do it?" John later got the impression "that [Mick] figured out a way while she was filming *Valentino*."[84]

Warren was still talking marriage when Michelle returned to Los Angeles. She had never looked more soignée or lovely. Warren's prospective stepdaughter, Chynna, was now eight, with long blond hair and blue eyes. Somewhat disturbed by having seen her father, John, shooting up heroin in London, Chynna climbed into bed with Michelle one night and asked, "Mommy, do drugs kill you?" Though the scene around John Phillips was drenched with every recreational drug from coke to intravenous smack, Warren somehow managed to remain squeaky clean. Michelle, after heavy acid use in her early days in the Mamas and the Papas, had distanced herself from drugs, and she was a protective, committed, and affectionate parent.[85]

One day Warren and Michelle's public display of carnality had the unwitting effect of propelling the antsy David Geffen further along his path to becoming Hollywood's preeminent power broker. Geffen was sitting poolside at the Beverly Hills Hotel with Warren and Michelle when the couple's amorousness got out of control. Some distance away they were being observed by director Marty Davidson and realtor Bob Tisch, whose son Steve would later produce *Forrest Gump*. "Warren and Michelle were necking at a cabana," Davidson recalls, "and David was just looking around, as if he were a little uncomfortable. Warren kept kissing her, and finally David spotted us and jumped up and came over to our table. I think he was glad to get away from them." Geffen proceeded to charm Bob Tisch, persuading him to "adopt" him and help him become a captain of industry.[86]

The primary bond in the unlikely pairing of Beatty and Geffen was a mutual obsession with power. Though a success in the record business, Geffen longed to be an important figure in movies, and in the mid-1970s, he used his connection with Warren to butter up Warner Bros. mogul Ted Ashley, telling him that his buddy Warren had tipped him off about some hot properties that could make a lot of money for the studio. Impressed, Ashley hired Geffen, hoping he'd reinvigorate the flagging studio.[87] Geffen was named vice chairman of Warner Bros. and would prove useful to Warren when he needed to raise money for his projects.

Geffen looked to Warren for an intimate kind of mentoring, often sharing his emotional issues, which were complex and painful, since Geffen was still concealing his homosexuality. He and Warren had Joni Mitchell in common. Warren had romanced her, but it was Geffen who discovered her and turned her into one of the recording industry's enduring stars. Geffen confided that he wasn't happy with his homosexuality, and Warren sent him to his shrink. Before long, Geffen was seeing Dr. Grotjahn five times a week, and later appeared to find heterosexual bliss with Cher, who became his mistress.

Cher and Warren participated in a surprise birthday party for Geffen in the Grand Trianon Room in the Beverly Wilshire Hotel, at which Cher sang "Happy Birthday to You," "All I Really Want to Do," and "Mockingbird." Entertainment also included a knife thrower, a cyclist, two mimes, a fire-eater, two wrestlers, and a fortune-teller. Among the seventy guests were Bob Dylan, Robbie Robertson, Ahmet Ertegun, Jack Nicholson, Ringo Starr, and Mo Ostin. A gullible Hollywood celebrated the odd couple's happiness.

Cher's decision to leave a straight husband, Sonny Bono, in order to take up with Geffen, who would shortly come out as a full-fledged gay, understandably threw her into emotional bedlam. Trying to help her cope, Geffen sent her to his and Warren's shrink, Dr. Grotjahn, but it turned out to be a serious blunder. Cher soon ditched Geffen for heterosexual Gregg Allman, a heroin addict strong on masculine sex appeal and kick-ass rock.

The diminutive Geffen went ballistic, telling Cher he wanted his presents back and threatening, "If you see me walking down the street, you better cross over to the other side." Not one to be easily intimidated, Cher retaliated by telling *Time* that Geffen was a "short, ugly man." Though accompanied by a smiling Warren and Michelle during a stroll down Sunset Boulevard, an unshaven Geffen looked anxious and miserable.[88]

Warren was torn between his loyalty to two feuding friends, but he opportunistically sided with Geffen, who, though unfamiliar to the public, was a Hollywood power to be reckoned with and far more useful than Cher. While with Warren one day, Geffen broke down in tears, bitterly complaining that his shrink should never have taken on Cher as a client. Dr. Grotjahn, of course, had only done so at Geffen's insistence. Finally the beleaguered doctor had to fire Cher. Geffen checked out of the Beverly Hills Hotel and moved into Warren's house on Mulholland to mend his broken heart.[89] Or was it his ego? In would-be macho Hollywood, a town often ruled by homophobic homosexuals, Cher had been the perfect gay blind.

When Warren and Michelle decided at last to get married, Michelle chose the most romantic setting conceivable for the ceremony: the island of Bali, in the far-flung Indonesian archipelago. On the way, Warren had second thoughts and started dropping obvious hints about marriage being a "dead institution."[90] Notwithstanding his public humiliation of Natalie Wood, he rarely was ungentlemanly enough to walk out on women, but he knew how to goad them into leaving him, by simply refusing to conceal his restlessness and boredom. He and Michelle stayed at the Bali Hai Hotel, where they were jarred out of sleep at three o'clock one morning by a long-distance call from St. Louis radio station KMOX host Gordon Currie, who wanted to know if they were married yet. "How the hell did you find out what hotel we're staying at?" Warren demanded. "Even my agent doesn't know."[91]

Still single, they returned to the U.S., looking anything but romantic. They went to a party at Marianne Hill's house, and Warren started mingling with other guests after Michelle ducked into the bathroom. Approaching a beautiful woman who was chatting with her date, he rudely positioned himself between the woman and the man. "Don't I know you?" Warren asked. The woman's escort, cowed by Warren's fame, backed away. She politely informed Warren they'd never met, but he went into his shy act, lowering his head, muttering something inaudible, kicking at the floor. Finally, he offered her a cigarette, but she said, "No, thank you. I don't smoke." He didn't either, he replied, but she remarked that she'd just seen him puffing on a cigarette. "That's only because I'm nervous," he said. "I'd really like to get to know you better." When she pointedly reminded him that he'd arrived with another woman, he said, "Yeah, Michelle. Have you seen her?" "I don't think so," she replied, which sent a dejected Warren wandering off toward the kitchen.

In the following days, reporters kept asking Warren and Michelle what had gone wrong in Bali. He complained that the press was acting "like anxious mothers," trying to push him into wedlock.[92] Stung by his words, Michelle retorted, "He feels that marriage isn't a happy, productive way of life. He prefers not to be involved. He prefers shallow, meaningless relationships—he thinks they're healthier, or at least the only kind he can have. I don't respect his lifestyle, but I don't try to judge him."[93]

At a party, Michelle recognized some craftsmen who'd been doing a job at Warren's house. "Warren's a royal prick," one of them told her. Later, speaking on condition of anonymity, he revealed that Warren's business manager had gone over their bill and criticized each expenditure, telling the workmen that various jobs were "premature . . . not necessary . . . not authorized." He cut the bill down and said, "Take it or leave it or you won't get anything." At the party, the workmen told Michelle, and each other, "Don't get mixed up with those horrible people again." Michelle replied, "We all got fired at the same time."

On January 21, 1977, the *Los Angeles Herald Examiner* reported that the Beatty-Phillips affair was "off and on . . . right now . . . cool but friendly, rather than romantic." By May, *People* was running stories about Warren and Kate Jackson, who was collecting ten thousand dollars per week for the weekly *Charlie's Angels* television series. With her sudden breakthrough, Kate was worried about "the brown Mercedes, Beverly Hills address, and all the other trappings that go with a TV success. . . . Warren has a good perspective on the business and keeps me from going over the edge. But we're just friends." At forty, he presented himself as a showbiz veteran, full of sage advice for new stars, especially pretty ones. When Diane Lane first broke through, she met Warren with some friends, and he later called her. She confided that she had certain worries about the movie business, and he said, "If you're going to talk to anyone please talk to me, you know I'm experienced." As it turned out, Lane didn't want to date him, because, as she put it, "I don't like being part of a harem." He handled the situation so tactfully that Lane could later say, "I needed the comforting knowledge that I didn't have anything to worry about from him."[94] Once she felt safe, she "got some counseling from him," she said. Evidently the aging Don Juan was having to work twice as hard for twice as little.

The next man in Michelle Phillips's life, after Warren, was a programming director for a radio network in the southwest named Bob Birch, who seemed to lead a stable, conventional life. But when she married again, she chose plastic surgeon Steven Zax. Apart from daughter Chynna and stepdaughter Mackenzie Phillips, her children include a son, Austin, and an adopted son, Aron. She continued to work, appearing on *Knots Landing* and in various soap-opera roles.[95]

Years later, Warren ran into Chynna Phillips at the home of Jack Nicholson's daughter, Jennifer. Chynna had grown up, and was now singing in the group Wilson Phillips, which included Carnie and Wendy Wilson, daughters of Brian Wilson of the Beach Boys. The girls would win a gold record in 1990 for their debut single, "Hold On." By 1992 Chynna had had enough of Wilson Phillips, and announced, "I have goals, I have aspirations, I'm leaving." By 2000, Chynna, now thirty-two, was married to William Baldwin, thirty-seven, one of the acting Baldwin brothers, and raising a baby daughter, Jamison Leon Baldwin.

Some of Warren's affairs never technically ended, or even faded away. In 1976, Goldie Hawn married Bill Hudson but Goldie wanted an open marriage and remained close to Warren, over her husband's protests. Recalls Hudson, "I'd answer the phone and this voice would say, 'Hi, is Goldie there?' After a month or so I said to her, 'Everybody knows we're together, who is this guy?' And she said, 'It's Warren.' And I said, 'Isn't it weird? We're in love and he's calling you and you're still giggling.'" Later, Hudson, who sired Kate Hudson with Goldie, said, "Hollywood is this living orgy." "You can't even have a barbecue without somebody there that you slept with. It's really pathetic. It's a feeding frenzy of ego."[96]

Early one morning, Warren called L.A. socialite Gail Hensley's daughter, Pamela, who was employed as an actress at Universal and portrayed C. J. Parsons on *Matt Houston*. "You wanna fuck?" he asked. She didn't. Just as often, the reverse was true, and he was prey to the bold new breed of Hollywood power women. After co-producing *The Sting* in 1973, Julia Phillips was trying to figure out "who to fuck next"[97] when Paul Schrader, the screenwriter of *Taxi Driver*, told her, "In Hollywood you're supposed to fuck up." Since Julia and her partners Tony Bill and Michael Phillips already had won the prestigious Best Picture Oscar, that didn't leave many candidates at her exalted level, except, she figured, Bob Evans and Warren Beatty. Evans was "too tan" for her taste, but Beatty would do, she decided. Spotting him at a party, she tried, in her shock-attack way, to hit on him, telling him about meeting Julie Christie at Paul Williams's beach house, "a dark hovel heavy with the scent of incense." Christie, Phillips said patronizingly, had been "warm and relaxed, if a tad nonverbal. A perfect audience for me." With subtle disdain, Beatty pointed out that Julia and Julie were quite different. Julia compounded her faux pas by openly criticizing Julie. "Well, let me put it this way," she said. "I did all the giving and she did all the taking—does that turn you on?" Evidently not. They didn't have sex, although, as she later wrote, "Warren tries to fuck everybody."[98]

Though Julia possessed the requisite Oscar, her kind of guerrilla aggressiveness turned him off. The glamorous and talented Diane Keaton was more his type. In the 1970s, immediately after ending her affair with Woody Allen, Keaton began dating both Warren and Al Pacino. Warren was also seeing other women. According to author Pamela Des Barres, he had a hand in the breakup of Don Johnson and Melanie Griffith's marriage. After it "smashed apart," wrote Des Barres, "I had been the one to move Melanie into her swell new Hollywood apartment while she bawled her eyes out. I think Warren Beatty had something to do with it. . . . She married another hunky actor, Steven 'Rocky' Bauer, and seemed content and semi-domestic."[99] Not for long, however. After Melanie's marriage to Bauer ended, she and Don Johnson got together again, and then she married Antonio Banderas. Meanwhile, Don Johnson was living with Patti D'Arbanville, and they had a son named Jessie. Don became the latest player in the high stakes Hollywood game of change-partners-and-dance.

When a sexy new novel, *Fear of Flying,* by Erica Jong, was making the rounds of the studios, Warren became interested. He called Julia Phillips, who had optioned it, to ask about the author, who looked very sensual in her dust-jacket photo. "Well," said Julia, "she's more Sue Mengers than her photograph on the jacket would indicate." Warren wanted Erica's phone number anyway, and Julia gave it to him. Later he told Lee Grant that *Fear of Flying* should be a porno movie, and at a party at Goldie's, he saw Julia Phillips and added that the movie of *Fear of Flying* should feature "see-through dildos and vibrators." Lee Grant commented, "Can you imagine the casting couch?" Julia shrugged, thinking, No different from any other.[100]

In the early seventies, Ali MacGraw, star of *Goodbye Columbus* and former wife of Paramount production chief Robert Evans, was one of the most desirable and sought after women in Hollywood. No sooner had Ali's marriage to Steve McQueen hit the rocks than Warren called Bob Evans, panting for Ali's dark and sinuous body, but reluctant to incur the wrath of the powerful Evans. "Your ole lady, she's free," Warren said. "Do you mind if I call her?" He didn't bother to call Steve McQueen, an old rival—for both women and movie roles—because McQueen had never, despite major stardom, been a member of Hollywood's power elite. Years later, recalling Warren's nerve, Evans said, "I couldn't believe his words." He knew that Warren was still involved with Diane Keaton and said, "If you weren't living with Keaton, Ali would be the best thing that could ever happen to you. She's too good a dame to hurt for the sake of a notch. You've asked me, so I'm telling you—pass."

Word of Ali's availability passed quickly among the Don Juans of Beverly Hills. Two minutes after Warren's call to Evans, Jack Nicholson rang, asking Evans if *he* could date Ali. "Whaddaya think, Keed? Now that your ole lady's free, is it worth a dial?" This time, Evans said, "Call her if you want, but you're with Toots [Anjelica Huston], Irish, and Ali's too vulnerable for you to play it shady. Got it?" Without hesitation, Nicholson, who was just as disinclined as Beatty to offend anyone at the studios with deep pockets, said, "Got it!" Years later Evans remembered, "The difference was, one called and called, and the other passed. Who do you think called? Who do you think passed? Let's just say, Nicholson called another lass."[101]

"Love," as Ali observed in *Love Story*, the movie that made her a star, "means never having to say you're sorry." Though the line caught on, it was more flip than true. Had she apologized to Bob Evans for leaving him for Steve McQueen, she might have had a future in Hollywood after *Love Story*. But when she and

McQueen plunked for the leads in *The Great Gatsby*, Evans, who was still running Paramount, said, "The two-hundred-and-fifty-pound cleaning woman
who scrubs toilets would play Daisy before Ali got the part."[102] The roles went
to Robert Redford and Mia Farrow, and Ali was finished in films except for
dreck like *Just Tell Me What You Want* and an occasional TV movie. Bob Evans
married Catherine Oxenberg, but it was all over in twelve days.[103]

Throughout much of the 1960s and 1970s, Warren Beatty and Steve
McQueen were among the most bankable male stars in Hollywood, competing
for the best roles. When the producer, David Foster, had cast Warren in *McCabe
and Mrs. Miller*, Steve had been deeply offended. Foster was McQueen's former publicist, and it outraged the actor that Foster hadn't offered him the role
first. "Oh, so you think Beatty's a fucking better actor than me?" McQueen
snarled. Complicating matters was the physical proximity of the two stars;
Warren and Steve lived in suites down the hall from each other at the Beverly
Wilshire. Steve considered Warren to be "pompous," according to his producer friend, Phil Parslow. "Warren was white collar and limousines and Steve was
blue collar and motorcycles."[104] Both were rich; McQueen was pulling down
three million dollars per picture, with 15 percent of the gross. Financially,
Warren was in a class by himself, at least among actors, owning, as producer,
huge chunks of his pictures.

A native of Beach Grove, Indiana, McQueen was born on March 24, 1930,
and came from a broken home. Always feeling his "life was screwed up before
I was born," he ran away with the circus, stole hubcaps, fell into gangs, and in
1945 was court-ordered to the California Junior Boys Republic at Chino. There,
he turned his life around and became an inspiration to other troubled boys.
Ironically, though later a gutsy action hero, he lacked self-confidence, and was
easily intimidated. Faye Dunaway, his co-star in *The Thomas Crown Affair*, said,
"He stimulates that cuddly feeling. He's the misunderstood bad boy you're sure
you can cure with a little warmth and some home cooking."[105]

One day Warren found himself on the same elevator with Steve in the
Wilshire and decided to ignore him. Steve had stolen Ali MacGraw from
Warren's buddy, Bob Evans, who later recalled, "Ali was looking at me and
thinking of Steve McQueen's cock." According to the rules of "the club,"
Hollywood honchos don't shoot each other out of the saddle. When Warren

snubbed him in the elevator, Steve stood behind him and made a goofy face, placing his thumbs in his ears and sticking his tongue out. Inside, he was crushed that Warren hadn't spoken to him; he knew Warren was his opposite in many ways, but he "respected the fact that Beatty grabbed ahold of *Bonnie and Clyde* when it was sinking in the mud and made himself the producer and made that picture work," Steve's friend Phil Parslow revealed. "He just loved to kid Beatty."

"Steve was so real, you could have mistaken him for a fireman," says Karen Bihari, who knew both McQueen and Beatty. "Steve raced motorcycles with my uncle Joe, who lived around the corner from him in Brentwood. Steve would take his bike up Kenter Avenue, above Sunset. Finally the neighborhood installed speed bumps. His stunt man introduced him to the world of dirt bike races. We'd go to the races in Torrance, and Steve would compete. It's called 'motocross,' the dirt bike races. Sometimes he won, but it was all just for fun. The Czech teams, who had the most fabulous bikes, stayed with my family, and Steve would hose off everyone's bike."

In 1977 Warren was going with a leggy Nina Blanchard supermodel named Barbara Minty. A dark-haired knockout, she was the daughter of a minister and had come of age in the bosom of the church. Barbara's modeling career made her rich and gave her a patina of L.A. sophistication, but she remained basically natural and unaffected. "Barbara was not part of the 'Hollywood crowd,'" said Pat Johnson, a karate instructor and fight coordinator on the *Teenage Mutant Ninja Turtle* films. "She was a naive farm girl. She did not give interviews. She stayed away from the limelight." Her discretion made her very compatible with Warren, but eventually, like most women, Barbara began to feel she was ready to settle down. Warren, of course, was no more suited for domesticity than ever. The very notion of stability still bored him.

One day, Steve McQueen saw Barbara Minty's picture in a fashion magazine, called and told her who he was, and asked for a date. As her relationship with the footloose Warren provided plenty of latitude, she accepted. After she rode behind McQueen on his motorcycle, her large breasts pressing into his back, he told a friend, "I knew this was the woman for me." Said Bill Maher, Steve's business manager, "She was Warren Beatty's girlfriend. Steve stole her away from him."[106]

Warren never had a chance. According to Loren Janes, who'd been Steve's stunt man on *Wanted: Dead or Alive*, Minty had a crush on Steve long before meeting him. She was willing to give up her career for him—and she did. During their affair, Steve was still married to Ali, and the *National Enquirer* threatened to expose Steve and Barbara's romance. He was frantic; Ali was the love of his life. "If he could have had Barbara Minty stashed away in a motel and have Ali in the kitchen, he would have been delighted," said Phil Parslow.[107] In the end, Steve cheated on everyone, even joining his former wife Neile Adams in Las Vegas, where she was appearing in *Can-Can*. When he finally chose Barbara, Ali went into a complete tailspin, but eventually found her way into a new life.

A strong positive influence on Steve, Barbara convinced him to become a born-again Christian. She was with him when he discovered he had inoperable cancer, which would end his film career in 1979. They were married on January 16, 1980, and when doctors gave up on him and told Barbara he was dying, she drove with him to Baja California in his pickup truck, in search of a miracle cure at a Mexican health spa. But Steve's luck had run out. There were to be no miracles.

Later, a tumor was surgically removed from his stomach in the Santa Rosa Clinic in Juarez, Mexico, and he died of an embolism on November 7, 1980. Barbara, who was with him at the end, received one million dollars from his twelve-million-dollar fortune, half of which went to his children Chad and Terry. "[Barbara] had her own money," said Pat Johnson. "Remember, she was a top model."

For Warren, she was one of the few girls who got away, and he never forgave McQueen. Despite his storied conquests, Warren's insecurity was so entrenched and pervasive that rejection struck at the very foundation of his identity, which was tenuous enough already. For many years, Warren and Bob Evans had shared the same physician, Dr. Lee Siegel, who one day, according to Evans, jokingly said, "Hate to tell you, Warren. Evans has got the edge. You're about equal in quantity, but he's about three points higher in *quality*." With those words, Dr. Siegel lost himself a star patient.[108]

Not content to give up on supermodels, Warren next went after the statuesque blond dazzler Jerry Hall. She remembers the exact day: May 21, 1977. She was attending a dinner in a Manhattan restaurant when Mick Jagger sat down next to her. Though he was to be her future husband, she was engaged at the time to Bryan Ferry, Roxy Music's quirky singer, who brought a world-weary sophistication to rock 'n' roll in *Stranded* and *These Foolish Things*. Warren, who'd also been invited to the dinner, walked by Mick and Jerry, sized Jerry up, and decided to make a play, though Mick was already on the make himself. Both men competed for her attention, and Mick, snubbing Warren, leaned over to say something private to Jerry. When Warren cut him off in mid-sentence, Mick snapped, "She's with me." Undeterred, Warren looked inquiringly at Jerry, who said, "I'm not with anyone. I'm engaged. I just happen to be at this dinner." "Now, Warren, listen, man," Mick said, dragging Warren over to a telephone. Mick called someone and told them to fix Warren up with another model. In his forties, Warren had to realize that seduction was no longer automatic.

Still a world-class trophy for rich middle-aged divorcées and older celebrities on the prowl, Warren met HRH Princess Margaret of England at a private party upstairs at the Bistro Gardens, then one of the most exclusive restaurants in Los Angeles. The younger sister of the Queen of England, Princess Margaret had been strikingly beautiful before ruining her looks with whisky and fast living in the jet set. Though required to live among royals, she'd always had an yen for sexy-looking men, regardless of class, and Warren still qualified.

At the Beverly Hills social gathering that day, HRH was supposed to be seated next to Frank Sinatra, the most desirable position at the table, but she went out of her way to juggle the arrangement, ending up next to Warren.[109] "She was a very unhappy woman," said royal watcher and U.K. journalist Richard Mineards. "She was looking for some sort of solace, be it sexual or otherwise, and I remember there were two names that came up a lot: Warren Beatty and Mick Jagger." Mineards said Warren later went to the Caribbean island of Mustique, a tropical paradise where Margaret had a piece of land and a home. "You had a lot of jet-setters going down there," Mineards added. "Princess Margaret liked the celebrity world and fitted into it more because she was a little more frivolous than the queen; she could be, because she doesn't have the responsibility of the monarchy."[110] She also enjoyed an affair with Jack Lemmon.

Another woman of noble lineage, Tricia Pelham Clinton Hope, who lives in Palm Beach, Florida, and whose father was the Duke of Newcastle, recalled in an interview in 2000, "Warren was fascinated by who I was. He was like, 'Oh, my God—*money*!' Like all Aries, he has a big thing about money. It was like, 'Well, you're not a movie star, but there are only twenty-seven dukes.' It put me in the right club, so to speak." Pelham and Clinton, Tricia explained, are family names of the dukes of Newcastle. "I met Warren through Polanski," Tricia continues. "We had a date on a Sunday or a Saturday afternoon, and we went to the Beverly Hills High School track because he was getting ready to do *Heaven Can Wait*. I had to sit there and watch him run around the track."

Afterward, they went up to his penthouse. "There was no way that I was going to sleep with Warren," says Tricia. "I knew better. I knew too many people that he had slept with. I'll never forget his charm—extraordinary, bright, interesting man, devastatingly good looking and funny. We went down the elevator, and he was flirting with every woman, yet he was still very much with me. Most men you'd want to kill, but you expected this from Warren, because of his romantic reputation. He played on that *big* time. Every once in a while, he would call, and [we'd] have these silly conversations. It would be eight o'clock on a Saturday night, and he'd expect you to drop everything and go running over there to the Beverly Wilshire. At that time, this was definitely not a man who was into any kind of serious thing unless you were famous."[111]

In a seventies *Rolling Stone* cover story, Warren claimed to be the fastest phone dialer in the world. When Bob Evans saw the piece, he told Warren his son Joshua was faster, and could easily "out-touch-tone" him. "I'll wipe him off the street," Warren said. They arranged to have a dial-off between Warren and Josh in Evans's Beverly Hills screening room, which had two phones. When Warren arrived, he said, "Where's the fuckin' runt?" Josh joined them, and he and Warren started dialing. Josh proved to be the fastest finger in the West. A sore loser, Warren didn't speak to the boy for more than a year.[112]

He was enjoying another break from moviemaking, and this one lasted two years, during which he turned down the title role in *Superman*, as did Clint Eastwood and James Caan, because no self-respecting Hollywood matinee idol would wear the silly comic-book costume. Warren took it home, put it on, ran around his pool, and regarded himself briefly in the mirror before taking it off. In the end, the producers had to draft a newcomer, Christopher Reeve, who was perfect—and the movie was a huge hit. Vanity has probably done more actors out of blockbuster roles than any other single cause.[113] Warren then was announced as the star of Sir Lew Grade and John Woolf's *Stone Leopard*, a spy yarn, with Don Siegel directing, but the picture never materialized.

So Warren went back again to dabbling in politics. In September 1976, he was at the Farmers Market in West L.A. to launch Voter Registration Week, hoping to sign up one million Californians for the November 2 election. In October, he and Louise Fletcher, Oscar-winning star of *One Flew Over the Cuckoo's Nest*, were seen at a political fund-raiser. In his choice of film projects, he was assiduously following advice given to him by politicos at the 1976 Democratic National Convention: "If you have any political ambitions, stay clear of porn."[114] He had been pursuing Paul Schrader's screenplay *Hard Core*, which concerned a Midwest businessman who flies to L.A. to retrieve his porn-actress daughter. Warren said he wanted either Mike Nichols or Arthur Penn to direct, but suddenly dropped the project. Paul Schrader was furious.[115]

Warner Bros.' Ted Ashley discussed doing a Howard Hughes picture with Warren for six months and finally concluded a deal. A billionaire womanizer, Hughes's sexual conquests in Hollywood (Bette Davis, Olivia de Havilland, Katharine Hepburn, Ava Gardner, Lana Turner, Jane Russell, Jean Peters, and countless others) exceeded even Warren's, and, like Warren, Hughes was reclusive and spent most of his life in hotel suites. The Hughes project would remain on the back burner for years. In 1976, CBS-TV made Warren an offer to play Hughes from ages twenty-five to seventy in a two-night, four-hour film, but negotiations broke down, and then-newcomer Tommy Lee Jones got the part.[116]

In 1977 Warren showed exactly how far he was willing to go to protect his reputation. The TV show *Blueboy Forum*[117] ran a teasing ad promising "the lowdown on Warren Beatty," with some allegedly blue material supplied by actor Justin Ormond. After Warren's attorneys and those of station manager Gene Inger went head to head, certain segments were edited out of the show. *New York* magazine reported the bleeping, saying the attorneys "saw eye to eye."[118]

On March 28, 1977, Warren co-emceed the Oscar ceremony at the Dorothy Chandler Pavilion, produced by William Friedkin. He shared the podium with Ellen Burstyn, Jane Fonda, and Richard Pryor. He'd twice before appeared on Oscar night as a presenter, but this was his first hosting assignment. Faye Dunaway, the year's Best Actress winner for *Network*, told the *Los Angeles Herald Examiner* that Warren and Jack Nicholson still cruised the Sunset Strip, "twin chauvinists—picking up broads."[119] But nothing could detract from the stature

Warren had won in the industry's power elite. By 1978, his reputation was so unassailable that *Time* called him "Mr. Hollywood."

He was still highly regarded in national political circles as someone who could be counted on to round up support among powerful Hollywood figures. Rick Burke recalls, "In 1979, when Ted [Edward Kennedy] was getting ready to run for president, the failed attempt, we were trying to drum up support from some of the celebrities known in the past to be friendly to the Kennedys. We were in Los Angeles, and we first visited Barbra Streisand, asking her to do a show for us, a benefit, a political function, and she was reluctant, saying something about not wanting to perform for crowds. Then we went to Warren Beatty's home. When we arrived, there must have been half a dozen attack dogs circling the perimeter of the house. All hell broke loose when we rang the doorbell, with those dogs barking. I stood there with Ted [Kennedy] and a Secret Service agent, all of us wearing three-piece suits. The door opens, and there is Warren Beatty in his underwear, dripping wet. I thought, How odd—he answers his door this way? But, fine. We went in, and he still didn't change. Instead, he brought us out to the hot tub, and there was a woman in it, wearing a bikini. Warren just jumps in with the woman. It was awkward, us in our suits and he in his underwear with this babe. I looked around and saw Jack Nicholson standing in a corner, and he's also in his dripping wet underwear. Jack had on boxers, Warren, briefs. Jack was with a woman, just flirting away. Then he comes over to the hot tub, and we get into a discussion, me, Ted, Jack, and Warren, about Ted's political future. They didn't seem to be enthusiastic about it, by the way. We asked them to appear at a fund-raiser, and they didn't decline, but also didn't commit.

"Ted wanted to take a shower and freshen up for his next appointment. Warren said, 'Why take a shower? Just get into the hot tub.' So Ted told me to go out to his car and get a fresh change of clothes. While I was out there, this girl shows up, and I said, 'Jesus, what are you doing here?' She says to me, 'Ted asked me to meet him here.' She knew Warren, too, for when she got into the house, she and Warren exchanged hugs and kisses. Ted said, 'Here you are,' and went over to her. They embraced and disappeared into one of the bedrooms.

"A few minutes later, they emerged, wearing towels. Then, in front of all of us, they dropped their towels and, naked as can be, just jumped into the hot tub. Warren, Jack, and I just watched and talked to them from the sidelines, and after about fifteen minutes, they got out of the tub, put on their towels, and went to get dressed. Speaking of Ted, Warren said, 'Now, there's a guy I like.' Warren and Jack had big grins, like Ted was one of the club members. Club of womanizers."

Tricia Pelham Clinton Hope recalls being with Nicholson the night he won the Oscar for *One Flew Over the Cuckoo's Nest* (March 29, 1976). "We all went afterward to Michelle Phillips's apartment, and Warren was there. I sat in the living room with Jack on one side of me and Warren on the other. I turned to Jack and said, 'Where's your little golden man?' Warren almost choked. 'What do you mean?' Jack asked, and I said, 'Didn't you get a little golden man tonight?' Jack was usually so drunk by that time of night he couldn't even remember his name, but finally sort of got it."[120]

Warren proved somewhat less simpatico with born-again Jimmy Carter than he did with Ted Kennedy. Carter sprang from Georgia's State House to become the leading candidate for the Democratic presidential nomination, and he was casting about for a potential running mate. In July, he still had a month before the convention in New York City, and he utilized the interim to raise funds to wipe out his growing debts, to work up a platform, and to decide on a running mate. He returned briefly to Georgia that summer, "to go to the same Sunday school class, and eat barbecue chicken, and come to Billy's filling station"[121]—not exactly Warren Beatty's kind of guy. After meeting with Walter Mondale in Plains, Georgia, Carter flew to New York for the Democratic National Convention in July 1976 at Madison Square Garden.

Warren lost out on the social event of the convention, which was *Rolling Stone* publisher Jann Wenner's party for the Carter staff. Unfortunately, Wenner's East 68th Street town house proved too small for the crowd that showed up, waving purple-and-white invitations. Those who managed to get in had left the convention's opening session early, but such latecomers as Warren were turned away, due to Manhattan fire laws proscribing overcrowding. Warren stood hand in hand in the street with Representative Bella S. Abzug (D-NY), waiting an hour as luckier guests, drinks in hand, looked from windows at the growing chaos outside. Inside, guests feasted on cold whitefish, roast beef, and green salad with croutons, and Warren and Abzug finally gave up and walked away through the angry throng, which was yelling, "We want

Wenner!"[122] Police had to be called in to quiet them down. Wenner was later castigated for poor planning.

Carter was nominated for the presidency the following day, and although Warren had been rumored for the vice presidential slot, Carter chose Mondale as his running mate, and Warren returned to the West Coast. On August 22, Carter came to L.A. and visited Warren's penthouse lair in the Beverly Wilshire for a party, surely the unlikeliest person ever to set foot in the notorious love nest. The presidential candidate had come from a dinner hosted by Universal's Lew Wasserman and organized by Bob Strauss, a Texan and boss of the Democratic Party. At the dinner, Hollywood's leading moguls grilled the candidate on tax shelters. They weren't about to part with campaign funds until they were certain their interests would be protected by the White House.

At the party for Carter at the Beverly Wilshire, Warren's carefully picked guests included Faye Dunaway, Diana Ross, Hugh Hefner, Sidney Poitier, Robert Altman, Dennis Weaver, Peter Falk, Norman Lear, Tony Randall, and Neil Simon. Introducing them to Governor Carter, Warren identified his friends as the cream of moviedom's liberals, describing them as "pinkos, leftists, commies," and they all had a "rising enthusiasm" for Carter.[123] The candidate was not particularly amused. Looking over the glamorous crowd decked out in jewels and Rodeo Drive fashions, Carter referred to them as "the big shots . . . you and people like you and like I was," implying that he had undergone, at some point, a profound sea change that differentiated him from their brand of frivolous liberalism.

Warren's friends asked "fatuous" questions, according to a Carter biographer, Peter G. Bourne. The candidate replied with politely phrased banter, while also lecturing them as if they were infidels and he the only true Christian west of the Rockies. The party heated up when Jerry Brown arrived. Carter tried to show off in front of him, delivering a passionate harangue; he was sick, he said, of lobbyists who cared only for their clients, like doctors and lawyers, and nothing for destitute people. "There's a need for public officials—presidents, governors, congressmen, and others—to bypass the lobbyists and the special-interest groups and our own circle of friends who are very fortunate, and try to understand those who are dependent on government to give them a decent life."[124]

Unfortunately, he was preaching to the choir at Warren's. The actors were not only liberals but militant ones. Carter's outburst would have made more sense had he aimed it at Lew Wasserman and the fat cats who were trying to grab self-serving tax breaks.[125] The rich movie crowd so unsettled Carter that, as he left L.A., he gave up his limousine and told the Secret Service that he'd do the rest of his campaigning in an ordinary sedan.

When Hefner gave Carter a chance to explain his beliefs in the pages of *Playboy*, Carter made the mistake of relaxing on a lazy summer day and going a little too far in his effort to show what a regular fellow he was, telling interviewer Robert Sheer, "I have looked on a lot of women with lust; I've committed adultery in my heart many times. . . . Christ says don't consider yourself better than someone else because one guy screws a whole bunch of women while the other guy is loyal to his wife." Then he went on to identify the following acts as sins: "sexual intercourse outside marriage [and] homosexual activities." In a single interview, the peanut farmer from Plains succeeded in offending virtually the entire voting populace, from fornicators like Warren to gays like David Geffen, and most particularly he outraged his own constituency, the southern fundamentalists, who scorned his talk of "screwing" and "shacking up."[126] All in all, Jimmy came off sounding about as presidential as his cornpone brother, the beer-guzzling Billy.

Both Warren and Shirley MacLaine vigorously campaigned for him, and Shirley would remain close to the first lady, Rosalyn, long after Carter moved into the White House. Explaining his advocacy of Carter, Warren said, "What I feel is that there is a general and dangerous mood in the country of people withdrawing from trying to help one another, that is manifested in the so-called tax revolt in California, the lack of interest in the Equal Rights Amendment, and a general reactionary turn throughout the country." Clearly he was on the side of the angels.

After Carter had been president for a while, Warren realized that no real progress was being made, and warned, "I think people are getting into a dangerously selfish mood, and they will pay a price for that. We will pay a price for that. I think Carter has had the unfortunate position of having to deal with that and with a Congress that seems to be answering the tax-revolt mood of its constituents by abandoning welfare projects and other areas in which the government is the only hope for the improvement of life of those less fortunate. People are giving up on solving society's problems, and for that reason, I think we need well-organized leadership for valid liberal causes. And I think Carter is developing this ability."

Unfortunately, Carter didn't have a clue about how to run the federal government. In December 1978, Democratic agenda leader Michael Harrington said, "It's a weird period for liberals. In many respects this is like the calm before the storm. The problem is the conventional liberal wisdom of the past doesn't work anymore. This is like 1931. Just as the conventional wisdom of the 1920s was totally shattered by the Depression, the conventional wisdom of the 1960s has been shattered by inflation."[127] By the end of his term in office, Carter's approval rating had fallen to 22 percent. Warren and the Hollywood liberal contingent felt betrayed by Carter's centrist government, which turned its back on the McGovernites of the Democratic Party's left wing. Warren lamented, "What animated Hollywood in the '70s was politics. You can mark the end of that with the election of Carter. There's nothing that can destroy the Democratic Party like a Democrat."

In the next presidential election, Carter was no match for Ronald Reagan, even though the former Warner Bros. contract player (*King's Row*) may have already been suffering from early symptoms of Alzheimer's disease.[128] Reagan easily won in the television debates, telling Carter, "There you go again," rebuking the incumbent for harping on his lack of qualification. By January, Reagan was in the Oval Office, having received 489 Electoral College votes to Carter's 49.

The Democrats would have been better off running Beatty in '76, and the thought crossed Warren's mind more than once.[129] Either way, a movie star ended up in the White House, while Jimmy Carter, exploring the potential for good that is available to a former chief executive, became the best ex-president in American history, bringing dangerous conflicts to resolution throughout the world. Ultimately he was hailed as "the American Gandhi."[130]

However ineffectual Warren had found Carter as president, he was proud of his active role in having swept Carter into the White House. Thereafter, whenever people introduced Warren as an actor, he quickly corrected them, saying, "I don't think of myself as an actor. I think an actor acts. Albert Finney is an actor, he acts all the time. I act, I produce, I'll try to write something, I'll be a politician. . . . I'm a sometimes actor, an unconcentrated actor."[131]

He was still trying to decide whether running for political office would require more of him than he had or was willing to give. The prospect was unnerving, and he went back to the movies. He had several projects in development, inspired by a feisty but well-intentioned public dressing-down given to him by the movie industry's favorite curmudgeon, Katharine Hepburn. Calling him the king of Hollywood of the mid-1970s, she'd scolded him for not putting his wealth and power in the film capital to some positive, world-shaping use. "I was a little depressed at the time," Warren said. "A couple of my friends had died . . . I thought something that was clean and funny and romantic would be a good way to spend an hour and a half."[32] It seems astonishing that the best he could come up with was *Here Comes Mr. Jordan*, Robert Montgomery's 1941 fantasy about a prizefighter and amateur saxophonist who goes to heaven by mistake when he crashes in his private plane.

That the creator of *Bonnie and Clyde* and *Shampoo* should take the path of least resistance, recycling stale, irrelevant material rather than blazing new trails, was another indication of burnout. Warren tried to justify his artistic laziness by saying, "There's nothing inherently negative about doing a remake. What is it they say, that there's only five basic plots? When you're developing any screenplay, you're always aware of all the other things, films, plays, whatever that you're either stealing from or resisting, but mostly resisting." To raise money for the film, he called in a favor from David Geffen, who was still in power at Warner Bros., and was still consulting Warren's shrink. He told Geffen about a couple of old movies he wanted to remake. One, *An Affair to Remember*, was a 1957 tearjerker starring Deborah Kerr and Cary Grant, which itself was a retelling of 1939's *Love Affair*. The second was *Here Comes Mr. Jordan*, which Warren intended to resurrect as *Heaven Can Wait*.

The latter became his first directorial assignment, a job he took ᴏnly after Peter Bogdanovich, Mike Nichols, and Arthur Penn turned it down. He'd argued with Bogdanovich for months about how the picture should be directed, until finally the director of *Paper Moon* and *The Last Picture Show* told him, "Warren, I'd like to dance with you, but I'm going to have to leave." In search of a scenarist, he hired Elaine May to inject the script with dollops of her famous sardonic wit. Grateful to find work again after having been blackballed following her fight with Barry Diller over *Mikey and Nicky*, May recalled, "It was sort of difficult for me to get directing jobs because I seemed sort of crazy. They accused me of taking the negative. But then I wrote *Heaven Can Wait*, and everything was all right. Hollywood doesn't care what you did as long as you're making money for them."[133]

But somehow *Heaven Can Wait* didn't have the distinctive Elaine May sound, possibly because Warren insisted on collaborating, which may have diluted the caustic streak in May that had galvanized such previous scripts of hers as *The Heartbreak Kid*. Warren kept her on board, according to one associate, mainly because she was the kind of "smart, funny, cynical urban person he likes to have around."[134]

Originally he'd planned to give the lead role to Muhammad Ali, but when the boxer proved unavailable due to other commitments, Warren decided to assume the role himself. In view of his own athletic experience, he told Elaine May to change the character from a boxer to a football star, though surely by now, in his forties, he looked a little long in the tooth for gridiron glory. His choice of a mop-top haircut was also unfortunate; bangs on middle-aged men are not advisable unless they're deliberately trying to resemble Margaret Mead.

Casting the film's feminine lead, he considered twenty-year-old Stephanie Zimbalist, daughter of actor Efrem Zimbalist Jr., but eventually told her, "You'd make me look too old." He turned to his former girlfriend, the incandescent Julie Christie. Curtis Harrington, director of *Night Tide* and *Who Slew Auntie Roo?*, recalls that relations between Warren and Julie by now were somewhat frosty. "When I was putting together Iris Murdock's *Unicorn,* I wanted Julie Christie for the lead, and went to the set of *Heaven Can Wait,* in which she was playing a schoolteacher. She was very upset with Warren; they were breaking up, and she was in a bad temper. I was talking with Warren sotto voce, and he told me, 'Julie is watching us. You'd better cool it. She will be angry at you for speaking to me.' In the end, she turned down the script, saying, 'It's the part of another schoolteacher.' "

Dick Sylbert, whose brother Paul designed the production, says, "Warren wouldn't do anything for power in that sense, getting his co-star to fall in love with him for a better performance. What he would do is get the best person for the role he could possibly get. Julie Christie *saved Heaven Can Wait.* In the last scene it was like somebody coming in at the bottom of the ninth with a tied-up score and hitting a home run. You know, she's that good—and they weren't even together then."

As the snappish and volatile David Geffen's power at Warner Bros. went into decline, the Warner top management started distancing itself from Geffen's pictures, including Warren's project. "Ashley and [Frank] Wells began to lose interest in *Heaven Can Wait*," wrote Geffen's biographer Tom King, "and were dismissive of Geffen after a poorly received screening of *The Late Show,* a movie starring Lily Tomlin and Art Carney that Geffen had shepherded."[135] Soon, Ted Ashley was demanding that Geffen be fired, saying, "It's either me or him." The following day, Geffen was out at Warner, after less than a year. *Heaven Can Wait* was now in trouble. Warren could tell, because Frank Wells wouldn't let him have the watercolor he wanted for his office. In retaliation, Warren told Warner Bros. that he needed one day to shop *Heaven Can Wait* around to the other studios. It took just one phone call for him to line up a deal with Barry Diller at Paramount.[136] The deal breaker at Warner was Warren's refusal to come up with a budget for the movie's expensive "heaven" scene. Frank Wells wouldn't give the green light for principal photography without the numbers.[137]

Heaven Can Wait was now safely in the hands of friends at Paramount, studio chief Barry Diller and independent producer Robert Evans, and Warren was good at waltzing both execs. "Barry had his pets and his favorites," said the late Don Simpson. "He loved to play with Beatty and Redford, while a lot of other things fell through the cracks." Though Diller was famous for his hardboiled running of the studio, Warren "devoted his considerable charms to wooing Barry Diller," wrote Peter Biskind.[138]

One day at Paramount, Warren asked Bob Evans to drop by his office. He trusted Bob's marketing savvy and wanted his opinion on the advertising poster, which showed Warren in jogging pants and sneakers, angel's wings sprouting from his back. When Bob arrived, industrial magnate Norton Simon, who was married to Jennifer Jones, was already there. An art connoisseur, Simon told Warren that the poster was "extraordinary. Too good for a film ad." Turning to Evans, Warren said, "Well?" Evans replied, "Uh-uh . . . no *cojones*. Your sweatpants, there ain't no crease. Looks like you're sporting a pussy." Warren immediately scrapped the entire advertising campaign. The cost was "north of half a million," said Evans, who called it "by far the most expensive *crotch retouch* in cinema history."[139]

Warren eventually tossed out Elaine May's script and brought in Buck Henry for rewrites. He also named Henry co-director, as if anyone could co-direct with Warren Beatty. "He's easy with people and has the ability to keep things rolling along," said Beatty, "and I *knew* we needed that. I worry and get uptight. Buck insists on having a good time. He won't *not* have a good time." Henry's own statements indicate that he was having anything but fun. "We had plenty of disagreements," he said. "When Warren wants to do something his way, he has it all figured out. So you goddamn well better be prepared to argue your case if you differ with him."[140]

In a piece of imaginative if highly unlikely casting, the role of Mr. Jordan, the heavenly bureaucrat, was slated for former senator Eugene McCarthy. Fortunately, this cloying bit of insider whimsy was junked, and Warren gave the role to James Mason.

"I can't believe you're still making these fucking dumb movies," Julie Christie told Warren, "when, I mean, there are people all over Europe making fabulous films, about real things, Fassbinder and so on, and you're still doing this shit."[141] He knew she was right. But he also knew his limitations. Despite his kibitzing on the sets of his previous films, he was an inexperienced director, and perhaps thought he needed this simple-minded film as a learning experience. He leaned heavily on the advice of the entire company. "The production designer, the cameraman, an actor will drop a remark that'll keep you going for another few days," he said. He even went to Bob Towne, asking him to polish the script. Mostly he leaned on Julie, later admitting, "I don't know that I could have functioned without Julie in *Heaven Can Wait*."

Though Towne had sworn he'd never work with Warren again, he agreed to try, but after one scene, gave up, telling Warren that his only interest these days was breaking through as a director. He was tired of being a writer in a town that held authorship in low esteem, even Scott Fitzgerald and Nobel laureate William Faulkner, both of whom had been underpaid and largely ignored during their stints in Hollywood. Towne's directorial project would be *Greystoke: The Legend of Tarzan, Lord of the Apes*. Anthea Sylbert, a production executive at Warner, was in charge of the picture. Soon, Towne lost interest in the Tarzan story, and started working on a movie about lesbian athletes, *Personal Best*. As the film got under way, he realized that he, like Warren on the *Heaven Can Wait* set, had taken on too many responsibilities, trying single-handedly to fill three roles—producer, writer, and director. "When he really couldn't handle it," recalled Towne's assistant, Patty James, "then he would be on the phone to Warren."[142] Towne also relied on his psychiatrist, Dr. Martin Grotjahn, whom he shared with Warren, Geffen, and, formerly, Cher.

After David Geffen's unsuccessful stint at Warner, he became an independent producer, and Towne took *Personal Best* to him for financing. Geffen consulted Dr. Grotjahn, who warned him that Towne was "crazy." But then, Grotjahn added, Geffen was crazy, too, and advised him to go ahead and bankroll Towne's picture. As filming got under way, Towne morphed into a Warren Beatty clone and "was chasing the girls," said his film editor, Bud Smith. "He was basically a playboy, he loved women." And he loved spending money. In 1980, Warren lent Towne one hundred thousand dollars, the first in a succession of half a dozen six-figure loans. Towne was having an affair with his star, Mariel Hemingway, while battling with his backer, Geffen.[143]

By the late 1970s, Geffen's life had turned into a mess, both personally and professionally. A denizen of the hard-partying disco scene in New York, he was hanging around Steve Rubell's Studio 54. "Even as he was deep into the most sexually promiscuous period of his life, having sex with countless young men, Geffen still felt uncomfortable about being gay," wrote Tom King. Diagnosed with a supposedly cancerous "atypia" on his bladder, Geffen feared that he was going to end up wearing some sort of drainage device, but fortunately the diagnosis proved incorrect. Thoughout his troubles in the seventies, a few good friends stood by him, including Warren, Marlo Thomas, and Carrie Fisher. Striking a deal at Warner, Geffen went back into the record business, but what he really wanted was to be a movie producer.[144] Warren was clever not to discount him, for Geffen's power would continue to grow. When Towne and Geffen clashed on *Personal Best,* the former proved less adept than Warren at handling the prickly mogul. Towne and Geffen ended up in litigation, and *Personal Best*, on release, turned into a sixteen-million-dollar turkey.[145] The salad days of the New Hollywood that Beatty and Towne had helped launch were numbered.

Meanwhile, Warren had been busy preparing for his jock role in *Heaven Can Wait.* He had to get himself back in shape to play football for the first time since high school. He put in eighteen-hour days, working as actor, producer, co-director, and co-writer. "It ain't easy," he said. Perhaps a less taxed and tired director could have prevented the friction that developed on the set between costars Julie Christie and Dyan Cannon after the latter demanded alphabetical listing in the credits. "Julie and Warren aren't speaking either," said one insider. "You'd never know they were once lovers. Warren isn't speaking to his co-director Buck Henry, co-star Charles Grodin isn't speaking to anybody. James Mason, who plays God. . . . is staying above it all."

Ironically, his least venturesome film became one of his most successful, increasing his personal fortune by fifteen million dollars. The buzz started early, thanks to a celebrity-packed press screening, which was held at the Academy of Motion Picture Arts and Sciences theater in Beverly Hills, and attended by L.A. Rams owner Carroll Rosenbloom, LeVar Burton, Alan Ladd Jr., Daniel Melnick (producer of *All That Jazz* and *That's Entertainment*), Linda Ronstadt, Art Garfunkel, Steven Spielberg, Henry Winkler, Sylvester Stallone, David Frost, and Cheryl Tiegs. Both *Newsweek* and *Time* were vying to put Warren on the cover. According to *Newsweek*'s Charles Michener, Warren began by lobbying the editor of *Newsweek*. Then, cagily, he went to *Time* and told the editors that *Newsweek* had approached him for a cover. *Time* took the bait, offering him *their* cover. Some insiders say that Warren preferred *Time* because of its larger circulation, but according to Michener, "[Warren] just had to honor the wishes of Barry Diller [Paramount chairman], who wanted to punish *Newsweek* for our *Grease* review."[146]

Recalls Dick Sylbert, "*Heaven Can Wait* was the best picture commercially he ever made. I thought it was a brilliant movie, maybe the only brilliant remake of a movie ever done. The nicest thing that I know about Warren among the leading men is his willingness on screen to make fun of himself. That's actually cool. He does that wonderfully well. There's no playing the fool in [his subsequent films] *Love Affair* or *Ishtar*. There's a lot of it in *Reds*, a lot of it in *Heaven Can Wait*. He's always willing to play the fool really charmingly. People like it." The public liked Warren in *Heaven Can Wait* to the tune of a seventy-seven-million-dollar box office, making it one of the major earners of 1978. The critical reception was generally favorable:

"Beatty and Elaine May have zipped out a heavenly script filled with funny sky-lines," said critic Gene Shalit. "Beatty is marvelous." Both Warren and Dyan Cannon received Oscar nominations for their performances, but he lost in the Best Actor category to Jon Voight for *Coming Home,* and Dyan lost in the Best Supporting Actress category to Maggie Smith for *California Suite*. Warren and Elaine May were nominated for the Oscar for Best Screenplay Based on Material from Another Medium, but the prize went to Oliver Stone for *Midnight Express*.

When Shirley MacLaine came on stage to present the Best Actress Award to Jane Fonda for *Coming Home,* she attempted to cheer up Warren by joking, "I want to take this opportunity to say how proud I am of my little brother, my dear, sweet, talented brother. Just imagine what you could accomplish if you tried celibacy!"[147] Sitting in the audience with Diane Keaton, he must have cringed at his sister's crudeness and cruelty.

According to Oscar historian Anthony Holden, Beatty set a record in the annals of Oscar history with *Heaven Can Wait*. Orson Welles's 1941 sweep of the nominations for Best Picture, Actor, Director, and Screenplay for *Citizen Kane* was a feat unmatched until Beatty's *Heaven Can Wait* in 1978. (Neither Welles nor Beatty were winners.) Shirley's career was also on the upsurge, *The Turning Point,* a year before, and *Being There,* a year later, having revived her flagging fortunes.

Heaven Can Wait seems to have hoodwinked most of the critics, save Pauline Kael, who wrote, "It doesn't represent moviemaking—it's pifflemaking. Warren Beatty moves through it looking fleecy and dazed, murmuring his lines in a dissociated, muffled manner." Kael was usually in Warren's corner, but she scorned the movie as a "prefab" picture, "image-conscious celebrity moviemaking," and ridiculed Warren as an "elfin sweet Jesus" and a "baby-kissing politician." He resented Kael's betrayal, and, according to Buck Henry, took revenge on her in a way that almost destroyed her. He dared her to come to Hollywood and try making movies herself, and she took him up on it, accepting a development deal he arranged for her at Paramount. Not surprisingly, Kael, who knew nothing of moviemaking from a practical standpoint, was a joke in Hollywood, and soon retreated to her critic's post at *The New Yorker*. She never recovered her full authority as a critic or potency as a writer, and was savagely attacked by Renata Adler in *The New York Review of Books*. Referring to Warren's machinations, Buck Henry said, "We're talking about manipulation on a level unknown to man. This is so Machiavellian, even I can't quite believe it, except that it was Warren."[148]

Having regained his power in his forties, Warren reflected, "I think there's a moment in time when you stay up too late and wake up the next morning saying, 'God, I really am older.' "[149] And richer—*Bonnie and Clyde, Shampoo*, and *Heaven Can Wait* brought him one hundred million dollars. The National Association of Theater Owners named him 1978's Producer and Director of the Year,[150] but the honor was somewhat compromised by the fact that it had been negotiated on his promise to appear at the organization's awards ceremony at the Americana Hotel in New York City. Warren and two other celebrity honorees who'd agreed to the same condition, Jane Fonda and Burt Reynolds, dutifully appeared on the appointed night, but when Warren went to the podium to accept his prize, he seemed rattled and quickly fled the stage. He was much more comfortable flirting with two cute little girls, whom he referred to as "two beauties." They were the nieces of NATO's publicity director, Karen Libbett.[151]

Ironically, Warren's highly visible financial gains, his idiosyncrasies on the set, and the excesses and fiscal irresponsibility of such other directors as Michael Cimino and Francis Ford Coppola would spell doom for the New Hollywood.[152] From the wings, less talented men like production executive Michael Eisner, who watched enviously as Warren got rich, deplored the New Directorcentric Hollywood. The era of action flicks, comic strips, and cartoons was nigh, and it would mark the twilight of movies as an art form. The New Hollywood had been the flame that burned most brightly just before total extinction.

But Warren's belief in romantic love remained undiminished. In 1978 he was besotted with the elusive Diane Keaton, who'd just won an Oscar for her charmingly ditzy performance in *Annie Hall*, a film directed by her former lover Woody Allen. But it was in her next film, *Looking for Mr. Goodbar*, in which she played a sex addict not unlike Beatty, that she impressed Warren so much that he set out to make her his partner, in both his life and work. In 1978, paparazzi pursued them along Manhattan streets a few blocks from Keaton's house. Warren told her to duck her head, shouting at photographer Ron Galella, "I'm not going to make it easy."

He tried to use his influence to help her acquire a condo in River House on East 52nd Street, perhaps the most exclusive address in Manhattan, just a few blocks from Shirley MacLaine's home. The tenants rejected Keaton, and the imbroglio was reported in *New York* magazine under the headline NO RM WITH VU FOR WARREN'S GAL. His other gal, Julie Christie, had fallen in love with rocker Brian Eno.[153]

According to *Us* magazine, Warren was in New York "writing a novel."[154] Nothing more was heard of this foray into fiction. He looked great, however, and an *Us* reporter referred to his "flush tones." Warren explained that he'd gained weight while directing *Heaven Can Wait*, and in order to lose it, he'd dieted on string beans and broccoli. "The diet not only reduces me, it flushes me out," he said.[155]

The year 1978 had been one of his best, but perhaps a modicum of humility was needed to balance the accolades. Ever ready to shrink famous egos, the *Harvard Lampoon* included Warren in its "Movie Worsts" list of the year, giving him a special citation, "The Remember-You-Saw-It-Here-First Award," calling him "that pudgy, self-preening angel of banality, whose—for lack of a better word—performance in an upcoming film biography of John Reed will be—for lack of a worse word—execrable!"[156] Warren took it good-naturedly, and even showed up for the presentation.

CHAPTER SIX

WARREN BEATTY NAKED (PART II)

WHEN JACKIE Kennedy Onassis came back into his life in the late 1970s, Warren Beatty, who'd always been into status sex, was still an energetic—if aging—Lothario. She and Warren dated for a while. Warren himself, when quizzed by *Entertainment Tonight* in 1997, denied having had sex with Jackie. As one of the most secretive, least forthcoming public figures in the world, Warren could hardly have been expected to confirm it.[1]

The former first lady had settled into an apartment on Fifth Avenue in New York following the death of her second husband, Aristotle Onassis, and worked as an editor at Doubleday. Fond of entertaining, she invited Warren on December 20, 1978, to a Christmas party, which was also attended by Andy Warhol and Bob Colacello of *Interview* magazine and numerous other celebrities. A longtime friend of Jackie's, who spoke on condition of anonymity, recalls, "Jackie was annoyed. She didn't realize that Warren was going to drag along

Diane Keaton. She fancied Warren, but as one would a toy. It was certainly not serious. Though he was political, she complained to me that he was inarticulate. 'I can't get him to put four words together to make a complete sentence,' she said. 'You'd have to be a psychic just to know what's going on in that head of his.' Still, he was rather handsome, and she thought he would make a good trophy for the evening. But, then, he showed up with another woman."[2]

During the course of the evening, one of the women guests confided to her hostess that she'd heard Warren say he'd been intimate with Jackie. The enraged Jackie marched over to Warren and accused him of being indiscreet, but he immediately denied everything. Jackie dropped the subject, having spotted Bob Colacello standing nearby, and fearing that he'd report the confrontation in *Interview*. Jackie's woman friend later recalled, "Jackie never trusted men, perhaps because of the way she'd been lied to by Jack Kennedy, or maybe because she knew what a cheater her father was. Where poor Warren Beatty was concerned, she had tried and convicted him before even hearing his first protestation. After that holiday gathering, he was banished from the kingdom of Jackie Kennedy Onassis, never to return."

Warren remained infatuated with blue-eyed, brown-haired Diane Keaton, whose remarkably high, round cheekbones and aura of intelligence and mystery were precisely to his taste. "Diane would go over to his house in London," says Sarah Porterfield. "He'd be on the phone with one of his little chickies. Diane would say, 'If you're not off the phone in fifteen minutes, I'm walking out of here.' Diane didn't take any shit from him, and that was how she eventually lost him."

Warren sensed Diane would be a catalyst, as indeed she soon was. For years he'd wanted to film a biography of John Reed, a dynamic young journalist from a privileged background who, in the early years of the twentieth century, became profoundly involved in social issues and labor struggles. As a political idealist, Warren was drawn to this period of American history, when men like Reed and Lincoln Steffens passionately believed America could realize its dream of liberty, equality, and justice for all. John Reed had become increasingly radicalized while reporting on the Eastern Front in World War I, and later he went to Russia, becoming an active supporter of the Bolsheviks. *Ten Days That Shook the World*, his eloquent firsthand account of the Russian Revolution, which would steer the events of the next seventy years, through the end of the Cold War, made

Reed a legend to Communists everywhere. "A hero like Reed appeals to me because he really gave himself to a great struggle, then got totally sapped by its bureaucracy and died," Beatty explained. "There was something a little bit ridiculous about him. I try not to ignore my own ridiculousness. Those old-fashioned heroes are embarrassing. Besides, I think I'm as noble as any of them."[3]

The somewhat diffuse statement, so typical of Warren's scattershot conversational style, does not begin to suggest the courage, intelligence, and emotional depth of the movie he would create in *Reds*, which, more than any film ever made, captures the intellectual ferment and excitement of one of the finest periods in American history—the radical movement of the early 1900s, which attracted the best and brightest minds of the time, all of them bent on bringing equality to all people. Warren's fascination with John Reed sprang from his ongoing immersion in politics and the question of whether he had what it takes to run for elective office and bring about some of the liberal changes he believed in. The central question of his life, as he phrased it, concerned the "abdication of your personal life for a political life and whether it's fruitful, and if it is, how fruitful is it? How much do you have to give up?"[4] In the end, the hyperanalytic artist in Warren would analyze himself out of running for office, while such less altruistically motivated showbiz colleagues as Ronald Reagan, Clint Eastwood, and Sonny Bono raced ahead of him, becoming, respectively, president of the United States, mayor of Carmel-by-the-Sea, and U.S. congressman. Even Elizabeth Taylor got into the act, promoting a then obscure husband, John Warner, who'd never held elective office, into the U.S. Senate.

Warren's plans for *Reds* proceeded at a snail's pace. Back in 1976, scouting for a screenwriter, he'd decided on forty-one-year-old playwright Trevor Griffiths, author of the screenplay for Elizabeth Taylor's *The Comedians*. They met at London's Claridge's Hotel, but Griffiths, a Marxist with an Andre Previn–type mop and a casual air, was asked to leave the conservative, tradition-bound hotel for not wearing a necktie. Refusing to accept the stuffy rule, Warren stunned the manager by offering to buy Claridge's.[5] The playwright was allowed to stay, and shortly began the first draft, calling it *Comrades!*

In the course of developing the material with Griffiths, Warren eventually decided that the playwright was focusing on the political aspect of the story to the detriment of the romantic and literary elements, and took over the screenplay himself, assisted by Elaine May and Robert Towne.[6] It wasn't as crass and megalomaniacal as it sounds; Reed's experience was truly wide ranging, including a passionate relationship with the little-known leftist Louise Bryant, a kind of Greenwich Village Madame de Staël who was courted by both Reed and literary giant Eugene O'Neill (Warren's boyhood hero). In this instance, Warren was right to intervene if *Reds* was to capture the full richness of the subject.

He went to Paramount for backing, confident that studio owner Charles Bluhdorn would have forgotten their shouting match after Warren enriched Paramount's coffers with *The Parallax View* and *Heaven Can Wait*. "A picture about a Communist who dies?" asked Bluhdorn. "What's it going to cost?" Warren told him thirty million dollars. "Do me a favor," said Bluhdorn. "Go to Mexico, spend one million dollars [on the picture], keep twenty-nine million dollars for yourself. Please, don't make this picture."[7] In the end, Bluhdorn backed him but remained skeptical.

Nor did his friends understand his passion for the subject of John Reed, with the exception of Diane Keaton, who shared his interest in political reform and intellectual history. A high-strung, nervous woman whose fingers were often fussing with her hair or stroking her nose or waving aimlessly, almost uncontrollably, Diane was a willowy five-foot-seven, with delicate bones. By the time she met Warren, she was already a Broadway star (a veteran of *Hair* and *Play It Again, Sam*) and a celebrated Oscar winner. A Southern California native, she was born Diane Hall in January 1946, and grew up with two sisters and a brother in Santa Ana, just south of L.A., where her father was a successful civil engineer, realtor, and operator of a consulting company. Her mother, Dorothy, had gone as far as Mrs. Los Angeles in the Mrs. America contest, and Diane had got her first yen for the stage while watching her mother compete. She wanted to be a singer and learned to vocalize by accompanying Judy Garland and Doris Day recordings. In the ninth grade, she blacked out her front teeth and delivered a smashing rendition of "All I Want for Christmas Is My Two Front Teeth." By high school she won the lead in *Little Mary Sunshine*. Despite being pretty, she "never had much success getting dates."[8] There was something strangely coy and inaccessible about her. "I don't think she wanted many people to know her," said one friend. "[Her facade] was always attractive enough that you didn't care if it was an act. And I never thought she herself was that aware that she was doing it. Which made it even more attractive. I'd describe her as just being very private."

After briefly attending Santa Ana College and Orange Coast College, Diane left for New York, where she studied with Sanford Meisner at the Neighborhood Playhouse in 1965. Summer stock led to membership in Actor's Equity, where she was informed that she should change her name, since a Diane Hall was already registered. She took her sister's given name and her mother's maiden name, becoming Dorrie Keaton. By the time she met Woody Allen, she was twenty-two, had changed her name to Diane Keaton, and was living in a cheap apartment on Manhattan's Upper West Side. She won the romantic lead in his play *Play It Again, Sam*, and also won Woody. "I'd seen him on television before, and I thought he was real cute," she recalled. Woody found her utterly unconventional, noting that she "would come in with, you know, a football jersey and a skirt . . . and combat boots and, you know, over mittens," but she was "very charming to be around and of course you always get the impulse with Diane to protect her."[9]

Though Woody was married to actress Louise Lasser (*Bananas; Mary Hartman, Mary Hartman*), he became Diane's lover and Svengali. Finding her mind to be "completely blank," he undertook her literary education and offered to pay for her to see a psychiatrist. She leapt at the chance. Though Diane lacked self-confidence, she was gifted with all the insight and empathy Woody lacked. "I never had a good understanding of people," he admitted, but "she has an uncanny understanding of people—when they are vulnerable, when they are covering up, when they are hostile."[10]

When she picked up her Best Actress Oscar for *Annie Hall* in 1978, she was wearing a Victorian gown, a long skirt with a layered tunic, a high-necked blouse with a rose attached to the bodice—and boots. "Annie Hall" fashions swept the world. Like Katharine Hepburn, Keaton was a rare Hollywood original, much loved by the public, but her personal life would always have a bittersweet quality. Relationships rarely lasted, including the one with Woody, who could be detestably condescending. She never could seem to find "somebody who thinks of me as an equal," she complained. "Breaking up happens to everybody, so no one should feel like a failure when it does happen. . . . You still have a lot of affection for this person but you both know that too much time and change have taken place. . . . Life is time and change, and it just cannot always be worked out, no matter how much affection there may be."[11] Woody quipped that he should never get into another relationship in which one of the partners was himself.

She leased an apartment overlooking Central Park on Manhattan's West Side, and shared it with three cats. Then, in the fall of 1978, Warren, who adored her in *Annie Hall*, rang, whispering into the telephone. Later he recalled, "I loved Diane Keaton. She made me laugh and made me cry. . . . If she had not made *Reds*, I do not know what I would have done."[12] Warren always liked to involve his girlfriends in his projects, to make them partners. Jack Nicholson, who often referred to Warren as "The Pro," said, "Just look at how many movies The Pro has made with his girlfriends. Of course, there are classic pitfalls. Making a movie is psychologically brutal."[13] Not until Diane agreed to play Louise Bryant, John Reed's wife, was Warren galvanized into action, and *Reds* at last went into production. The intense emotional reality that Keaton, as an actress, was capable of summoning would humanize Warren's political movie and keep it from becoming a dry, didactic tract. "In a film with political implications," he remarked, "she searches for what's true in a person and absolves the situation of being preachy or propagandistic. In other words, she has a built-in bullshit detector." In their private time together, she took him along when she visited her family. As a child, Diane had pantomimed the story of Bonnie and Clyde, taking the role of Clyde Barrow, and her family screened their 8mm home movies of her performance. "Warren broke up," said her father Jack Hall. "He wanted to see her over and over."

He was deeply touched by Diane's vulnerability, remarking, "Diane has a great sense of the terror that a woman can feel who has an insecure identity. And she has a great sense of the comedic aspects of that terror." They got along much better before the shooting started than afterward, when Diane, as Reed's mistress, was required to confront many of the issues that lay unspoken and unresolved between her and Warren. "I'm tired of living in your margins," Louise says to John Reed. "I'm not taken seriously when you're around." In the movie, Louise becomes "boring, clinging, miserable." When Jack Nicholson, who played Eugene O'Neill, was asked if Louise and Reed would have lived together, happily ever after, had Reed not died at the age of thirty-three of typhus and kidney failure, he said, "No way!" According to a London journalist, Diane had turned down two marriage proposals from Warren by February 1980. Jack Nicholson developed a crush on Diane, but Warren's best friend did not betray him, managing to control his actions, if not his feelings, toward Warren's new flame. Falling "in love with Miss Keaton," Jack said, "isn't hard." In *Reds*, the characters they played were involved in a love triangle while summering in Provincetown, Massachusetts.[14]

Back in New York, Warren sandwiched dates with Diane between outings with Mary Tyler Moore, Hope Lange, fashion model Janice Dickinson, and various unknowns. "A good friend of mine said that she came to see him at the Carlyle Hotel," recalls Sarah Porterfield. "He had some girl there, and he told my friend to sit in a chair and tell him what to do to the other girl. He'd say, 'Should I grab her hair? Should I grab her ass? Should I fuck her in the ass?' She said, 'Yeah, yeah.' Then at some point she realized he was hurting the girl, not meaning to, but it was painful for the girl, so my friend said, 'No, no,' and he stopped."

In L.A., "Warren was all over Cher at a party," Sarah Porterfield continues, "but Cher wouldn't leave with him. After Cher turned him down and left the party, he started trying to make it with these two little lesbians. He kept coming on to them and coming on to them, until finally one of the lesbians said, 'What the fuck do we need you for?' "[15]

Sharon Washington, the girl who telephoned Warren after spotting him in his car on Sunset Boulevard years before, revealed the details of their liaison for the first time in the fall of 2000. At his penthouse at the Beverly Wilshire that day in the early eighties, she remembers, "He took my hand and we went inside, and he asked if I was hungry. He'd had a lunch prepared—tea and a little something to munch on. It was very hard for me to eat in front of him, but I tried. All I could get down was a couple of grapes. I could hardly hold my teacup. Then the interruptions began, the phone constantly ringing. He was happy to hear from most of the people, and I thought, He has a lot of friends, he's there for a lot of them, and from his conversations I could tell that he has a really remarkable memory. . . . He was very kind, and I began to feel comfortable."

After eating, they went to the bedroom. "I sat beside him on the bed, and we kissed, lying back on the sheets. I took off everything on top, and he pulled his sweater off. There was not a lot of hair on his chest. He was thin, and pale, but firm. His arms seemed small to me but muscular. He was a good kisser. 'Is this how you saw things?' he asked. 'Tell me about your fantasy.' "

She said she liked for lovemaking to be "very gentle," and later recalled, "He was extremely gentle with me. He's very much into caressing. He talked in my ear, his lips moving against my earlobe, his mouth against my ear as he talked.

'Is this what you like?' he asked. He touched me in different places, always telling me I was beautiful. I could see through his jeans that he had an erection. He never put my hand on his penis.

"Everywhere he touched me, it was with a very light touch, and he told me to tell him whenever I needed anything. 'The main thing,' I said, 'is I want to be around you. I want to be your friend.'"

Respecting her youth, inexperience, and nervousness, he didn't pressure her into having sex. "We talked for a while, but our conversation was not about him. It was all about me and my interests, likes, and dislikes. We talked about my family, especially about my brother, about books, because I love to read. Then he said he had something he had to do, and I told him I had already made plans as well."

They chatted in a friendly, easy way as they dressed, and finally said goodbye. When she next heard from Warren, he said that he was just calling to check on her, see if she was okay. "He asked me about birth control on the phone, and I told him that I'd never taken contraceptives." Then he called her again and said, "This is what we are going to do. We're getting back together again." He wanted her to come to the Beverly Wilshire, and a short time later, she appeared at the front desk and asked for Mr. Beatty. "It was evening," she says, remembering her arrival at his suite. He greeted her wearing jeans, a brown belt, and a white shirt. The phone started ringing again, as it had on their first visit. "I was jealous," she continues. "I was so insecure, knowing that he was talking to women, even though nothing of a sexual nature was said. I assumed at the time—but later realized I was mistaken—that every woman who called him was involved with him romantically. A lot of them, I learned as we talked, were just friends."

Finally the phone stopped ringing, and at last Warren kissed her. He helped her undress, and they got on the bed, which wasn't very comfortable, and he lay on top of her. "I remember him being hard, but not completely hard," she says. "I loved his hair. There was definitely chemistry between us. He was gentle in his lovemaking, but there was real passion. He fulfilled something for me. His body was not hot. But he was passionate."

Sharon assured him she was all right. At various intervals in their lovemaking, he'd again stop and ask if she was okay. "You're beautiful," he told her, and he asked if he was doing everything she'd envisaged in her fantasies of him.

"He went down on me for a while. He looked at me while he gave me oral sex. I was embarrassed. It was like you don't really know him, but you feel you do. My feelings were much deeper than his, I believe. I remember doing him, and then he got harder."

When he entered her, he was not wearing a condom. "It wasn't so easy to start, because I'm very small, but he wasn't rough at all." Even at the height of passion, Warren was thinking of his partner. "He asked me if he was hurting me. Warren was a great lover. From the first moment, everything was focused on me. When we made love, his ego was not in the room.

"Afterward, he didn't ask, like many men, 'Did you enjoy it?' because Warren had made sure that I was okay, that I was taken care of, that I enjoyed myself. He did not ejaculate inside of me. He pulled out, which was thoughtful, because I did not take any precaution. We lay there for a while, without any clothes on. I thought we were going to make love again, because he began to get aroused. Then, he looked at his watch and kissed me. We kissed like we were going to make love again, but he said, 'I have to make a phone call. It's time.' "

He went to the next room, and then came back to the bedroom after using the phone. Warren and Sharon talked "about thirty minutes," she recalls, "about certain things in the film industry. Then he helped me get my stuff together. I had begun to feel like I was in the way, knowing that any minute the phone would ring, and he'd be talking to someone else. He walked me to the door and kissed me. 'I'll talk to you and I'll see you again,' he said."

The following day, he called to check on her. "How are you?" he asked. "I want to see you. I'm going to try to have you come up to Mulholland." Then they chatted like old friends. "He has a wonderful sense of humor. We laughed all the time. I didn't ask a lot of questions about him. I could tell he was an extreme-ly private person. On the phone with others, I'd noticed he was careful what he said to whom; certain things I would hear him tell some people and not others. I'm as private as he, and I think he knew he didn't have to discuss whether I would get pregnant or talk about him. He knew he didn't have to with me. And he didn't talk about the other women in his life."

Significantly, he failed to mention a definite date for her to visit his Mulholland home. A week passed, and when she didn't hear from him, she rang the Wilshire. He said he would call her back, and promptly did so. "I have to leave," he said, explaining, "I have to go to Europe for a little while. If you need anything, call me. As soon as I get back, we'll get together." Another week passed, and Sharon called again, leaving a message. Returning her call, he asked, "Is everything okay?"

"Fine," Sharon answered.

"Look," he said, "I'm coming back in a couple of weeks, and I only want you to call if it's an emergency."

Then she saw a photograph of Warren and Diane Keaton in a newspaper. "Are you going to marry her?" Sharon asked, the next time she spoke with Warren. He told her to stop being so "off the wall," and added, "I don't know where you're coming from anymore. We have to end this conversation right now." It was the end of the relationship as well. She realized he "wasn't about to handle my mood swings or my jealousy." Later, when she was invited to a party at Jack Nicholson's, she didn't go. She knew Warren would be there, and that whatever happened would be bad for her—whether he ignored her or wanted to see her again, she could only lose.

His sixteenth picture in twenty years, *Reds* was Warren's magnum opus, and it should have been his swan song, had he wanted to end his career on a high note. To complete this ambitious epic of the sweeping revolutionary movement that changed the face of Europe and much of the rest of the world, he had to finagle many more millions of dollars from Charles Bluhdorn and Barry Diller, using his charm to convince these capitalistic moguls to continue supporting his paean to Communism. Only Beatty, a past master at manipulating the gays, bisexuals, cokeheads, lechers, and the rest of the kinky lot that ran the studios of the New Hollywood, could have pulled off such an irony-drenched feat.

Again he selected Richard Sylbert to design the production. "It's 1980," recalls Sylbert, "and he and I were walking along a railroad track one hundred and twenty-five kilometers above the Arctic Circle, setting up something that we would shoot the following winter, because it's going to be covered in snow, but we have to get it all organized while there's no snow, so we could see it. We were walking down this long railroad track, and you see nothing, and then you see two people coming down the track, a man and a woman, and they get closer, and it's like the shot on the camel in *Lawrence of Arabia*. They're getting closer and closer and closer and at about a hundred feet away, Warren starts to look at her. About seventy-five feet away, the woman says, 'Warren?' It was *her* [a beautiful dark-haired Finnish woman he'd romanced in a hotel room in Cannes in the sixties, when he'd been promoting *The Roman Spring of Mrs. Stone*]. He was thrilled, and he thought it was so funny.

"Warren and I were once sitting in France when we were over there doing *Reds*. And Joan [Collins] was there with her pals. Her book had just been published about Warren and vitamin oils and all the constant sex. He looked at me and then looked at her. 'You gotta admit,' he said, 'she's got a lot of class.' I liked Joan, and so does he."

Warren was not adept when it came to dealing with the Russians. Communist bureaucrats demanded to review the script before permitting him to shoot in the Soviet Union. He turned them down and made the picture in Finland and Spain. Filming finally commenced on August 6, 1979. "The first day of principal photography, Warren broke out in red blisters all over his lips," says Sarah Porterfield. There were whispers about herpes. "There's a girl in our group [Phyllis Major, now deceased] who complained she had gotten a yeast infection from him," Porterfield adds. "Because he was so sexually active, he was passing yeast infections back and forth to his girls. He was called by a mutual friend and told of this, and he got really upset that this was going around."

Work on the picture would continue over the next couple of years, often without a shooting script. "Warren Beatty is *mysterium tremendum,*" said actor Edward Herrmann, who played Max Eastman, John Reed's editor at the left-wing activist publication *The Masses*. "We never saw a script. We could have been shooting *Casablanca* for all we knew."[16] Adds Dick Sylbert, "From the day Warren walked on a set in a movie, it was his agenda, there was gonna be no nonsense. And that's the way he lived his life. His way. I don't know what Frank Sinatra did, but Warren Beatty really did it his way. If Warren's job was to write the movie, he would never finish it. Never. It takes him long enough to do a movie. [At the same time] this guy was the most considerate human being I've ever met. Considerate as a director, writer, person, everything. [Cinematographer] Vittorio Storaro was trying some very dangerous stuff in three sequences in *Reds*. One was a factory scene with a lot of smoke. Later we're looking at the monitor and Warren says, 'Vittorio, are you sure about all that smoke?' 'Ah, don't worry,' says Vittorio, 'it's going to be fine.' The film had to go to Italy to be processed, so it was weeks later before you saw the rushes. About three weeks passed, and as I'm watching the rushes of this scene, I notice Vittorio shrinking down in the chair. As soon as the rushes are over, he jumps up and screams, 'Oh, my God! I have to go call Warren! The film is a disaster!' He gets Warren on the phone and says, 'Something terrible has happened.' Warren says, 'Are your children all right? Is your family okay?' Vittorio says, 'No, no, Warren, it's too much smoke in that thing.' Warren says, 'Vittorio, it's only a movie.' "

Not everyone found Warren so thoughtful. When he insisted that Maureen Stapleton, who played Emma Goldman in *Reds*, do fifty takes for a simple piece of business, she finally screamed at him in exasperation. On another occasion, he called for yet another take after she'd delivered a rousing speech in the rain to a huge crowd. "Are you out of your fucking mind?" Maureen yelled, and in support of her, the entire crew broke into cheers. As Bob Towne later put it, Warren "works everybody to a frazzle" but always "wins them back."[17] Elaine Dundy, author of *Finch, Bloody Finch*, later told Warren, "Maureen always gives sympathetic performances, but her Emma Goldman has exactly the right edge. How did you pull that performance out of her?"

"I hired her son Danny to work on the film," Warren said.[18]

His affair with Diane Keaton made their working relationship difficult. During months of filming, he tried to control her every movement and utterance on screen. Keaton is too good an actress for intrusive directing, and eventually she rebelled, scowling at him on the set, fighting him off, and shaking her copy of the script in his face. Some observers took Warren's side. "It was not easy directing Diane," said writer Jerzy Kosinski, who played the Bolshevik leader Grigory Zinoviev. Others tried to remain neutral. George Plimpton, who played Horace Whigham, a powerful publisher, recalled, "Warren was very fastidious. He did thirty or forty takes, all the time. Diane almost got broken. I thought he was trying to break her into what Louise Bryant had been like with John Reed."[19]

The real problem was Warren's ego—Diane outperformed him in every scene they appeared together in. Moreover, some say she was directing *him*. Wrote David Thomson in *Film Comment*, "Beatty is not the easiest actor to play with: he can be chilly and hidden on screen—not so much out of vanity as caution. Some actresses have wilted in his presence, but Keaton assaults him, reads him the riot act, mauls him until the actor-producer-director rediscovers his own charm."

He received some help in the rewriting of *Reds* from his old friend Elaine May, who was brought in, as she'd later be on Dustin Hoffman's *Tootsie*, to improve the script. Though she declined to accept a credit on any project that she didn't initiate, she relished her growing status in the industry as a script doctor.[20]

Dick Sylbert recalls, "Finally, we're coming to the end. Warren's dying—he's got to die in the Russian hospital set. It's going on, and on, and on. Vittorio Storaro's family was in London, and each time he'd come home, his kids would be hanging out the window, and they'd yell down to him, 'Pa! Pa! Is he dead yet?' Because they wanted to go home. He'd say, 'No, not yet, but he's very seeck.' Finally, after two more weeks, Vittorio comes home and the kids ask if Warren is dead yet. 'Yep,' says Vittorio."

In Sylbert's observation, Warren carefully thought out every move he made as a producer. "Everything about Warren was calculated. *Everything* went through the machine, the pros and the cons. 'If I do this, what'll happen?' 'If I say this, what'll happen?' " Eventually his compulsive work habits backfired, undermining his health. The eighteen months he spent filming and editing *Reds* left him so depleted he was unable to see the picture through to a successful release. Nor did his affair with Keaton survive the shoot. When the film wrapped, she went off to co-star with Albert Finney in a picture about the breakup of a marriage entitled *Shoot the Moon*, giving what many critics considered to be her finest performance to date. Alan Parker, her director, recalled, "If anyone mentioned Big W, she'd just walk away. There was no way she was going to share all that."[21]

Excruciatingly exacting as he could be, it was Beatty's producing, writing, and directing of *Reds*, rather than his acting, that turned the project into a brilliant, *Citizen Kane*–type collage of drama and documentary footage, a panorama of a thrilling period in recent history, full of hope and idealism. (Woody Allen's *Zelig*, in which interviews with real people were juxtaposed with archival illustrations and newsreel outtakes, was intended as a sendup of *Reds*).[22] Elaine Dundy remembered that Warren's mind "was like a steel trap," which was what was needed to hold the huge production together. "Maureen Stapleton was visiting me in my apartment," she recalls. "I'd taken her to see Beryl Reid in a lesbian play. Warren joined us later at my place. 'I met you once,' he said to me. 'I was with Vivien Leigh, and later I saw a preview of your daughter's [Tracy Tynan's] film.' I remember thinking, 'It's a producer's job to be very good with memory and figures.' "[23]

Unfortunately, shooting *Reds'* 750,000 feet of film did not leave Warren with the necessary energy to protect and promote his film the way he had *Bonnie and Clyde*. He more or less finished *Reds* and threw it to the wolves. Jerzy Kosinski, who, with his girlfriend Kiki von Frauenhofer, shared Warren's cold-water two-bedroom house during location shooting in Finland, said Warren was "exhausted. Coughing all the time. Sick. Emaciated." Working eighteen-hour days, he lost thirty pounds and suffered terribly as he toiled straight through bouts of chronic laryngitis and a tubercular cough.

When the picture went over its twenty-million-dollar budget, Paramount production chief Barry Diller stopped talking to Beatty. As costs rose to fifty-five million dollars, a bunker mentality prevailed both in the executive suite in L.A. and on Beatty's overseas sets. Rumors of another *Heaven's Gate*—at forty-four million dollars,[24] the costliest egg ever laid by the New Hollywood—began to spread. Warren made a crucial mistake when he decided not to talk to the press, motivated no doubt by a desire not to exacerbate an already explosive situation, and afraid of further imperiling his picture by annoying the studio. But in clamming up, he sacrificed all the free publicity that would have accrued from hundreds of stories. His offbeat picture badly needed all the publicity it could get if it were to succeed at the box office.

Diller took part of the blame, later explaining that the studio had misunderstood the picture from the start. "No preproduction was done on the film; we had to start immediately because of the availability of the actors. So it was always catch-up. It was originally budgeted at twenty million dollars. It should have been budgeted in the high twenties or low thirties. . . . We fought. . . . You can't work in that process unless you fight. If you have a point, the only way to make it is with a certain level of viciousness or the other person doesn't know you mean it. You have to show you care." Nonetheless, in stonewalling Warren, he admitted, "My behavior was unfortunate." Behind the carefully chosen words may have been a wish to strangle Warren, but at this late date Diller knew that candor was less important than damage control. Besides, he'd laid off much of the film's cost on a U.K. tax shelter.[25]

When Diller saw five hours of rushes on Thanksgiving 1979—mostly Diane's scenes—he was impressed and threw all his weight behind the picture, but some of the harm proved irreparable. "Every movie is like a war," said designer Richard Sylbert, and though Warren was a seasoned "field marshal," he was suffering from terminal burnout insofar as *Reds* was concerned. Workaholism is a serious disease when permitted to run riot, and in *Reds* he'd let his obsession take over his life. There was something pathetic in his admission, "I don't know what I do for fun. I don't say work is one thing and fun is another. I have fun working, I hope, and if I don't have fun working, I'm not happy."[26] Work had become his god, a false one that permitted him to lose himself completely, and perilously, in the life of John Reed.

His ill-considered refusal to screen the film for *Life* cost him a major spread in the magazine, which canceled its story on *Reds*. His ban on press previews resulted in the loss of cover stories in both *Newsweek* and the *New York Times* Arts and Leisure section. He lost thousands of column inches in the press and free time on television by alienating reporters, explaining, "I find it better policy in general not to do interviews, and instead let the film, you know, kind of speak for itself." In her NBC *Today* spot, Rona Barrett referred to Warren as a person "who is often credited with playing the media the way Isaac Stern plays the violin." Then why, Rona asked, was he deliberately sabotaging *Reds*? As Warren's silence began to fuel speculation that the picture was a costly, out-of-control bomb, Michael Eisner, then president of Paramount, tried to come to Warren's aid, telling reporters, "Warren is a responsible filmmaker who's going over schedule with responsibility, and going over budget by about fifteen to twenty percent. . . . [An out-of-control production goes] two hundred to four hundred percent over budget." But in a Paramount memo, Eisner lamented the studio's decision to greenlight Warren's epic and, using a baseball metaphor, cautioned studio executives against trying to hit home runs with would-be blockbusters.[27]

Reds received numerous Oscar nominations, but Beatty's publicity embargo also extended to refusing to stage a campaign for the Oscars. This was another grave miscalculation. Because of the nature of the Oscar balloting, producers are expected to advertise, hold screenings, and in general court the industry for votes.

One of the longest pictures ever made, there were 130 hours of footage to consider when principal photography was completed. It took editors Dede Allen and Craig McKay, working closely with Warren and a corps of sub-editors at JRS Productions on West Fifty-fourth Street in Manhattan, nineteen months to bring the footage down to a running time of 199 minutes. Thanks to recent technology, the film was edited on videotape, permitting splicings to be viewed with-in minutes. Once a decision was reached regarding what was to go into the final cut, the editing process took place on actual film.

In the fall of 1981 a screening was held on the thirtieth floor of the Gulf + Western Building in Manhattan's Columbus Circle, attended only by Warren, Diller, and Bluhdorn. Fortunately the latter loved the picture, and he dined with Warren and Diller in the screening room, talking until 1 A.M. and promising full backing. After a November 9 screening for other Paramount executives, serious doubt was expressed about the film's marketability. Exhibitors later voiced sim-ilar reservations.

In view of the studio's nervousness, it was fortunate for Warren that he had "final cut"—the contractual privilege of controlling a motion picture's length and form. At three and one half hours, *Reds* was just fifteen minutes shorter than *Gone With the Wind* and faced the same resistance from theater owners, who could only show a movie of that length once on weeknights and three times a day on weekends, severely limiting ticket sales. David O. Selznick, producer of *GWTW*, had waged the biggest publicity campaign in movie history to over-come these strictures. *Reds* needed much the same sort of hoopla for healthy box-office receipts as well as Oscar wins. *GWTW* also received an exclusive run in special venues, but Paramount announced it would open *Reds* simultaneously in four hundred theaters, which led reporters and movie commentators to specu-late that the studio was maneuvering to get big audiences before the picture was stiffed by bad reviews. Warren's ostrichlike behavior in the face of a bloodthirsty press seemed incomprehensible. The younger Warren of *Bonnie and Clyde* would have been in there slugging—and scoring knockouts.

He was equally intransigent when ABC, who offered to pay $6.5 million for TV rights, asked to cut ten minutes from the film's unwieldy length in order to finish the broadcast in time for the local news shows. Though $6.5 million would have helped Paramount defray the hefty production costs, Warren refused to budge, effectively killing the deal. It seemed irrational and unnecessary, since the film could easily be seen in its entirety on videocassette. His stubbornness was more than a little suicidal, since it virtually assured no one would ever again give him final cut. Was he subconsciously trying to render himself unemploy-able due to burnout? Some of his remarks sounded defeatist. "At a certain point, you feel a little silly about trying to retain nine minutes of a film. . . . Acting and directing movies are hard enough for me anyway. You feel foolish enough when you are trying to keep a ninety-five-thousand-ton soufflé from falling, so we have to go through some rituals in order to keep our dignity in this work."

Reds was emphatically a work of dignity and a work of art, its only failure lying in Warren's lack of entrepreneurial skills. A producer is responsible for the total picture from inception through promotion and distribution. In assuming the producer's role at this point in his life, he'd seriously overreached his area of competence. But if he was not equal to the job of putting *Reds* over with the public, he succeeded in creating a masterwork. When *Reds* was released on December 4, 1981, critic David Israel wrote, "Warren Beatty has made his lasting mark on film, has provided the innovation, has become the man who created the movie as journalism and journalism as the movie." Everyone who mattered, except for Pauline Kael, agreed that *Reds* was a tour de force. Kael wrote in *The New Yorker*, "It's because of the way *Reds* wavers and searches for what it's trying to say that it needs this length." Rex Reed complained that John Reed "changed nothing, made no impact, and influenced no succeeding generations. . . . Why should we remember him?" But the film's few detractors were buried under an avalanche of praise. *Vogue*'s critic called it "a staggering, brave, romantic, intelligent, and peculiarly subjective movie. . . . The blame for its freshness, its candor, its fearless use of elision and ellipsis, must come to rest with Beatty." *Time*'s reviewer wrote that *Reds* "combines the majestic sweep of *Lawrence of Arabia* and *Doctor Zhivago*—David Lean and Robert Bolt's mature and exhilarating epics—with the rueful comedy and historical fatalism of *Citizen Kane*." Kenneth Tynan called it "an old-fashioned love story that few moviegoers will have any difficulty recognizing or embracing."

Shortly after the film was released, Elaine Dundy ran into Warren in New York. "I was on Fifth Avenue," she says, "and on a side street in the fifties, where Mr. Kenneth's salon was, I saw Warren walking with Mary Tyler Moore, three days or so after her son committed suicide. I told him the picture was wonderful and congratulated him again on directing Maureen so well."

By April of 1982 the *New York Daily News* was reporting that *Reds* was "doing dismally," playing to an average of fifty-seven customers per performance at ten New York City theaters. As critics in the industry accused Warren of being a prima donna, Robert Benton, his old *Bonnie and Clyde* collaborator, commented, "There is a part of him that is an outlaw. He's chosen to be aloof.

I think he's always remained outside the movie business. He's never won an Academy Award."

Reds would change all that. In March 1982 Warren received the Directors Guild of America award for best feature film, a sure sign that he would be the leading contender for that year's Oscar for Best Director. Accepting the citation at the Beverly Hilton in L.A. he lauded his leading lady, Diane Keaton, as one "whose acting integrity can hold a movie together," and he also singled out Jack Nicholson, "whose integrity can hold a director together."

When the Oscar nominations were announced, Reds received a whopping twelve, the most since A Man for All Seasons in 1966. Warren became the only person in movie history twice to win multiple nominations as producer, director, actor, and co-writer.[28] Surely, many predicted, this would be Warren's year. On Oscar night in April 1982, he escorted Diane to the annual telecast. Both Warren and David Puttnam, producer of Chariots of Fire, believed that the winner of the Costume Design statuette would indicate how the other awards would go for the rest of the evening. When Morgan Fairchild announced Chariots' Milena Canonero as the winner, Puttnam beamed, and Beatty disconsolately buried his face in his hands. "What the heck were our costumes, after all?" Puttnam exulted. "A few shorts and singlets. I knew from that moment that things looked good for Chariots. It was the end for Beatty and Reds."[29]

Not entirely, for the Beatty Oscar jinx was at last over. Warren won his first Oscar not as an actor, but in the elite Best Director category, which placed him in the same company with Hollywood legends like Lewis Milestone, Frank Capra, Leo McCarey, Victor Fleming, William Wyler, Elia Kazan, George Stevens, and John Ford. The filmmaker with whose work Warren's Reds could most accurately be compared was the generalissimo-like British director David Lean, winner of Academy Awards for The Bridge over the River Kwai and Lawrence of Arabia. Though Lean did not win an Oscar for his superb direction of Doctor Zhivago, that film's large-scale, surging drama influenced Warren as he was envisaging his epic-size Reds.

Both Warren and Diane Keaton were nominated in the acting categories. Warren lost to Henry Fonda for On Golden Pond and Diane to Katharine Hepburn, Fonda's co-star in the same film. Warren and Trevor Griffiths were nominated for Best Screenplay Written Directly for the Screen, but they lost to Colin Welland for Chariots of Fire. Jack Nicholson, who played Eugene O'Neill in *Reds*, lost the Best Supporting Oscar to John Gielgud for *Arthur*. "The Academy has been a little reticent to give [Warren] his due," said Nicholson. "They think he's a little too pretty and cute."[30] There was one acting win— Maureen Stapleton did take the Best Supporting Actress prize.

In accepting the Oscar for Best Director of 1981, Warren paid special tribute to Diane Keaton and then figuratively kissed every capitalist ass that had been involved in funding his Communist manifesto. "I want to name Mr. Barry Diller, who runs Paramount . . . and Mr. Charles Bluhdorn, who runs Gulf + Western and God knows what else, and I want to say to you gentlemen that no matter how much we may have wanted to strangle each other from time to time, I think that your decision, taken in the great capitalistic tower of Gulf + Western, to finance a three-and-a-half-hour romance which attempts to reveal for the first time just something of the beginnings of American socialism and American Communism, reflects credit not only upon you; I think it reflects credit upon Hollywood and the movie business wherever that is, and I think it reflects more particular credit upon [the] freedom of expression that we have in American society, and the lack of censorship we have from the government or the people who put up the money."

Later he told the press, "I see myself as a very tired person as a result of this. I don't know what I'm going to do immediately, but it's a flattering question." It felt "good," he added, to clutch an Oscar at last. Despite his personal victory, the evening did not, as he'd wished, belong to *Reds*. Despite the film's multiple nominations, it was eclipsed by the dark horse, *Chariots of Fire*, which won four Oscars to *Reds'* three and took the coveted Best Picture award. "I think we were treated very nicely," said Warren, but the less diplomatic Puttnam belittled Warren's Best Directing Oscar by dragging the losing *Chariots* director, Hugh Hudson, up to the stage with him when he accepted the Best Picture statuette. "Hugh is without doubt a better director than Warren is, or ever will be," Puttnam later told columnist Marilyn Beck. "And so are Steven Spielberg and Louis Malle. . . . [Beatty's Oscar was] the academy's acknowledgment that a gorgeous actor, a pretty boy, could raise fifty million dollars to make that lumbering picture."

With that ill-advised fulmination, Puttnam, who was British, alienated the Hollywood Establishment, which dumped him before the decade was over. Hired as CEO of Columbia Studios, Puttnam was fired after little more than a year. British filmmaker and author Nicholas Kent identified the six powerful figures in Hollywood most responsible for Puttnam's downfall: Warren, Dustin Hoffman, Bill Murray, Bill Cosby, Michael Ovitz, and Ray Stark. All of them resented Puttnam's charge that agents and stars inflated the cost of moviemaking by demanding exorbitant fees. "Hollywood eats outsiders for breakfast," observed attorney Peter Dekom. "Hollywood does not want to change, and since Hollywood is a town in which you have to get certain talent to work with you, if you come out alienating that talent, then the change you wish so very much to implement will never occur."[31]

But Puttnam was correct about one thing; *Reds* was not worth what it had cost the studio. The film never recouped Paramount's thirty-three-to-fifty-million-dollar investment. It needed to gross seventy-five million dollars just to break even. Though it was briefly the number-one box-office attraction in major cities, rural audiences did not care to learn about how the Soviet Union had come about. In the final analysis, *Reds* earned twenty-one million dollars, half its production cost, and Paramount bitterly complained that if Warren had been willing to promote the film as he had his others, another twenty-five million dollars would have been forthcoming, and he would have swept the Oscars. According to an industry insider, Beatty "may have committed the biggest faux pas in the last fifty years of filmmaking" by refusing to campaign for the Oscars or do publicity for the movie. Another accused him of "high perversity: only a shell-shocked showman declines to promote the biggest picture he has ever made."[32]

But that is exactly what he was: shell-shocked, having bitten off more than he could chew in deciding to direct, produce, write, and act in *Reds*. Some degree of megalomania was involved. Despite the honors that *Reds* received, there was an unmistakable aura of doom surrounding the picture, due less to its disappointing box office than because it symbolized the Götterdämmerung of the New Hollywood. The picture that usually received the blame for killing it off was *Heaven's Gate*, but it was Warren, as much as Michael Cimino, who presided over its dismantling. "The film that caused the crisis could have been [William Friedkin's] *Sorcerer* or [Coppola's] *Apocalypse Now* or [Spielberg's] *1941* or even [Beatty's] *Reds*," wrote Peter Biskind. "So far as the ambition and budget were concerned, Cimino didn't do anything Friedkin, Coppola, Spielberg, and Beatty hadn't done." Producer Jerry Hellman blamed the end of the New Hollywood on the tyranny of the director and the corresponding trivialization of producers and studio executives. "The director is in creative respects the most important part of the team. But directors are not producers, by and large, and if you look at the cost overruns and films out of control, and huge, terrible movies being made by guys with two credits like Cimino, you begin to see how they built a disaster in there."[33]

Increasingly, auteurs like Beatty and Coppola would be replaced in the driver's seat by such younger studio executives as Diller, Eisner, and Jeffrey Katzenberg, men who were good at saying no—and often little else. The new breed had been trained in network television. Once they wrested Hollywood from Beatty, Scorsese, Coppola and other hometown boys, their reign at the studios would spell the end of movies as an art form. Says director John Milius, "The stuff that brought it all to an end came from within. Diller, Eisner, and Katzenberg—they ruined the movies." Hollywood would become a factory grinding out remakes, recycled comic strips, and other "high concept," or simplistic, fare that could be pitched to studios and distributors, and ultimately the public, like soap or cereal. Mutating from New Hollywood pioneer to high-concept schlock-meister with *Gremlins* and *Jurassic Park*, Spielberg said, "If a person can tell me the idea in twenty-five words or less, it's going to make a pretty good movie." The era of the sequel, the prequel, the look-alike, and the crash-and-burn action flick would leave little room for art. Most of the dynamic directors of the seventies—Friedkin, Bogdanovich, Ashby, Schrader, and Penn—were burned out. While some of them survived into the eighties and nineties, such as Beatty, Scorsese, George Lucas, Brian De Palma, Spielberg, and Altman, only Spielberg would completely cross over into the new regime, founding a major studio, DreamWorks. Warren, who'd always been a part of the system, would adapt, but he'd produce only one more significant movie, *Bulworth*.

Despite his personal and artistic exhaustion after *Reds*, Warren recovered his health, thanks to the generally wholesome regimen of his lifestyle—no drinks, no drugs, plenty of healthy food and exercise. Peers like Hal Ashby fell victim to the cocaine blitz that hit the industry in the seventies (and still rages). When Ashby reappeared in Hollywood after years of reclusiveness, Warren helped him get into Johns Hopkins for treatment of pancreatic cancer, urging him to undergo surgery for the removal of tumors. His chemo treatments were unbearably painful. He died in the late 1980s at age fifty-nine.

Shirley MacLaine, who'd starred in Ashby's *Being There*, spoke at his funeral, which was held at the Directors Guild on Sunset Boulevard. Warren, Bruce Dern, Andy Garcia, Jerome Hellman, and Bud Cort were among the mourners. Though underestimated by critics, Ashby was loved by the Hollywood community. Even in his sad later years, "actors killed to work with him," wrote Peter Biskind, who added that Ashby's funeral was "a wake as much for Hal as for themselves, for their dreams, for the best years of their lives."

Another casualty among Warren's friends was Roman Polanski, who had to flee the U.S. due to a sexcapade with a minor. In 1979 Polanski was arrested in Los Angeles and charged with unlawful sexual intercourse with a thirteen-year-old girl.[34] Though he was having a comeback, and scheduled to direct *The First Deadly Sin*, a major production, Polanski seemed determined to self-destruct. In his forty-fourth year,[35] he had the bad judgment to shoot a *Vogue Hommes* spread on adolescent girls, a thinly disguised ruse to meet nubile Lolitas. During one session, a thirteen-year-old[36] he later referred to as "Sandra" took off her blouse, flaunting the fact that she wasn't wearing any undergarments. "She had nice breasts," Polanski later recalled. During a subsequent session, Sandra told him she'd been having sex since she was eight. He asked if she'd be willing to come to Jack Nicholson's house, where they could enjoy some privacy. He knew that Nicholson was traveling, but he also knew that Nicholson's mistress, Anjelica Huston, might show up at any moment.

Though Sandra was a minor, Polanski fed her Cristal champagne. "When I asked her to remove her blouse, she did so without hesitation," he said. He asked her to change into another outfit and "was very aware of the flash of nakedness as she slipped the dress on. . . . I could sense a certain erotic tension between us."[37] Leading her out to the Jacuzzi, he watched her undress, took a few pictures, and stripped and jumped into the pool when she invited him in. Later they retired to the bedroom and dried each other off. Polanski began to kiss and fondle her. "She spread herself and I entered her," he said. They were going at it when Anjelica arrived. He withdrew before climax,[38] and then he and Sandra dressed and left.

The following day, he was arrested as he walked out of the Beverly Wilshire Hotel. According to Shelley Winters, who'd recently co-starred with Polanski in *The Tenant*, he'd been set up from the start, a victim of the conservative Hollywood Establishment, which wanted to be rid of him.[39] The LAPD charged him with rape and took him back to Nicholson's house, armed with a search warrant. Nicholson was still away in Aspen, but he was later hauled in by the police for fingerprinting. Anjelica also fell into the trap that Polanski had unwittingly set, showing up at Nicholson's Mulholland Drive house just as the police arrived. They proceeded to search her, and found cocaine in her purse. She had to go to the police station along with Polanski. Later, her lawyers negotiated her release on condition that she testify against Polanski. She was only too happy to do so. "I couldn't really blame her for accepting the deal, though it left me feeling slightly bitter," said Polanski.[40]

At the grand jury hearing, Sandra testified that Polanski gave her a Quaalude in addition to the champagne before having sex with her. He was indicted on six counts, including rape, "an act of perversion (oral copulation with the sexual organ of a child)," and sodomy. Again, Polanski was ostracized in Hollywood. His agent, Sue Mengers, turned on him,[41] and the joke around town was that his next picture would be *Close Encounters of the Third Grade*. He pleaded guilty in court, telling the judge, "I had sexual intercourse with a person not my wife, under the age of eighteen."[42] While awaiting sentencing, he was remanded to Chino State Prison for ninety days for psychiatric testing. He found himself in a filthy cell with a flush toilet.

Oddly, he enjoyed prison life, feeling more contentment than he'd ever known. Though he was granted early release after serving half his time, he still faced a sentencing that could return him to prison. Warren and Jack Nicholson planned a party to celebrate his release on probation, but Polanski bolted, flying out of LAX on a British Airways plane to London. Judge Laurence Rittenbrand issued a bench warrant for his arrest. If Polanski ever returned to America, he'd face up to fifty years in prison. From that day on, he has lived in exile, a fugitive from justice.

Nicholson, desperate for a director for *The Two Jakes*, a sequel to *Chinatown* that he and Bob Towne developed, visited Polanski in Paris. Harrison Ford, star of Polanski's *Frantic*, who, according to the *Star*, reportedly likes strippers[43] as much as Nicholson likes the L.A. Lakers, joined them for several nights on the town, and later it was reported that Nicholson was using his influence with the L.A. judiciary to end Polanski's exile and get him back to work in the U.S. Nothing came of it. "The spirit of laughter has deserted me," Polanski wrote in 1984, from his Paris apartment on the Avenue Montaigne, just off the

Champs-Élysées. Unintentionally exposing the depth of his self-hatred, he added, "I am widely regarded, I know, as an evil, profligate dwarf." Most touching of all was his admission, in the coda of his 1984 autobiography, that even his tremendous drive and sense of artistic mission had been diminished. "I seem to be toiling to no discernible purpose," he wrote, revealing the ultimate spiritual bankruptcy of a life driven by lust and ambition.

Many women, attracted by his notoriety, still wanted to meet him. "I have never hidden the fact that I love girls," he told *Paris-Match,* "and I will say once again for all, I love very young girls."[44] It sounded like a personals ad for nymphets. He eventually married actress Emmanuelle Seigner, had two children, and recovered his zeal for moviemaking, turning out *Death and the Maiden* and *The Ninth Gate,* the latter starring Johnny Depp. Though the films didn't succeed, international honors were heaped on him, including a seat in the august Academie des Beaux-Arts that previously had been occupied by Marcel Carne, director of *Children of Paradise.* Steven Spielberg offered him the opportunity to direct *Schindler's List,* but he declined, fearing that working in the remains of the Krakow ghetto, which he'd escaped at age six, would be traumatic. An icon in his native Poland, he finally returned to his homeland in 2001, at age sixty-eight, to shoot *The Pianist,* Wladyslaw Szpilman's autobiographical account of the Holocaust, as experienced by a young Jewish pianist and composer in the Warsaw ghetto. Made in English, the film was financed by France's Canal Plus cable television channel, and produced by Polanski's old friend, Gene Gutowski. "It is the most important film in my career," Polanski said.

Jack Nicholson's seventeen-year love affair with Anjelica Huston ended when he got actress Rebecca Broussard pregnant with their daughter, Lorraine. He and Rebecca later had a son, but, predictably, Jack soon moved on to greener pastures.

Another of Warren's friends, Robert Evans, was, like Polanski, getting into trouble with the law: on July 31, 1980, he pleaded guilty to the misdemeanor charge of cocaine possession.[45] Charles Evans, Bob's brother, and Michael Shure, Bob's brother-in-law, bought five ounces of cocaine for nineteen thousand dollars from undercover narcotics agents in New York on May 2. Although Bob was three thousand miles away in California during the transaction, he pleaded guilty to cocaine possession on July 31, in New York. Bob later explained, "Though it was [Charles's] hand caught in the cookie jar, it was me who said, 'Let's buy it, put it in the vault.'" Bob Evans had once brought Paramount

Pictures out of the graveyard with *The Godfather,* but now the studio disowned him, issuing a terse disclaimer: "Evans is not an employee of Paramount and has not been an employee of Paramount for four years. He is an independent contractor producing pictures for us." Other business associates were more supportive, particularly Robert Altman, director of Bob's latest film, *Popeye,* who poured an entire carafe of red wine over a *New York Daily News* journalist's head and said, "Been reading your column for the past month, my dear. 'Cocaine' Evans is my partner. Next time call him Bob." Hauled into court, Evans was given a year's probation in exchange for promising the judge to produce a thirty-second antidrug message to be aired within the year as a public-service commercial on TV.[46]

For the most part, Warren and other members of what some called the Pussy Posse remained loyal to Evans. The regulars on Evans's tennis courts included Nicholson, Bob Towne, Dustin Hoffman, and Robert Duvall. They customarily bet one thousand dollars a set. One day in the 1980s, both Warren and Nicholson sat on the sidelines, watching a doubles match between Bob and Charles Evans and Ted Kennedy and John Tunney. The Evans brothers won the first two sets, but when a TV producer named Wendell Niles Jr. bet a thousand dollars that the Evanses would be defeated in the third set, Ted Kennedy took off his back brace and went to work. He and Tunney demolished the Evans boys, 6–2.[47]

In the 1980s, when Bob Evans attempted to resuscitate his career by producing a new film, *The Cotton Club*, studio financing was no longer available to him, and he turned to dubious sources, including a drug racketeer, to raise twenty million dollars. The drug dealer was murdered, it was rumored, over a cocaine theft. Bob was implicated in what came to be known as the Cotton Club murder case. Later, his movie *The Cotton Club* flopped, a forty-million-dollar disaster, and Evans's career went on hold.[48] The company he'd formed with Nicholson and Towne to produce *The Two Jakes* collapsed in animosity. Towne had tried to get rid of Evans, but Nicholson had remained loyal. Hearing of the acrimony between the partners, Paramount, which had been eager to produce the *Chinatown* sequel, pulled out. A million dollars had already been spent on set construction, and creditors sued the former partners for three million dollars. Eventually Nicholson both directed and starred in the film, but he admitted that it would have been better with the still-banished Polanski directing.

In Los Angeles, Warren attended a dinner party for twelve at Jennifer Jones and Norton Simon's house in Malibu. Cary Grant and Carol Matthau were seated directly across the table, and Grant covertly pointed to Warren and asked Mrs. Matthau, "Do you see him?" She nodded. "I used to be him," said Grant. A clever and very popular woman—often identified as Truman Capote's inspiration for the fictional courtesan Holly Golightly, in *Breakfast at Tiffany's*— Mrs. Matthau later wrote, "Needless to say, I spent the rest of the dinner telling Cary he was much, much too magnificent to have ever been Warren because that is what that statement called for, and I do know how to play tennis. That was the ball he wanted to bounce back and I continued to do it throughout dinner."[49]

Though Warren might have looked good to the doddering, embittered Cary Grant, he was not happy. The new palimony laws had Hollywood's Don Juans in a dither, and it was entirely possible that one of Warren's casual sex partners might try to hold him up for millions of dollars in court. Becoming almost paranoid, he stashed his money as far away from California as he could, opening several Swiss bank accounts and complaining how unfair it was to have to "pay half your assets to a woman you've been in a romantic relationship with. . . . From now on, if any former lady love wants to find my money, she'll have to search all over the Swiss Alps to get it." Hard words for those he'd been most intimate with, and yet he could also say, "It's very lonely for me to live without a woman, without relating life with or to another person. . . . Life means so much more when it's shared."[50] No doubt the growing number of single households in America found his remark pathetic and politically incorrect. So did some of the women he'd shared his life with. "So we had an affair?" Bianca Jagger snapped. "You must be pretty bad. I don't even remember you."[51] NBC news anchor Jessica Savitch certainly remembered him, but was hardly bowled over. Jessica struck Warren as the perfect mate—attractive, intelligent, and independent minded. Her boss, Ray Timothy, president of NBC-TV, once described her as having "a certain Edith Piaf quality, almost a Judy Garland quality, which not every paid reader had."[52] When Warren first asked her out in 1982, she turned him down. But she couldn't get him out of her mind, and eventually they began an affair.

Like Warren, Savitch had never known contentment. She'd risen from obscurity in 1977, as anchorwoman at KYW-TV in Philadelphia, to the top of the broadcasting heap, as NBC's Washington correspondent on the *Nightly News*. With no more worlds to conquer, she ruefully reflected, "There has not been a single moment in my career when I didn't say, 'Is this all there is?' . . . Success does not have to bring happiness. Success brings success." Her marriage ended in divorce, and her second husband, gynecologist Donald Payne, killed himself following Jessica's miscarriage in 1981.

She was one of the first of the glamour-gal anchors, along with Barbara Walters and Diane Sawyer. Though it did not detract from her popularity with the viewing public, her liaison with Warren damaged her credibility within the media. She often flew to L.A. to be with him, and it was rumored in broadcast circles that she took drugs to overcome jet lag. "She was wound just tighter than a two-dollar clock," said Tom Brokaw, who'd once done a stint with her on the *Today* show. Other associates at the network, from producers to makeup artists, noticed that Warren inevitably called her just before airtime.[53]

Savitch could be as flirtatious with women as with men. She had had several serious lesbian attachments, including an affair with another woman newscaster, but a producer at NBC remarked that Savitch was so distant and cold he "couldn't imagine her having any sexual relationship with anyone."

She surprised her NBC *Frontline* producer David Fanning by dashing out of her office one day and saying that "Senator Gary Hart, a great friend of Warren Beatty, had just called and offered to fly across the country to meet her." Though Warren's affair with Savitch had ended, he was obviously setting her up with Gary Hart. No doubt Savitch felt like Goldie Hawn when the latter said in *There's a Girl in My Soup,* "They were passing me around like a plate of cakes, take a nibble and pass it on. It's not very nice, being passed around."

NBC exploited Savitch for her sex appeal, using her to attract more viewers to the *NBC Nightly News.* When her coke habit caught up with her, the network quickly abandoned her, giving the anchor job to Connie Chung, and kicking Savitch downstairs.

Warren tried to help her, arranging for her to detox at the Sonoma Mission Inn, a celebrity health spa. In 1984, after some plastic surgery on her chin and nose, she holed up at Warren's house. According to David Fanning, the plastic surgery ruined her distinctive Roman nose, and her face no longer had "the right proportions. She had taken the bump out, which was what made the planes of her face work."[54] Moreover, she was obviously anorectic. Soon, she was going on camera stoned on champagne and coke, freaking out before millions of astonished viewers. What was left of her shattered career quickly evaporated. She died in a tragic accident when her newspaper-executive boyfriend, Martin Fishbein, drove their rented station wagon into a canal in Pennsylvania, near the Delaware River. Ed Bradley and Sue Simmons were the only well-known persons at her funeral in Atlantic City. Again, one of Goldie's lines from *There's a Girl in My Soup* was apt: "That's me, the disposable girl. Use me and throw me away."

Warren's relations with his sister remained civil if somewhat aloof. "He's always somewhere, and I'm always somewhere else," Shirley said. "We hardly get to see each other lately." She treated their parents to a visit to Nathan Pritikin's Longevity Center in Los Angeles, and Pritikin helped Kathlyn Beaty's diabetes. Warren wanted to assist his mother and father, but they remained as independent and proud as ever. According to Shirley, Warren often said that if he offered them a million-dollar house in Hollywood with a staff of servants, they would be insulted and turn it down, saying, "We wouldn't live here! We want our *own* house on our *own* block back in Richmond, Virginia!"[55] When his father fell ill with leukemia, Warren saw to it that he was treated at Johns Hopkins, and Ira Beaty survived a few more years, finally dying on January 14, 1987.

One of Warren's stranger dates in 1983 was seventy-nine-year-old Lillian Hellman, who, blind, crippled, and with a permanent pacemaker, was obviously dying. "Warren took Lilly out to dinner," recalls Hellman's companion, Peter Feibleman, who adds that Hellman later remarked, "I think I've come to interest Warren. I don't know why—I can't imagine that a lot of women interest him, except sexually." When Feibleman asked her how many males had intrigued her, except sexually, she replied, "Not many. Most of us live by pretending to be more interested than we are."[56]

The year 1983 marked a splashy resurgence in Shirley's career, capped by the Best Actress Oscar for *Terms of Endearment*. Characteristically, on accepting the award, the fifty-year-old diva didn't bother to pretend humility, or even modesty, announcing, "I deserve this." For once, she was right; it was her fifth nomination, and the Academy Award for her many-splendored portrait of Aurora Greenway, mother of a dying girl, was richly deserved, though it would have made equal sense going to her co-star, Debra Winger, who ennobled the screen as Emma, her daughter, and was also up for the Best Actress Oscar. Off-camera, during filming, the two rival leading ladies had duplicated heir mother-daughter animosity, taunting and tussling during a heated rehearsal. Jack Nicholson, who played Shirley's horny, potbellied lover Garrett Breedlove, an over-the-hill astronaut, used his considerable diplomatic skills to separate his not always compatible co-stars. He liked them both. The husky-voiced Winger, a liberated spirit "a lot like me," Nicholson said, spent some time "swathed in black spandex" around his house, and Shirley, his best friend Warren's older sister, naturally received his respect. He'd had a hand in getting her the role, not an easy task, since she was no longer bankable. Jennifer Jones (Mrs. Norton Simon) controlled the screen rights, contemplating a comeback as Aurora, but when Nicholson signed for the picture, he created a package that proved attractive to the studios and assured jobs for both Winger and MacLaine. On Oscar night at the Dorothy Chandler Pavilion, a grateful Shirley acknowledged Nicholson from the podium. "To have him in bed was such middle-aged joy," she said. Then she simultaneously complimented and rabbit punched Debra Winger, referring to the younger star's "turbulent brilliance," a crack viewed by many as symptomatic of their competitiveness.[57] Nicholson was well paid for his many services to *Terms of Endearment,* receiving nine million dollars—and the Best Supporting Actor prize, his second Oscar.

To cash in on the publicity, Shirley began to write a book about reincarnation and opened a song-and-dance show on Broadway. During the performance, she produced her Oscar from behind a grand piano on the stage. Warren attended the show at Manhattan's Gershwin Theater on May 10, 1984, and Shirley pitched most of the performance directly to him. Later, he went backstage to congratulate her. "He paid me such a compliment," she said. "You know Warren: he doesn't throw compliments around. . . . He said, 'You're not dipping into your capital this time. You're using your interest.' " Of the two siblings' overbearing egos, hers was still the hardest to take. "Philosophically celebrating myself is what I am into," she boasted.[58]

Shirley's finished manuscript on mysticism and reincarnation was rambling and harebrained. When Warren first heard that she was about to go over the top and publish *Out on a Limb*, her book of paranormal musings, he went to Atlantic City, where she was doing her nightclub act, and tried to dissuade her, taking along Pete Hamill and Bella Abzug. Undeterred by this delegation of sober intellectuals, Shirley submitted her dizzy book to Random House, but editor Jason Epstein turned it down, explaining that he wasn't in the business of defrauding the American public.[59] When the book finally came out on a less illustrious list, it became a number-one bestseller. With decades of notoriety behind her, anything with Shirley MacLaine's name on it would have been a bestseller. For all who disagreed with her, she had a pat answer: "Intellectual cynicism is a sickness."

In Shirley's second *Time* cover story—May 1984—the magazine wrote, "The lovable kook with the carefree sex life and oddball ideas has been transmuted into a role model of a self-possessed, successful woman at fifty." Her relationship with Warren remained "perhaps the most intense, enduring, unresolved and potentially explosive relationship in her life," *Time* revealed. In response, Warren said, "As for what goes on between Shirley and me, you can safely call it complicated. . . . Manners were not invented for nothing."[60]

He briefly dated Mary Tyler Moore, but seemed more serious about Daryl Hannah, later the girlfriend of John F. Kennedy Jr. Daryl had emerged as a star in *Splash*, a film with which Warren had a curious history. Bob Towne had long been working on a script called *Mermaid,* and Warren was set to star in it with Jessica Lange, Ray Stark producing and Herbert Ross directing. But Towne kept fooling around with the idea and stalling in his customary way, until he was scooped by *Splash,* another mermaid story, starring Hannah and a young Tom Hanks, directed by Ron Howard. The film was a huge success, launching several major careers.

Occasionally Warren thought of reviving his romance with Diane Keaton or Julie Christie. "Actually," says Dick Sylbert, "Julie and he are very close friends." Diane wasn't available; by 1987 she was again Al Pacino's mistress. "Diane is real special," Pacino said, "a true *friend*, which is what I look for. I love her spontaneity and sense of humor." After taking Pacino home for dinner with her family, the Halls, Diane commented, "I think it would be wonderful to see myself with one man for the rest of my life. I don't know if I can, though." The following year, the *Los Angeles Herald Examiner* wrote that the forty-two-year-old Diane was pregnant. "Low profile though their relationship may be," the reporter alleged, "Pacino is definitely the father." Shortly thereafter, a miscarriage was reported.[61]

Perhaps the last word on Warren's crucial relationships with Christie and Keaton came from Dick Sylbert, who said, "Warren and Julie were very close. She's very happy right now [the fall of 2000]. She lives her own life. She didn't play this game. This was *not* her game. She'd cry whenever she had a chance about being in Hollywood.

"Diane Keaton, I think, wanted to get married and have children. I don't think Warren misled anybody. I don't think he went in saying, 'Someday, honey, you'll wear a ring.' It's just not like him. Common denominator with the women he's dated: They won an Academy Award. He went for people at the top, but Julie and Diane were the wrong people for him. I know them both well. They knew there would never be a marriage, and if there were, it would never work."

In 1984 and again in 1987 Warren leapt back into politics, supporting the presidential aspirations of Colorado senator Gary Hart. After graduating from the Yale divinity and law schools, Hart had practiced law in Denver, later becoming active in the Democratic Party. He and Warren became friends when they campaigned together for McGovern during the 1972 presidential election.

In 1984 Hart made his bid for the presidency. Leaning heavily on Warren's advice, the candidate and the actor were on the phone almost daily. Political concerts were no longer in style, so Warren moved from impresario to an advisory position closer to the center of Hart's circle. Always in awe of Warren, Hart listened to his opinions about key issues and consulted with him on speeches. Warren came to relish the role of power broker as much as any fictional part he'd ever played on screen, but after the booing debacle that had greeted his speech at Candlestick Park in 1972, he chose, in 1984, to remain behind the scenes, making no public appearances.

Running under the banner of "new ideas for a new generation," and endorsing nuclear-arms control, cost-effective approaches to defense spending, and reshaping the economy through such measures as tax reform, Gary Hart made strong showings in the New England and western primaries. At the San Francisco Democratic National Convention, Warren was an official delegate. He was everywhere in evidence, chatting with George Lucas, and dating CBS television reporter Diane Sawyer. Hart included him in on all key decisions, and Warren wrote his speeches. Hart lost. In retrospect it's clear that the candidate would have been wiser not to rely so heavily on a movie star/playboy for political advice. Walter Mondale became the convention's choice, and in the fall elections, he lost to Ronald Reagan. Some of Warren's show-business colleagues speculated that he always chose to back losers, perhaps out of a compulsion to prove himself better than his heroes. Certainly that had been his pattern with such mentors as Samuel Goldwyn, Sam Spiegel, Arthur Penn, and Charles K. Feldman.

Warren was again involved in 1987 when Hart became the favorite for the Democratic presidential nomination. Hart's enemies began to take note when Warren allegedly lent Hart $265,000 to purchase 135 acres, which Hart somewhat prophetically named Troublesome Gulch.[62] It was also noted, even among Hart's Democratic supporters, that the candidate on occasion stayed at Warren's Mulholland Drive house, a sexual seraglio where Hart was introduced to other well-known womanizers—Jack Nicholson, for one. Sometimes Hart used Warren's house when the latter was not in residence, and Hart's enemies suggested that the very married senator was sleeping around on his wife.

Some members of Hart's inner circle begged him to keep out of Los Angeles altogether, but Hart ignored them, saying, "If people wanted to say there were orgies going on up there and I was chasing starlets, there was nothing I could do about that." There was plenty the fifty-year-old Hart could have done about it, like eschewing the L.A. fleshpots, but he remained loyal to Warren even when another of his show-business supporters, Robert Redford, dropped out of his camp. Hart's worst error, according to Redford, was entangling himself "with the Hollywood set . . . because he ended up thinking he was invisible."[63] Entertainment leaders continued to withdraw their financial support, and screenwriter Joe Eszterhas later wrote that Hart's "binding friendship with Warren destroyed him. Gary, the joke was, wanted to be Warren—the greatest Hollywood swordsman since Milton Berle, and Marilyn [Monroe] had once said Uncle Miltie had the biggest willard she'd ever seen—and Warren wanted to be Gary, the serious social thinker."[64]

Warren was not the right man to advise Hart about the possible dangers of a libertine lifestyle, since Warren refused to accept, as he told a reporter from *Ladies Home Journal*, that "my *supposed* lifestyle would hurt me or my candidate. Maybe twenty years ago, but not today. I don't believe the majority of people in this country are interested in whether you are married or not or what your sexual preferences are."[65] He could not have been more wrong, and his naïveté on this point made him a distinct liability to Gary Hart. As underground rumors of his infidelity circulated, the candidate recklessly challenged the media to "follow me around" to check on reports of philandering. Three weeks into his campaign, the *Miami Herald* did exactly that, camping outside Hart's Washington town house, and later revealing that a young woman had stayed overnight with him while his wife was in Denver. Hart denied everything, denouncing the *Herald* piece as preposterous and inaccurate.

Stage two in the brewing sex scandal erupted when photographs surfaced showing Hart with sexy twenty-nine-year-old swimsuit model Donna Rice sitting on his lap during a rollicking cruise to Bimini on the aptly named yacht *Monkey Business*. A former beauty-pageant winner, Rice had met Hart at rocker Don Henley's Aspen, Colorado, home on New Year's Eve 1986. During their Bimini frolic, after consuming quantities of alcohol, Gary and Donna jumped up on the stage at a nightclub called the Compleat Angler, Gary playing the maracas while Donna sang. Later, after a wine-drenched steak dinner, they spent the night together in the master bedroom of the eighty-five-foot yacht. As Hart held the model in his arms, he confided that he'd twice separated from his wife and had reconciled only to run for president. Later, he'd marry Donna, he promised, and make her his first lady. The dalliance sank his campaign.

None of the many reporters on the story was ever able to establish a connection between Hart's womanizing and Warren's circle. When the scandal broke, many supporters immediately defected, but Warren was on the phone to Hart all day. Patrick Caddell, a key figure in the campaign, rushed to Mulholland Drive for a crisis session with Warren, remaining through dinner. A press conference was announced, and Hart followed Warren's advice to remain in the race, admit his wrongdoing, and persuade his wife to forgive him.[66] At the last minute, Hart learned that the *Washington Post* was poised to publish more evidence of his affair with Rice. He owned up to his "fool mistake"[67] and watched his presidential dreams evaporate, withdrawing from the race.[68] At the time, such invasive poking into a statesman's private life was almost unprecedented. The JFK scandals had erupted only after his death; chairman of the Ways and Means Committee Wilbur Mills's affair with dancer Fanne Fox was uncovered by police who caught them in a drunken spree on public roads in 1974; and chairman of the House Administration Committee Wayne Hays was exposed in 1976 by his own mistress, Elizabeth Ray, who revealed she was paid fourteen thousand dollars a year to have sex with him.[69] Gary Hart's downfall marked the first time that a living politician was subjected to such a relentless investigation, but it would become the predominant American political style, culminating in the impeachment of President Clinton following his affair with Monica Lewinsky and the exposure of future President George W. Bush's arrest for drunken driving.

Amazingly, Hart later reentered the 1988 presidential race, his wife by his side. According to the *New York Post*, Warren told him that he had every right to keep his private life and political activities separate, and should try again.[70] After eight years of Reagan extremism, anything was preferable to another four years of Republicans. "Let the people decide," Hart said. "The voters are not dumb." But his reentry in the race was regarded as a joke, and he pulled out again after only a few weeks.

Any hopes Warren may have harbored for a cabinet post were dashed, though he had no remarks for the press. According to Beatty biographer David Thomson, political pundits found "a self-destructive recklessness in Hart that had been influenced by Beatty. Some say inspired. Mentioned in all such studies, Beatty [began] to emerge as a laconic, rootless Mephistopheles. Two political careers finished."[71]

Though Hart was destroyed, Warren was far from convinced that his own political career was over, and he took care not to anger the Democratic Party, working dutifully, if not very enthusiastically, for Michael Dukakis, the party's eventual nominee for the presidency. More active participation on Warren's part was neither wanted nor sought by Dukakis, though his cousin Olympia was the well-known actress who played Cher's mother in *Moonstruck*. Michael Dukakis lost in the fall election.

Warren found himself disillusioned by an electoral process that tortured good men like Gary Hart and Joe Biden (the latter was caught plagiarizing a speech). But Jack Nicholson, undaunted by the Hart fiasco, told *Rolling Stone*, "I'm a Hart supporter because he fucks. Do you know what I mean?"[72] Nicholson was a follower of Wilhelm Reich, a former colleague of Freud's who believed that coitus could cure all of society's ills.

Behind Nicholson's sex obsession, according to his biographer, was the fact that "he couldn't shake a lifetime feeling of vulnerability. He always had a 'sister-mother' thing with the opposite sex. Beauty was a particular Achilles heel for the New Jersey hanger-on who never got to date the pom-pom girls and twirlers."[73] Jennifer Lee wrote that "drinks, drugs, and dicks don't mix—not with Jack, anyway." Nicholson could get violent on occasion. "When he was through with me he began to slap me," claimed an L.A. hooker. "Maybe it was the drugs . . . but he hauled off and hit me hard. . . . 'Take it easy, tiger. Easy, easy,' I kept repeating. He kept slapping."[74] Although the hooker was used to being knocked around during S&M calls, she was terrified of Nicholson because he reminded her of "the Devil," perhaps due to his chilling performance as Jack

Torrance, the murderous caretaker in Kubrick's supernatural shocker *The Shining*. He told the hooker that "lots of people" had pointed out his resemblance to Satan, whom he'd play in 1987's *The Witches of Eastwick*.

For Warren, who was approaching fifty, the mid-1980s marked the beginning of lifetime-achievement awards conferred by prestigious film institutions. Diane Keaton was present on September 10, 1984, when Warren's oeuvre was honored at the Toronto Film Festival. Others who came to toss bouquets and accolades included hosts Gene Siskel, Roger Ebert, Penn, Towne, Nicholson, and Kosinski. At first Warren sounded like someone who'd drifted in from Ganymede, remarking in his diffuse fashion, "When one has become a familiar face, it endows one with responsibilities to respond to questions. It's one of the things you have to go along with when you become a performer or a household word or a sex symbol."[75] He never seemed more stunned or helpless than when he tried to be amusing. But then he went on to deliver some prepared comments that surprised the gathering with their clarity and astuteness; he said he was concerned for "the future of pictures that deal with ideas, given the decreased attention span and the lower median age of moviegoers. It's a crisis affecting the style of filmmaking. . . . Long movies like *Reds* and *Gandhi* and *The Right Stuff* may become extinct. Investors are not excited about participating in them." When pressed to reveal his own plans, he said that the script for his biopic of Howard Hughes was complete, but again the project languished, though he was still mentioning it, in the 1990s, as a vehicle for Madonna as Jean Harlow and Annette Bening as Jean Peters.

For all his talk of "pictures that deal with ideas," most of the films he produced after *Reds* were relatively mindless. His next project starred Molly Ringwald. With the rise of the Brat Pack in the eighties, Miss Ringwald, teenage star of *The Breakfast Club*, had appeared in a string of box-office hits, eventually adorning the cover of *Time* magazine. Warren briefly considered putting her in a movie version of Edie Sedgwick's life, based on a book co-edited by George Plimpton, but instead he cast her in *The Pick-up Artist*, costarring Dennis Hopper, who played her alcoholic father. Reviewers buried the picture, and it soon faded from the theaters. Dennis Hopper survived both alcoholism and drug addiction in his own life, and was blackballed by the Establishment twice, but Warren never turned his back on Hopper, and a few years later gave him some valuable career advice. "It's time you play a straight part," he said, "someone whose problems are caused by outside forces, not from internal things."[76] A number of strong supporting roles followed.

Warren remained one of the richer men in Hollywood and was able to take another of his sabbaticals, going to New York and checking in at the Ritz Carlton. Julia Phillips, who was in New York filming one of her post–*Close Encounters of the Third Kind* bombs, was staying across the hall from him, and was annoyed when he tried to get her ousted from her suite. He wanted it for his current girlfriend Isabelle Adjani, but Phillips thought, "Why move me when it's just for appearances—why worry about appearances when you're Warren Beatty and have gone to all this trouble to get this cocksman rep?" Ellie Peters, a vice president of the hotel who liked to mother Phillips, refused to move her out of her rooms, after which, according to Phillips, Warren got "even more cordial." Later, when she ran into him in the lounge, he was not with Adjani. He stood up to greet Phillips, deliberately blocking her view of his date, but Phillips looked "around his chest and [saw] Molly Ringwald's fat mouth. How does this guy avoid jail?"[77]

A few days later Warren was lunching with publicist Lois Smith in his favorite banquette at the Jockey Club, going over promotion plans for *Ishtar*, a feeble farce about two untalented tunesmiths marooned in the mythical kingdom of Ishtar. Recalls Dick Sylbert, "He's done more pictures with me than anybody else (seven). But I ain't stupid. I didn't do *Ishtar*. My brother [Paul] did that."[78] *Ishtar* would represent the nadir of the careers of everyone involved in it.

Julia Phillips came into the Jockey Club alone that day, and Warren motioned for her to join them. "So tell me, Julia, don't you ever have an inclination to knock on my door late at night?"

"Not in the least," Phillips said. Not to be dissuaded, Warren added, "Well, what would you do if I knocked on your door?" She replied that she'd tell him to go away. He then suggested a threesome with Phillips and her fourteen-year-old daughter, Kate.[79]

"We're both too old for you," Phillips said. In the end, "Neither Kate nor I sle[pt] with Warren," she added.[80] Warren also had a yen for Drew Barrymore, the child star of E.T. who had blossomed into comely womanhood. Warren had never lost his interest in Drew's mother, Jaid, whom he'd first met in the sixties, and he hit on her again when Drew was a teenager. In the years since their first encounter Jaid had been busy, enjoying affairs with Kiefer Sutherland

("We made love all night nonstop"), James Taylor ("like fire and rain, hot and drenched in sweat after finishing"), Sean Penn ("a great kisser"), Jim Morrison ("a wild lover"), Kris Kristofferson (who made her feel like "a real woman, sexy"), and Jackson Browne ("tender and kind"). "I was at Chasen's restaurant on Sunset Boulevard with Drew," she recalled. "Warren invited us over and we joined him. He got very flirtatious. He started kissing and caressing me and eyeing Drew. Finally, he said he was very much into sleeping with one of us, or even both of us."[81]

Drew, her mother pointed out, was only fifteen years old—legally, morally, and in every other way emphatically a minor. "Okay then," Warren said, "how about just you?"[82]

Jaid's "no" wasn't the only one he heard around this time. By 1986, the middle-aged star was getting used to an occasional rejection. In October, while staying at the Ritz Carlton in Manhattan, he asked Jennifer Lee to come up to his room. She later wrote, "I decide that I don't want to sleep with him, so I don't." Later, she made the mistake of mentioning Warren's name during a *People* interview, and he chastised her when he saw her at a party in December, remarking that he "hated" the article. She thought, "Maybe it's because I don't want to sleep with him anymore. Fuck him and his Greta Garbo act."[83]

Ishtar, co-starring Dustin Hoffman, was a picture with very little on its mind, and, along with *Howard the Duck* and *Heaven's Gate*, it stands as one of the more odious blunders in movie history. Almost as bad for Warren, it revealed he was no longer a beauty. According to David Thomson, the 1987 film "shows how far Beatty's face is dissolving in indecision, lofty reticence and discreet soft focus. He has the presence of a stander-by, someone overlooked." Few have ever bothered to see *Ishtar* through to the end.

His first mistake was handing over the writing and direction to Elaine May, whose reputation as a classy genius had about run its course. Far behind her were her cabaret triumphs as Mike Nichols's partner and her brilliant movies *Enter Laughing* and *A New Leaf*. "The secret we share," she once said of herself and Mike Nichols, "is that neither of us really likes people very much—they have no reality for us. The reason we're not very funny in a group is because we have this kind of communication, and people are always telling us they feel left out. It's something we can't seem to do anything about."[84] The heyday of the wonderfully caustic sick humor she and Mike Nichols had invented was long gone, and all she had left was shaggy-dog stories like *Ishtar*.

Warren was paid six million dollar for his indifferent work as star and producer. After a difficult location shoot in Morocco and outlandish production costs of forty million dollars, what he and Elaine May delivered in the end was a five-hundred-thousand-pound soufflé.[85] At least, he had the beautiful Isabelle Adjani as his costar. He'd first met her when she was working for Polanski in 1976 in *The Tenant*. Though her acting would never match her reputation as a classic international beauty, Warren, at his most besotted, called her "the most gifted person for the screen I have ever known."[86]

In the film, a road movie in the tradition of the Bing Crosby-Bob Hope-Dorothy Lamour series, Adjani plays Shirra Assel, a terrorist trying to overthrow the U.S.–backed Emir Yousef, ruler of a Middle Eastern country. Beatty and Hoffman, two down-and-out Manhattan singer-songwriters, arrive on the scene after securing a gig in a Morocco nightclub. Adjani romances Beatty, involving him in her plot to unseat the Emir of Ishtar; CIA agent Charles Grodin enlists Hoffman to work for the other side, and in the upshot, Beatty and Hoffman, innocently pitted against each other, are marooned in the desert, pursued by all sides.

In retrospect, after the terrorist attacks on America on September 11, 2001, *Ishtar*'s bumbling CIA functionary wandering around the Sahara on a blind camel seems stupendously relevant. But personally, despite repeated attempts, I have never been able to watch more than thirty minutes, due to *Ishtar*'s lethal combination of bad acting and flat jokes.

Filming was completed on March 16, 1986. On March 30, Warren turned forty-nine. That he emerged from the debacle of *Ishtar* with a shred of credibility in Hollywood was a tribute to his macho magnetism, which had won him such a well-entrenched position in the Establishment that not even the ignoble *Ishtar* could dislodge him. "Colossally dunderheaded," was the verdict—on the film, if not on Warren—of the industry's trade paper *Hollywood Reporter*.

Although the *New York Times* critic Janet Maslin found *Ishtar* "likable [and] good-humored," most of the press trounced it. The *New York Daily News* called it "an amiable mess," blaming "May's lackadaisical, hit-or-miss direction." In his syndicated column that was printed in the *New York Post,* Roger Ebert wrote, "The movie cannot be said to have a plot. It exists more as a series of cumbersome set pieces. . . . It's not funny, it's not smart, it's interesting only in the way a traffic accident is interesting. . . . There's nothing of Hoffman's wit and intelligence in *Tootsie*, no suggestion of Beatty's grace and good humor in *Heaven Can Wait,* no chemistry between two actors who should be enjoying the opportunity to act together. No life." According to *Variety*, the film never got "beyond a lame concept propped up by two name talents." Referring to *Ishtar*'s roots in the 1940s Hope-Crosby comedy *The Road to Morocco*, Mike McGrady of *Newsday* said the film should be retitled *The Road to Ruin.*

After a disappointing box office, the film was dumped, to make way for more likely features. "*Ishtar*/disastar" became an industry joke, frightening film-makers away from romantic comedies. Even worse, as months and then years passed, the joke didn't go away, and *Ishtar* would be mentioned in connection with every big-budgeted flop that came along, like Kevin Costner's 1995 turkey, *Waterworld*, which the media dubbed "*Fishtar*."

By the unwritten laws of the industry, heads had to fall after such an expensive mistake. Beatty and Hoffman were too useful to be sacrificed, and so director/writer Elaine May became the scapegoat, not without some justifi-cation, according to Paul Sylbert, who said, "Elaine reduced us all to ineffectu-ality. Storaro, myself, Beatty, who is a good director. We were all nullified by her fears. People who are frightened get really defensive, so nobody could help her at a certain point. Beatty was so angry. His control is magnificent. He knew if he blew up it would all stop and nothing would happen, so he backed off."[87]

The film helped bring down a studio regime. Coca-Cola, then the owner of Columbia Pictures, reshuffled its feature-films division. Francis (Fay) Vincent, who'd given the initial green light, was absorbed into the main Coke division, and studio chief David Puttnam, an old adversary of Warren's, bailed out of Columbia with a billowing golden parachute.[88]

Some industry observers suggested that this would be a good time for Warren to make a graceful exit from active moviemaking. When his car dis-appeared from the parking lot while he dined at a Sunset Boulevard café, a jest made the rounds that he couldn't afford to pay the valet. "No one believes that story," wrote David Thomson, "but the business now has many brave enough to be seen enjoying Warren's decline. This is a mood and a time in which such a star might easily withdraw."

Some speculated Warren was undergoing a midlife crisis. His friend Jack Nicholson fared much better in the 1980s, turning out seven films, including *The Shining* and *Terms of Endearment*, while Warren devoted his energies to "politics, power, and pussy,"[89] completing only two films, both highly questionable in terms of public appeal and industry bankability—*Reds* and *Ishtar*. His reputation accordingly plummeted both with the studios and the public. In a *Premiere* magazine survey, he now ranked forty-fifth in the list of Hollywood's most powerful people, far beneath Nicholson, Redford, Sylvester Stallone, Michael Douglas, Arnold Schwarzenegger, Tom Cruise, and Danny DeVito. Insiders began to smirk at the mention of his name. The advent of women's lib had made his kind of Don Juan passé. As Joe Eszterhas said, "Women got tired of hearing about how many women the Kielbasa Man—Wilt Chamberlain (twenty thousand)—or Warren Beatty or JFK or Mick had used . . . and they got justifiably pissed off. . . . Cocksman became a pejorative word. . . . Men weren't talking anymore about banging their brains out and moving on to the next piece of tail. . . . They were talking about 'failure to communicate' . . . 'lack of commitment' . . . 'emotional fatigue.' "[90]

Among other things, *Ishtar* seemed to advertise the fact that Warren was not aging well.[91] The *Village Voice* critic scolded, "He's a bit long in the tooth to engage in the adolescent skittishness about sex, hetero and homo, that adds a dose of painful infantilism to the massive ineptitude of the movie as a whole."

Mad Dog Beatty needed a comeback, and he adroitly set about staging it, both as a filmmaker and a lover. In the latter capacity—a Don Juan at fifty—he needed a spectacular girlfriend to prove that he could still cut the mustard, and soon he would target a rock star who was the world's number-one sex symbol. It would hardly achieve the desired effect, the world finding it rather sad that the old man was still acting like a kid, and that he had not established a single emotional root in all his philanderings. Instead, over the years, he had latched onto whatever temporary "family" with whom he happened to be shooting a film—the actors and crew—and when it wrapped, he moved on to the next film and the next surrogate family. Occasionally, he'd attach himself to the families of such friends as Dustin Hoffman, who remarked, "Lisa and I both like him, but he makes us sad and we don't quite know why. There's an essential loneliness in him. I'm not surprised he is considering a movie about Howard Hughes. I mean, I see him dying alone with nobody there to love him or hold his hand. It hurts to think about that." And Shirley MacLaine's daughter, Sachi Parker, said, "I feel his loneliness. I don't know if it's true, but I feel he's living in this big house at the top of a hill with no one to share it, or his life." Shirley herself, referring to Warren's "psychological dilemma," said he should have heeded her advice and married Julie Christie years ago.[92]

Julie had a full new life on her farm in Wales, and in time she'd enjoy a long-term relationship with journalist Duncan Campbell. Though she disliked Hollywood, she frequently flew to Los Angeles to spend time with Campbell after he took a job there.[93]

Warren had been smart to keep powerful friends like Jeffrey Katzenberg and David Geffen through all the vicissitudes of their careers. Katzenberg stood him in good stead after *Ishtar*, offering the backing of the Walt Disney Studios. Warren definitely would not go hungry in Hollywood. Geffen was also in a powerful position, having rebounded with a vengeance, producing such Broadway hits as *Cats* and *Dreamgirls,* and launching rock bands like Guns N' Roses. Geffen Records made him hundreds of millions of dollars. With friends like that, Warren's place in the Establishment was solid, for few indeed dared cross Geffen. When Geffen's mother, Batya, a brassiere manufacturer, died in 1988, Warren attended her funeral, sitting in Stephen S. Wise Temple off Mulholland Drive next to Hollywood power brokers including Barry Diller; Allen Grubman, a lawyer in the music business; Joel Schumacher, director of *St. Elmo's Fire*; and superagent Sandy Gallin. Joni Mitchell was also there, along with Geffen's tall, handsome erstwhile lover Bob Brassel.[94] Among the lesser lights in attendance was agent Sue Mengers, whose luster had dimmed with the arrival of a new generation of agents like Michael Ovitz.

Warren was present the night that Geffen finally came out of the closet and began to live openly as a gay. During the AIDS crisis that had begun in 1981, Elizabeth Taylor had pointed out that many of the people who ran Hollywood were gay, and she began a one-woman campaign to flush the industry's power gays out of the closet in order to garner support for her AIDS charities. Geffen was the first of the moguls—and by 2000 still the only one—to come forward and declare himself. It happened after Warren introduced him as the speaker for the AIDS Project Los Angeles Commitment to Life banquet, which was held during the eighties at the 6,251-seat Universal Amphitheater in Hollywood.

At the AIDS event, after entertainment supplied by Elton John, Liza Minnelli, and Billy Joel, Warren rose to present Geffen, who had contributed a fortune to the AIDS cause, with the Commitment to Life award. "The analogy of David and Goliath is hard for me to ignore," Warren said. "As David's societal contribution mounts, and business, political, and religious Goliaths blink in the aim of his slingshot, his intelligence focuses and his anger mobilizes. And a mobilized David Geffen is something that you want working *for* you, not *against* you."[95]

As the audience stood and cheered, Geffen strode to the podium and hugged Warren. "Thank you," he said. "Thank you, Warren." And then came his long-delayed disclosure. "As a gay man, I've come a long way to be here tonight." Hollywood would never again be the same homophobic place. The crowd at the Universal Amphitheater, representing the cream of movie-industry liberals, went wild, applauding and whistling. Years before, Geffen had represented the rock group Crosby, Stills, Nash and Young, but they'd had their differences over the years and rarely spoke to him. The day following the AIDS banquet, David Crosby told Geffen, "I've always been so ready to jump into your shit when you were wrong. I thought that when you did something right, I should let you know. I watched you on TV last night, and I was really proud of you. I thought that was a real stand-up move."

Other Beatty buddies were faring less well. By 1989 one of Warren's staunchest supporters, Robert Evans, had committed himself to Scripps Memorial Hospital, a "loony bin" in his own description, just north of San Diego, "to prevent the possibility of suicide."[96] After an attack of claustrophobia, Evans escaped from the depression clinic, and Jack Nicholson helped him buy back his old home. By 1991 Evans was sufficiently recovered to get a job as a producer at Paramount, the studio he'd headed twenty-five years before. Warren came to a party in Evans's office on the lot at Christmas 1991, along with Nicholson, Faye Dunaway, Raquel Welch, photographer Helmut Newton, and Ali MacGraw. "You know, Keed," Nicholson said, using his nickname for Evans, "you were ten thousand to one."[97] Evans's professional comeback, at age sixty-two, proved disappointing; the best he could come up with was the slick, uninspired *Sliver,* a middling Sharon Stone vehicle.

Warren's output was equally undaring and derivative. Instead of making the intellectual movies he'd espoused at Toronto, he continued to fool around with exactly the kind of mindless claptrap that he'd denounced at the festival. Dusting off an old project, he announced he'd film the jejune comic strip *Dick Tracy,* which he'd been tinkering around with since 1975. The original production had been abandoned when Warren clashed with the director, Walter

Hill, who'd since guided *48 Hours* to the screen. Hill saw *Dick Tracy* as a realistic gangster flick, but Warren had in mind a stylized hybrid—real people presented as if they were animated figures in a cartoon come to life. In 1985 he acquired all rights to the Chester Gould property. It remained in development for another five years. For much of this time he was talking to Martin Scorsese about directing it. They finally hammered out a deal, agreeing on a "joint" final cut, a contradiction in terms, since the deal ceded ultimate approval to Scorsese in case of a disagreement. Scorsese signed it, but Warren, who would have all the labor of finding studio backing and making the picture happen, never signed the agreement. The only thing they could agree on was to call it quits.

In addition to assuming the lead role, Warren would both produce and direct. One day he received a call from the rock star Madonna, then the hottest ticket in the world. It marked the beginning of one of his randiest and most demeaning relationships.

He had always liked them young. "The chicks, the cruising—he, Nicholson, and Roman Polanski had been the great predators," said a top Hollywood agent. "When I was at parties in the seventies, Polanski was scraping up girls, including thirteen-year-olds." Now it was almost the 1990s, and Warren, in his fifties, was still drawn to women half his age, including the Material Girl herself.

Recalls a Hollywood insider, "Madonna told me that Warren took her to dinner at the Ivy on their first date. He wore tinted glasses, she thought to try to cover his crow's feet. They were quite a pair, this fifty-three-year-old sex symbol of the past romancing the present-day sex symbol. For dessert, she ordered and ate both flavors of ice cream. Later, Warren telephoned her and noted that she seemed to be a woman who liked variety in life, at least in regard to ice cream. Had she ever made it with a woman? he asked. She told him it was none of his business. He asked her if she wanted to be with a woman."

If that was his game, he had certainly come to the right place. Madonna Louise Veronica Ciccone, the daughter of a working-class Italian-American father and a French-Canadian woman named Madonna, was afraid of nothing, willing to try anything, and had openly wooed women, including comedian Sandra Bernhard.[98] Her first amorous exploits, at age eight, had been with girls. "That's really normal, same-sex experimentation," she said. "You get really curious and there's your girlfriend, and she's spending the night with you and it happens."[99] Born on August 16, 1958, in Bay City, Michigan, her ambition since childhood had been "to rule the world." By the time she met Warren, she ruled, if not the world, then at least the rock 'n' roll sector of it. She was, indisputably, the biggest and brashest female star since Janis Joplin.

"Before their next date," continues the Hollywood insider, "Warren telephoned from the car and said he was a half mile from her house. 'Take off your blouse,' he said. At the next light, he called and said, 'Take off your underwear.' His voice was hypnotic. After calling her at every stoplight, he made a final call as he pulled into her driveway. 'Get in bed and wait for me,' he said. He loved phone sex, and Madonna thought she was going to have the best sex she'd ever experienced.

"He had a lot of sexual fantasies, and she liked that. 'He knows a woman's body so well,' she said, 'that he can pinpoint the day of your cycle.' "

Unfortunately for Madonna, Warren "turned out to be a premature ejaculator. She said he came before she even had time to turn the sheets down. Another time they had sex on top of his piano, but once again he pre-ejaculated. She said here she was, looking forward to a concerto, and all she got was the minute waltz. He was too fast, in her estimation, and he washed his hands compulsively. She thought he should tone his body up, so she suggested he get liposuction. He was very insulted."[100]

During the fifteen-month course of their affair, Madonna crossed the line from being just young enough to excite Warren to being just old enough to bore him. Madonna liked them young, too, but she'd made an exception for Warren. Why? Her unresolved issues with her father, Tony Ciccone, had left her looking for a sugar daddy. As a child of four she'd crawled into bed with her parents and slept between them. The following year, when her mother died of breast cancer, Madonna continued sleeping with her father, later stating, "Like all young girls I was in love with my father and I didn't want to lose him. I lost my mother, but then I was my mother . . . and my father was mine."[101] When Tony Ciccone remarried, Madonna's resentment and anger would last for decades, a baleful influence on her relations with men. Paradoxically, she would also seek her father's approval, but in a most self-defeating way. In her teens, she behaved outrageously—bumping and grinding, flashing hairy armpits, having sex at fifteen with seventeen-year-old future truck driver Russell Long—convinced that if her father could accept her on her own terms, he would prove his love.[102] At the same time, she knew he would fail to pass this test, and she could continue to harbor her anger and resentment, endlessly recycling it. In short, she had a whale of an Electra complex, and Warren became an unwitting enabler. She had other uses for him as well. As one of the most influential and resourceful figures in Hollywood, he was capable of salvaging her chronically anemic movie career. They would proceed to exploit each other in the Tinseltown tradition immortalized by Joyce Haber in her novel of power and sex in Hollywood, *The Users*.

"Warren, I really want this part," Madonna said, referring to the role of Breathless Mahoney, a brazen, peroxided bistro spitfire who tries to steal Dick Tracy from his lady friend, Tess Trueheart. In the latter, lesser role, Sean Young had initially been cast. "I basically was sexually harassed by him," she later complained. She "blew the whistle"—talked to the press—and "paid a very, very big price . . . being fired by Warren Beatty."[103] Tess would ultimately be portrayed by Glenne Headly, who had appeared in *Dirty Rotten Scoundrels* and was once married to John Malkovich. For the role of Breathless, Warren was thinking of *Batman*'s Kim Basinger or perhaps Kathleen Turner, who provided Jessica Rabbit's voice in *Who Framed Roger Rabbit?*

Since Madonna's debut movie, *Desperately Seeking Susan*, which had originally been intended for Diane Keaton, the singer's film career had gone nowhere, but Warren had always had a yen for her. In 1984, he had called *Desperately Seeking Susan*'s director, Susan Seidelman, trying to date Madonna. Seidelman remembers that Warren asked her if he could view the dailies. "He came to the editing room and watched some scenes. He was obviously intrigued by Madonna. Watching his face watching hers, I knew he wanted her. From that point on, I had a premonition that someday they would be together."[104]

He offered to go out with the five-foot-four, 115-pound, 32–23–33 Madonna to discuss *Dick Tracy*, but she declined, knowing that if she put him off, he'd crave her all the more. "It took me weeks to get a date with her," Warren recalled, and she later explained, "The best way to seduce someone is by making yourself unavailable. . . . You don't fuck them for the first five dates. Let them get closer and closer, but definitely don't fuck them."[105] They finally met when Sean Penn brought Madonna—on their first date—to a party Warren was giving. Hollywood's most gifted and dysfunctional young actor, a hard-drinking, gun-toting punk, Penn had once shot the watch off girlfriend Elizabeth McGovern's wrist. "Sean took me to Warren's house," Madonna said. "I guess he wanted to show me off—I'm not sure. I didn't know L.A. at all. I remember meeting a lot of movie stars that night, like Mickey Rourke." To his later regret, Penn also introduced Madonna to future rival Sandra Bernhard, a bizarre bisexual comedienne. Since Penn was a member of the Brat Pack, Madonna and Sandra decided to call themselves the Snatch Batch, later welcoming Jennifer Grey, star of *Ferris Bueller's Day Off* and *Dirty Dancing,* into their circle.[106] On that first night, Madonna was so smitten with Penn that she paid little attention to Warren, but subsequently she kept them all on a string, juggling Sean, Sandra, and Warren to suit her whim.

During the marriage of "the Poison Penns," as Madonna and Sean became known, the actor's violent temper raged out of control, inflamed by the relentless réclame of Madonna's superstardom, not to mention her kissing Sandra Bernhard in Manhattan's lesbian bar, the Cubby Hole. Madonna's popularity far eclipsed Penn's, and he resented the paparazzi who followed in her wake, paying little attention to him. After stoning two photographers, he faced assault charges, entering a no-contest plea and receiving a ninety-day suspended sentence and a fifty-dollar fine on two misdemeanor charges.[107]

Another issue in the marriage was Madonna's fortune, conservatively estimated at the time at seventy million dollars (Penn was worth five million dollars). Determined to dominate her, he reportedly wanted co-starring rank in her picture *Evita*,[108] but in the end Antonio Banderas became her leading man. Finally, Penn's ego couldn't take the punishment of being Mr. Material Girl any longer, and their marriage began to disintegrate.

Madonna turned to John F. Kennedy Jr., who soon was licking low-fat whipped cream off her legs during sex.[109] Madonna pronounced him "unbelievable. A perfect specimen." But she lost all respect for him when she realized that his mother, Jacqueline Kennedy Onassis, called all the shots in his life, and the last person Mrs. Onassis wanted to see her son, the natural heir to Camelot, wed was a rock star—a married one at that. Nevertheless, Madonna and JFK Jr. were caught trysting in Hyannis Port. Nor was Sean Penn idle; he went tomcatting with Brat Packers Timothy Hutton and Judd Nelson. In time, Madonna and John-John parted. After he confronted her a couple of times—"*What the hell is wrong with you?*" he'd shout, right in her face—it dawned on her that JFK Jr. was temperamentally just another Sean Penn, a hopeless hothead, and she'd had enough of that in her marriage. Understandably, John-John was equally afraid of the fiery Madonna, and told his friend, law school classmate Chris Meyer, "She scares the hell out of me." According to Meyer, she was already over Kennedy by the time he dumped her one night at a fashionable restaurant on Manhattan's West Side.

Madonna resumed her pestering of Warren for the role in *Dick Tracy*, but he explained that a dozen other actresses, all more qualified than she, were up for the part, including Michelle Pfeiffer (he didn't add that he couldn't afford Pfeiffer, nor that both Kathleen Turner and Kim Basinger were unavailable)."I saw the A-list and I was on the Z-list," Madonna recalled. "I felt like a jerk." One reason Warren was reluctant to cast Madonna was, no doubt, that his buddy David Geffen had tried to sign her for a film called *The Fabulous Baker Boys*, but she hated it, dismissing the screenplay as "mushy." Michelle Pfeiffer assumed the role of the nightclub singer, and Geffen's film became a box-office hit.

Warren's financial angel for *Dick Tracy*, Jeffrey Katzenberg, later a partner of Geffen's, was not convinced that Madonna's identity as a rocker wouldn't spoil the movie's credibility with conservative audiences. Finally, Beatty and Katzenberg decided that her unprecedented popularity with the younger generation—the most significant demographic factor in the moviegoing public— more than offset her liabilities. The Chester Gould comic strip had long been out of circulation and was completely unknown to teenagers, but if anyone could get them into the movie houses, even for an anachronism like *Dick Tracy*, Madonna could—or so they thought. They overestimated her pulling power; despite her clout as a rocker, she would never amount to much as a movie star, lacking almost everything required for screen presence: acting talent, personality, a large head, and a great face.

Determined to win the role at any cost, Madonna offered to perform for union scale—$1,440 a week, for a total of $27,360—instead of her customary multimillion-dollar salary. (Even had they been available, neither Kathleen Turner nor Kim Basinger would perform in a sixty-million-dollar-budget film for under two thousand dollars per week.) If the picture earned out, Madonna would be in for hefty percentages, but that would cost Warren nothing up front. Seeing an opportunity to bring the picture in under its sixty-million-dollar budget, he finally surrendered. The occasion was a dinner date at the Ivy restaurant in L.A. Madonna was wearing a slithery black leather jumpsuit unzipped as far south as the Ivy would allow and a matching leather cap. "I know you've heard a lot of terrible things about me," she murmured, "and I'm here to tell you that they're all true. How about you? I've heard a lot about you. True?" When Warren remained silent, she said, "Just as I thought. All true." He loved her wit, which was so right, he thought, for the role of Breathless, and when he took her home that night, he kissed her outside her door and allegedly said, "We have lift-off."[110] According to a friend of Warren's, he hired her that night.

Sean Penn was furious, because Madonna had promised to have their baby in 1989. Put it off for at least a year, she begged, but when he discovered that she'd concluded the picture deal, he became so violent that Universal security guards had to drag him from her bungalow. Sean stalked Madonna and Warren on their dates, noting that they always ended up at Warren's house. Penn parked his car outside Warren's gate and waited for her to leave, and he was still sitting there at dawn.[111] Madonna confided her marital woes to John Kennedy, who rang Penn from New York and threatened to pulverize him if he laid one hand on Madonna. Penn replied that he'd report Kennedy's threat to the police, and later chastised Kennedy for cuckolding him.[112] Sandra Bernhard jumped into the fray, asking Madonna, "What the fuck are you doing to yourself?" Madonna replied, "I still love Sean."[113] Later Penn broke into Madonna's Malibu home, assaulted, bound, and gagged her, and left her bruised and bleeding for nine hours. Finally she broke free, escaped to the Malibu sheriff's station, and swore out a complaint. Later, she hid from Penn in the home of her manager, Freddy DeMann. Penn was arrested, and one week later, Madonna dropped all criminal charges. Penn denied Madonna's version of their contretemps, claiming that all he did was threaten to cut her hair off. He admitted to a friend that whiskey was his undoing.[114]

Though two decades older than Madonna, Warren was exactly what she wanted at this juncture, with certain reservations. "Warren was like a fairy godfather," said one observer. "She could hardly believe she was involved with him. She said, 'I'm with this guy who's been with some great women who put up with this sorry, premature ejaculator. It takes me thirty seconds to get all my clothes off, and it takes him thirty seconds to come.' " Another source quoted her as saying, "Warren should have been a psychiatrist or a district attorney. When he wants to know somebody, he goes out of his way to investigate. You feel like you're under a microscope. You're not used to people spending that much time trying to get to know you. But it's admirable. Everybody ought to examine the people they're going to work with as intensely as he does."

Working with her was probably the least part of Warren's motive in hiring Madonna. He'd romanced Brigitte Bardot when she'd been the world's most desirable woman, and now that Madonna had inherited the same title, he went after her. Approaching his senior years and fast losing his looks, he perhaps needed verification of his virility more than ever. "Sometimes," he told a reporter, "I look at myself in the mirror and say, 'Man, I am with Madonna! She makes me young.' "[115] He showered her with presents—dresses, gowns, bikini panties, Lejaby bras—and, although she kept them, she scolded him, pointing out that she wasn't some starlet he could control through bribery. After all, she was "very wealthy" and could afford to buy her own bras. But she loved being pampered and made Warren promise to take her on his next shopping spree.[116]

Apart from his power to cast her as Breathless Mahoney—and his impressive credentials as a father figure[117]—what was Warren's attraction for Madonna? His appeal to her was more as the legendary Casanova of Hollywood. Though his performance in bed was brief,[118] he always made sure that she was completely satisfied, patiently discovering her requirements. A studio technician who observed them the night Madonna recorded "Hanky Panky" referred to "Beatty's favorite sport, spanking."[119] After her affair with Warren had been going on for a while, Madonna said, "Sometimes I think he's been with the world's most beautiful, most glamorous women. I go, 'Oh, my God! Oh, my God!' . . . Then there is the side of me that says I'm better than all of them." As the world's allegedly preeminent lover, Warren was uniquely in a position to confirm that Madonna was the world's greatest lay. "He's into all aspects of sexuality," she confided. "He has no restrictions. He says to me, 'If you misbehave, I'll just have to spank you.' I love that. Everything to him is living out his sexual fantasies." She had a few fantasies herself; as later revealed in her book *Sex*, she found anal intercourse to be "the most pleasurable way to [have sex], and it hurts the most, too." She was also into dogs; toe sucking; S&M; shaving pubic hair; oral sex; being a dominant lesbian; and being raped while dressed as a schoolgirl.[120]

According to one source, "She enjoyed the rumors that Beatty was bisexual." Madonna loved nothing more than demolishing stereotypical thinking on sexuality and gender. "I don't know that he's ever slept with a man," she told an *Advocate* reporter. "But he's certainly not homophobic. I asked him once, 'Would you ever sleep with a man?' and he said he was sorry that he hadn't but that now because of AIDS he felt it was an unsafe thing to start exper-imenting with."[121] Another aspect of Warren's appeal for Madonna, who liked to bully her boyfriends, was that, unlike Sean Penn, Warren could be pushed around.[122] No matter how much she taunted the philosophical, tolerant Warren, she knew she'd never get an unwanted haircut or a fat lip. At worst, he'd just walk out until he controlled his anger. "I understand rebellion," he said. "So I understand Madonna."

But if he understood her so well, their relationship would hardly have been the constant battle it was. When she nagged at him to work out with her, he reminded her that she'd often denounced people who judged others by outward appearances. "How dare you judge me?" he said. "It works both ways, you know."

"If you want to be fat and flabby, Warren, fine by me . . . You older guys are too sensitive."[123]

Furious, he started to reply but checked himself. At the time, they were sur-rounded by people at the L.A. *boite* Club Nouveau, and he was wary of making a scene. Instead, he drained his brandy glass and bolted, leaving her alone at the table. "That is *so* like my father," she said. "He is *so* like my father!" She got even the next day, telling Warren in a restaurant, "Keep your stupid remarks to your-self." He replied, "Oh, Christ! Grow up!" Wayne Gretzky, the hockey star, who was sitting nearby, saw her reach in her purse and throw a Snickers bar at Warren. Dashing to their table, Gretzky admonished, "Hey, you two, knock it off, will ya?" Within a few minutes, a repentant and solicitous Warren was cut-ting up Madonna's food and fork-feeding it to her. On another occasion, when she demanded a Diet Pepsi at a five-star restaurant and threatened to leave when informed no such beverage was available, Warren gave the waiter five hundred dollars to go to the nearest convenience store and fetch a Diet Pepsi. At such moments, Madonna thought, "My God, we're just *perfect* together."

After dining at the Sushi Cove restaurant near his house on Mulholland, Madonna asked him, "Have you ever done it with a man?" Instead of answer-ing her, he offered to set her up with a lesbian. "It will be my present to you," he said. "I'll get you a woman." At Warren's invitation, Sandra Bernhard joined them for dinner the following night at the Sushi Cove. "Warren, you know that Madonna and I share *everything*," Sandra said. "Don't you?" Later Sandra recalled, "His eyes lit up like a kid in a candy store. A wild ride, I thought to myself. A very wild ride."[124]

Madonna showed him her new, $2,950,000 aerie in the Hollywood Hills, where her living room ceiling featured a heroic rendering of male genitals—a Langlois nude of Hermes, Cupid, and Diana that had been painted originally for the palace at Versailles. *Arts and Antiques* listed Madonna as one of the "Top 100 Collectors" in the United States; she owned an eclectic array, ranging from Keith Haring to Picasso, and over her bed hung a Robert Smithson abstract, her very first acquisition, which she dubbed her "guardian angel." In her office, black-and-white portraits of nude women by noteworthy photographers were positioned near her desk. Like Warren, she wasn't deeply into drugs, restricting her recreational substances to an infrequent sleeping pill, champagne, and cigarettes.

Warren produced *Dick Tracy* for Disney's Buena Vista corporation, hiring Jim Cash and Jack Epps, Jr., to write the screenplay, Vittorio Storaro to photograph it, and Dick Sylbert to design the unconventional, highly stylized sets. To compose the songs, he recruited Stephen Sondheim, the leading figure in the American musical theater, who'd been Warren's friend ever since composing the theme for *Reds*. Apart from Madonna, Headly, and Beatty, the all-star cast so far included Dustin Hoffman, Kathy Bates, Dick Van Dyke, James Caan, Michael J. Pollard, Charles Durning, Mandy Patinkin, and Paul Sorvino.

For the pivotal role of Big Boy Caprice, the world's largest dwarf, Warren contacted Al Pacino and took him to lunch one day in January 1989 at Dan Tana's Italian restaurant on Santa Monica Boulevard. Drinking Pelegrino and talking intently, Pacino pointed out that Big Boy had never been an important continuing character in the comic strip, but Warren said he'd beef up the role for Pacino, who'd always longed to play comedy. "Al is one of those centrifugal people that cause good acting around them," Warren said. The two actors had much in common, including Diane Keaton, Pacino's latest co-star.

During the shooting of *The Godfather Part III*, also filmed in 1989, Pacino and Keaton had shared a villa in Rome. Like Warren, neither Diane nor Pacino had ever married, still wary of emotional commitment. "I was almost married a couple of times, and don't know what happened," Pacino said. "I've certainly had long-standing relationships that *felt* like marriages. Why didn't I propose? I hate to say this, but marriage is a state of mind, not a contract. When I think about the law and marriage, I ask myself, 'How did the cops get in on this?' "[125]

Diane Keaton said, "Sure, I'm hopeful. I mean, I'm not dead yet. . . . I would like to be a parent, but I'm a little old to be having children. . . . The best way to do it would be to adopt a child." Like Warren, both Keaton and Pacino yearned for intimacy but so far had proved incapable of forming a lasting partnership.

During their affair, Pacino and Keaton fought, evidently over the former's refusal to make the arrangement more permanent. *Godfather III* was already in chaos because of leading lady Winona Ryder's nervous collapse. Diane began showing up on the set with her eyes too puffy for filming, apparently having wept through the night. "Our relationship at times has been complicated," admitted Pacino. On completion of filming, he returned to New York, where he visited the director Sidney Lumet. "How about Diane?" Lumet asked. "She's a terrific girl. Why don't the two of you get married?" Pacino laughed and shook his head. Observed a Hollywood agent in 2000, "Diane Keaton has had affairs with all the leading men of Hollywood, from Woody Allen to Al Pacino, but they all ended, and she is finally the spinster mom of an adopted baby. She is all nerves, a bundle of nerves and insecurity." By 2001, her son Dexter was five years old, and she had adopted yet another boy, Duke, six months old. Now fifty-five, Diane said, "When I was young, I honestly believed in some ridiculous way that you would find someone who would be the person you lived with until you died. I don't think because I'm not married it's made my life any less. That old maid myth is garbage."[126]

Pacino would eventually enjoy a continuing relationship with Beverly D'Angelo, who played Patsy Cline in *Coal Miner's Daughter* and Chevy Chase's wife in *Vacation,* but he still didn't settle down in any conventional sense, preferring to maintain separate quarters at Shutters, a Santa Monica beachfront hotel, while Beverly lived in the Hollywood Hills.[127]

When Warren tried to cast Pacino in *Dick Tracy,* he finally resorted to the same technique that had snared Jack Nicholson for the O'Neill role in *Reds*. "Who do you think I should get for it?" Warren asked. "Cut the crap, Warren," Pacino said. "If you want me to play it, then just ask. And, by the way, the answer's yes."[128] When principal photography at last began, Pacino stole every scene he appeared in. His turn as a dancer with a line of chorus girls in a night-club was a classic. No other actor in the film could hold a candle to him.

Tension was not long in developing on the set between Warren and Madonna, who brought their issues as off-screen lovers to the workplace. "She was great," recalls Sylbert. "I had worked with her before on a music video, and had got to know her very well. When she walked on the *Dick Tracy* set, she said,

'Oh, Dick, what's going on?' There was nothing going on at first, but she's a wonderful, hard worker, a real trouper. She's serious, she puts it out. She was very funny to have around, because the more she and Warren got together, the more the picture took off. It's just like Gary Merrill and Bette Davis [romancing on the set] in *All About Eve*—don't forget, all of that comes out in the movie. And it was no different from Warren and Diane in *Reds*, or Warren and Julie Christie—it all works. It's all calculated. He never makes a mistake of that kind. Madonna was great, and she wouldn't take any of his shit. One night we were out at this lake up there at Universal, doing a green screen shot, and it was getting cold, and it was going on and on, and Madonna says, 'Warren, you know, I'm losing my hard on, Warren.' The whole crew broke up. Warren could do that—you could lose your hard-on. Fifteen takes!"

As the boss's mistress, Madonna knew she could get away with anything, just as Warren had when he'd been the apple of William Inge's eye in *A Loss of Roses*. "What is this shit?" she fumed when she first heard the Sondheim tunes. "I can't sing this. It isn't me." On being informed they were the work of the esteemed author of "Everything's Coming Up Roses" and "Send in the Clowns," she reconsidered, though she still groused about their "chromatic wildness." She finally conceded, "They're brilliant, but really complex." Warren even brought Sondheim to the studio to coach her. Eager to see his songs at last break through, via Madonna, on MTV, which had previously had no place for his Broadway show tunes, Sondheim showed Madonna how to shape a lyric. Critics had not previously considered her a significant song stylist, but *New York Daily News* music critic David Hinckley later called *I'm Breathless* "easily the best record Madonna has made." She had Beatty and Sondheim to thank for an important breakthrough. She also owed a debt of gratitude to Warren for teaching her how to become a better businesswoman, taking up his suggestion that she start her own record label.[129]

Though Madonna matched Warren's workaholic perfectionism and was willing to do forty takes to get her big production number with Al Pacino right, she hated having to wait between takes while Warren laboriously set up his shots. Since they made no secret of their affair and smooched on the set, she felt free to nag him in front of everyone, saying, "Come *onnnn*. Hurry up, *Old Man*!" Controlling himself in the face of insubordination, he called her "Buzzbomb" but treated her the same way an indulgent parent would treat a spoiled, tyrannical child, with reluctant deference. One of the crew quietly grumbled that Warren was "pussy-whipped." During filming, he was caught in Madonna's dressing room in a highly compromising position.[130]

"Warren was there for her recording of 'Hanky Panky,' " says Sarah Porterfield, who knew studio engineer Brian Malouf. "The song is about spanking, and Madonna told a friend that Warren always teased her that he wanted to spank her. Brian Malouf says it got really steamy, as if Warren and Madonna were in a world all their own. Though she called him a huge disappointment in the sack, Madonna and Warren were happy for a while. He paid for a full-time masseuse for her. On May 16, 1989, he presented her with a six-carat engagement ring. They were dining out, and he was so happy, he tipped the waiter at the restaurant one hundred dollars. Madonna wore the ring on the middle finger of her left hand to conceal the fact that she was engaged, because she was still married to Sean Penn. But she filed for divorce in January."

After work each day, they necked openly at fashionable clubs. For Madonna, familiarity bred contempt. On the set, when Warren attempted to defuse one of her tantrums, she shrieked, "Don't *touch* me!" Then, waving a Marlboro Light like Bette Davis, she strode off the set. One night after work, she took him to a gay hustlers' hangout in South Central L.A. Inappropriately dressed in a Versace suit, Warren was reluctant to go to the dance floor. "Hey, Pussy Man," she said, "come on out here." She felt perfectly at home, dressed in boxers' shoes, shorts, and a hooded sweatshirt under her blue denim jacket. "No, I'm just fine," Warren said. "I can't even breathe, let alone dance." Madonna started dancing with two women and yelled at Warren, "I shoulda' come here with Rob Lowe. Now, he's a guy who knows how to party hearty."

Though obviously mismatched, "there is a ridiculous inevitability to Warren and Madonna," thought Julia Phillips, after sighting the unlikely lovebirds at a party for Freddy DeMann. At first, Phillips hadn't recognized that it was Warren standing next to the rock star, later recalling, "Her skin is so porcelain it glows. I wonder for a moment if she is on a first-name basis with the Vampire Lestat. If anyone is, it is she. There is a short, bespectacled man with good hair standing next to her. It takes me a moment to recognize Warren. Warren is usually tall and dominates a room, but in this situation he is a dim bulb in the aura of her supernova. He looks like Ron Meyer, star of CAA, not Warren, Star. I touch his arm and he smiles. He is glad to see me. I lean across her to exchange kisses in the air. She ignores me. 'I don't believe you're here,' I say. . . . He looks down at his shoes. 'I'm here,' he says to the ground. I straighten up to half-look in her direction. She ignores me. She is in a skin-tight halter dress that stops above the knee and is somewhere between flesh-tone and gold lamé. She is wearing very high heels, with sparkles up the heel. Her hair is white. She looks great, and it is better to look good than to feel good. She puffs-puffs at a Virginia Slim. 'Warren Beety,' she says in an exaggerated New York whine, 'let's move down to the next level.' This is the way the world ends, not with a bang but a simper."[131]

For Madonna, the liberal Beatty was a relief after the homophobic, chauvinistic, uptight Penn, who'd never have accepted her self-described "flirtation"[132] with Sandra Bernhard. "Warren is open to everything sexual," said one friend. "If anything, the hint of bisexuality probably aroused him." He didn't even object when Madonna and Sandra caressed each other during a benefit at the Brooklyn Academy of Music. After the show, Madonna and Sandra continued to stimulate each other publicly at a theater party at Indochine restaurant. Their friendship eventually ended when Madonna stole Sandra's girlfriend, nightclub owner Ingrid Casares.[133] Years later, at a New Year's Eve party in Miami, Madonna and Gwyneth Paltrow let themselves go while dancing and kissed each other full on the mouth.[134]

As far as Warren was concerned, Madonna could dyke it up as much as she liked, but he drew the line when she came on to other males. Especially off limits were personal friends like Jack Nicholson. Since Jack's triumph in *Batman,* he was the town's major star, and, like Madonna, was an impassioned art collector. As a Mulholland Drive neighbor of Warren's, he had easy access to Madonna, and they soon discovered they shared a mutual love for the painter Tamara de Lempicka. Jack told Madonna about haunting the Manhattan auction houses, scouting for his favorite Impressionist painters. "He was intrigued by Madonna, and Madonna was flattered by his attention," said a neighbor, "but Warren wasn't happy at all when he heard they were dating. The bottom line was she wasn't going to do anything to jeopardize *Dick Tracy.*"

After such casual flings, Madonna always came back to Warren, despite her reservations about him. One day, holding up her thumb and index finger an inch apart, she complained to a secretary at Warner, "They're all like this." Warren continued to lavish presents on Madonna, giving her an Ilse Bing photograph for her thirty-first birthday. It showed a corps of dancers, and one of them was striking a pose, trying to outshine the other chorines. "She reminds me of you," Warren said.

"I can't imagine why," Madonna replied.

One day, accompanying her to an audition for the video of her song, "Express Yourself," Warren noticed that she was rude to the dancers, remarking about one of them, "Look at the bulge in this guy's tights. What's *that* all about?" Turning to one of the choreographers, Warren said, "Man, she's rather a bitch, isn't she?" "Yeah, well—" the choreographer said. "Or maybe she's just showing off for me," Warren concluded.[135] Rumors of a Beatty-Madonna wedding persisted, and Warren told friends that Jack Nicholson would be his best man and Sandra Bernhard would be Madonna's maid of honor. But they continued to fight, and at the Ivy one evening, after Madonna told him, "Keep your stupid opinions to yourself," Warren paid the bill and left. Alone at their table, Madonna glared at the other patrons and yelled, "Stop staring at me." In San Antonio on a studio publicity junket, they stayed at La Mansion del Rio Hotel, and Warren spent most of his time calling Jack Nicholson and complaining that Madonna and Sandra Bernhard were planning an elaborate wedding, and Sean Penn was on the phone cussing him out for hitting on his ex-wife. "I'm too old for this," Warren said. "old enough not to want to look foolish." Barbra Streisand rang and told him he was "crazy for falling for a young floozy." His elderly mother, Kathlyn, said Madonna was completely unacceptable, and her opinion still held considerable sway with Warren. Madonna tried to win over Warren's mother, without success. "It's no wonder," Madonna said. "Look at how many women she has seen with her son. She probably didn't approve of any of them, either."[136]

Was that the reason Warren had never married—no woman could live up to mom? Certainly his sister had lived in a kind of bondage to their mother. Kathlyn Beaty spent her final years with Shirley in California, and after Kathlyn's death at the age of ninety in May 1993, Shirley revealed that it had taken her sixty years to come to a resolution with her mother. Sixty years! The length of the struggle was the measure of its death-grip desperation, but in the end, Shirley was able to speak generously of her mother, calling Kathlyn "my insistent inspiration, the person whom I acted for, and in the end the one who released me from her own dreams."[137] There may have been a release of sorts for Warren, too, for he would at last marry in 1992, the last year of Kathlyn's life.

As he began editing *Dick Tracy* in 1990, Madonna left on her infamous Blond Ambition tour, threatening to grab her crotch on stage like Michael Jackson had done in his *Bad* video. "Well, you should," urged her choreographer, Vince Paterson, who added, "you have more balls than most of the men I know." The tour would break every rule about sexuality, cross-sexuality, and religion that the guardians of public morality had been enforcing for centuries. Madonna's forte was not as an actress, as *Dick Tracy* would once again demonstrate, but as an iconoclastic rocker who combined music, fashion, theater, and performance art—all in trailblazing concerts.

Putting the tour together in New York, far from Warren, she felt free to run riot in Club Nine, which was located in a penthouse in Manhattan's west fifties. Radiant in a gold tinsel wig and a black sheath, Madonna arrived with three Latinos in slave collars. The management required all male customers to be able to demonstrate, at the door, genitalia measuring up to the name of the club. Madonna's escorts had no trouble qualifying, especially after she whipped out her tape measure. She then attached a leash to one boy's reproductive organ and led him to the nearest bed.

Madonna returned to L.A. before taking the tour on the road, and she and Warren dined in the front booth at Adriano's in Bel Air. They also were seen at Spago, La Scala, Louis XIV, and at Citrus on Melrose Avenue, where Madonna sat on Warren's lap. She never bothered to defer to his conservative ways, and he uncomplainingly accompanied her to deafening discos like Club Louis. When she felt like dancing with a girl, he watched from a distance, the antithesis of the violent Sean Penn, who'd have dragged the girls out by the hair. Like Warren, Sandra Bernhard was always hanging around, and often she and Madonna would go to the toilet and swap clothes. At Sunset Boulevard night spots, they sometimes ran into Jack Nicholson, still partying while Rebecca Broussard remained at home, pregnant with their baby."[138]

Rumors began to spread that Warren and Madonna weren't authentic lovers, but just dating to promote their film. In the Hollywood of the 1940s and 1950s, such studio-arranged "romances" had been common, like the celibate teaming of Elizabeth Taylor and Tab Hunter or Joan Collins and Gardner McKay. Warren denied the charge, saying, "She's no accident," and Madonna went on record in *Vanity Fair*, telling Kevin Sessums, "Sometimes I'm cynical and pragmatic and think it will last as long as it lasts. Then I have moments when I'm really romantic." Such moments were fewer and fewer for Warren, who sometimes held the phone two feet from his ear when she called, wincing at the sound of her voice. One day he brought a friend home at lunchtime, but Madonna said, "And who is this?" Warren asked if she'd mind if the man, who was a business associate, joined them. Madonna did indeed mind, and imperiously informed Warren that she'd need proof that the man didn't work for "the fucking *National Enquirer*." Warren glanced at his friend and said, "Charming, isn't she?"[139] The two men left together, and Madonna presumably lunched alone. Eventually, she went to David Geffen for advice, and he told her to see a shrink. "I have this feeling that I'm a bad girl and I need to be punished," she later confessed in a *Vanity Fair* interview. "The part of me that goes around saying, 'Fuck you! Fuck you! I'm throwing this in your face!' is the part that's covering up the part that's saying, 'I'm hurt. And I've been abandoned and I will never need anyone again.' I have also not resolved my Electra complex."[140]

She left for her rock tour, opening to thirty-five thousand hysterical fans near Tokyo, and cavorting, in her "Like a Virgin" number, with two topless males wearing pointy brassieres over their muscular pectorals. Madonna appeared to be masturbating as she writhed on a prop bed on stage. "I was exorcising myself of the guilt of the Catholic Church over sex and masturbation," she explained. To Warren's delight, she tirelessly promoted *Dick Tracy*, singing soundtrack numbers like "Sooner or Later" and "Now I'm Following You." In the latter song, a duet with Warren, his taped voice was boomed across vast rock venues. In Madonna's climactic production number, the dancers were dressed in yellow trench coats from *Dick Tracy*, and previews of the film were projected onto gigantic stadium screens. At one point, Madonna turned to the audience and said, "Dick. That's an interesting name. My bottom hurts just thinking about it." Sondheim's songs were also plugged in her new album, *I'm Breathless (Music from and Inspired by the Film* Dick Tracy*)*, and a rock journalist described her S&M style as "*A Clockwork Orange* meets the Weimar Republic." There could be no question that Warren got his money's worth in hiring Madonna. Helped by two No. 10 singles, "Vogue" and "Hanky Panky," the album climbed to No. 2 on *Billboard*'s chart, selling two million copies in the U.S. and five million internationally. Warren threw a party at his home to celebrate, telling Madonna to "dress down" for his respectable friends, including Al Pacino, Michelle Pfeiffer, and Jack Nicholson. Madonna appeared in a bare-backed, black Halston gown, her hair in a sleek coif, and Warren asked his guests to listen to a recording of her singing a tune from the *Dick Tracy* soundtrack, "Something to Remember." Everyone applauded, and Madonna had tears in her eyes. She had so wanted Warren to be proud of her, and he was.

But their affair was as rocky as ever, especially after she discovered that he'd hidden an oil painting she'd given him behind a couch, because it clashed with his decor. In his absence one day, she hung the oil on his living room wall, and when he saw it, he exploded, accusing her of trying to control him. Severely damaged by such fights, their relationship would not survive her demanding rock tour. His commitment to *Dick Tracy* was at odds with her demands for emotional support on the road. Expecting Warren to travel with her when the tour came to the U.S., she dispatched a private plane to fly him from L.A. to Houston for her opening at the Summit arena. He refused to go. The incredulous Madonna delayed her performance for half an hour, unable to believe that Warren would defy her. He did not phone until after the performance, explaining that important *Dick Tracy* business had detained him. She hung up in a rage. Customarily a tireless party girl, she left her opening-night wingding after making a token appearance. Other celebrations had been planned in Houston as well, but she canceled and retired to her hotel suite.

Now that Warren was experiencing Madonna in full flight as a rock star, he did not always like what he saw. "He was uncomfortable with her lifestyle," says Sarah Porterfield. "She embarrassed him. At Jewels Catch, a seedy downtown nightclub, he was uptight when Madonna enjoyed dancing in front of him, with her jacket off, showing all her cleavage. There were some racy scenes [with Warren] in *Truth or Dare* [a documentary Madonna filmed during the tour], but Warren threatened to sue if Madonna used any of them. They were shot just for kicks." The full title of Madonna's film was *Truth or Dare: On the Road, Behind the Scenes and in Bed with Madonna*, and she screened it in Warren's home for friends, serving popcorn and sodas. Warren grimaced at a scene in the film in which he and Madonna are discussing a room-service meal, Madonna being her usual bitchy self, and Warren exercising his customary restraint. According to a friend who was present in the screening room, Warren's expression made it clear that he disliked the way he appeared, in the film, to be letting Madonna browbeat him.[141]

The following day, she heard from his attorney, who demanded that certain scenes be deleted. In a taped telephone conversation in the film, Warren said he loved her. At his insistence, it was cut, and Madonna later fumed, "I don't think he respected what I was doing or took it seriously. He just thought I was fucking around with some kind of a home movie." But Warren had been taped without his knowledge, which is illegal.[142] After he threatened to sue, they were doomed as lovers, but Madonna still held on to him, less out of affection than addiction to drama.

A friend of Warren's was with him one day when a call came in from her, and he told her he was busy working. "We were golfing," recalled the friend, who asked Warren if he loved her. "What is love, anyway?" said Warren. "I really don't think I know." Madonna was "fun," but he added, "my problem is that I'm easily bored."[143]

Throughout the rest of her rock tour, Madonna seemed testy, and by the time the show played L.A., she was screaming at everyone. When Warren ventured backstage, she was in the middle of a tirade, telling her roadies, "I'm singing a cappella and my fucking headset goes out and everybody thinks the fucking show is over with." Warren tried to fade into the woodwork, but members of her youthful entourage spotted him and called out, "Uncle Warren," and "Dad." "Don't hide back there, Warren," Madonna admonished. "Get over here. You stink. You pussy man, what's with you? Can you believe I have to do this every night? Are you going to be nicer to me now, Warren?"

Evidently not. They quarreled, and she revoked his complimentary tickets for her last two L.A. shows. In humiliation, he called some buddies he'd planned to take along and told them not to come.

As the *Dick Tracy* release date approached, Madonna tried to upstage Warren, implying that she was the picture's true star. "Most people don't associate me with movies," she crowed in *Newsweek*. "But I have a much bigger following than Warren does, and a lot of my audience isn't even aware of who he is." When talk-show host Arsenio Hall asked her on national television, "What does Warren Beatty have that we don't have?" she replied, "About a billion dollars."

"Joan Collins once called Warren sexually insatiable," Arsenio said.

"He was twenty at the time," Madonna fired back, implying that Warren had lost some steam, and adding, "Aren't all twenty-year-olds insatiable?"

When Madonna's tour reached Boston, her only heterosexual dancer, Oliver Crumes, replaced Warren in her affections. "He was a toy for Madonna," said one of her gay dancers. "He was dumped and he gagged, and we laughed because we knew it would happen."

Warren and Jack Nicholson tried to visit her when the Blond Ambition tour played New York, but Madonna refused to let them in her dressing room, sending out a message that she had a headache. "She was really just pissed off in general at both of them," said an observer. Later she consented to see Warren, evidently still desiring him. When a girl in the crew flirted with him, Madonna immediately terminated her. Warren co-hosted the show's New York farewell party with Madonna at the Palace de Beauté on Broadway, and then she took her show to Europe. Altogether she played to two million people in ten countries.

During this time, *Dick Tracy* was being advertised to the tune of ten million dollars, but Madonna lost interest in the movie when she realized her musical sequences had been slashed in the final cut. "Warren *is* a pussy," she fumed. "He's a *wimp*."

The Walt Disney Studios expected *Dick Tracy* to be the big box-office hit of the summer, Disney's answer to Warner's *Batman*, one of the most successfully publicized movies of all time. As *Reds* had shown, publicity was Warren's fatal shortcoming in the new blockbuster era of saturation merchandising. With his disdain for hype, he was increasingly out of step with the industry. He knew very well that both *Ishtar* and *Reds* were destroyed by unfavorable publicity, which he'd been either unwilling or incapable of countering, and this explained why he at last reversed tactics and went all out promoting *Dick Tracy*. *Batman* had triumphed over all the other 1989 summer releases, and Disney expected Warren to claim the same box-office trophy during the following summer.

He had fierce competition: Arnold Schwarzenegger's *Total Recall*. The Austrian bodybuilder had always exhibited a natural gift for waltzing the press, generating precisely the kind of media hype that Warren couldn't abide. As a result, Schwarzenegger was the media's darling, prized for the good-natured way he made the public his partner in all his enterprises. The two superstars went head to head on Barbara Walters's TV special on the night of the Academy Awards. The contrasting attitudes of Beatty and Schwarzenegger demonstrated their differing outlooks on the nature and responsibilities of showmen in the new, high-concept Hollywood, where the producer's main job was to shoehorn comic strips and thinly veiled sitcoms into publicity and merchandising niches.

Warren's TV performance was less than sizzling. As the Walters interview began, he assumed his old adversarial role, and it was clear that he hadn't changed in his disdain for the media—a bias guaranteed to sabotage every interview. His demeanor betrayed his reluctance to appear on the show at all, and his depressing responses showed that he intended to limit the discussion to his oeuvre proper, excluding personal revelations. When Walters pressed for intimate details, he clammed up, indicating that such questions were extraneous to the quality of *Dick Tracy*.

When Schwarzenegger came on, the Walters special sprang to life. While Warren had seemed ill at ease, Schwarzenegger gleefully seized the opportunity to flog his goods on free worldwide TV. He quickly took charge, making Walters's work easy, which she loved him for. As a man who'd married into America's royal family, the Kennedys, he was in an enviable position, and he cooperatively chatted about his wife, JFK's niece, Maria Shriver, revealing that his mother-in-law, Eunice Shriver, insisted that his baby daughter, Katherine Eunice, was pure Kennedy, while his own mother claimed that the child was 100 percent Schwarzenegger. Walters, and the viewing public, relished his warm open manner. In the following days, the public flocked to his movie, making it the summer's top grosser—$120 million in the U.S. alone.[144]

When *Dick Tracy* opened in the nation's theaters, Al Pacino turned out to be the only good thing in it, apart from Dick Sylbert's colorful, capacious designs. Pacino, under Warren's skilled direction, added another facet to his already formidable talent, emerging from *Dick Tracy*, and later from *Sea of Love*, as "a looser, lighter Pacino." Warren's acting was wooden, and his face looked as if it were melting. Clearly he was not aging for the camera nearly as well as such earlier leading men as Clark Gable, Spencer Tracy, James Stewart, Gary Cooper, John Wayne, and Cary Grant, all of whom retained their appeal well into their middle years. Increasingly, audiences would be uncomfortable watching Beatty making love on screen to women half his age. Audiences had also fidgeted when a wrinkled, leathery-faced Robert Redford got amorous with Debra Winger in *Legal Eagles*. Of their generation, only De Niro, Pacino, and Hoffman—those whose talent was more than skin deep—would survive the ravages of aging.

Critics were evenly divided about *Dick Tracy*. David Ansen of *Newsweek* called the film "a class act: simple, stylish, sophisticated, sweet. This comic strip come to life is not like any other movie Warren Beatty has made, and yet his personality is stamped on every carefully considered frame." But Madonna, Ansen complained, was "smashingly unsubtle as the *femme fatale*." *Variety* found the film to be "curiously remote," and Warren "passive and listless." In the *New York Times*, Vincent Canby called the movie "a grand exercise in cinema imagination and wit for their own sake. Mr. Beatty and Richard Sylbert, the production designer, evoke the timeless 1930s of the early comic strips with studio settings of exceptional humor." David Denby, writing in *New York* magazine, found Warren too old for the role, referring to "the lines in Beatty's face," but the critic acclaimed the movie, referring to it as "a charming and beautifully designed work of American popular art—by far the most beautiful of the recent big cartoon-strip movies." David Edelstein of the *New York Post* disagreed, writing that "Beatty and his crack team of designers have aestheticized the life out of their *Tracy*. It's a macho cop picture with the soul of an interior decorator." Kathleen Carroll of the *New York Daily News* remarked on the mismatching of Warren and his leading lady. "There's so little onscreen chemistry between Madonna and Beatty that the reports of their recent real-life romance seem greatly exaggerated. Madonna may have plenty of moxie on the concert stage, but in this case she somehow lacks the electrifying allure of a movie star and her scenes, for all her effort, tend to fall flat."

As the movie played to diffident audiences across the country, Warren and Madonna continued to court in public, although journalists still doubted their sincerity. Friends vouched for them, one even saying, "She definitely screwed his brains out. Of that I am absolutely certain. But that doesn't mean that they were ever in love. Madonna doesn't want *maturity* in a man. She likes them young. That whole time, Madonna carried a torch for Sean."

As Katzenberg poured Disney's millions into marketing *Dick Tracy*, *Newsweek* decided to devote a cover to the film. Warren wanted the entire cover to himself, telling *Newsweek* he'd cooperate only if Madonna were excluded. The magazine was crestfallen, hardly savoring the prospect of an entire cover devoted to Beatty's withered visage, which no longer sold copies. Editor in chief Rick Smith called Katzenberg, insisting that Madonna appear with Warren— or no cover. Katzenberg gave him the go-ahead, supplying a still from the movie featuring both stars. When Warren saw the cover, he was infuriated. In reptilian Hollywood machinations, Katzenberg had trumped him. Nor was Madonna happy; when she realized that Warren had attempted to betray her, she tore into him, accusing him of blatant womanizing. But, surely, no case of a pot calling a kettle black had ever been so open-and-shut.

With the fading of Warren's allure, he changed his attitude toward the press.

Ironically, now that reporters no longer clamored for him, he made himself available, even hiring one of the most powerful—and hard-boiled—press agents in the business, Peggy Siegal, described by *Los Angeles* magazine as the "Doyenne of the Dragons." When *Vanity Fair* editor Tina Brown assigned Herb Ritts to photograph Warren for an issue, Warren readily agreed, though he later proved somewhat grumpy during the shoot. One of Ritts's assistants allegedly showed Warren her breasts in order to get a smile out of him.[145] Sometimes Peggy Siegal's hardball tactics did not work to Warren's advantage. On one occasion she denied *Vogue* access to Warren as a way of punishing the magazine for having described the work of another of her clients, Mel Gibson, as "ill-informed, half-baked and unfunny."[146]

Departing from his longtime policy of reticence regarding personal matters, Warren sat still for a probing *Rolling Stone* interview, but he was so guarded when quizzed about Madonna that the reporter, Bill Zehme, led off his story by writing that to "interview Warren Beatty is to want to kill him." After that, the article went downhill, demonstrating that Warren remained as inept as ever at promoting his films, despite his new hunger for attention and his willingness to be interviewed.

Though *Dick Tracy* racked up domestic grosses of $110 million, making a killing for both Warren and Madonna, it had cost forty to seventy million dollars to produce, and fifty-four million dollars to market. Disney was not pleased. In an interoffice memo leaked to the press, Katzenberg kvetched, "*Dick Tracy* made demands on our time, talent and treasury that . . . may not have been worth it."[147] The public slap stung Warren, who pointed out that *Dick Tracy*'s cost was half as much as such contemporary blockbusters as *Days of Thunder* and *Die Hard 2*. Some observers felt Warren's movie was too fragile for Disney's massive promotional effort, which amounted to hype overkill.

Disputing Katzenberg's figures, Warren said, "They got the costs back on cassette sales alone. . . . I thought [Katzenberg] might be the most capable manager I had ever known in Hollywood. He treated me very well. Perhaps too well . . . It could be that there was something basically frustrating in that he had to put up with someone who had complete artistic control in his contract. They don't ordinarily have to deal with gorillas like me." Though Katzenberg did nothing to reverse his negative spin, he more or less apologized by sending Warren two white doves in a golden cage, an olive tree, and a chocolate dart board with his own face on it.

Warren's affair with Madonna ended no better than his romance with Katzenberg. Ultimately he found the singer, who was all of thirty-two, a bit too old for his taste, and took up with a twenty-two-year-old actress. "He tossed me aside like a piece of old meat," Madonna moaned. She retaliated by walking up to a well-built young man on the beach at Malibu, and putting her cigarette out on his back. He was twenty-seven-year-old Tony Ward, a popular nude model for gay magazines. Madonna's cruelty turned him on. Short and muscular, he looked exactly like Sean Penn, and Madonna was ecstatic. Pinching his nipple and patting his butt, she said, "I think I can balance my glass on your ass. . . . A nice change from Warren."[148]

When the latter reappeared in her life and demanded fidelity, she said, "Go to hell," and later threw away a cheap brooch Warren sent her for her thirty-second birthday. After fifteen months, the Pro and the Buzzbomb were history. When someone asked her about Warren, she scoffed and said, "Who? Oh, you mean that guy I did that movie with? The last I heard, he was in a home somewhere."[149] She suspected that he was the source of a very accurate account of their breakup that appeared in the press. "He loves publicity, no matter what he says, especially if it makes him look like a big shot," she said.[150] Throughout their affair, and long before it, Madonna had been on a heedless, headlong ego trip, but she was about to crash and burn. With the publication of her trashy nude book *Sex*, in which she declared, "I love my pussy," her forgettable album *Erotica*, her scandalous foul-mouthed appearance on *The Late Show With David Letterman*, and the tasteless, mediocre *Truth or Dare*, the public at last turned on her, deciding she'd finally gone too far. Columnist Molly Ivins wrote that Madonna was "someone you wouldn't take home if she were the last woman left in the bar." Eventually, the indestructible star reinvented herself, giving birth to two children, marrying a British film producer, and launching the wildly successful Drowned World Tour.

Back in March 1991, she was scheduled to sing Stephen Sondheim's Oscar-nominated "Sooner or Later (I'll Always Get My Man)" from *Dick Tracy* at the Academy Awards ceremony. Having shed Tony Ward, she was between love affairs, and in search of an escort who'd help her create a sensation. After briefly considering such former lovers as Prince and Warren, both of whom she now hated, she settled on Michael Jackson, who'd just scored a $1 billion record deal with CBS, cinching his reputation as the king of pop. Though Michael Jackson had no respect for Madonna as an artist, he was enough of a marketing expert to appreciate the potential publicity of an Oscar appearance with her, and he agreed to discuss it over dinner at the Ivy. Madonna later told the *Advocate*, "I keep telling Michael Jackson, 'I'd love to turn Jose and Luis [her dancers] on you for a week. They'd pull you out of the shoebox you're in. Anybody who's in a shoebox in the closet cannot be in one after hanging around with Luis and Jose. Or me, for that matter." Though appalled, Michael consented to hang around Madonna just long enough to cash in on their date at the Oscars.

Wearing twenty million dollars worth of diamonds, a skin-tight white beaded strapless Bob Mackie gown, and trailing a snow-white ermine boa, she arrived at the Shrine Auditorium on Michael's arm. During the presentations, they sat in the front row until she took the stage to sing "Sooner or Later," which went on to win the Academy Award for Best Song. Apart from Sondheim's triumph and Dick Sylbert's winning the Best Art Direction–Set Direction Oscar, *Dick Tracy* was almost totally ignored. Pacino was nominated for his superbly grotesque cameo but lost the Best Supporting Actor award to Joe Pesci for *Goodfellas*.

Later that night, arriving at Swifty Lazar's annual bash at Spago in West Hollywood, Madonna immediately abandoned Michael and rushed to Warren's side, blowing into his ear and whispering to him. The shrewd Madonna knew that, in this roomful of Hollywood power hitters, Warren's star far outshone Michael's, and she behaved as if she and Warren had never broken up. Diana Ross finally rescued the abashed Michael, who was standing alone and ignored. Warren permitted Madonna to continue flirting with him, since his date for the evening, model Stephanie Seymour, had stood him up. After a while, Warren and Madonna drifted apart, and he began to cruise the crowd. A foxy, round-faced woman who looked as if she might have been the model for Columbia Tri-Star's logo, a Statue of Liberty look-alike holding a torch, caught his eye. In an interview several years later, Dick Sylbert said, "Warren and I saw Annette Bening for the first time at the Oscars, the year that I won for *Dick Tracy*. She was with Ed Begley. I looked over at her and I said to Warren, 'Interesting girl.' And he said, 'Ooooh, yeah.' It was the first indication I had."

Miss Bening, an offbeat newcomer, was the odds-on choice that night for Best Supporting Actress in *The Grifters*. She lost the Oscar, but the nomination supplied her with one of the essential qualifications for becoming a Beatty girlfriend, in case she was interested. With one or two exceptions such as Madonna,

Warren's girls had always been Oscar-caliber actresses, since he still required, in a woman, not only beauty but brains, talent, and status—qualities to enhance his own reputation. Annette had all that, and more: a huge ambition. Years ago, in 1976, at the height of Warren's freewheeling days, Goldie Hawn had predicted, "Warren will marry. It will take a very special woman. She'll have to be non-smothering and non-clinging. And strong! The stronger the woman, the better her chances of holding Warren."[151]

Such a woman now had Warren in her sights.

CHAPTER SEVEN

YES, YES, ANNETTE

"THE WAY Annette Bening got Warren," says Sarah Porterfield, "was, she got pregnant. What Annette had going for her as far as Warren was concerned was popularity—all his women whom he's had relationships with have either won Oscars or been nominated except for [actress] Pleasant Skye and Michelle Phillips, though [the latter] had Grammys.

"Annette started cranking out babies as quickly as she could so that in the event he dumps her for the next co-star, she's got child support on Warren's kids. You can't convince me she's through having babies."[1]

Another old friend had a different view concerning Warren and the woman he chose when he finally got married, well into his middle years. "There was no way it wasn't going to work with Annette," says Dick Sylbert. "He married himself a straight American girl, another Presbyterian or whatever. It wasn't going to be any other way. That's all he didn't have—children. There are two ways to live your life: Warren chose one of them and it's not without its own wisdom. First way, to get married at twenty-one, like everybody else in the whole world, have four children and then go and play. By that time you're limping. And the other choice is to go and play first, reap the wild wind, sow the seeds, whatever you want to call it—Don Juanism—and then get married and have a family. Warren doesn't do anything that isn't calculated. He had every right to do his life that way. Now he has four children and a wife. And I know for a fact his adolescence lasted more than most people's. And Annette knows, because that's what he said to her: 'I've had a very long adolescence.' "

Fairly early in the career of the perky, blue-eyed, slim, fine-boned, ambitious Annette Bening, she was looking for an apartment to rent. The Gersh Agency was handling her at the time, and someone in the office told Annette about Ron Bernstein, then a Gersh agent, who'd been looking for an actress to rent the guest house in back of his home on North Sierra Bonita Avenue in Hollywood. She called Bernstein, and they briefly discussed his rental. In the end, she decided she wanted to live in another neighborhood, but before hanging up she asked Bernstein if he knew anything about Virginia Hill, the Hollywood starlet and party girl who became mobster Bugsy Siegel's mistress, and on whose front lawn Siegel was executed, gangland style, on June 20, 1947, with three bullets in his head.

"That took care of the next hour or so," recalled Bernstein in 2000. "I'd once produced an RSO [Robert Stigwood Organization] movie on Virginia Hill, and I knew Judy Feiffer, who'd known Virginia Hill in Mexico. Annette mentioned she'd come to town to audition for the role of Virginia Hill."

Annette's homework paid off. Warren Beatty, set to star in the latest biopic about Bugsy and Virginia Hill, was smitten by the bright, clean-cut girl with the short, gamine-style sandy hair. In a strange way she was rather beautiful, except when she was tense, and then her face appeared clenched, her mouth turning down at the corners. They had almost met a few years before, in 1988, when he'd been casting *Dick Tracy*. He'd seen her around and was sufficiently stirred by her odd, unconventional appeal to put out some queries. "I had heard about Annette," he said, "and you know, you have opinions of certain people's opinions."[2] A meeting was scheduled, but he had to cancel (he was still involved with Madonna at the time). A second meeting was arranged, and this time *she* canceled.

After honing up on Virginia Hill with Ron Bernstein, Annette met Warren at Santo Pietro, the restaurant in the Beverly Glen Center, a minimall not far from his office. By then her résumé was looking somewhat better. Though she'd been rejected for *The Sheltering Sky* and fired from an ABC pilot, she'd appeared in a Dan Aykroyd flop, *The Great Outdoors*, in 1988, followed by more impressive credits, such as *Valmont* in 1989, *Postcards from the Edge* (a cameo), and *The Grifters* in 1990. She was thirteen years into her career when she met Beatty that day, and he told her that Barry Levinson, the director, and James Toback, the scenarist, wanted Michelle Pfeiffer to play Virginia Hill. "No," Warren told them, "I think Annette Bening would be perfect. I'm having lunch with her tomorrow." Annette told him that her agent hadn't wanted her to meet him because he was sure Warren was just going to hit on her.

"And it turned out he was right," Warren recalled.[3] She got the role, and he knocked her up.

Of the hundreds, perhaps thousands, of women he'd known, Annette was probably the most stable, the least sentimental, and therefore the least romantically or sexually demanding. For a womanizer like Warren, marriage to a safe, sane woman would assure that no future dalliance of his would contain the threat of commitment or permanence. He once said that he desperately wanted to deserve Annette's love, and the way to do it, he reasoned, was to be good to her. Would that be possible, given his sex addiction and history of promiscuity? She tried to make it easy for him to change, retaining her willowy figure even while carrying his baby.

What drew Annette to the much older Warren? "He's smart and fun and interesting," she said.[4] Not a word about his looks, which were no longer impressive. But Warren and Annette were suited in more crucial ways, having nothing to do with sex, appearance, or romance. Both basically insecure persons, they understood each other. Warren had always secretly suspected he was a laughingstock, and Annette felt unattractive, boring, and worthless unless she scored every role she went out for.[5] Socially, as the wife of a reigning mogul, she'd be assured of a place at the top of the L.A. heap.

Her ambitions simmered beneath a deceptively casual exterior. Shirley Bening, Annette's mother, observed that Warren loved Annette "because she doesn't behave like an actress. She's not always *on*. She's still herself."[6] Born on May 29, 1958, Annette spent her early childhood in Topeka, Kansas, and grew up wanting to be an actress. Both of her parents were performers, her mother a paid soloist in the church choir and her father, Grant, an inspirational moti-vator who taught salesmanship at the Dale Carnegie Institute. Annette was the fourth of Shirley and Grant's children. "It was a good family, but we had our problems, just like everybody else," Annette said. "Basically, we are all really close."

The family seldom went to the movies, and never to the theater, but Annette had a love of playacting. By the time the family moved to San Diego, she was seven and already performing in her own childhood play-games. "If you set up the room and you were playing dolls, or if you were a pioneer woman outside grinding berries—if things were going well, you forgot about real life, and there was this ecstatic experience of freedom," she recalled. "I think that's a univer-sal phenomenon of creativity. Every once in a while, after you've worked and worked and worked and worked, you find a groove, and for that little moment of time, there is no work. It's a very rare thing, but it's what sucks you in and keeps you coming back." She studied ballet but gave it up as a teenager, though her interest in acting persisted.

At San Diego's Patrick Henry High School, she was asked to act out the role of a victim during a routine disaster-preparedness exercise held on the football field. She was supposed to lie on a stretcher and wait for a helicopter to arrive and evacuate her, but she turned it into a performance worthy of Sarah Bernhardt. "Suddenly I found myself really experiencing it," she said. The helicopter pilot watched her histrionics for a minute and told her, "Whoa, take it easy." Coming back to reality, Annette was embarrassed, but the acting bug had ineluctably taken hold. Anne Krill, her drama teacher, wasn't much more impressed than the helicopter pilot, and later recalled, "She had loads of inter-est in things other than drama."

Indeed she did. Scuba diving was more fun for Annette in her teenage years than theatrics. Ms. Krill gave her a C in drama, but that didn't stop her from appearing in a school production of *Godspell*. "All the boys liked her," said a class-mate. She was slim, merry-eyed with mischief, and tousle-haired, and she'd been blessed with an elegantly sculpted bone structure, if not conventional prettiness. She neither wore nor needed much makeup. According to many, she had the shapeliest and longest gams seen since Betty Grable's. All that, and she could cook, too. At seventeen, to support her scuba expenses, she worked on a boat off San Diego "in a tiny galley," her mother remembered. "I couldn't believe what she had to work with, [but Annette became] a very good cook. I know she's good with light pasta dishes."

After graduating from high school a year early, she spent her freshman and sophomore years at San Diego Mesa College, where she signed up for the course in women's studies and began to develop a political consciousness. Perhaps as a result, her politics would always retain a shade of ivory-tower unreality, and this limitation would restrict her usefulness to Warren, in 2000, when he entered the political arena as a potential candidate for the U.S. presidency. After completing her work at the San Diego college, Annette left home, earning her B.A. in theater at San Francisco State University. In 1980, she was one of forty students accepted at that city's reputable American Conservatory Theater. A long and rigorous apprenticeship lay before her; at ACT she studied and performed in repertory for five years. Bravely, and despite feelings of self-doubt and insecurity, she flew to New York in 1984 to participate in the annual "league auditions," in which the four most promising drama students were given an opportunity to perform in front of theatrical agents. Annette was not at her best. She was still wearing her hair long, a style not suited to her round face. She had a chipped tooth, which her gummy smile did nothing to conceal, and she was convinced that she was a tad overweight for the stage, though the fear was grounded more in neurosis than reality. Part of the blame for her failure in Manhattan was ACT's, she thought, later explaining, "My acting school was all about character. The idea of just going in and being myself . . . that terrified me."

Surrendering to her terrors, she retreated to San Francisco, having gained nothing more during her New York sojourn than empty, polite promises from an agent. It would have been a depressing time had it not been for J. Steven White, an actor and director at ACT, with whom she fell passionately in love. They began living together in 1981, but she didn't tell her parents that her "roommate" was also her lover. She continued to act, broadening her repertory with such challenging roles as Lady Macbeth, Juliet, and Emily in Thornton Wilder's *Our Town*.

Wearing her mother's formal white wedding gown, she married Steve White in 1984 in San Diego. This was her first marriage, the one undertaken for love. The following year, Annette and Steve made a huge joint decision about their careers, leaving ACT to try their luck in Colorado, where they went to work at the Denver Center Theater Company. The majestic Rockies have a salutary effect on most people, but not Annette, who felt completely cut off from the mainstream of American theater, though she was appearing with the Colorado Shakespeare Festival. The real problem was her marriage, which had run into trouble by 1986.

Peter Donat, who performed with her during her tenure at ACT, vacationed with her and Steve, and his recollection of the experience indicates that the passion had drained out of their marriage. "She was intensely interested in any sport," said Donat, "especially windsurfing. She went out again and again."

After a year in the mountains she fled to New York, again trying trying to get her career on track. Her absence did not make J. Steven White's heart grow any fonder. Whenever opportunities opened up for Annette in Denver or California, she did not hesitate to commute, feeling that she could spend her life in regional theater with occasional Broadway roles, but she was strongly drawn to New York, finally settling down in a friend's apartment. "It was a big closet," she said, "in a really cool building."

Inevitably, her marriage suffered, and finally J. Steven White gave up and returned to San Francisco. Stephen Tyler, who studied with Annette in San Francisco, said, "Annette has never been subservient, that's for sure. Once, it came up in a class discussion that women sometimes have to give up their careers to keep their husbands. Annette spoke right up and said, 'If my husband can't accept my career, then he's history.' "

New York rewards those who don't rush it, who are willing to stick around and become a part of the scene. As her marriage waned, her career began to blossom. She made important connections, including Alan Ball, who worked "off-off-off-off" Broadway, scripting wild material for a comedy troupe, and would later provide some of Annette's strongest material—*The Grifters* and *American Beauty*. By 1986, she was playing the lead role in Tina Howe's *Coastal Disturbances*, and when it opened on Broadway, the *New York Times*'s Frank Rich wrote that Annette projected "the mystery of a woman floating ambiguously but passionately between love and nervous collapse." The theater capital at last knew who Annette Bening was, and awarded her a coveted Tony nomination. She also received the Clarence Derwent Award for Most Outstanding Debut, and appeared in Michael Weller's *Spoils of War*, playing the girlfriend of co-star Kate Nelligan's ex-husband and infusing the role with thoughtfulness and intelligence.

Her earlier remark that any husband who couldn't accept her career was "history" proved sadly prophetic. More and more, White was fading from her life. She couldn't afford to spend much time with him in California because, despite her Tony nomination, she was still too new in the theater to command top roles or even steady work. She filmed a television pilot for ABC in 1987, but when the show went on, it was with another actress. Annette found the experience "devastating. It confirmed every insecurity that I had. 'I'm not sexy. I'm not funny. I'm not any good at all.' " For many months in the late eighties, she pulled every string, worked every contact she had, lobbied furiously and tirelessly to land the lead in Bernardo Bertolucci's film *The Sheltering Sky*, adapted from a highly regarded literary novel by Paul Bowles. With her combination of romantic appeal and neurotic edginess, she was perfect for the role based on the suicidal writer Jane Bowles. The story, fictionally tracking the dissolution of Jane and Paul Bowles's unconventional marriage, somewhat paralleled the ordeal Annette and Steven White were going through as their own marriage disintegrated. As critic Rex Reed wrote, the film was about "the death of love, the loss of illusions, but mostly about the terrible consequences of what can happen when you wander too far away from the world you know with nothing but the sky for a compass."

At this point in her life, Annette too had wandered far from her home and her husband, and had very little to show for it. "I was just scrambling, trying to get work and make it good," she recalled. But she was gradually losing Steve White, and would be left with nothing, neither career nor marriage. The *Sheltering Sky* role went to a more established actress, Debra Winger, and the pain of Annette's loss was all the keener when the film, though not commercially successful, was hailed as a "masterpiece, one of the greatest films of all time," and Winger's acting was lauded as "impeccable." Annette had an affair with actor Ed Begley, Jr.,[7] and was depressed when she discovered he was two-timing her.[8]

Fortunately, she had supporters in New York who encouraged her and kept her focused. "She just had it," recalls Tina Howe. "Everyone knew she was going to be a star." Occasionally she'd see a good film, like *The Killing Fields*, in which she could imagine herself being cast. "I thought, 'There are people in those movies, and somebody has to be in there, so maybe I can possibly do it.' " Finally, in 1988, she landed a major role in Dan Aykroyd's *The Great Outdoors*. It was not an entirely auspicious debut—the movie was a box-office and critical flop—

but at least she'd displayed her considerable abilities on screen, and the following year Milos Forman gave her the splashy leading role in *Valmont*, a remake of *Les Liaisons Dangereuses*. Though the film was a loser at the box office, Annette's portrayal of Madame de Merteuil, a decadent aristocrat, was outrageously sexy, and she came across as a brash and dynamic screen personality.

When she moved to Hollywood relatively late, at thirty, she right away was asked, "So how does it feel to be an older actress?" Customarily, newcomers— such as Julia Roberts, Leelee Sobieski, Cameron Diaz, and Julia Stiles—are closer to their teens than they are to their thirties, so Annette battened down for another struggle. That left little energy to devote to her personal life, and her marital crisis worsened. She and Steve White got divorced in 1991 due to her professional ambitions.[9] She had never experienced anything as intense as the loss of the personal life she'd been trying, however intermittently, to build, and later described her divorce from Steve as "the most painful time in my life."[10]

In the early nineties, meaty roles continued to come her way. Mike Nichols, one of the screen's hottest directors, permitted her to steal some of Meryl Streep's thunder in a scene in *Postcards from the Edge*. She made an even stronger impression in *The Grifters* as Moira Langtry, co-starring with Anjelica Huston and John Cusack. Slender and comely, a svelte five-foot-seven, *The Grifters'* skimpily clad and sometimes completely unclad vamp impressed her costumer, Richard Hornung. "With everyone else there's always something wrong," he said. "Their torso is too long, their thighs are fat. With her there's nothing you can't show, because she's sort of fabulous everywhere." Pauline Kael called her "a sex fantasy come to luscious life . . . a superb wiggler." Annette's competition for the Oscar in 1990 proved too strong—Whoopi Goldberg walked off with the statuette for *Ghost*.

Summoned to audition with Robert De Niro in *Guilty by Suspicion*, she made an indelible impression because "she had no nerves," recalls director Irwin Winkler. "About halfway through the reading, Bob looks at me and gives an almost imperceptible nod, like, 'Wow, she really is something.' " She won the role, playing De Niro's ex-wife in a HUAC blacklist story.

In 1991, thirteen years into her career, Annette was at last in demand as a leading lady. "Thank God fame didn't happen to me until I was thirty," she said later. "By then, I had some coping mechanisms. I never went through what must be very tricky—to be very famous, very young. It was still a lot to go through to learn how to become a public person, but it wasn't something that I had to do when I was twenty-two, like my husband [Warren] did. I had never really considered myself glamorous." On screen, more than glamour, she projected inner beauty, enormous confidence, and authority. Filming *Regarding Henry* with Harrison Ford, she played a devoted wife and mom with utter conviction, holding her own with the industry's top leading man. More than that, she was emerging as a true screen original, as uniquely herself as a Bacall or a Claudette Colbert. Mike Nichols, who was directing her again in the Harrison Ford film, attempted to define her quality: "She's confusing, because she's so perfect. Her kindness is perfect, her technique is perfect, her relaxation is perfect." There was a buzz around Hollywood about her: she was the girl of the moment. This brought her to the key turning point of her career, and if she hadn't met Warren, she would have continued going straight up, toward superstardom. But she did meet Warren, and it would never be the same.

With all the excitement about her, it was inevitable that he would be the next man in her life, because he always had to have what was hottest and newest. "It's like a drumbeat," he said, explaining how his obsession with Annette developed as her status in Hollywood soared. "Someone has a tone in their voice when they speak about somebody. Real talent and real intelligence and wit, the best voice in the world, the best body, the best face, and the best appreciation of a joke . . . How can anyone be so gifted?" In view of her Oscar nomination and status as Hollywood's new leading lady of choice, he had to have her. After all, he had his reputation as "the great seducer"[11] to uphold. Unwittingly, he was kicking off the new Hollywood trend of older men–younger women pairings, which by 2000 would include Jack Nicholson, sixty-three, and Lara Flynn Boyle, thirty; Michael Douglas, fifty-five, and Catherine Zeta-Jones, thirty; Jerry Seinfeld, forty-six, and Jessica Sklar, twenty-eight; Billy Bob Thornton, forty-four, and Angelina Jolie, twenty-four; and James Woods, fifty-three, and Alexis Thorpe, eighteen. James Woods frankly admitted that he felt obliged to make Miss Thorpe, an aspiring model, a star, and added, "It's a total myth that you lose your interest in sexuality as you get older. I'm more potent now than I ever was."[12]

Annette once said that she liked brave people who took risks, and though *Bugsy* was just another big-budget gangster film, she was impressed by Warren's past accomplishments, the significant gambles he'd taken with *Bonnie and Clyde*, *Shampoo*, and especially *Reds*. She was a bit of a risk-taker herself, especially in the unpretentious way she assumed the mantle of movie stardom. Unlike such previous generations of leading ladies as Elizabeth Taylor, Joan Crawford, and

Lana Turner, who wouldn't dream of setting foot outside the house in less than full star regalia—mink, jewels, and gloves, even in the heat of summer—Annette wore casual clothes, usually white cotton pants, rubber platform flip-flops, and a white shirt knotted at the waist, or a three-quarter-length corduroy jacket over black leggings or pedal pushers. Her hair was slightly mussed, her face without makeup. The only actressy touch was her big sunglasses and her little white BMW convertible. For dinner at her favorite restaurant, Ago, a sleek, highbrow showcase on Melrose Avenue co-owned by Robert De Niro, she might don a black cashmere shawl, but she rarely got herself up any fancier than that. One was more likely to find her browsing the labyrinthine stacks at Book Soup, across from Tower Records on the Strip, than frequenting such trendy L.A. spots as Les Deux Cafés on North Las Palmas Avenue.

She was in her early thirties, Warren in his early fifties, the day he fell in love with her at Santo Pietro restaurant in 1991. "It took about ten minutes," he remembers. "Maybe five. And I felt very conflicted because I was so elated to meet her, and yet at the same time, I began to mourn the passing of a way of life. I thought, Oh, everything's going to be different." Part of him wanted to hold onto his bachelorhood and freedom, but the shrewder part knew that, at his advanced age, this was probably his last chance to score the hottest new star, and at the same time save himself from becoming a laughingstock as a ridiculous old lecher. "When I was in my twenties and thirties, there were certain things that were irresistible," he said. "And then into my forties and into my fifties. Being adolescent never got boring to me. And that fortunately came to a conclusion, not a moment too soon. I stood a good chance of reaching the end of my days as a solitary, eccentric. . . . fool."[13] He feverishly set about selling himself to her. "I went into my peacock syndrome and couldn't shut up. I did everything but stand up and do a soft-shoe on the table."

After lunch, they went for a stroll beside the Beverly Glen minimall, about a third of the way down from Mulholland Drive. Her agent had told her that he was "meeting every actress in Hollywood" in the process of casting *Bugsy*, but she saw the effect she was having on him, and kept walking along the cul-de-sac, which was directly behind his office. She told him all about her close-knit family, and Warren suddenly found himself opening up as never before.

She wasn't particularly bothered by his reputation as a womanizer. After all, he was practically a senior citizen, and she realized that it was his past that had brought him finally to her. It had taken all those affairs to teach him, she hoped, what he needed to know about living. "Whatever got him to where he is now is fine with me," she said. "Nobody ever changes anybody else, I do believe that."[14] The last thing she wanted to change, naturally, was his lofty status in the Hollywood Establishment. But what she did not reckon on was the precious momentum she'd lose, mired in the demands of domesticity and motherhood. For Annette, potential superstar, Warren was not so much career magic as career poison.

Ecstatic, he could have been describing himself and Annette instead of Bugsy and Virginia when he told a pal, "Bugsy was very promiscuous until he met Virginia Hill. When they got together, he never went after another woman. He found someone who accepted him for who he was."

Finally, Warren and Annette said goodbye that day at the minimall, and he went upstairs to his office and found Jim Toback in the cutting room. "What did you think?" Toback asked. All Warren could say was, "Whoa!" Toback resignedly thought, "It was very clear who would get the part."

Much as Warren was driven to seduce her, for once he restrained himself. He didn't want to put her under any pressure, so that she could have a chance to shine in *Bugsy*. On the set, they worked together in perfect harmony, perhaps because Warren, for a change, was not directing, having realized that directing himself was a form of onanism, while being directed by someone else was a form of intercourse.[15] The very able Barry Levinson of *Diner* fame was in charge, and Rex Reed would later note, "Beatty gives his best performance in years, probably because he wisely left the direction in someone else's hands; he's charming, unpredictable, reckless, and romantic. Annette Bening, full of passion and wiseguy wisecracks, plays gun moll Virginia Hill with such energy and spunk the chemistry is apparent and juicy. Their love scenes don't look like acting."

Toward the end of the shoot, her parents came to visit the set, and Warren invited them to his dressing room for lunch. He was favorably impressed that they'd been married forty years; it boded well for the future he envisaged with Annette, who struck him as "an actress who's human." When her parents left, he told her, "I'm not making a pass at you, but if I were to be so lucky as to have that occurrence happen, then I want to assure you that I would try to make you pregnant immediately."[16]

His goofy proposition, so cheeky and yet quaintly Victorian in its staid phraseology, was "very precious" to Annette, whose desire for children was more urgent as her biological time clock ran out. Shirley Bening said that Annette "knew early on she wanted to be a mother. She said if she couldn't have kids physically, then she'd adopt." According to one Hollywood source, Shirley advised Annette to make Warren fall in love with her before surrendering to his charms. "She played him like a violin," says the source.[17] Adds Dick Sylbert, "They got together, and I remember something about a diamond ring—she sent it back. Earrings—she sent them back. That was unusual."

Warren and Annette had one more scene to film before the picture wrapped, and he suggested. "If we went to dinner it wouldn't be so much pressure on either of us." When he inquired if she, too, wanted a child, she waited a few minutes and then said yes. "Well," he said, "I would like to do that right away." When asked years later if they'd had sex that night, Annette replied, "Umm . . . very quickly. Because we were . . . trying."[18]

Warren added, "There was never a moment of not, in effect, being married to Annette." When she discovered she was pregnant, she was set to play Catwoman in *Batman Returns*. She lost the coveted role, which made an even bigger star of her replacement, Michelle Pfeiffer. Annette's timing, as far as her burgeoning career was concerned, could hardly have been worse. Her precious pre-forties years—a movie actress's only prime—were flying, and there wouldn't be any more cracks at superstar-making megahits like *Batman Returns*.

Madonna, for whom David Geffen had found a therapist following her affair with Warren, was beside herself when she learned of Annette's pregnancy. "First Sean went off and fathered another woman's child, and now Warren," said a friend of the rocker's. "It left her feeling hurt and confused."[19] Eventually, Madonna would have a baby, Lourdes, with her Hispanic trainer.

Meanwhile, Warren was enjoying life with an intelligent, talented woman. Pillow talk with Annette was always scintillating, because they could share so much. "If I'm having a problem with a person or I'm needing a little encouragement, I'll talk to him," she said. "We're very different kinds of actors, in a way. But he likes what I do a lot, so he's very, very supportive and encouraging." He liked what she did in the kitchen, too. For the weight-conscious Warren, who'd never developed middle-age spread, the light pasta dishes Annette specialized in were ideal. When he dined out without her, he tended to splurge on calories, as *Variety*'s Peter Bart noted at a luncheon ("Beatty loves to eat, relaxed by his heaping portions of risotto, fish, and steamed vegetables").[20]

On July 6, 1991, Warren attended a birthday party for David Geffen, newly crowned the richest man in Hollywood. Having joined MCA at a particularly fortuitous moment, Geffen's shares in the company made him a billionaire after the Matsushita takeover. His forty-eighth birthday was celebrated at Sandy Gallin's house in Malibu, and present were most of the stars he'd advised over the years, including Warren, Madonna, Michael Jackson, Joni Mitchell, Jackson Browne, Elizabeth Taylor, and Carrie Fisher, as well as the movie industry's top brass—Diller, Katzenberg, Ovitz, and Eisner. Noticeably absent were the two rock groups he'd worked with who'd never forgiven Geffen for certain business dealings that rubbed them them wrong way: the Eagles and Crosby, Stills, and Nash. New Age guru Marianne Williamson, long a friend of Geffen's, delivered the birthday blessing, asking that the youthful mogul's billions be accompanied by serenity and peace of mind. Then she added, "May we all be as rich as David in our souls."[21]

In 1991, Warren was nominated for the Best Actor Oscar for *Bugsy* in a strong field that included Anthony Hopkins, Robert De Niro, Nick Nolte, and Robin Williams. Apart from his nomination as Best Actor, he was also nominated as producer. This brought his grand total of Oscar nominations to thirteen over some twenty-four years: four as actor, three as co-writer, four as producer, and two as director. When a reporter asked Annette if his accomplishments intimidated her, she said, "I guess I felt that I was on my own path before I ever met him. Maybe if I hadn't gotten my own aspirations in line at a young age, I would have been more vulnerable to that kind of insecurity."

In view of his record number of Oscar nominations, the industry at first expected *Bugsy* to make a clean sweep of the awards. "Once the voters actually saw the picture," wrote Oscar historian Anthony Holden, "the disappointment quotient grew. Wasn't this a somewhat two-dimensional, cardboard-cutout gangster, despite the hype suggesting that Beatty the actor had never showed more range?" There was also something profoundly wrong with the whole picture, which presents the founding of Las Vegas as some sort of manifest destiny, the fulfillment of an American dream, and a great contribution to modern life. In reality, if authors Sally Denton and Roger Morris, former members of the National Security Council under Presidents Johnson and Nixon, are right in their study, *The Money and the Power: The Making of Las Vegas and Its Hold on America, 1947–2000*, the Nevada gambling capital is "the nexus" of "international corruption at the highest levels of business and government," and has poisoned

American life at every level. Once again, as in *Bonnie and Clyde*, Warren's simplistic approach to his subject matter, and his tendency to idealize the characters he played, had glamorized crime and criminals.

In early 1992, well before the Oscar ceremony, Annette gave birth to their daughter Kathlyn. Recalls Dick Sylbert, "They weren't married when they had the child." During Annette's first trimester, she was "very sick at first and very cranky and I felt awful," she recalled. She gained a lot of weight but remained healthy. However, she lost her desire to work, and the sudden disappearance of this driving force in her life reduced her to a state of fear and confusion. *"Is this going to go away and not come back?"* she wondered. She stayed in touch with old friends from ACT in San Francisco, and was amazed to learn that she was the only woman in her graduating class to have a baby. On some days, noted an interviewer, "the expressive blue eyes from the glossies are slightly clouded by a bit of early-pregnancy fatigue."

Following the birth of Kathlyn, who was named after her paternal grandmother, Warren and Annette were married in March 1992, at the height of the Oscar voting period, inspiring speculation that the nuptials were designed to sway the academy Warren's way. "Small wedding," Sylbert mused, "few people." For a while at least, marriage seemed to transform Warren. "I think stability is part of what Warren saw in Annette," says Shirley Bening. Sandee Hirst, a high-school chum, agrees, pointing out that Warren fell in love with Annette "probably because she's real down to earth." Bob Evans said, "Until his marriage, Warren stood alone as the single most competitive person I've ever known. His obsession in life was to be *first*—first with the new hot girl in town, preferably model or starlet; first to be shown the new hot screenplay, the new hot role, or for that matter the new hot anything—as long as it was new and hot."

His life fell into two distinct phases, Warren now maintained, "before Annette" and "with Annette." But many Hollywood insiders wondered what he would do when she was no longer "new and hot." Would he go chasing after the latest sex goddess, as he'd done with Brigitte Bardot and Madonna, compelled to add yet another notch to his belt? His idea of honor had always permitted infidelity. "Before Warren got hitched to Annette Bening (who is one sensational lady)," said Evans, "for years he had been terribly orthodox when it came to hitting on a pal's lady: *never on Sunday*. Ahhh . . . but Monday through Saturday was different. Then it was a religious experience. No wonder he's called 'the pro' by his friends (or those who think they are)."[22]

An even bigger difference in his life than the advent of Annette was his daughter Kathlyn, on whom he doted. Womanizers make great dads, especially for daughters, because they love women so much. The daughters feel this energy—this masculine adoration and support emanating from their fathers—and almost invariably grow up feeling beautiful and loved. Often (like Caroline Kennedy, for instance) they find exactly the right kind of man and eventually have happy homes.

On Warren's fifty-fifth birthday, March 30, 1992, he attended the sixty-fourth Academy Awards with Annette, who'd been three years old when Warren first brought Natalie Wood to the Oscar ceremony. In the intervening years, he had produced and starred in five films that had garnered fifty-one nominations from the academy, an extraordinary record. Since he had been rebuffed by his peers for *Dick Tracy*, Hollywood pundits predicted the industry would compensate by honoring him for *Bugsy*. Warren attempted to project an attitude of indifference toward the Oscar contest, explaining, "I go for the enjoyment of seeing the people that I've worked with and know, with the understanding that it's all slightly masochistic. . . . It's enjoyable in the way that bobbing for apples is enjoyable. You can't take the game too seriously."

Though Annette wasn't nominated for *Bugsy*, she was heartened by the response of the crowd when she and Warren arrived at the auditorium. Obviously, she had not been forgotten by the public or the industry. She could tell from the excitement she stirred that, despite her absence from the screen due to motherhood, she still had a crack at superstardom. She was not, however, on the same level of fame as Warren. "I don't really get recognized, not like Warren," she admitted. "We were entering the building and he was opening the door, and this woman on the other side just stopped dead and said, 'I love you.' It was so funny."

As the Oscars were passed out, Warren's odds began to decline when Harvey Keitel, nominated for his supporting role in *Bugsy*, lost to Jack Palance, who'd played a cowpoke in *City Slickers*. When the Best Actor winner was announced, Warren lost to Anthony Hopkins for *The Silence of the Lambs*. Perhaps it was just as well. His family life required the kind of time and attention he could never have given it in his obsessive *Reds* days, when he'd wanted to turn out the greatest movie ever made. An Oscar for *Bugsy* would probably have driven him to try to top himself professionally, instead of attending to the personal responsibilities he'd taken on (the picture's only Oscar wins were in the less illustrious categories of Art Direction—Set Decoration and Costumes). Now Warren could relax and be Mr. Mom.

Commercially, *Bugsy* disappointed TriStar Pictures' Mike Medavoy, who'd greenlighted the film despite Warren's rudeness at one of their initial confabs. "Look at you," Warren said. "You've got to get in shape and you've got to start dressing better." Then he pointed to his own lean body, black suit, cashmere sweater, and suede shoes. Relations between the two men did not improve as the picture progressed. Though Warren listed himself as one of the producers and participated in preproduction matters such as casting, locations, and budget, once the shooting started he left all the producing chores to partner Mark Johnson and focused exclusively on his acting. When filming was completed, he reverted to producing, putting "sometimes hourly pressure" on Medavoy to make the film a hit. If displeased, he'd tell Medavoy, "How can you be in the business? You are lazy."

Medavoy's downfall at TriStar was in part associated with *Bugsy*. When the picture opened to a lukewarm box office, Medavoy was away from his desk, enjoying a cruise down the Nile, and Warren sometimes made five calls a day to Peter Guber, chairman of Sony Pictures, TriStar's parent company, complaining about Medavoy and asking for better marketing efforts. TriStar sank forty-three million dollars into making the film and another fifty million trying to sell it. The public continued to turn a cold shoulder, and TriStar lost almost thirty million dollars. "Guber was plotting how to get rid of me," says Medavoy. The ax finally fell a couple of years later, when Medavoy's resignation was requested, shortly after he asked one of Guber's executives, "Who do I have to fuck to get off this train?"

If Bugsy demonstrated that Warren's name could no longer assure a big opening at the box office, his reign as the world's favorite playboy had also passed. For a while, gossip columnists wondered who they'd write about now. Then along came Leonardo DiCaprio, who celebrated his phenomenal success in the 1990s by playing pickup basketball with Will Smith, Mark Wahlberg, Tobey Maguire, and Freddie Prinze Jr. and hanging out in nightclubs with his "posse." Leo's inseparable crew included Maguire; Harmony Korine, the *Gummo* boy auteur; levitating magician David Blaine; actors Ethan Suplee (*Chasing Amy*, *American History X*), Jay Ferguson (Burt Reynolds's wisecracking son on *Evening Shade*), Josh Miller (Keanu Reeves's little brother in *River's Edge*), and such other aspiring stars as Lukas Haas, Kevin Connelly, and Scott Bloom, and the posse's Shirley MacLaine–type mascot, Sara Gilbert (*Roseanne*). When Leo came under criticism for his wild ways, *New York Post* columnist Richard Johnson wrote, "It has been a long time since I've had so much fun reporting about a celebrity. He is only following in the grand tradition of Jack Nicholson and Warren Beatty. Leave the kid alone." Predictably, DiCaprio showed up at Hefner's mansion, and told Hef his dream was to be in the Grotto, in the Jacuzzi, at 3 A.M.[23]

Still fascinated by politics, Warren advised Democratic presidential candidate Bill Clinton in 1992 to jazz up his speeches by yelling "fuck" a few times.[24] Unlike George McGovern and Gary Hart, Clinton ignored the movie star's advice and won the election. In January 1993, Warren and Annette were in the celebrity contingent at the inauguration party. During his two administrations, Clinton demonstrated, above all, that a politician, if shrewd enough, could maneuver himself out of damaging revelations about his sexual life. The danger of such exposés had no doubt been one of the obstacles that kept Warren from running for public office. Clinton's extraordinary example of survival may have inspired the nervous movie star to reconsider a life in politics. Whatever the reason, he was definitely open to the possibility of running for public office.[25]

Annette wasn't surprised, knowing his fondness for fame. "It's the only thing he's ever known as an adult," she said. "He's just very comfortable with it. I really admire him, and I admire his desire to do things, to make a statement." Her own interest in politics was pretty much limited to being a disgruntled Democrat, one who didn't care for what the party had become in the nineties. "I read my stuff," she said, "but I'm not nearly as informed politically as he is."

One of Hollywood's most popular and visible couples, Warren and Annette looked happy at *The New Yorker*'s 1994 first-Hollywood-issue party, which was held under a white tent in the garden of the Bel Air Hotel, where editor Tina Brown entertained three hundred guests. The Beattys cuddled for photographers. At a nearby table, Shirley MacLaine was laughing with Anjelica Huston. Tina's love of show business, so evident in her previous post as editor of *Vanity Fair*, had by now seeped into virtually every periodical in the U.S., provoking such magazines as *Time* and *Newsweek* to devote more cover stories to actors and actresses. At her party at the Bel Air, Tina ruled over table thirteen, where the guests included Steven Spielberg and his wife Kate Capshaw, Michael Ovitz, Ralph Fiennes, Barbra Streisand, and United Artists studio chief John

Calley. Said producer Joel Silver, "This is as much Hollywood power as *anyone* can muster."

The 1994 Los Angeles earthquake devastated the Beattys, destroying their home. Instead of repairing the house, they bought a sprawling, Spanish Mediterranean mansion on Mulholland Drive and moved in immediately. "We're still drawing plans and changing," Annette said six years later. "And we keep adding rooms."

She got pregnant again that year, and stopped drinking as she always did when carrying a baby (caffeine-free diet Coke was her customary beverage). "He doesn't smoke," she said of Warren, "and he actually barely ever takes a drink— I wish he would more! But, yes, he does take good care of himself." With a gentleness he somehow drew from the depths of his narcissistic soul, he buoyed her up during her pregnancies, putting her welfare and interests above his own. She was never less than 100 percent certain that he adored her.

Their bliss was shaken when Connie Chung, who had once been linked with Beatty, chose this moment to subject Warren and Annette to a mischievous interview on network television. Annette was not amused when Chung embarrassed her with allusions to Warren's newfound taste for monogamy. "I was so surprised by the questions she was asking," recalled Annette, "partly because I hadn't been doing interviews in years, and also I was tired and thinking of the baby. So it was partly my naïveté to be surprised. But she did a nice piece, including things like Warren's comment about not dignifying the question, which I felt she didn't have to do."

On another occasion, again referring to Warren's reputation before their marriage, Annette frankly and sensibly said, "We both have friends from before we knew each other, and that's a big part of our lives." But strains hit the marriage after the birth of their second baby, Benjamin, in 1994. Annette had managed to sandwich in a film, *The American President*, between pregnancies, and it was a hit. As a spirited environmental lobbyist who nabs a widowed chief executive, played by Michael Douglas, Annette reminded critics and moviegoers of such legendary romantic comediennes as Jean Arthur and Carole Lombard, actresses whose inimitable intelligence and charm had not been seen in Hollywood in several generations. After Annette's convincing performance as a U.S. first lady, a worshipful press crowned her "the thinking man's sex symbol."

Changing diapers no longer held quite the same appeal, and during the

Christmas holiday season, a fight erupted between Annette and Warren. He had told her to remain at home for the sake of the kids, but she angrily informed him that she'd never again sacrifice her career. Their public feud occurred in an L.A. hotel elevator, spilling out into the lobby, where one of the guests said, "My God, what was that fight about?"[26] For one thing, it was about a failure in communication. "He is not communicative in the least," observed Warren's former associate David Hart. "He has these old-time attitudes that people don't dissect their relationship. But Annette is into careful dissection. . . . He wouldn't even agree to go to a marriage counselor."[27]

Despite emerging conflicts, there were broad areas of compatibility that saved the marriage. "If you fall in love and you're with someone and it's working, your life simplifies," she said. "That's one of the joys of it. You make your choices based on this relationship. The anxiety is lessened, because you know your priorities." On the day that Benjamin slept seven straight hours for the first time, Annette rejoiced and went shopping. Kathlyn, who was two years old, was "very affectionate with Ben," Annette said. "But I do notice she's a little more demanding with me."

Apart from their mutual devotion to the children, Warren and Annette shared deep ideological and political affinities, placing them in total harmony on many issues. He even shared her enthusiasm for cranky, unpredictable feminist Germaine Greer, whom Annette admired because Germaine was "unafraid to be bold" and "infuriating sometimes, but at least she's out there." Warren's friend Garry Shandling said, "They are meant to be together. I am meant to be with my dog, Shep, with whom I have perfect chemistry."

Annette sometimes kidded Warren about his scrupulously healthy habits. At Four Oaks restaurant on Beverly Glen one day, the largely vegetarian Warren kept eyeing a tasty morsel on her plate. "What is it?" he asked. "Goat cheese," she replied. Finally he reached over with his fork and said, "I think I'll try some." "Good!" Annette said. "Live it up, Warren."

For such a classy, civilized actress, she had a pronounced bawdy streak. Though a feminist, she poked fun at overly defensive women who insist on political correctness, accusing them of "prude-y feminism." She once said, "What, we can't be nasty bad girls? We have to be pure and better than men?" She liked to think of herself as someone who'd rather stick her neck out than remain safe.

But the couple's attempt in the mid-1990s to establish themselves as an acting team was ill-advised from every standpoint, artistically, commercially, and even personally, for it placed additional strains on the marriage. The unfortunate co-starring vehicle they chose following *Bugsy* was a romantic trifle called *Love Affair*, which, like *Heaven Can Wait*, was another of Warren's soulless remakes, this one based on Leo McCarey's 1939 weepie, which in turn spawned the maudlin 1957 *An Affair to Remember*, starring Cary Grant and Deborah Kerr. In addition to playing the protagonist, an ex-jock turned sportscaster and skirt chaser, Warren produced and co-wrote with Robert Towne. Actress Carrie Fisher, who, following *Shampoo*, *Star Wars*, and *The Burbs*, reinvented herself as a script doctor pulling down one hundred thousand dollars per week, was called in and asked to add her brand of irony to the leaden script. Though Fisher had been able to punch up *Lethal Weapon 3* and *Sister Act*, she disappointed Warren, and later Barbra Streisand on *The Mirror Has Two Faces*.[28]

No writer or rewriter, not even a Nora Ephron or a James L. Brooks, could have salvaged such maudlin material as *Love Affair*, but the Beattys were convinced that it summed up all they felt for each other. Certainly the plot was autobiographical enough, tracing the reformation of a media star who's a sex addict until he meets a woman who inspires him to be faithful. One journalist called it "the most public love letter ever written by one intensely private person to another." Annette gushed to a reporter, "Thank God my life turned out this way!"[29] When another writer remarked on the parallel between the womanizer Warren plays in the film and his fabled liaisons with endless beauties, Annette said, "The movie, obviously, invites the comparison. People wonder about you, and so maybe it satisfies the question about what these two people might have said to each other. But I want to say to them, 'Hey, it probably was like when you met the person you fell in love with.' " Unconvinced, the writer reflected, "Hmm, that would be a pizza joint rendezvous with someone two decades your senior who seems as likely to commit to one partner as the moon is likely to choose a different orbit."[30]

Some sources said that the rift in the Beatty marriage deepened when they worked together on *Love Affair*.[31] David Hart recalled, "A shapely blonde who Warren hadn't seen in a while suddenly appeared out of nowhere. Warren was trying to be nice, so he brought her into his trailer and talked with her. But Annette showed up just as the two of them were leaving his trailer. She went off the deep end."[32]

Annette told him, "You don't take bimbos to your dressing room."[33] A few days later, trouble erupted again when Madonna visited the set. Annette's friend Diane Girodano said, "Madonna likes shock value. She came by to check out how the marriage was faring. She never believed that Warren would ever be able to settle down. She showed up in a tight little miniskirt with plenty of cleavage showing and spent an hour sweet-talking him. But Madonna told me that she wasn't serious at all. When she broke up with Warren, she'd had enough of him."

That's not what it looked like on the set that day. Madonna tarried for an hour or more, and Annette went into a slow boil. Finally, Warren had to tell Madonna to leave, and she scribbled her phone number on a scrap of paper, tucking it into his belt buckle. As her hand brushed his trousers, Warren blushed and laughed nervously. Annette glared at them. "If looks could kill," recalled Diane, "Madonna would have been long buried. That's when Annette laid down the law and told him, 'No more visits from Madonna.' She didn't want Madonna anywhere near the set. Finally, Warren just told Madonna, 'Look, if you love me as much as you say you do, stop talking about me to the media . . . and please stop calling me.' This delighted Madonna, and reconfirmed for her what she always has said about him, that he's a wimp."[34]

There were also artistic differences between Warren and Annette, and they flared up on the set. Says a technician who worked on the film, "Warren is a perfectionist. He drove Annette nuts with take after take, and by giving her unsolicited advice on how she should act. She put up with it—she had no choice—but she was disgusted by the time they were done. He made her do one take twenty times, until she finally said, 'Enough! I have had enough, Warren!' and she stormed off the set."[35] Annette told a friend, "I didn't think I would ever get through it. Warren was so incredibly difficult to work with."[36] Co-star Pierce Brosnan added, "Warren is very sweet, but once he gets obsessed with something, he's impossible. The first day of work, I couldn't believe it. I thought it would be a simple scene between Annette, myself, and Warren. Suddenly, we were on the twentieth take."[37] But the loyal Annette insisted to the press, "I love being directed by Warren." The nominal director of the movie, Glenn Gordon Caron, was clearly not in charge.

Working with Katharine Hepburn, who also starred in *Love Affair*, was difficult. "She's intimidating," Annette revealed. "And that was integral to the part.

She has that star quality that people talk about. In her own life it's hard now, because she's quite old. So to see this life that happens before the camera, the grace, the way she charms and emphasizes those words. I was taken aback. It was great." But later Annette's discomfiture was detected by *USA Today*'s movie reviewer, who wrote, "Playing opposite Hepburn, Bening looks nervous in their scene. She was."[38]

The Beattys quarreled again when Warren declined to make personal appearances to promote the film. "She now feels that if Warren had gotten up off his butt, they might have had a hit," said David Hart.[39] Friends predicted the marriage had already run its course. Warren's "biggest mistake," says Stephen Tyler, who went to San Francisco's Conservatory Theater with Annette in the 1980s, was telling Annette to give up her career.[40] Annette denied it, but she couldn't wait to get back to her own career, her own agenda rather than Warren's. "I'd like to do Beatrice in *Much Ado About Nothing*," she said, indicating her eagerness to stretch her talent until it embraced Shakespeare. She also set her sights on George Bernard Shaw. "Maybe *Man and Superman*," she said. Obviously she missed her pre-Warren fire-and-ice, tigress roles. "What I liked about *The Grifters* is that the nudity was comedic," she said. "It would scare me to have to be sexy and dramatic. But if someone handed me a script that was as weird, offbeat, independent, gritty, then absolutely." Clearly she was in open rebellion against vapid fare like *Love Affair*.

Discounted by *Variety*'s Peter Bart as "a textbook exercise in narcissism," *Love Affair* was Warren's worst miscalculation in the 1990s. He no longer had the looks to bring off a romantic leading-man role, and he must have known it, for cinematographer Conrad Hall shot the film in shadows, silhouettes, dim light, and fuzzy reddish glows, apparently to conceal the attritions of time. Instead, Warren ended up looking like a Chinaman with a sunburn, and poor Annette, so attractive in her other films, was barely recognizable, resembling a hungover Ida Lupino in some scenes and a venerable Sylvia Sidney in others. In a sequence set in a hospital, she was a dead ringer for the late River Phoenix. She could hardly have looked worse had the producer issued explicit instructions to the cameraman and lighting technicians to destroy her career. Her superb body was abominably costumed, swathed in bland, shapeless pants or homely dresses, evidently to deemphasize her youth—and the yawning gap between her age and her co-star husband's.

USA Today reporter Marco R. della Cava interviewed her and was surprised to discover that, in real life, her beauty and allure were still intact. "The seductress still sizzles," he wrote. "Something in the way she smiles exudes a promise of adventure. Her appreciative giggle—which once prompted husband Warren Beatty to 'defy anyone to leave the room when she's laughing'—can still fire the libido at a moment's notice. Bening, thirty-six, is unassuming in a merlot silk blouse and black mid-thigh skirt, tights and boots. Other stars may radiate more glamour, but few pack such playful sex appeal." The director of *Love Affair*, Glenn Gordon Caron, caught none of her magic.

Warren's choice of material had never been worse, a classic example of how one man's vanity could lead him to reject a surefire career resuscitator like *Misery*, which he was offered, and which went on to become one of the most popular films of the decade, in favor of *Love Affair*. *Misery* offered him an unglamorous but great character part, while *Love Affair* allowed him to masquerade as a ladies' man. The leading character in the Stephen King shocker was a writer named Paul Sheldon, not at all romantic but a character-driven role that provided an opportunity to show he could still act. Recalls *Misery* director Rob Reiner, "Warren Beatty worked with me for a couple of months on the script and he kept pressing me on plot points. I told him that the audience wouldn't notice but he kept pressing me to plug up the holes. And I did. Whatever you think about the film . . . there's nothing where you can say, hey, that's not possible, that couldn't have happened."[41]

At the time, Bette Midler had been approached for *Misery*'s female lead, a psycho who, in the King novel, sadistically amputates Paul Sheldon's feet. After Warren's defection from the role, Reiner went after Harrison Ford, Michael Douglas, Dustin Hoffman, Robert De Niro, Al Pacino, Gene Hackman, Kevin Kline, Richard Dreyfuss, and William Hurt, but they all said no. Richard Gere was deemed perfect for the part, but in 1989, when Reiner was casting *Misery*, Gere was considered a has-been, with seven straight flops following *An Officer and a Gentleman* and preceding his comeback in *Pretty Woman*. Reiner considered James Caan but knew of the actor's substance abuse and consequent reputation as difficult. Desperate to work again, Caan assured Reiner, "I'll pee in a bottle for you. I will pee in a bottle every day."[42] When Caan finally won the part, Bette Midler dropped out, telling the producers, "I ain't doin' no pitcher co-starring with Jimmy *Caan*." Kathy Bates assumed the role, and copped the

Best Actress Oscar. Caan turned in a sterling performance. Recalls Donfeld, "The following year, Midler, desperate for another film project, signed on for Mark Rydell's *For the Boys*. Her co-star? James Caan, who never let the diva forget the fact she'd thrown away an Oscar. He walked around the set between takes sneering at Midler and mock-whining, 'I ain't doin' no pitcher with James Caaaaaaaaan!' "

Had Warren stuck with *Misery,* his career would have taken a dynamic new direction. Says Donfeld, "He's notorious for taking pictures to the starting gate and leaving, from *What's New, Pussycat?* to *Misery.*" When Bob Evans suggested Warren for the lead in Joe Eszterhas's *Jade,* Eszterhas almost had a coronary, later writing, "The word on Warren in Hollywood was that he had unmade more movies he'd been involved in than he'd made. . . . Warren would commit to do a movie and then he'd work with the writer to rewrite the script. Then he'd work with the director to redo the schedule. Then he'd work with the cinematographer to redo the shots. . . . When everything had been redone to his satisfaction, he'd pull out of the movie. . . . The studio, exhausted, would tire of the project. . . .'It's got the clap,' as they say in Hollywood—and the movie would never be done."[43]

Fortunately for Eszterhas, Bob Evans decided he couldn't afford Warren's asking price of eight million dollars and hired TV star David Caruso for *Jade*, saving himself six million dollars.

Because she was only sporadically available for filming, Annette's work in the nineties was disappointing, apart from *The American President*. She managed to knock out two more movies—*The Siege* and *In Dreams*—before the birth of their third child, Isabel, in 1997. "Now, I've been through the cycle a few times, disappearing and coming back," she said. "I realize there's an ebb and flow." After bearing healthy children, and then facing the challenge of raising them while pursuing a full-time career, she was often asked by interviewers if she intended to stop working until the children were grown. "I don't see life like that," she replied. "I don't see children as the end of anything." But she added, "You know, there are times it's complicated, in terms of juggling all the stuff that's going on." Often pregnant, she spent most mornings throwing up, and then went to the supermarket, surrounded by her children and enduring the curious stares of startled shoppers. "She's a brilliant actress and woman—two things that I'm not," said friend Garry Shandling. Although Annette had been raised to "care what people thought about you," she was smart enough, once she became a celebrity, to ignore criticism. "Because you really can't control what people think," she said. "What I do worry about is my children. I feel responsible to help them deal with it." When her oldest daughter commented on an admiring magazine article she'd seen about her mother, Annette told her, "This idealized notion people have about me is not the whole story." Another thing she had to deal with was the children's aunt, Shirley MacLaine.

An occasional visitor at Mulholland Drive, bearing gifts for the nieces and nephews she never thought she'd have, Shirley was as thorny as ever, part McMurtry heroine and part Steel Magnolia. What effect, Annette wondered, would three movie stars in one household have on impressionable kids? After seeing a puff piece about her mother in one of the slicks, Kathlyn said, "But she's the one who lost her temper last night and threatened to start spanking me." Both Warren and Annette worried sometimes about their children growing up rich, because they'd both come from middle-class backgrounds, and they didn't know how to bring up privileged children. They decided it was best not to take them to other rich children's parties in Beverly Hills—big-budget productions held on tennis courts and resembling carnivals. "Considerably out of proportion from what's appropriate, from my point of view," said Annette. "So I don't do that. If anything, I'll probably overcompensate." The fact that both parents worked so hard would perhaps impress on their children the necessity of having an occupation and being self-supporting. "They have to do their own chores," Annette revealed. "They have to earn what they get. The good part for us, at least, is that we both work really hard and they see that." Behind those words was the anxiety of a conscientious mother in a era when other celebrities' kids were getting into terrible messes: Pierce Brosnan's son, Elvis Presley's daughter, Ryan O'Neal's son, Debbie Reynolds's daughter, President Bush's daughters, President Clinton's brother, Michael Douglas's son, Mary Tyler Moore's son, John Phillips's daughter. Considering the world the Beattys inhabited, Annette's concern was understandable.

There was one aspect of celebrity that Annette thoroughly enjoyed. It was, after all, the life she'd chosen. "I'm a celebrity and I'm participating in it," she said. "Everyone has a choice and that's important for people to remember. And it can be nice. People say nice things to you. They're glad to see you."

Warren, who'd once feigned contempt for the press, no longer bothered to conceal his love of attention, and even courted the friendship of *New York Daily News* gossip columnist A. J. Benza, who once began a conversation a with a publicist by saying, "I need some dirt on somebody. You gotta find me some dirt. Find me dirt and I'll print your lame item." Bob Evans was hosting a small party at his home, and invited Beatty, Benza, Robert Shapiro, Sean Connery, Anjelica Huston, Christian Slater, Jon Peters, Beverly D'Angelo, Michael Des Barres, Geraldo Rivera, Jacqueline Bisset, Jack Valenti, Beverly Johnson, and Chazz Palminteri. At one point in the evening, the eagle-eyed Benza noticed that Michael Viner, owner of Dove Books, had crashed the party. Viner at the time was publishing an exposé of Evans, Beatty, and other Hollywood playboys. Eager to curry his famous host's favor, Benza rushed up to Evans and said, "Why would the publisher have the balls to come to your house tonight?" Enraged, Evans said, "I'll break his ass. That weasel." Evans rounded up Beatty, and the two of them cornered Viner. Later, Evans took Beatty and Benza into his bedroom and said to Benza, "You did me a solid, kid. A real solid. Can you imagine the gall of that cocksucker?" Turning to Warren, he put his hand on Benza's shoulder and said, "This guy is one of us, Warren. He's one of the guys." Warren stroked his chin and nodded sagely. "I see that," he murmured. "I see." Benza immediately wanted to "talk girls" with Warren.

The columnist would later rise to moderate recognition as the hard-boiled host of TV's *Mysteries & Scandals,* but standing next to Warren that night, he got as mushy as an adolescent autograph hound, thinking, "Fuckin' *Warren Beatty,* man!" Benza all but trembled when Warren handed him his telephone number and asked him to call. "That sort of thing kills me," Benza later gushed.[44]

Though Warren obviously set A. J. Benza's heart aflutter, he was wrinkled and unmistakably faded, and his once magnificent mane was no longer lustrous. *George* magazine poked fun at his sagging skin, but he was still, in his sixties, a bit of a sex symbol, as Paul Newman had been in the 1970s. After conversing with Beatty, agent Dorris Halsey offered an explanation of his still discernible appeal. "Bert Fields has long been Beatty's lawyer," said Dorris, "and still is. I was at a memorial at Mel Brooks's when Bert's wife died, and I talked with Warren. He gave total attention to what I was saying: that's the secret of his charm."

To look fit on such occasions, Warren followed ever more stringent diets, trying to cope with the passing years and the natural slowing down of his metabolism. In the summer of 1998, he went to the Four Seasons Hotel in New York and ordered an "oil-free egg-white omelet with vegetables." Then he left his table and went into the kitchen to supervise the five-star chef.[45]

Later the same year, he ran into Madonna at a party he hosted at Moomba for Robert Downey Jr.'s *Two Girls and a Guy*. "Warren is very bitter about his romance with Madonna," says Sarah Porterfield. "He fell head over heels in love, and later was angered by Madonna's chatting about the most intimate details of their affair. The day after the party at Moomba, he called her and asked, 'What are you doing today?' She found she had plenty to do."

For Annette, there remained the question of how to cope with Warren's old playmates. As long as men like Jack Nicholson were on the loose, Warren was in danger of relapsing into a sybaritic life. She appointed herself matchmaker for Nicholson and actress Lara Flynn Boyle, who played Helen Gamble, a tough-as-nails assistant district attorney on David E. Kelley's hit TV show *The Practice*. "Oh, please," Lara told an interviewer. "The whole country has a love affair with Jack. Why can't I?"

After they became lovers, Lara explained, "I needed a dad who would make me feel like the most wonderful little girl in the world."[46] Thirty-three years Nicholson's junior, Lara—whose mother (and career manager) named her after Julie Christie's character in *Dr. Zhivago*—was as ballsy as the character she played on TV—"like Tallulah Bankhead on speed," according to one Hollywood wag. Having sex with her, confided ex-boyfriend David Sherrill, a sometime actor, was "like trying to jack off a bobcat with a handful of barbed wire. She was too wild for me, bro."[47] In a tête-à-tête, Annette cautioned Nicholson that if he didn't make some sort of commitment, Lara, who often quoted Gloria Steinem's line, "A woman needs a man like a fish needs a bicycle," would eventually drift away from him. She'd divorced her husband of a year and a half, John Patrick Dee III, grandson of legendary Columbia Records A&R man John Hammond, and gone on to affairs with Kyle MacLachlan, her *Twin Peaks* co-star, and Richard Dean Anderson (*MacGyver*); she was allegedly behind the breakup of Harrison Ford's marriage; and Bruce Willis was said to be waiting in the wings. "Jack is solo, solo, solo," Lara said. "And he should always be. He can stimulate me mentally, too, you know," she said,[48] and elsewhere she added, "It's not bad sleeping with Einstein."[49] Annette kept after Lara, telling her that playing hard to get was the only thing that worked with rolling stones like Warren and Jack.

But had it really "worked" with Warren? Columnist Janet Charlton wrote,

"Annette wants Jack to be as happy as she imagines her husband Warren is." Annette told Warren to warn Jack that he'd better consolidate his hold on Lara, but in May 2001, Lara was seen smooching with *Gideon's Crossing* hunk Eric Dane.[50] "She is not a Good Girl," said Boyle's *Practice* co-star, Dylan McDermott. "Lara is a throwback to Marlene Dietrich and Bette Davis and those kinds of Hollywood dames. That's why older guys are attracted to her." "The Chief," as Nicholson was known, was again unattached. Lara then decided she needed a love interest in *The Practice* to spice up the prim character she played, and stunned the producers by requesting Beatty rather than Nicholson. She even asked the latter to sound out the former regarding a role on the show, but, unsurprisingly, Nicholson refused.[51] Before long, Jack and Lara were back together, traveling to Russia, where they had tea with President Vladimir Putin; attended the tennis matches at Wimbledon; and took Jack's three children to L.A.'s Staples Center to watch Michael Flatley's *Feet of Flames*. They became Hollywood's perennial on-again, off-again lovers, and to many observers marriage seemed unlikely. "It is difficult to imagine a woman of Boyle's appetites sitting up there in the hills, sharing muffin recipes with Annette Bening," wrote *Talk* magazine.

It looked for a while in 1999 that Annette, who'd played a president's wife in the movies, might get a shot at the real thing. Oddly, right-wing social gadfly and sometime author Arianna Stassinopoulos Huffington floated Warren's name as a possible candidate for the White House. "We need someone who can pull the nation around the fire and draw us together," said Huffington, evidently oblivious to the cold shoulder Warren had turned to the public for decades. In one of his most characteristic exchanges, after Joan Dew of *Redbook* urged him to shed his cloak of secrecy and say something that "would make you more human," he told the reporter, "But I have no need to seem more human."[52] Those few words summed up, more than anything else he'd ever said, his unsuitability for public office, but he somehow convinced himself to lay siege to the White House, and huddled in smoke-filled rooms with Bob Evans, Pat Caddell (a Jimmy Carter pollster and later consultant for television's *The West Wing*), Gary Hart, and Ms. Huffington.[53] Not everyone took Mrs. Huffington, who'd risen to prominence by marrying a socialite who later revealed his homosexuality in a 1999 *Esquire* profile, seriously. "It's easy for someone who has maids making her beds to talk about voiceless Americans," said Bob Mulholland, a California Democratic Party official. "Most Americans get a kick out of somebody like her preaching to the rest of us."[54] Along with Pat Caddell and Richard Walden, head of Operation USA, which used Hollywood connections to penetrate countries like Cuba, Warren was very much a part of the scene at Huffington's Brentwood home, and attended her party for Norman Mailer's wife Norris Church, on publication of her first novel, *Windchill Summer.*

Some in the film industry were horrified at the notion of Warren as president. What about his "satyriasis, his praying mantis need for woman flesh, his narcissism . . . his megalomania . . . priapism and male nymphomania?" asked Joe Eszterhas, who was even more concerned about the effect Warren's perfectionist nature would have on the running of the government. "Would he want to redesign the lasers in the Tomahawk missiles? Would he veto every bill unless he could sit down and rewrite it with Trent Lott and Dennis Hastert? Would he take two years and seventeen speechwriters to deliver *last* year's State of the Union address?"[55]

Annette was more comfortable with the idea of her husband's candidacy, believing in Warren and emphatically sharing his dislike of the Clinton administration's policies. At first she'd admired Hillary. After listening to the first lady's speech on health care, Annette said she was "knocked out. Mrs. Clinton told a story about a child who was ill. I was moved to tears. [But later], if I showed up at an event, she would make sure that I was brought up and that she had time to see me. I saw how politically deft she was, and I was not completely seduced by that. And then there's my disappointment over the administration, how they ended up. I have a lot of mixed feelings about [Hillary's running for the U.S. Senate]. She always appears to be doing what's politically expedient in the most transparent way. That whole thing about the clemency with the Puerto Rican terrorists and how she claimed that she hadn't spoken to him about it, that was an example to me of just how you feel like there's prevaricating, there's lying. You just don't trust them."[56]

To some observers, Annette's political posture was idealistic and impractical, and no doubt it was partly responsible for Warren's failure when he decided at last to become a politician. As much of a political purist as Annette, he'd watched in anguish as President Clinton compromised on issue after issue, gutting welfare and adopting most of the planks of the Republican platform.

Bulworth, Warren's 1998 campaign-finance-reform comedy, was unique in the annals of Hollywood filmmaking, bearing no resemblance to previous political films, like the relatively polite *Mr. Smith Goes to Washington* and *State of the Union.* "Most [political] films, like *Running Mates,* pander to the audience's wishes. The rare exception is Warren Beatty's underrated 1998 film *Bulworth,*" wrote the *New York Times* two years later, in a story about the Democratic National Convention, which was held in 2000 at the Staples Center in Los Angeles.

Bulworth relates the story of a senator who sells out his ideals to lobbyists and becomes so ashamed of himself that he puts out a contract on his own life. In the few hours left to him, the senator gives the public some straight talk, delightfully delivered in rap style ("As long as you can pay, I'm gonna do it all your way—Big money/Big money"). Comedy usually paralyzed Warren, but in this raw, trenchant, abrasively satiric film he hit his stride as a first-rate comic actor. He also directed, and co-wrote with Jeremy Pikser.

Though he was clicking in *Bulworth,* some at Twentieth Century–Fox found him "rude to everyone," said an anonymous co-worker. "He suggested to one production guy, an Italian, that he buy him a book to read about how to better deal with black people. Warren was going to rip him a new asshole. The Italian guy and everyone else said he was crazy. He used to spend hours at the office hovering over people at their computers. They made up this shirt, 'I survived Bulworth.' " The T-shirt bore this message on the front: "I worked on *Bulworth* and all I got was _____. (a) an ulcer; (b) psychosis; (c) a migraine; (d) facial tics; (e) all of the above." The anonymous co-worker continued, "They all hate Warren now. He micromanaged every aspect. He would come there unannounced and he would stay for hours until way after dark. People would have to just leave. Warren would still be there harassing them.

"He told the head of publicity and the VP overseeing the project, 'Come over.' He was going to screen the movie, show a first cut of the film, and go over stuff regarding the campaign, promos, and junket items. So they get there and Warren is very ingratiating, but they don't start the movie right away. He asked them, 'Are you hungry? We'll have a snack. Meet my wife, the kids.' So they meet the wife and kids, play. By this time it's six or seven o'clock, time for dinner. He asks them if they want to go swimming. So finally they're like, 'We'd like to see the movie.' They don't get to see it until midnight. They're like hostages. I always joke, 'You were taken hostage by Warren Beatty. At least it was in a Mulholland mansion.' They roll the movie at midnight and it's over at two o'clock, and he wants to talk and make them a snack in the kitchen. At three o'clock in the morning, they are dropping their keys on the floor, you know, signaling they're tired. Finally, they're like, 'We're leaving. We have been here for twelve hours.' Apparently he doesn't need much sleep."

The anonymous colleague added that Warren was a devoted homebody. "He's so into the wife. He's not looking at anybody else. I never heard he fooled around with any women on the set. In fact, the total opposite."

Warren later explained how he made such an uncompromisingly truthful movie in *Bulworth:* "Something happened to me, gradually, which made it no longer possible to avoid the truth. You can't really make jokes like that, unless you're willing to have your invitation to the table rescinded. And I had become more and more willing to have that invitation rescinded. I had become a Bulworth Democrat." As far back as the 1960s, Leslie Caron had said, "If you woke him in the middle of the night, before his defenses were up, if that is ever possible, and asked him what he wanted to be, I think he would say, 'President.' I don't think he'll stop until he's president."[57] But already in *Bulworth,* whether he ever ran for office, he was fulfilling the function he had defined for himself back in 1974, when he'd told reporter Judy Klemsrud that an artist is "an alternative government." *Bulworth* was the funniest and best political film since *The Great Dictator,* the Chaplin classic that also combined slapstick, satire, and social commentary.

Sometimes reluctant to promote, Warren came out of hiding to push *Bulworth* in the summer of 1998. As *Variety*'s Peter Bart once said of both Beatty and Robert Redford, "When they wanted to talk about something, they were in your face. When problems arose, you couldn't get them on the phone."[58] Warren agreed to meet Bart at an Italian restaurant near Twentieth Century–Fox, the studio releasing *Bulworth,* for lunch, and Bart later wrote, "Ask Warren Beatty why he decided to tackle *Bulworth,* and you are all but inundated by a blizzard of words relating to the political process, the responsibilities of celebrity, the nature of personal commitment, and so forth."

Almost immediately Warren attacked Bart for writing in *Daily Variety* that morning that stars' twenty-million-dollar salaries and percentage cuts were excessive. "The column is simply wrong," Warren announced. "The star system is at the center of Hollywood, and these salaries are at the center of the star system." Bart pointed out that one of the main points Warren made in *Bulworth* concerned the unfair apportionment of income in the U.S. "A tiny minority makes the big bucks and the rest of the nation isn't doing any better than they did one or two generations ago," said Bart. "That's your thesis, right?" Without missing a beat, Warren replied, "Stars are different."

He seemed "edgier and more evasive than usual" that day. "If there's one thing a star deplores," Bart noted, "it's being ignored, and Beatty began to work feverishly to attract attention to his movie." He went to Cambridge and lined up Harvard intellectuals behind his film, flew to the capital to enlist the support of political pundits, and appealed to Julian Bond of the NAACP. Sam Donaldson and Cokie Roberts let him show *Bulworth* clips on ABC's *This Week,* marking the first time that an actor had been permitted to hawk his movie on a high-minded political forum. Tim Russert interviewed him on *Meet the Press,* and Warren even went on the Howard Stern show. Inevitably, the shock jock asked him about his sexual conquests, and Warren clammed up. "God, you're a lousy interview," Stern said.

His principal backer at Fox was studio executive Tom Sherak, who invited Warren, Annette, and their three children to his house to celebrate Passover. Warren took to calling him "my rabbi," but still feared that they'd never get the crucial support of studio owner Rupert Murdoch.[59] Peter Bart warned that no one in the industry "besides Sherak and Beatty believed that *Bulworth* was anything but dead on arrival."

The press, however, was solidly behind it, David Ansen of *Newsweek* writing, "Like Bulworth the senator, Beatty the director is throwing caution to the wind, producing a genuinely political movie in an era deeply suspicious of political passion . . . savaging Hollywood as well as Washington." The *New York Times* hailed it as "one of the best political satires of recent years. . . . The satire of *Bulworth* is more scathing than all the hollow speeches about people and power. The film has adult complexity and political opinions."[60]

Unfortunately, demographics were against *Bulworth*. Warren had assumed his cool mastery of rap would win over the younger audience, and that blacks would appreciate the senator's flirtation with an African-American woman (especially as played by gorgeous Halle Berry). In researching the film, he courted such gangsta rappers as Tupac Shakur and Dr. Dre, later proclaiming, "Rap music is the language of social protest. They are poets and they must be heard."

According to Suge Knight—the chief executive of Death Row Records, imprisoned in 1996 for parole violation after he beat up a man in a Las Vegas casino—Warren spent some time attempting to penetrate the rap scene, "hanging out" but mostly making a "pest" of himself.[61] It's likely that Warren relied more on videotapes of *Def Comedy Jam,* HBO's comedy series, than going into the bowels of the inner city. Even so, he came up with some impressive moves, but few blacks liked him. In *Newsweek* in May 1998, N'Gai Croal wrote that "for all the hype that Beatty is brave and politically incorrect, he simply peddles paper-thin stereotypes. . . . A failure as both political and cultural satire, *Bulworth* is interesting only as a look into the bizarre subconscious of a filmmaker who wanted to say something but couldn't figure out how."

Without young people or blacks behind it, the movie was seen only by a narrow segment of the older audience. Clearly they loved it—the *New York Times Magazine* gave Warren the cover, breaking a long-standing bias against showbiz types—but the older segment represents a fraction of the movie-going public. Though it was his best film since *Reds, Bulworth* was a commercial disappointment. His anonymous co-worker at Fox says, "He hated that the film didn't do as well as it should." But it brought him unexpected political dividends. He'd always assumed that the movie, radical to its angry, boiling core, would get him kicked out of the Democratic Establishment, but instead, a delegation of prominent liberal Democrats, some of them from the Gore and Bradley camps, begged him to run for the presidency. David Letterman thought he'd make a better vice president, joking on his TV show, "Warren Beatty has vast experience in screwing people and leaving them happy. That's why he'd make a good running mate for Al Gore."[62] Garry Shandling advised Warren, "If you get elected, make sure you get your name above the title of the country." Arianna Huffington put Warren to work, along with Ron Silver and comedian Bill Maher, launching the shadow conventions that accompanied the Republican and Democratic national conventions in 2000, giving expression to millions of voters who'd been excluded from the national dialogue.

Warren had always been convinced that politics was the only way to make a more compassionate, equable world. That Lyndon Johnson had been prevented from implementing the Great Society by the Vietnam War "was the great tragedy of the past forty-five years," he said, "because it did much harm to a way of thinking which people began to call 'bleeding-heart liberalism,' 'big government stupidly throwing money at problems.' " To reinvent the Great Society he could have used an Eleanor Roosevelt–type wife capable of transforming ideals into reality. According to one friend, Annette urged Warren to enter the race. "She played to his ego," said the source, "and managed to give Warren a new purpose and vitality by encouraging him to throw himself into what was once just a mere hobby: politics. The once-hunky *Shampoo* star will be in his eighties when his kids reach college. Because of this there has been a definite power shift between the Beattys. Today Annette obviously is the big breadwinner in the family. Warren tinkered with his troubled movie project *Town & Country* for almost two years and he hasn't had a bona fide hit since 1991's *Bugsy*."[63]

For all Annette's encouragement and support of Warren's political activism, she was too aloof and elitist in her attitudes to be of much help to a possible candidate for the presidency. "I am still reluctant to use my celebrity, to just show up at a place and draw attention to a given issue like abortion rights or Amnesty International," she said. "Part of it is time with my kids, and if I'm not working, I'm just basically doing them." But what better use for her second-rank stardom than to use it to alleviate human suffering? Why was it so important to clutch "my celebrity," as she called it, to her bosom, where it accomplished nothing but personal ego gratification. With such a self-absorbed disposition, and however admirable her domestic priorities, she would never make it into the proactive political ranks of such movie stars as Jane Fonda, Paul Newman, Marlon Brando, Harry Belafonte, and Martin Sheen, all of whom generously and sometimes bravely lent their celebrity to such worthy causes as peace and racial equality, putting their lives on the line at freedom marches and demonstrations.

She was willing enough to lend her celebrity, such as it was, to Warren's cause, and she was at his side on September 30, 1999, the day that marked the apex of his political career. As talk of his possible candidacy for the presidency steadily gained currency, Warren addressed Americans for Democratic Action in Los Angeles, receiving the organization's annual Eleanor Roosevelt Award for "a lifetime of creative and political integrity." Joe Eszterhas called it "the biggest Hollywood event until the cocktail party for the Dalai Lama. . . . Half of [Bob] Evans's whorehouse was there, applauding." Also in attendance were Beatty-for-President supporters Faye Dunaway, Dustin Hoffman, Jack Nicholson, Courtney Love, and Gloria Allred, who filled the ballroom of the Beverly Hilton, along with 150 reporters. The first baleful sign that Warren wasn't presidential timber was his wimpy handshake. "Not pumping hands like . . . the old-style macho pols," said Eszterhas, "but touching them a little fey, Euro-trashy, almost New Age."

Introducing the guest of honor, Dustin Hoffman promised that, if elected president, Warren wouldn't make the mistakes of other chief executives. "Unlike Bill Clinton, he would have never trusted a twenty-two-year-old girl to be discreet."[64] Taking the microphone, Warren automatically disqualified himself for the presidency by rambling on in what the New York Times generously referred to as "his trademark halting and epigrammatic style." "I had in mind a different kind of lighting," Warren said. "Could we get the candles going again?" But if his levity was offputting and inappropriate, his agenda was impressive: single-payer health care, diplomatic recognition of Cuba, environmental safeguards for the third world, and full public financing of campaigns. America could do worse than elect a man who held such beliefs.

If only he could have taken himself more seriously, he might have had a chance, but he couldn't, which had always been his problem. In concluding his speech, he offered some advice to an imaginary drum majorette who was considering running for president. "Look, drum majorette, there's no harm in thinking about this, however unlikely it may be. But whatever you do, go ahead and speak up. Speak up for the people nobody speaks up for. If you speak up well, maybe you'll influence the party, maybe you'll influence the candidates that are running. And who knows what else. And remember, drum majorette, don't delude yourself into thinking that it's got an awful lot to do with you. It doesn't. It's the time that you're living in, and a temporary vacuum that allows you the privilege of being heard. And one more thing, drum majorette. When those plutocrats start with you, when you start hearing those moneyed, honeyed voices of ridicule and reaction, let them call you coy, let them call you flirtatious, but keep talking."

Everyone who'd advised him—whoever the image-makers and spin doctors were—deserved the firing squad. Imagine JFK or RFK—or Humphrey, McGovern, Gary Hart, or even Bulworth, for that matter—invoking a drum majorette as the central metaphor in a keynote political address. Here was a man committing political suicide in plain sight.

Though Warren was right on target in saying that neither Al Gore nor Bill Bradley were really liberals, many who'd taken him seriously as a possible candidate were disappointed, wondering why he hadn't come on bold, courageous, and brilliant, like Bulworth. Instead, he gave them warmed-over Frank Capra. But his platform was sound, and his first notices as a politician were surprisingly good. The *New York Times* wrote, "Warren Beatty held an enthusiastic crowd of Hollywood's liberal elite in the palm of his hand for half an hour Wednesday night as he denounced the influence of money in politics and the rightward drift of the Democratic Party and insisted that its Presidential candidates not forget society's least fortunate, whether or not he runs himself."[65]

The *Washington Post* editorialized, "In 2000 it might just take a Beatty candidacy to slay the money beast."[66] John F. Kennedy Jr.'s *George* magazine was all for the "political hunk," but advised Warren to get a makeover; he needed to turn in his slick Hollywood duds and look more like Harry S. Truman to "sell himself to Middle America," and while he was at it, the sixty-two-year-old actor should stop dying his hair, since voters preferred the honesty of silver locks.[67] Along with two other dark horses, Warren made the cover of *Newsweek,* which headlined, "The Wild Bunch: Ventura, Beatty and Trump Stir Up Campaign 2000." *Newsweek* staff pundit and former Clinton aide George Stephanopoulos wrote, "Beatty's not-quite campaign may be the ultimate pseudo-event. . . . He's not really an actor running for president; he's an actor playing an actor thinking about running for president." The *Wall Street Journal,* usually conservative, chimed in with a pro-Beatty editorial. A reporter asked Annette how she'd feel if Warren became president. She replied that she certainly wouldn't stop acting, because "what's great about being an actor is that you can stop and start." Perhaps an actor could stop and start, but a superstar couldn't, as her own punctured career amply demonstrated.

Former Reagan consultant Roger Stone asked Warren to run on the Reform ticket, but Warren replied that America didn't need a third party; it needed a second party. "No, I'm a Democrat," he said. "I'm not going to do that." Stone then approached Donald Trump, who agreed to run. The *New York Times Magazine* gave Beatty, Trump, and several other wild cards their October 24, 1999, cover, headlining, "Slam! Bam! Sham! The phony spectacle—and genuine promise— of Reform Party politics." *Times* political journalist James Bennet wrote patronizingly, "Even a pop-culture candidate can have an idea or two worth wrestling with. . . . Warren Beatty insists he wants to save the Democrats' soul, not mold the Reformers', though he has equivocated just enough to keep some members hoping."[68]

He continued to tell the Democrats no when they urged him to enter the New Hampshire or California primary. His reasoning was logical enough—he'd been approached too late in the game to put together a professional political organization, which customarily requires a full year. Acting in accordance with his own principles, he would be forced to reject special-interest funding, without which, however, he was bound to fail, and he feared that his agenda would be tarnished forever, that the public would say, " 'Look, Mr. Movie Star was up here and tried to do something with these issues and look how unpopular they are.' Well, I don't believe that."

Obviously he didn't have the time, energy, will, or desire to go directly to the public and ask them to finance his campaign. It was sad, because his platform would have been good for the nation, espousing campaign finance reform, Medicare for everyone, increasing teachers' salaries and rebuilding the educational infrastructure, and ending, through world trade sanctions, environmental abuse and cruel labor practices. In September 1999 he announced that it was "extremely unlikely" that he would run. Several months later, he said, "I'm not running now."

TV talk shows offered him free time, but he declined them all. "What I have to say is not particularly pleasant to hear," he remarked. His political beliefs would be "characterized as strident, and . . . the window of acceptance for that is narrow. I think you have to use judgment about how it can be maximized. Should I do more? The answer to that question is, I don't know. I mean, I just don't know."

Buck Henry thought it just as well for Warren, and for the world, that he didn't run. "Easygoing is not a quality he has," said Henry. "You know how presidents age in office? If Beatty was president, either he would be dead after the first year or the country would be dead."[69]

When old political allies approached him looking for endorsements of their own candidacies, he declined to support either Gore or Bradley. "They're all good men," he said, "but none of them are saying enough of the things that need to be said."[70] Moreover, Gore's eventual running mate, Senator Joseph I. Lieberman, was one of the Senate's most virulent critics of Hollywood, accusing filmmakers of "market[ing] death and degradation to our children." Rising to Hollywood's defense, Warren said, "I don't think it's possible to attribute the high level of mayhem in this country to movies and music."[71]

However, both Warren and Annette joined other Hollywood notables when the Democratic National Convention was held the following year in L.A.'s Staples Center. Tommy Lee Jones, Jimmy Smits, and Dylan McDermott spoke from the podium; Warren and Annette joined Sarah Jessica Parker and Sean Penn on the convention floor; Paramount CEO Sherry Lansing served as one of California's delegates; Christie Brinkley was there as a New York delegate; and in the stands sat *American Beauty* producer Bruce Cohen, Ron Howard, Rob Reiner, Brian Grazer, Steven Spielberg, Jeffrey Katzenberg, and David Geffen. Later, at producer Lawrence Bender's swank Holmby Hills party, hosted by the Creative Coalition and *George* magazine, the Hollywood celebrity contingent came out in full force, supporting the fund-raiser for Christopher Reeve's Paralysis Foundation. On the lawn of Bender's spacious mansion, lawyer Robert F. Kennedy Jr. and Secretary of Housing and Urban Development Andrew Cuomo mingled with Camryn Manheim, Salma Hayek, William Baldwin, Michael Douglas, Frances Fisher, Robert Forster, Harry Hamlin, Milla Jovovich, Julia Louis-Dreyfus, Jennifer Love Hewitt, Miramax's Harvey Weinstein, and Fox Searchlight's Peter Rice.[72]

At another party, in Mandeville Canyon, John Travolta told President Clinton, "I only wish we could have you for another eight years." Over at the Playboy Mansion, Warren's friend Arianna Huffington embraced a beaming Bryant Gumbel. On the set of *The West Wing,* first daughter Chelsea Clinton attended a reception and chatted with Martin Sheen and Dule Hill. There were also parties at David Geffen's; the Santa Monica Pier; Streisand's Malibu compound; the San Fernando Mission; the Conga Room; the Sunset Room; and at the homes of NBC executive David Corvo, supermarket magnate Ron Burkle, and Haim Saban, the Egyptian-born Israeli who built a six-billion-dollar entertainment empire on the kids' cartoon *Mighty Morphin Power Rangers. Los Angeles Times* political journalist Shawn Hubler wrote, "The idea at these was to draw a range of lawmakers who might be chatted up now, or later at the Capitol."[73] Warren no doubt rued that all the revelry was in Al Gore's behalf, not his own.

Annette was still a little disappointed that Warren hadn't donned his rapper's gear from *Bulworth* and hit the hustings. "I know people have a fantasy that somebody is going to stand up and behave that way," she said. "I felt it, too. I felt incredible enthusiasm, excitement, and just joy at the prospect that he could sort of get out there and say things that nobody else was going to say. But unfortunately that's only part of the equation. If there is anything that can really screw you up about fame, it is trying to run after people's expectations. Warren never promoted himself as being this beacon of hope that everybody wanted him to be."[74]

Had his venture into the real world of politics achieved anything at all, like pushing Bradley to the left, which would of necessity also have pushed Gore to the left, and perhaps salvaged something for the liberals? Not according to Democratic strategist Mark Mellman, who said, "Beatty is a guy of enormous convictions and a strong moral compass, but the notion there was a strong public demand for a Beatty candidacy is ludicrous."[75] He was probably right, but he begged the question of what would have happened had Warren been willing to drum up campaign funds from his fans, or thrown prudence to the wind and talked like Bulworth at his most honest and inspired. That was what one of Warren's admirers at the *New York Times,* Caryn James, called on him to do, and when he disappointed her, she chided him for his "teasing flirtation with a presidential run."

Garry Shandling had the last word: "Each of them [Warren and Annette] would make a great president. And each of them would make a great first lady. I aspire to be either one of them." In squandering the power of his celebrity, Warren did not serve his country well.

Warren's association with David Geffen continued to pay off, especially after Geffen formed DreamWorks with Spielberg and Katzenberg. Annette's strongest role ever came in 1999 in the DreamWorks production *American Beauty,* a sendup of contemporary family life in which she and Kevin Spacey portray an unhappy suburban couple. Her old friend Alan Ball wrote the script, and his ironic, witty vision of America as a place of lost dreams and twisted desires appealed to her greatly. "I've made movies I cared about just as much as this one," she said, "but they never quite came together. I think this one has."

She was fortunate to have Kevin Spacey playing opposite her. "It was very special, very harmonious," she said, "and it isn't always on a movie set." Though his was the more sympathetic role—hers was brittle and unappealing—he spurred her on, according to director Sam Mendes, who observed, "It was one of those lovely things where two gifted actors were being good for each other as much as for anything else."

Both Bening and Spacey were nominated for Oscars. "There are movie stars," Spacey said, "and then there are actresses who happen to have become them, and Annette is a great actress." *Mirabella* hailed her performance as "an astounding feat of comic art." In the now famous "asparagus scene," Bening improvised her long, manic monologue—a wife bitching at her husband—and Sam Mendes and Alan Ball incorporated it into the script, word for word.

After filming *American Beauty,* she returned to the theater, playing Ibsen's demanding *Hedda Gabler* at the David Geffen Playhouse in Los Angeles in 1999. Getting to the theater every day caused some emotional difficulties because of "the kids," she admitted, and she could have taken the production to Broadway save for her determination not to pursue a full-time stage career until the children grew up a bit more. But she definitely wanted to do more theater, feeling that she was ready to assay even Chekhov. Unsurprisingly, she was not eager to work again with Warren, explaining, "Once you're a married couple, you have to think carefully about what work to do together." No one, she said, wanted to see an old married couple making love, not even Tom Cruise and Nicole Kidman in *Eyes Wide Shut.* She was mindful of a radio commentator who'd said, "Before they were married, we watched *Bugsy* and we were all interested. But once they got married, well, did you see *Love Affair?*"[76] For Annette, the only exception to the rule would be "Richard Burton and Elizabeth Taylor because it's likely that they would be arguing and having sex at the same time."

When her work schedule was intense, Warren took over at home, changing diapers and even doing laundry. He had dinner ready for her when she returned from work. "After one particularly grueling shoot," said a friend, "Annette crawled home from a day on the lot. Warren was making popcorn while the kids were making 'art projects' out of construction paper and the Sunday funnies. As Annette came in, Warren said, 'Well, look who's here, kids, it's Mommy. You remember Mommy, don't you? She must be here for a visit.'"[77] Annette broke into a wide grin, hugged the children, and kissed Warren.

His success these days was as a family man. When Annette was asked what kind of father he was, she replied, "He loves it. He wants as many [children] as I want to have." Added a friend, "He's totally gone off the deep end into fatherhood. He laughs about the kids having food fights, how Kathlyn is doing in school, a funny thing Isabel said, and what kind of trouble Ben got himself into. He's still involved in pictures, still keeps an office in Los Angeles to develop scripts—but he's happy to relegate the 'star' role to Annette while he makes breakfast and picks up toys. Warren told me: 'I'm proud of all the films I've written or directed or starred in. But the best things I ever did are running around my house right now. I get more rewards from my kids than I could get from a hundred Oscars.' "[78]

Photographed while playing outside with the children in early 2000, Warren and Annette appeared to be having as good a time as the kids. Isabel had inherited Annette's round funny face, brown hair, and bangs. Seven-year-old Kathlyn was very much Warren's daughter, long and lean, with the rosy complexion and grave handsomeness he'd displayed *Splendor in the Grass*. Her fine blond hair was worn in a long braid down to her waist in back. She loved to read, especially Harry Potter books, but was discriminating enough to inform her dad that *Dick Tracy* was "silly." With six-year-old Ben, the mother's genes again predominated; on him, her offbeat eyes were almost Asian looking, and he had her round face rather than his father's huge brow and creased cheeks. In his knee socks and full tunic, he could have sprung from a Victorian children's book. The parents were comfortably casual for their afternoon romp with their offspring, Warren in a brown sport jacket, white turtleneck, and Levi's; Annette in a blue denim Levi's jacket and black slacks, her long black cashmere shawl wrapped around her neck.

In March 2000, Annette said, "When I turned forty last year, I felt very reflective. I felt like it was a time to sort of sit back and look at my life." After taking stock, she realized that neither husband nor career headed her personal inventory of assets. "I really felt grateful that I had my kids," she said. "The most profound, gut-level feeling I had was *I've had three children. That's just incredible. Good for me.*" No doubt Warren regretted the crack he'd once made about fortyish women. "My notion of a wife at forty," he'd said, "is that a man should be able to change her, like a bank note, for two twenties."[79]

The fourth baby would be the last, Annette insisted. This pregnancy was just like the first; she was ill early on but by the end, she felt good, "like I can conquer the world. I've got to get this baby *out*." Nonetheless, with respect to having more children, she announced in March 2000, "This is the end of the road." She was not at all sentimental about childbearing, and said, "At the end of the pregnancy, you are so filled with hate and bitterness and rage—at least I am—that all you want is to get it out. It never occurs to you to say, 'Oh, gee, if only I could stay pregnant another few weeks.' "[80]

Thanks to Warren's multimillions, they could afford a battery of nannies and assistants, but on Sundays Annette was often seen grocery shopping at the sprawling outdoor Farmers Market on Fairfax Avenue in Hollywood, alongside such other celebrities as Jon Voight, Ellen DeGeneres, and Anne Heche. "Annette Bening comes here and buys veggies for her husband's dinner," a merchant explained.[81] At home, the domestic staff was "smart and loving and caring and responsible," Annette said. "That's how I do what I do." Just so the kids would know who their mother was, she decided to take on two parenting tasks, and fulfill them rigorously: she drove them around the city, and she was always there at bath time. When she and Warren took the children to restaurants, they told the waiters in a friendly but firm voice that they couldn't chat. The little time they had for the children was too precious to share with strangers. "You can't dawdle," she said. "For the most part, we're left alone."

To some observers, Warren continued to evince little passion for his career, content to let the forty-one-year-old Annette be the family's celebrity. And he continued to accede to her direction of their domestic life. "Annette keeps the household running like a Swiss watch, divvying out chores and giving orders to the staff and Warren," said a close source. "Warren never utters a peep of protest because he absolutely loves his new job and he's still ga-ga over Annette."

In one respect, the Beattys were like any other couple: they had spats. "Sometimes, we might disagree about how things go around the house or domestic stuff, like anybody else," she said. "How things are done, how things are run."[82] In early 2000, she dropped her ban on making another movie with Warren and avowed, "I would love to do something with him again. I'd like to do something he directs."[83]

Though some skeptics had thought *Bulworth* his swan song, he started his new film, *Town & Country,* in 2000. It was written by Michael Laughlin (another Leslie Caron ex), directed by Peter Chelsom, and co-starred old Beatty flames Goldie Hawn and Diane Keaton, as well as Nastassja Kinski, Andie McDowell, Jenna Elfman, Marian Seldes, Tricia Vessey, Josh Hartnett, Charlton Heston, and Warren's best friend, Garry Shandling. The latter also was in Annette's new film, *What Planet Are You From?* a wacky, nonsensical Mike Nichols production presumably about how women humanize men. *What Planet Are You From?* was summarily—and rightly—dismissed by critics as a total loss.

Warren's picture also was in trouble. Interviewed in September 2000, Dick

Sylbert said, "It's in the fourth year. And they're thinking of doing voice-over. The numbers at the previews keep going down. It's going to be up to Warren whether he does the voice-over. They've got a problem with the picture. It's one of those things that he got himself into that he might have been wiser not to. He got caught in this; Warren is not in charge of this movie. He is an actor in this movie. He said okay to the script, which has had four producers on it. It took him a long time to say 'yes.' We were both doing pictures for New Line, and I told him this picture I was doing was going to be brilliant, but it took 105 days to make it. He said, 'Gee, isn't that a long time for a comedy?' And I said, 'Are you talking to *me?*' "

For Warren, it was just like old times, when he'd had Paramount in a stew over the skyrocketing costs of *Reds*. *Town & Country* had been pushed back, the sure sign of a picture in trouble. Budgeted at fifty million dollars, the cost by 2000 jumped to seventy-eight million. A new ending needed to be shot, but no one knew if it ever would be. Some industry insiders blamed Warren, citing the same perfectionism that had complicated and prolonged much of his filmmaking. One New Line senior executive said, "He behaved badly, plain and simple. He claimed that the script had been changed from the version he had approved and, since his contract provided him with script approval, he insisted that Buck Henry be on the set to rewrite the movie. It's been a nightmare."[84] *Vanity Fair* called Beatty "the 800-pound gorilla on the set."[85]

New Line chief Mike DeLuca refused to lay the blame on Beatty, just as Barry Diller and Mike Eisner had refused to backstab him as a fellow member of the Hollywood "club," and just as *Ishtar* had been blamed on Elaine May. DeLuca admitted that *Town & Country,* like Elizabeth Taylor's fabulous white elephant, *Cleopatra,* had commenced shooting without a finished script, causing inevitable scheduling snafus. "We just rolled the dice and hoped it would work out."[86] DeLuca was indulging in the old Hollywood game of damage control, trying to prevent the picture from getting a bad press, but *Vanity Fair* wrote, "Hollywood buzz has pointed the finger at Beatty."[87]

Dick Sylbert continues, "There was a script that needed an enormous amount of work. If you want my personal opinion? It is basically in one sentence: A comedy of reconciliation. Now, you just take your little brain and think about the movies that have been made with the casts that have been brilliant. You have comedies of remarriage—thirties and forties—*Philadelphia Story*—you can't stop naming them, they're all brilliant. Then there were comedies of marriage like Frank Capra's *It Happened One Night.* There is no such thing as a comedy about reconciliation. Reconciliation is a tragedy. What you get in the end is the Clintons. That's the real problem. That's why no matter how many Band-Aids they put on it, it's in very big trouble. I can only think of one movie where a comedy with a reconciliation worked. It worked only because the entire first half of the movie is about two people who are very different falling in love—that's Spencer Tracy and Katherine Hepburn in *Woman of the Year.* 'I went out and fucked all these women and came back to my wife.' A geriatric *Shampoo.* Well, it's his choice. People make mistakes. Warren is a brilliant guy. He made a mistake in putting Garry Shandling in *Town & Country.* He made a mistake in *Love Affair.* He made a mistake in *Ishtar.* He's paying for *Town & Country* emotionally. He's very unhappy and I feel sorry for him. We had a conversation one night and I said to him, 'Do you realize how well you've done? This is baseball. If you get up to bat ten times and you don't hit it seven times you end up with a three hundred average and the Hall of Fame.' He looked at me and said, 'Holy Christ! I'm batting about five hundred.' He's very hard on himself. Perfectionism is the name of the game. You're either a compulsive-obsessive or you're not. Go do something else."

As William Goldman once pointed out, it's almost impossible to write Warren Beatty off. "He's *very* smart," said Goldman.[88] "Beatty understands the workings of the town better than anyone. He has been a force for forty years, has been in an *amazing* number of flops, and whenever his career seems a tad shaky, he produces a wonderful movie or directs a wonderful movie and is safe for another half decade."

Warren didn't want anyone writing him off as a politician, either. "Can I be effective at another time?" he asked in 2000. "Whether that is in a year, or two years, who knows?"[89]

On Oscar night 2000, when he accepted the Irving G. Thalberg Memorial Award from the Academy of Motion Picture Arts and Sciences—the industry's highest prize—his speech was characteristically diffuse and silly, even more inane than his Americans for Democratic Action address. Said one academy member, "With regard to his flaky delivery on accepting the Thalberg, I don't know what he'd had to smoke." Jack Nicholson was the presenter, and at one point he tried to help Warren, who was so nervous he was almost inaudible, by giving him breathing exercises. "Hup! Hup!" huffed Nicholson, urging Warren to project his voice.

Nicholson, an unreformed womanizer, was having his own problems at this time, slapped with a lawsuit by Catherine Sheehan. The trouble had started on October 12, 1996, when Sheehan and a friend were offered one thousand dollars each by Nicholson to have sex with him in his Mulholland Drive home. Afterward, he tried to get out of paying, but Sheehan insisted. "That brute threw me against walls and stomped my head," she alleged in a suit filed in Los Angeles Superior Court. "Jack Nicholson hired me for sex—then beat me so badly that I'm dying from my injuries."[90] He settled $32,500 on her in 1998, extracting a promise that she wouldn't try to get anything more from his forty-five-million-dollar estate, but as her alleged "brain inflammation" worsened, she had to spend ten to fifteen thousand a year on medications. "The damage is killing her," said Dr. William Baumzweiger, and her lawyer, Ira Chester, added, "We had no idea how badly she was injured at the time."[91]

Despite this crisis, Nicholson was in better shape at the Oscars than Warren, whose acceptance speech was one long non sequitur. Previous Thalberg winners—such industry pacesetters as David O. Selznick, Darryl F. Zanuck, Walt Disney, Cecil B. DeMille, Alfred Hitchcock, and Ingmar Bergman—had sometimes used the occasion to offer guidelines and challenges for the industry, and Warren could well have taken advantage of the opportunity to defend freedom of speech, which was under attack by politicians of both parties, all of them bent on blaming Hollywood for the nation's social ills, citing the proliferation of violence and sex in films. With the threat of political censorship looming throughout the 2000 presidential election year, it was time for a high-profile Hollywood spokesperson to remind the world that the artist's only obligation is to tell the truth about what the world is really like, what it is to be human, and what it's like to feel deep emotion.

Predictably, censorship quickly followed the Lieberman-McCain hearings in September, and by the following year, director John Stockwell was complaining that nervous studio executives compelled him to make cuts in *Crazy/Beautiful* that compromised the film's integrity. "Word came down pretty quickly that we were going to have to do whatever it took to get a PG-13 rating," said Stockwell. That meant trashing the scenes of Nicole, played by Kirsten Dunst, purchasing marijuana, of her using a water pipe, of her frankly revealing her sexual experiences. Stockwell couldn't even show Nicole taking a drink, which "was sort of tragic to me," he said, "because the movie is about a girl who is veering off the rails and who is truly struggling, and part of that is that she drinks and does drugs. I kept asking: Doesn't it matter what the overall message is? Doesn't the redemptive quality at the end mean anything?" In the new political climate following the McCain-Lieberman hearings, the answer was no. The extent to which *Crazy/Beautiful* suffered from censorship was sadly evident in the *New York Times* review. The critic lavished high praise on the film but concluded, "Because it starts off with so much promise, its eventual slide into melodramatic convention is especially disappointing. It's ultimately too cautious and responsible to live up to either the promise of its title or the talents of its cast."

Obviously, industry leaders like Warren should have been sounding warning bells, but on receiving his career-capping award, the Thalberg, he myopically restricted his remarks to the wife and kids, also blowing a kiss to all the girls he'd loved before. When he finally did turn to politics in his speech, he told academy members and the millions watching on TV, "Thank you so much for encouraging my voice in public affairs. Please forgive me if I've used it stridently or in fact not often enough. I'll try to do better." Clearly, he hadn't given up on public office. Lifetime achievement honors would continue coming his way, including, in April 2001, Blockbuster's World Entertainer Award, presented by Dustin Hoffman.

Annette would not be as fortunate. Touted for months as a shoo-in for the 1999 Best Actress Oscar for the DreamWorks studio's *American Beauty,* she lost the prize to a total newcomer, Hillary Swank. Annette's humiliation could hardly have been more public; she attended the Academy Awards ceremony despite being nine months' pregnant. What was the industry saying by singling her out as the only key figure involved in the making of *American Beauty* not to receive an Oscar (the film won Best Picture, Director, Screenwriter, Actor, and Cinematography)? That "club" wives shouldn't assume that marrying into Hollywood royalty rated preferential treatment? That the fantastic publicity she'd received throughout the year, including cover stories in several major national magazines, amounted to overkill? Or simply that the woman she portrayed in *American Beauty* was unsympathetic—and that Annette's performance was so over the top that it amounted to caricature?

Whatever the case, being the press's sentimental favorite hadn't won her the

Oscar. DreamWorks tried to cheer her up, commissioning a jeweler to create a special consolation Academy Award festooned with diamonds and valued at fifteen thousand dollars. Inscribed, "What Should Have Been . . . Best Actress," the statuette was holding a pair of garden shears, exactly as Annette's strident, violent harridan had done in *American Beauty*. Clutching his Best Actor Oscar, Kevin Spacey attempted to comfort her, observing, "In a little while you're going to be able to hold in your arms a rather more important object than an award."

Her defeat at the Oscar ceremony was a shocking rebuke and marked the beginning a streak of bad luck. After her Mike Nichols fiasco, *What Planet Are You From?*, Hollywood, and the press, seemed to lose interest in her. Good movie roles were so scarce for middle-aged actresses that she was tempted to pack up and take the whole family to Manhattan, where a Broadway play was being tailored for her. Warren, who preferred California to New York, urged her to find a TV series that would keep her in the west, and for a while she reportedly was considering a sitcom about a suburban mom who revives her career after her husband goes broke on Wall Street.

Though *What Planet Are You From?* was bad enough to destroy careers, the film occasioned a good joke from Garry Shandling. When Annette and Garry stripped naked for a shot during filming, a reporter asked, "What's it like to do a nude scene with your best friend's wife?"

"It was great," Shandling quipped. "She went home so turned on that they made love and Warren got her pregnant. That's why they're going to name the baby Garry, whether it's a boy or a girl."[92]

As usual, Annette suffered from morning sickness. "It's happened before," she said, "but I've always felt better after the first trimester." In fact, she quite liked being pregnant again, and said, "I feel exhilarated, kind of liberated." She'd been under a crushing year-long load of commitments: *American Beauty* was followed immediately by a four-week stage run in *Hedda Gabler* and the filming of *What Planet*. "I was just over-acted," she said. "If I had to come up with one more emotional moment, I was going to kill myself."

Overwork and middle-aged pregnancy left her sounding somewhat frazzled. She didn't always make sense. Discussing her pregnancy one morning at breakfast, she said, "You become kind of animal about how things smell. 'Is this something I can eat, or will it give me indigestion?' " But then she tore into a meal that would have choked a quarterback, wolfing down potatoes, bacon, scrambled eggs, and a bran muffin. In her free time, she ran to a yoga class, acting like any career woman trying to satisfy the demands of family and job. She couldn't always pull it off. "If I've been on the set all day putting out emotion, I'm pretty much drained," she confessed. "So when one of my kids asks for a fiftieth glass of water before bed, I just want to say: 'I don't have anything else left, you can't have any more water.' "

Warren's devotion to fatherhood was of course a great help to the expectant mother at this trying time. So were her parents, with whom she'd remained close, and who still lived in the house in San Diego where she'd grown up. Though something of an elitist, unsavvy in politics, and a bit too cold as an actress, her strong suit was continuity in relationships. "I'm convinced that Bening's down-to-earth quality is what helped her win Beatty," said Liz Smith. "In his long list of ladies, many have had intelligence, humor, and sensuality. But none could offer one vital quality: stability. Bening is a real woman."

Warren helped the kids with their homework, performed chores around the house, and served dinner to Annette. "I waited more than half a century to have children," the sixty-three-year-old Warren told a friend, "and now that I have them, I just want to be with them."[93]

When the baby, a girl, was born on April 8, 2000, weighing in at nine pounds, two ounces, they named her Ella Corinne. The baby shower was thrown by Annette's actress friend Victoria Foyt, who appeared in *Déjà Vu*, a film co-written by Foyt and Natalie Wood's old boyfriend, director Henry Jaglom. "Annette was happy to have the whole Oscar thing behind her," said Foyt. "She was able to relax and settle into baby mode. To have four kids, nowadays, is a lot if you're going to have any kind of career. *Most* people wouldn't handle it well, but Annette will handle it beautifully." Edward Zwick, who directed Annette in *The Siege* in 1998, agreed. "You'd be surprised," he said, "at how normal this process is—even for actresses."[94] With the arrival of Ella, the Beatty brood now numbered four, including Kathlyn, eight, Ben, six, and Isabel, three. At forty-one, Annette was spearheading Hollywood's midlife baby boom, joining such forty-something moms as Madonna, who, just before turning forty-two, gave birth to Rocco, later marrying the boy's father, thirty-three-year-old British director Guy Ritchie; Beverly D'Angelo, forty-nine, who gave birth to twins, Anton and Olivia, after she and sixty-one-year-old Al Pacino resorted to in-vitro fertilization[95]; Kim Basinger, who was almost forty-two when she delivered her first child, daughter Ireland Eliesse, before her marriage to Alex Baldwin ended; Cheryl Tiegs, who, at fifty-three, having failed to conceive a child with her fourth husband, Rod Stryker, a yoga instructor ten years her junior, had her eggs fertilized in another woman, who delivered twin boys, Theo and Jaden; and Sharon Stone, who was forty-two when she and her husband, newspaper editor Phil Bronstein, adopted their son Roan.[96]

Four months after the birth of the latest Beatty child, Ella Corinne at last began sleeping through the night without waking up her parents, and Warren and Annette celebrated by closing their bedroom door and going slightly wild. Earlier, they'd stopped in their limo at a sex shop in Hollywood and told the driver to wait for them. Inside the shop, they selected six hundred dollars' worth of equipment from the shelves, including costumes, sex toys, and massage oils. Later, back at Mulholland, they donned matching latex Tarzan and Jane outfits and played dress-up through the night.[97]

Obviously there was still plenty of sizzle in the marriage, and great fun to be had in rearing the kids, to judge from the look of Warren and his six-year-old son, Ben, at a Lakers–Chicago Bulls game in L.A. in December 2000. While Warren and Garry Shandling chatted amicably during halftime, young Ben, a blondish, boyish version of Annette Bening—and that's not bad—had a great time mugging and gesticulating for photographers. Warren looked like a man who'd found his niche: doting papahood. He was wonderful with his girls, too, drawing on years of experience and understanding gained while making love to beautiful women. With Ben, he became a typical Little League dad, showing up at ball games and cheering his son on.

Annette was sometimes seen around L.A. coping with baby Ella alone, or trying to. When a photographer snapped her leaving a coffee shop and then placing the infant in the front seat of her Mercedes SUV, a minor controversy broke out in the press. California law mandates that children under four years and forty pounds be placed in a car seat, and all car-seat manufacturers recommend that the seat be located in the middle of the back seat of a car if there is a passenger-side air bag, as in the Mercedes SUV.[98] On another outing, Annette took Ella and three-year-old Isabel to a coffee shop. Later, when she emerged with the children and went to the car, she carefully tried to balance Isabel's glass of milk atop the Mercedes, but while she secured the children in their seats, the milk toppled over, splashing the roof and leaking into the $90,000 vehicle's plush interior.[99]

For Annette, the dual demands of child-rearing and career building, especially now that roles were going to younger competitors, proved all-consuming. Though a feminist, she refused to take the usual Hollywood stance that men alone continue to command good roles as they grow older. "If women want to see more of those stories, they also need to *make* more stories," she said. "I don't think we should wait for somebody else to hand us the material." Certainly Annette wasn't waiting. But in an increasingly youth-seeking entertainment industry drawn to dewy beauties like Angelina Jolie, Reese Witherspoon, Renee Zellweger, and Jennifer Lopez, superstardom would forever remain just beyond her grasp. Bucking the trend, Annette continued to search for new material whenever she could, inviting scripts with parts for women with children. She did not, she complained to a reporter, have enough time to read as she'd done in the old days, when she'd chased after *The Sheltering Sky* for years. Perhaps it was just as well; superstardom hadn't helped Julie Christie any, at least insofar as winning Warren was concerned.

Annette left it up to her husband to do his full share of parenting, but he found time to show up regularly at L.A. sporting events and to ride his Harley-Davidson motorcycle daily along winding Mulholland Drive. Annette told him that since he'd passed age sixty-three, perhaps he should give up the Harley, but he reportedly told her, "No way."[100] He attended meticulously to his social duties on both coasts. When media mogul Barry Diller wed designer Diane Von Furstenberg on February 2, 2001, Warren was among the guests at the reception in Manhattan, along with Mike Nichols, Diane Sawyer, and Jerry Seinfeld's ex-love, designer Shoshanna Lonstein. On April 1, seated next to former first lady Nancy Reagan, he joined the ladies who lunch—also known as the Colleagues— and Saks Fifth Avenue for a benefit luncheon and fashion show for Children's Institute International, held at the Regent Beverly Wilshire, scene of many a past Beatty conquest. As they watched a swank runway preview of Chanel's spring/summer 2001 collection, Warren, in a brown suit and tan tie, leaned slightly toward Nancy, in her usual all-red ensemble, to catch her every word. In the same month, *People* magazine reported an encounter he had with former president Bill Clinton at a Lakers–Knicks basketball game. "Clinton was caught on tape with sometime critic Warren Beatty, who later stayed mum about their animated encounter," wrote *People*.[101] In the photograph accompanying the story, Clinton was glaring at Warren in apparent resentment and shock. After surviving numerous scandals during his administration, Clinton had refurbished his reputation and regained his popularity at the end of his second term, only to mess it up again by pardoning a pack of crooks on his final day in the White House. Warren, as both an older man and a Democratic Party benefactor, evidently used the Lakers game as an opportunity to lecture the bad boy of American politics.[102] At another Lakers game, Warren was sitting next to Magic Johnson when Shaquille O'Neal swished an astounding basket, and Warren became so agitated that he jumped out of his seat and dumped his beverage all over Magic. "It's the last time I sit next to you," Magic joked.[103]

Though Annette's career had faltered, she sounded like a fulfilled woman, remarking, "I always wanted a lot of kids. Ever since I was tiny. I just loved kids." She certainly had enough of them now, and she loved watching Warren nurture them. Baby Ella, like older sisters Kathlyn and Isabel, blossomed under his adoring attention, proving once again that womanizers can make terrific fathers, the kind whose daughters feel forever loved by men. "Warren has something rare: an understanding and an appreciation of women," Goldie Hawn said. "He genuinely likes us. He is not threatened by women and is generally quite devoted to us as persons."

He was equally effective with his son; at an April 2001 Lakers game, Ben and Warren huddled together, in matching blue denim jackets, Warren smiling broadly and leaning toward a delighted Ben, who was excitedly commenting on a play. With his new short haircut, Ben looked more like his mother than ever—utterly offbeat, but with a dash of all-American Tom Sawyer/Huck Finn merriment, a boy tailor-made to beguile and disarm any father. From all appearances, Warren was having the time of his life.

"He may get away with it," says Dick Sylbert. "Let me tell you what I think has happened. The story of Don Juan or Don Giovanni, a man who counted up the number of women he slept with, has been done many times over the centuries, and that was Warren's life. Eventually Don Juan was dragged into hell—that was his punishment. But in Pushkin's version, *Stone Guest*, the punishment is, he has to marry the girl and spend the rest of his life with her and have children. That's what Pushkin thought was the true punishment for this guy. In real life, Pushkin died in a duel defending his hooker wife's honor. She was a real swinger, but honor was very important in those days. He *died* defending his marriage. Now, that may be Warren's punishment. Four kids and a wife. But, my guess is, he's a happy man. You can write only two endings to *Don Giovanni*."

Or perhaps three. Granted, marrying Annette represented a turning point, bringing about a sea change, and she was right in her observation, "There's something internal that, for whatever reason, part of it the person and part of it fate, makes you ready for change in your life."[104] How much change remained to be seen. Former *Village Voice* reporter Blair Sobol said, "It was obvious they had no chemistry in *Love Affair*." When gorgeous—and decades-younger—Elizabeth Hurley stopped at his table at a restaurant in 2001, it was almost touching to see how eagerly he sprang from his seat to greet her, or, in 2002, how devotedly he supported his former leading lady, thirty-three-year-old Halle Berry, quietly whispering into the ears of movers and shakers that she should be given an Oscar for *Monster's Ball*. As for Annette, guests at a Hollywood party noticed her blushing under the admiring gaze of Australian heartbreaker Russell Crowe.[105] Marriage, like everything else in life, is a one-day-at-a-time affair. The media, most of the movie industry, and their fans wish the Beattys well.

Whether Warren would get away with *Town & Country*, a choppy, excruciatingly unfunny divorce comedy, was less certain. During production, reports persisted that he was at loggerheads with his director, Peter Chelsom, on the set, echoing the general perception of Warren as a demanding perfectionist. Bob Shaye, the chairman of New Line Films, appeared to blame Warren for the movie's troubles in the *Los Angeles Times*, but Pat Kingsley quickly issued denials in her client's behalf. Then Peter Chelsom chimed in, denouncing "mind games" played by superstars. "It's a mess," he said. "I have never seen so much money wasted."[106] Finally, heads started to roll. In early 2001, Michael DeLuca, president of New Line, was fired. "I had a pretty bad run of movies," said DeLuca, and he admitted that he and a woman had been caught in flagrante delicto at a high-profile Hollywood party and asked to leave, behavior that struck many as less than CEO-like.[107] A key Hollywood observer pointed to Warren and *Town & Country* as important factors in DeLuca's downfall. "He couldn't control Warren," said an agent. "Warren was able to push the director around. So the final cost may come in at hundred million dollars [columnist Liz Smith upped the ante to $120 million].[108] This may really be the end for Warren."

It was a familiar refrain, trumpeted after every flop Warren had ever appeared in. Unlike his more resilient friend Bob Towne, who successfully negotiated the transition from New Hollywood to high concept by scripting an action movie, *Mission: Impossible 2*, for Tom Cruise,[109] Warren let himself become an anachronism, appearing in *Town & Country* in silly hats and baggy, clownish pants. And his costumes weren't the worst of it. He and his makeup artists should have been scrambling for every piece of gauze they could find, instead of letting the naked camera lens expose, in semi-nude love scenes, the full effect of aging on his body. It was a little late for him to start building a career out of self-deprecation, like an addlepated Woody Allen. To say the Beatty act didn't work in this film was putting it mildly. According to the London *Express*, preview audiences could no longer accept him as a serial seducer. "At the test screenings moviegoers said they couldn't stand Beatty because he was only after one thing from women—sex—and he didn't seem like the sort of guy who would be able to get so much of it."[110]

When *Town & Country* opened in America in May 2001, it grossed a paltry $6.7 million. A key reviewer, the *New York Times*'s Stephen Holden, was surprisingly indulgent, according Warren's worst turkey since *Ishtar* a reluctant thumbs-up. Though the film's old-fashioned 1970s sensibility, which had worked so well in *Shampoo,* "the 1975 comic masterpiece," was unequal to the task of satirizing "marriage, adultery, and the battle of the sexes at the turn of the millennium," Holden found that he could still relish "Mr. Beatty's attitude of sheepish suavity, in which a raised eyebrow and a shuffling, half-apologetic delivery send intriguingly mixed signals of vulnerability and predatory intent."[111] If the Beatty act was back in business, it proved, if nothing else, that there's no man more endearing than a fool for love.

In the late summer of 2001, the Beattys went to New York City, which was basking in the last few precious carefree days before the terrorists' attack on the World Trade Center that changed American life forever. On August 12, relishing Manhattan's excitement, Warren and Annette plunged into a round of parties, theater evenings, and restaurant openings. They caught the incomparable Meryl Streep in *The Seagull* at the outdoor theater in Central Park, the same venue where Streep had electrified audiences almost thirty years ago in *The Taming of the Shrew*. The opening-night crowd, which included Meg Ryan, Mike Myers, Sarah Jessica Parker, and Matthew Broderick, got soaked by a summer storm. Huddling under an umbrella, the Beattys looked as happy as newlyweds, but unfortunately they also resembled a circus act, both of them done up in garish yellow outfits—L.A. bumpkins in a city well-known for understated elegance and tasteful dark clothes.[112]

But not even the rain—or inappropriate attire—could extinguish Warren's elation, for over the summer it became clear that *Town & Country* hadn't finished him off as a performer. He and the brilliant Sean Penn, who'd forgiven Warren for romancing his ex-wife Madonna, were part of an ensemble cast for the new David Rabe play, and they celebrated by having drinks with Calista Flockhart at Manhattan's Tao restaurant.[113]

Together again a few days later, Beatty and Penn attended the opening of the Manhattan restaurant Man Ray. At their table, Penn spent his time talking with Ed Norton, while Warren characteristically zeroed in on Penn's current wife, Robin Wright, who hung on his every word as he gently touched her shoulder.[114] *Plus ça change, plus c'est la même chose.*

When tragedy struck the city a few weeks later, Warren, like so many of his countrymen, did whatever he could to help. On September 24, back in L.A., he joined Leonardo DiCaprio, Samuel L. Jackson, and hundreds of other guests at the home of *The Mexican* producer Lawrence Bender for a benefit that raised $1.5 million. The money was later distributed to the families of World Trade Center victims and rescue workers.

Warren's heart, as it had been so often in his life, was in the right place.

PRESENT AT THE CREATION

THIS BOOK'S true parents are three remark-able L.A. women—Cathy Griffin, Pat Loud, and Dorris Halsey. It was Pat, matriarch of the prototypical TV reality series *An American Family,* who led me to the columnist and researcher, Cathy Griffin, and it was Pat who hosted a dinner party for the Los Angeles–area supporters of this large biographical undertaking. Intensive interviewing in Hollywood and abroad helped to give this book its insider clout, especially the accounts of professionals who worked on Warren's films and whose testimony lend to the narrative a special kind of intimacy—its you-are-there feel about moviemaking, whether it's experiencing Lady Olivier's tirade on the set of *The Roman Spring of Mrs. Stone* or trudging across a vast Arctic waste with Warren and his designer Richard Sylbert during the *Reds* shoot. My dedicatee, Dorris Halsey, who handles the estate of Aldous Huxley and seems to know everyone west of the Rockies, steered me in many productive directions and, on a personal level, was my delightful and witty companion throughout my L.A. stay.

It was Dorris Halsey who connected me with the costume designer Donfeld, a veritable gold mine of Hollywood lore and industry contacts. Donfeld in turn took me to Nan Morris-Robinson, the lovely daughter-in-law of Edward G. Robinson. Nan was in Hollywood when Warren arrived in the fifties, and she provided a unique picture of the Strip when it was first being cruised by a new breed of leading men, the "sensitive hunks" who emerged in the wake of James Dean. Largely because of her job with agent Henry Willson, Nan knew them all—Warren, Richard Beymer, Troy Donahue, Elvis Presley, and many other promising young actors who reached for the brass ring that only Warren would seize and hold for more than forty years, making him one of the longest running acts in show business. Nan was also able to paint vivid verbal portraits of director Roman Polanski and hairdressers Gene Shacove and Jay Sebring; from Warren's relationships with such men sprang his masterpiece, *Shampoo*.

In the summer of 2000, Ron Bernstein, the International Creative Management agent, kicked off my Hollywood trip for this book in the most auspicious way, taking me to a party given by Bruce Cohen and Dan Jinks, the producers of *American Beauty,* the Oscar-winning production starring Warren's wife Annette Bening. Ron's knowledge of the current Hollywood scene is extensive, and I am extremely grateful to have his good will and generous help.

Ron, too, is part of this book's immediately family—but the book would not have been possible had there not also been a much larger family that had gone before. Since I first began visiting L.A. professionally in the 1970s, as a publishing executive, then as a collaborator to the stars, and finally as an author in my own right, numerous persons have helped me negotiate the formidable social barriers of Beverly Hills. Without them, and the wealth of anecdotes I heard in their homes, I'd still be editing other people's books instead of writing my own. This larger family of good shepherds and guardian angels should also be acknowledged.

On one of my first New York–to–L.A. jaunts, in 1970 or 1971, when I was vice president of Coward-McCann, Ron Bernstein and I were guests of Julia and Michael Phillips at their beach house in Trancas, far up the Pacific Coast Highway, beyond the big beach at Zuma. The Phillipses met our plane at LAX very late one night and drove us, in a blinding downpour, to their home.

Everything about Julia was then fraught with drama, and, typically, when we arrived at the house, at the height of the storm, a desperate young man lunged at us out of the darkness. Covered with blood, he begged to be protected from a madman who'd just given him a ride, stabbed him, and was chasing him down the beach. Michael locked the poor soul in a utility room underneath the sun deck and called the police, who arrived in due course with pistols and rifles drawn and took the man away in a squad car. Julia looked at me and hissed, "See what bad New York vibes you've brought with you?"

Thankfully it was calmer the next day, and I took a long walk on the beach with Peter Bill, Tony Bill's towheaded four-year-old, a remarkable child who held up his end of the conversation like someone in his twenties or thirties. His parents, Tony and Antonia Bill, and aspiring screen writer David S. Ward were frequently at the Phillipses, and, over a breakfast of Julia's tasty *huevos rancheros* one morning, it dawned on me that they were all plotting some great new enterprise together. Little did I suppose at the time that it was nothing less than the New Hollywood, or that I was present at the creation, at least as an observer, of a revolution that would change Hollywood forever. A few years later, when I saw *The Sting,* I realized why the air had been so electric every time Tony, David, Julia, and Michael got together. David wrote *The Sting,* Tony and the Phillipses produced it, and they all took home Oscars, confirming the revolution Warren had started with *Bonnie and Clyde* in 1967.

During that same trip, Ron and I drove over to writer Arnold Margolin's home in Malibu for brunch, and Arnold introduced us to Jill Clayburgh, Margot Kidder, and Jennifer Salt, young actresses then just starting out but destined, along with Diane Keaton, Dyan Cannon, and Jane Fonda, to reinvent our concept of leading ladies, and shatter the movie stereotype of feminine beauty. Later we spent time at Tony and Antonia Bill's house in Brentwood, admired their swap-meet art deco furnishings, and took in a round of movie-industry parties, meeting other fledgling filmmakers. Though I had no idea that I'd one day be writing about Warren Beatty, I was already beginning my research into the New Hollywood, which figures prominently in this book, and which Warren did so much to define.

Later in the 1970s, as editor in chief of the Delacorte Press, I added Joyce Haber to my growing list of Hollywood authors, hammering out a six-figure contract with Swifty Lazar. The former wife of *Dynasty*'s Doug Kramer as well as the *Los Angeles Times* columnist who invented of the A-list, Joyce agreed to write a novel about Beverly Hills for me and Delacorte publisher Ross Claiborne, and as I helped her put together *The Users* over the next few years, I became a part of the scene at her Roxbury Drive house and the restaurant where she got most of her items, Ma Maison. Whenever this powerful and deeply troubled woman came to Manhattan to work with me, we spent our evenings with people like Frank Sinatra, Dani Janssen, Marlo Thomas, and Alison (The Night Bird) Steele. One night I escorted Joyce, Marlo, and Dani to a party in Halston's tower-like East Side townhouse. Warren Beatty wasn't there, but everyone else was, including Liza Minnelli, Martha Graham, James Jones, Margaux Hemingway, and Judy Garland's son, Joey Luft. This was the era of *Shampoo,* and tales of Warren's prodigious sex life were the talk of the cocktail party circuit. As Warren's future biographer, I was in the right place that night, listening to eyewitness accounts.

Another legendary columnist, Radie Harris, took me to dinner, at different times, with Elizabeth Taylor, Ingrid Bergman, Cary Grant, and Henry Fonda, and they'd all either known, worked with, envied, or adored Warren. It was my practice when I got home after such evenings to jot down everything I'd heard.

I first met Pauline Kael, a crucial figure in any account of Warren as an artist, at a dinner hosted by editor Peggy Brooks in her Gay Street townhouse in Greenwich Village, and I continued to see Pauline, the most powerful movie critic of her day, from time to time. For someone so searing in her judgments and fearlessly outspoken in delivering them—I once saw her tell screenwriter Larry Kramer, to his face, that he was "an asshole for exaggerating the 'Gladiatorial' section of *Women in Love*"—she could be surprisingly sweet and courteous. Another movie reviewer, Rex Reed, left Macmillan to be published by me at Delacorte (and later at Morrow). His eagerly anticipated profiles in the *New York Times* and *Esquire* were so popular that major stars stood in line to be interviewed by him (and sometimes, as in the case of Warren, skewered). When Rex and I organized his books, it was never in my office, but always in his elegant Dakota condo, where I'd sit in rapt fascination as he told me the stories behind the profiles. It was Melina Mercouri this, and Warren Beatty that— and all of it, of course, unwittingly became grist for the present book's mill.

At Delacorte I published two books by director Joshua Logan, one of

Warren's earliest discoverers, and at Josh and Nedda's glittering parties in River House, I mingled with the crowd, often with Pat Loud on my arm, gathering enough anecdotal ammunition to draw on for the rest of my life. The regulars at the Logans were Tony Perkins, Berry Berenson, Gloria Vanderbilt, Wyatt Cooper, Estee Lauder, Mary Martin, Jacob Javits, Abe Beame, Betty Comden, Adolph Green, Phyllis Newman, Margalo Gillmore, Eugenia Sheppard, and Carol Channing—and how they loved to talk! The same riches were there for the harvesting at Florence and Harold Rome's parties, where I met Ethel Merman, Walter and Jean Kerr, Arlene Francis, Al Hirschfeld and Dolly Haas, Ruth Goetz, Belle Kaufman, Yoko Ono, Frances Gershwin, Arthur Kober (who'd been married to Lillian Hellman), Mrs. Joseph Fields, and Judy Collins. Helen Meyer, president of Dell Publishing, introduced me to John Huston, whose daughter Angelica appears in the present volume. In those days, Warren's name seemed to drip from every lip, and I'm glad I was there to collect the stories.

Moving on to William Morrow and Company in the late 1970s, I signed Shelley Winters to write her autobiography, and thereafter, for two or three years, spent as much time at Shelley's places in Beverly Hills and New York as I did in my Morrow office. Through Shelley, I seemed to meet half of Hollywood—New and Old—from Lee Grant, Farley Granger, and Robert Wagner to Susan Strasberg (who described her affair with Warren over a brandy at Lainie Kazan's), Kyle McLachlan, and Laura Dern. I often stayed at the Beverly Wilshire Hotel while working with Shelley, and our editorial conferences customarily took place in the Wilshire's capacious swimming pool. Helen Chaplin, the hotel's warm and motherly publicist, was introduced to me by Hector Arce, co-author of Vincente Minnelli's autobiography. Warren Beatty was in residence in the penthouse suite. His doings were the talk of the hotel.

Morrow in those days was Hollywood's publisher of choice—the company behind bestsellers by Doris Day, Sophia Loren, Christina Crawford, Rex Harrison, and Roman Polanski, and I luxuriated in the entry Morrow gave me whenever I visited L.A. Many figures in the movie establishment educated me about Hollywood in their gracious homes, as they sat with me and pondered whether to accept a publishing contract and a hefty Morrow advance to write their memoirs. Hector Arce, the A-list's favorite writer at the time, took me to see the former Mrs. Charles Feldman (Jean Howard), and when Jean and I talked about Charlie that day, I never supposed I'd be writing about him as Warren's mentor, twenty-five years later. I also remember going to dinner at Mrs. Edie Goetz's with Hector, and meeting Skye Aubrey, Mrs. Edgar Bergen, Luis Estevez, and David Columbia. David, who later wrote Debbie Reynolds's bestselling memoir, would become a close friend and benefactor, one who would give me some of my best scoops, including a couple of unattributed ones in this book.

In the 1980s, as editorial director of G.P. Putnam's Sons, I signed Priscilla Presley, June Allyson, Ann Todd, and Stewart Granger, and in the course of working with them further laid the foundation for my life as a writer. I remember a magical evening in London—picking Ann Todd up at her flat in Melbury Square, going to the West End to see Maggie Smith in a play about Virginia Woolf, and later visiting with Maggie and talking about theater, movies, and everything under the sun. At a party for *Superman,* I spoke with Christopher Reeve, Valerie Perrine, and movie critic Alexander Walker, personable raconteurs all, and at cocktails at Anaïs Nin's, I chatted with Luise Rainer and her husband, publisher Robert Lusty, later committing everything they said to my notebook. One should try to be, as Henry James put it, a person on whom nothing is lost.

Back in Beverly Hills one day, Paul Rosenfield and I decided to pay a call on June Allyson, whose memoir I was editing at the same time Paul was researching a piece about her for *Calendar.* It was a sunny morning, and we hopped in Paul's vintage convertible, put the top down, and sped up to June and her husband Dr. David Ashrow's cottage in Ojai. Later on, in New York, I had a memorable dinner with June, David, and Van Johnson at La Côte Basque. All I had to do was listen—and remember.

While on another Putnam junket to Beverly Hills, what a wealth of tales I gleaned at Paul Jasmin's birthday party for Marisa Berenson at Georgio Moroder's house on Castle Place, talking with Barry Diller, Bud Cort, Swifty Lazar, Ellen Burstyn, and Brad Davis. Later, at a dinner at Christopher Isherwood and Don Bachardy's in Santa Monica Canyon, the guests included Tony Richardson, John Rockwell (or was it C. Thomas Howell?), and Rae Dawn Chong. E.J. Oshins took me to dinner at Paul Newman's restaurant, The Hamptons, with playwright Mart Crowley, who'd witnessed a dreadful fight between Warren and Natalie Wood, and I also met Natalie's sister Lana, who shared factual material about Natalie and Warren's affair. If you're going to write about Hollywood, especially about Warren Beatty, it's good to get your material from the horse's mouth. I can't thank them enough, these movie personalities I edited and sometimes collaborated with; they permitted me to enter their world, which would subsequently become the setting of my biographies. Be warned, a writer ends up using everything he hears, and I was always mindful of what Mae West once advised: "Keep a diary now, and it'll keep ya later."

For the present book, I am especially indebted to Tony Bill, who, although we hadn't seen each other in many years, graciously consented to be interviewed in his home in the Venice section of L.A. Tony continues to direct fine movies, and, as we sat in his library, surrounded by his collection of first editions of American novels, he shared invaluable insights.

With my agent, Al Lowman, I spent an unforgettable day at the St. Regis Hotel in Century City, watching two important figures in Warren's life—Joan Collins and Shirley MacLaine—cavort through repeated takes for *Those Old Broads,* with co-star Debbie Reynolds. Between takes, they talked with a reporter from the *New York Times.* Carrie Fisher, who wrote the film, and who appeared with Warren in *Shampoo,* was also present.

In all, some five hundred interviews were conducted for *The Sexiest Man Alive,* either by me or Cathy Griffin, in California, New York, and many points in between. I wish to thank everyone who cooperated, especially the following: Eva Marie Saint, Richard Sylbert, Curtis Harrington, Tony Bill, Phyllis Diller, Elaine Dundy, Tricia Pelham Clinton Clark, Valerie Allen, Sharon Washington, Marvin Paige, Lisa Purdom, Bruce Cohen, Claudine Albuquerque, Rick Burke, Karen Bihari, Richard Mineards, Alicia Corning Clark, Rona Barrett, Judy Feiffer, Jill Schary, J. Randy Taraborrelli, Leonard Stanley, Tom Culver, Rita Stone, Julia Pierpont, Paul Hewson, Jeremy Zimmer, Sue Pollock, Ann Rapp, Donfeld, David Columbia, Arnold Margolin, Leonard Stanley, Julie Payne, Roy Moseley, Dorris Halsey, Marvin Paige, Ron Bernstein, Nan Morris-Robinson, Nancy Gullo, and Jo Ann Ratterree Wacaster.

Thanks, too, to Padric Gibson, Brad Eaton, and the staff at Borders bookstore on La Cienega for giving me a party on publication of *The Most Beautiful Woman in the World,* which came out while I was in town researching Warren Beatty; to the *Hollywood Reporter*'s George Christy for devoting a column to me; and to KABC's Ed Adamko for arranging a television interview.

My gratitude, and warm wishes, to the superb staff at the Margaret Herrick Library, Academy of Motion Picture Arts and Sciences. The Academy's research center in Beverly Hills, on La Cienega Boulevard, is a mecca of comfort and courtesy for movie historians, thanks to the immaculate professionalism of Oscar librarian Barbara Hall, reference head Sandra Archer, Stacey Behlmer in special collections, and Eddie Baker in the core collection. After hours of pouring over production memos, diaries, and photographs, I often repaired to nearby Lawry's steak house, where waitress Jennifer Fetherston served me roast beef and told me what Elizabeth Taylor had said in my banquette the night before.

For personal favors, and for the pleasure of their company during the writing of this book, I am grateful to Jill Evans, Patricia Soliman, Elizabeth Ashley, Norman Bogner, Matthew West, Millie Perkins, Mrs. Joseph Cotten (Patricia Medina), Mrs. Edward Dmytryk (Jean Porter), Anna Lee, Taylor Negron, Ingrid Margolin, Holly Woodlawn, Sandford Birdsey, Marva Green, Marcia Nasitir, Dr. Mani Bhaumik, Everett Watkins, Sherry Arden, Andrew Ettinger, Steven Gaines, Wendy Tucker, Alan Keener, Mark Hefferan, Tom Salciccia, Jr., Philip Stuart Barber, Jack Martin, Fabrice, Larry and Pat Behnke, Linda Thomas, Dante DeJoio, Bill Manville, Jean Egan, Penny Ripple, William Apt, Felice Bogner, Gary Grunder, Allston and Pepper James, Nell Crisante, Jimmy Thomas, Fannye Mae Gibbons, Bettye McCart, Lewis Briel, and Patrick O'Connor.

To my biological family in Florida and Texas, my love and gratitude: Bill and Joyce Amburn, Lu and Bill Bradbury, Richard and Julie Amburn, Lynn and Jeff Amburn, and Richie and Sydney Amburn. My brother Bill and his wife Joyce deserve a special word of praise for helping me build, virtually from the ground up, a magnificent new office, near the banks of the Suwanee River. After many battles with recalcitrant carpenters, Bill and Joyce took over the construction themselves, laboring from dawn to dusk for many months, ultimately creating the work space of my dreams.

Finally, to those most intimately connected to this book, from its inception to its destiny, I have words not only of gratitude but of love: Al Lowman, my agent for almost twenty years; editor and publisher Diane Reverand, who bought the proposal and edited the final manuscript; Tom Dupree, who took over from Diane and finished the job; my copyeditor, Greg Villepique, whose incisive and relentless queries proved invaluable; and Matthew Guma and Yung Kim, who helped in countless ways.

Cy Egan, the veteran New York newspaperman, now of Tryon, North Carolina, has been my mentor and first reader for many years. He took the rough draft in hand and, as he has on all my books, improved every page.

Complete bibliographical information is given after the first reference to a source; thereafter, only the author's surname, title of work or name of periodical, and page number are given. Some titles have been abbreviated after the initial citation, e.g., David Thomson's *Warren Beatty and Desert Eyes* is shortened to *Desert Eyes*; Lawrence J. Quirk's *The Films of Warren Beatty* to *The Films*; Donald Spoto's *The Kindness of Strangers* to *The Kindness*, Peter Biskind's *Easy Riders, Raging Bulls* to *Raging Bulls*, etc.

The Academy of Motion Picture Arts and Sciences is referred to as AMPAS.

PREFACE

1. Sharon Washington interview conducted by Cathy Griffin.
2. Joe Eszterhas, *American Rhapsody*, New York: Knopf, 2000, p. 391, confirms mirrors in bathroom.
3. At least those twenty-five and over, and upscale, Warren's "market" as defined by a research firm hired by Mike Mahem, a film distributor who was asked by Beatty to find the best way to re-release *Reds* in the 1980s (see David Thomson, *Warren Beatty and Desert Eyes*, New York: Vintage, 1987, p. 421).
4. James Spada, *Shirley and Warren*, New York: Collier/Macmillan, 1985, p. 211.
5. Kate Myers and Benjamin Svetkey, "News and Notes: Warren Gets Pregnant," *Entertainment Weekly*, documents MacPherson, Hawn, Bergen, Chung, Streisand, Sawyer, Fonda, Mitchell, Adjani, Bardot, Caron, Jackson, Dunaway, Bateman, Moore, Collins, Cher, Van Doren, Christie, Ekland, Phillips, and Madonna. Barbara Hershey: documented in Jennie Louise Frankel, Terrie Maxine Frankel, and Joanne Parrent, *You'll Never Make Love in This Town Again*, Beverly Hills, California: Dove, 1995, p. xvii. Jean Seberg and Susannah York: Jeannette Walls, *Dish*, New York: Avon, 2000, p. 127. Brooke Hayward, models Carol Alt and Dayle Haddon, and Israeli

Sippi Levine: David Thomson, *Desert Eyes*, pp. 349, 424. Jackie Onassis and Princess Margaret: Cathy Griffin, also Thomson, *Desert Eyes*, p. 350. Robin Menken, an improvisational comedienne: Thomson, *Desert Eyes*, p. 368. Lillian Hellman: Blair Sobol, former *Village Voice* reporter, interview with author. Inger Stevens, Princess Margaret, Leslie Caron, Dewi Sukarno, Michelle Phillips, Julie Christie: *Playgirl*, June 1975. Vanessa Redgrave: Academy of Motion Picture Arts and Sciences, Margaret Herrick Library (Robin Adams Sloan, *Los Angeles Herald Examiner*, Warren Beatty file, May 4, 1975), and Henry Ehrlich, "Warren and Julie: Together at Last," *Look*, June 1, 1971, p. 74. Barbara Harris: David Columbia, formerly of Sardi's. Princess Elizabeth of Yugoslavia: Melvyn Bragg, *Richard Burton,* Boston: Little, Brown, 1988, p. 269. Jackie Onassis, Brooke Hayward, Keaton: Quirk, *The Films,* p. 57. Jackie Onassis, Christie, Adjani, and Keaton: James Kaplan, "Mother Superior," *Allure,* November 1998, p. 277. Bardot: "Warren Beatty and Annette Bening, Hollywood's Power Couple," *Yahoo! News,* March 24, 2000, p. 2. Elizabeth Taylor: "Warren Beatty: Has He Lost Sex Appeal?" *Examiner,* April 25, 2000, p. 22. It was the *National Enquirer* ("Ladies Men," p. 24, unsigned, undated article, circa 2000) that once linked Warren romantically with fifty-seven famous women.

6. John Kercher, *Warren Beatty*, New York: Proteus, 1984, p. 102.

CHAPTER ONE

1. "Sarah Porterfield" was interviewed by Cathy Griffin in 2000.

2. Kercher, *Warren Beatty*, p. 8.

3. Ibid.

4. Shirley MacLaine, *My Lucky Stars*, New York: Bantam, 1995, pp. 5, 8.

5. Jon Whitcomb, "The Healthy Ego of Warren Beatty," *Cosmopolitan*, February 1962, p. 14.

6. Thomson, *Desert Eyes*, pp. 18, 61. Shirley MacLaine, *My Lucky Stars*, p. 8.

7. Whitcomb, op. cit.

8. Suzanne Munshower, *Warren Beatty*, New York: St. Martin's Press, 1983, p. 8.

9. Thomson, *Desert Eyes*, p. 56.

10. MacLaine, *My Lucky Stars*, p. 8.

11. Spada, *Shirley and Warren*, p. 4.

12. Stephen Singular, *The Rise and Rise of David Geffen*, Secaucus, New Jersey: Birch Lane Press, 1997, pp. 7–8.

13. MacLaine, *My Lucky Stars*, p. 8.

14. Spada, *Shirley and Warren*, p. 112.

15. Kercher, *Warren Beatty*, p. 8. MacLaine, *My Lucky Stars*, pp. 20, 34. Thomson, *Desert Eyes*, p. 30

16. MacLaine, *My Lucky Stars* pp. 34, 194, 196.

17. Lawrence J. Quirk, *The Films of Warren Beatty*, New York: Citadel, 1979, 1990, p. 28.

18. Munshower, *Beatty*, p. 7.

19. Spada, *Shirley and Warren*, p. 5.

20. Spada, *Shirley and Warren*, p. 4.

21. Eszterhas, *American Rhapsody*, pp. 390–391.

22. Author interview with Jo Ann Ratterree, 2001.

23. Spada, *Shirley and Warren*, p. 40.

24. Eszterhas, *American Rhapsody*, pp. 389–390.

25. Spada, *Shirley and Warren*, p. 2.

26. MacLaine, *My Lucky Stars*, p. 8.

27. Peter Biskind, "He Stars, She Stars," *Vanity Fair*, February 2000, p. 117.

28. Quirk, *The Films*, pp. 9–31.

29. John Phillips and Jim Jerome, *Papa John*, New York: Dell, 1986, p. 221.

30. Spada, *Shirley and Warren*, pp. 5–6.

31. MacLaine, *My Lucky Stars*, pp 64, 66. Steve Parker and Sachi lived in his adopted country of Japan. Shirley and Steve separated officially in 1976 and later divorced. According to *People*, Parker "transferred millions of dollars to his girlfriend's account": *2001 People Entertainment Almanac*, New York: People Books, 2000, p. 488.

32. Munshower, *Beatty*, p. 13.

33. Ibid., p. 7.

34. John Parker, *Warren Beatty*, London: Headline, 1993, p. 22.

35. Thomson, *Desert Eyes*, p. 26.

36. Munshower, *Beatty*, p. 7.

37. Thomson, *Desert Eyes*, p. 50.

38. Beatty file, Hedda Hopper Collection, AMPAS.

39. Stella Adler: Peter Manso, *Brando*, New York: Hyperion, 1994, pp. 106–107, 111–112. Andrew Yule, *Life on the Wire: The Life and Art of Al Pacino*, New York: Donald I. Fine, 1991, pp. 108–109. Spada, *Shirley and Warren*, p. 19.

40. Cathy Griffin interviewed Rona Barrett in 2000. Also see Rona Barrett, *Miss Rona*, New York: Bantam, 1974, pp. 86–87.

41. Munshower, *Beatty*, p. 95.

42. Unsigned article, "The First Time Warren Beatty Ran for President," *Examiner*, October 26, 1999, p. 15.

43. Rafe Klinger, "Desperate Son Begs Ailing Dudley for Reunion," *Globe*, January 9, 2001, p. 10. "The Survival of Tuesday," *Time*, May 15, 1972, re: Weld and Lockwood.

44. James Spada, *Streisand and Her Life*, New York: Crown, 1995, p. 16.

45. Joan Rivers in a conversation with me after agent Arnold Stiefel sold me her book proposal and sample manuscript, *Pepper January: Comedy With Spice* (later published as *Enter Laughing*) when I was editor in chief of the Delacorte Press in the 1970s. Spada, *Streisand and Her Life*, pp. 53–54, wrote that the play *Driftwood* by Maurice Tei Dunn, was staged at the Garret Theater, but that Barbra and Joan didn't have a scene together, and the play wasn't about lesbians. Streisand played a tough barfly named Lorna, and Joan played the uptight Miss Blake. Diana's marriage and Rosalind's birth: Anne Edwards, *Streisand,* Boston: Little, Brown, 1997, p. 48.

46. Spada, *Streisand and Her Life*, p. 67.

47. Nellie Bly, *Barbra Streisand*, New York: Pinnacle, 1994, p. 31.

48. Donald Spoto, *The Kindness of Strangers: The Life of Tennessee Williams*, Boston: Little, Brown, 1985, pp. 110, 112, 300.

49. Editorial notes, the Delacorte Press, 1975. I published Josh Logan's memoirs, *Josh* and *Movie Stars, Real People, and Me*, at the Delacorte Press, where I was editor in chief from 1971 to 1978.

50. Thomson, *Desert Eyes*, p. 79.

51. Peter Collier, *The Fondas*, New York: G. P. Putnam's Sons, 1991, p. 120.

52. Dominick Dunne, "Murder Most Unforgettable," *Vanity Fair*, April 2001, p. 278. My interviews with Nan Morris-Robinson were conducted in 2000–2001.

53. *E: True Hollywood Story*, April 1, 2001.

54. "Secrets of Golden Oldies," *Globe*, June 5, 2001, p. 46.

55. Munshower, *Beatty*, p. 24.

56. Joan Collins, *Past Imperfect*, New York: Wings, 1978, 1984, pp. 113, 115.

57. Collier, *The Fondas*, p. 119.

58. Warren once told Hedda Hopper, "I did quite a few small parts in plays before I got into *Loss of Roses*." Beatty file, Hopper Collection, AMPAS.

59. Kercher, *Warren Beatty*, p. 10.

60. Julia Phillips, *You'll Never Eat Lunch in This Town Again*, New York: Random House, 1991, p. 160.

61. Collins, *Past Imperfect*, p. 121.

62. Whitcomb, *Cosmopolitan*, p. 14.

63. Joshua Logan to author.

64. Spoto, *The Kindness*, p. 341.

65. Munshower, *Beatty*, p. 19.

66. Kercher, *Warren Beatty*, p. 10.

67. Patrick McGilligan, *Jack's Life: A Biography of Jack Nicholson*, New York: Norton, 1994, p. 115.

68. Collins, *Past Imperfect*, p. 121.

69. Spada, *Shirley and Warren*, p. 211.

70. Collier, *The Fondas*, p. 117.

71. Warren G. Harris, *Natalie & R. J.*, New York: Doubleday 1998, p. 76.

72. Charlene Tilton, "Thumbs Down," *Globe*, April 3, 2001, p. 12. Gibson: Dominick Dunne's column, *Vanity Fair*, August 2001, p. 84.

CHAPTER TWO

1. William Ball Baer, editor, *Elia Kazan Interviews*, Jackson, Mississippi: University of Mississippi Press, 2000, p. 268.

2. Suzanne Finstad, *Natasha*, New York: Harmony, 2001, p. 222.

3. Spada, *Shirley and Warren*, p. 51.

4. Spoto, *The Kindness*, p. 300.

5. Quirk, *The Films*, p. 74.

6. Kazan revealed this in a talk at the Museum of Modern Art Department of Film, February 11, 1971. See Charles Silver, *The Films of Elia Kazan*. See also Finstad, *Natasha*, p. 215.

7. Baer, editor, *Elia Kazan Interviews*, pp. 84–85.

8. Finstad, *Natasha*, pp. 222–223, quotes Bob Jiras, Natalie's confidant.

9. Sam Kashner, "Natalie Wood's Fatal Voyage," *Vanity Fair*, March 2000, p. 220.

10. Finstad, *Natasha*, p. 192.

11. Ibid., pp. 120, 209–210.

12. Estelle Victoria Changas, *The Films of Elia Kazan*, UCLA master's thesis, AMPAS, p. 603.

13. Finstad, *Natasha*, p. 230, writes that Crowley was "a homosexual" and Natalie's "best girlfriend" and "caretaker."

14. Kashner, *Vanity Fair*, p. 223.

15. Finstad, *Natasha*, p. 211.

16. Ibid., p. 230; Redford quote, p. 222; "Mental Anguish," p. 223; "about thirteen," p. 222; Maguire/Kranze quote, p. 222.

17. Ibid., pp. 222, 230. Despite Kazan's account, Finstad denies that Warren and Natalie had sex during *Splendor*.

18. Kashner, *Vanity Fair*, p. 226.

19. Finstad, *Natasha*, p. 222.

20. Changas, *The Films of Elia Kazan*, p. 603.

21. Hollis Alpert, "What Goes on Here," *Woman's Day*, circa 1961.

22. Kashner, *Vanity Fair*, p. 223.

23. See Finstad's *Natasha* pp. 234–235, and in Pete Trujilla and Jeff Samuels, "The Day Natalie Wood Caught Robert Wagner in Bed—With a Man," *Globe*, May 1, 2001, pp. 24–25.

24. Finstad, *Natasha*, pp. 234–235; the source of the Joan Eliot story is a best-selling author and magazine editor who requested anonymity.

25. Lana Wood, *Natalie*, New York: Putnam, 1984, p. 61.

26. Finstad, *Natasha*, p. 238.

27. Changas, *The Films of Elia Kazan*, p. 670.

28. Finstad, *Natasha*, pp. 260–261.

29. "The Biggest New Name in American Entertainment—It's Warren Beatty," *Life*, November 3, 1961 (unpaged clipping, Beatty file, AMPAS).

30. Hedda Hopper collection, Harry Mines to Arthur P. Jacobs, October 26, 1960, AMPAS.

31. Munshower, *Beatty*, p. 31.

32. Baer, ed., *Elia Kazan Interviews* p. 149.

33. Changas, *The Films of Elia Kazan*, pp. 122, 155.

34. Kercher, *Warren Beatty*, p. 7.

35. Parker, *Warren Beatty*, p. 89.

36. Cher: "News & Notes: Warren Gets Pregnant," *Entertainment Weekly*, p. 15, undated clip, Beatty file, AMPAS. Paragraph "After PT": source for WB and RFK is Peter Bart, *The Gross*, New York: St. Martin's Press, 1999, p. 185.

37. William Lee Jackson, "Bye-Bye Beatty," *The Players*, Fall 1964, p. 55.

38. Dennis McDougal, *The Last Mogul*, New York: Crown, 1998, p. 302.

39. Faye Dunaway and Betsy Sharkey, *Looking for Gatsby*, New York, Simon and Schuster, 1995, p. 93.

40. P. J. Oppenheimer, "The Brothers Have It!" *Family Weekly*, April 8, 1962, p. 18.

41. Ibid., p. 110.

42. Peter Harry Brown, *Reluctant Goddess*, New York: St. Martin's Press, 1986, p. 237.

43. "Say What?" *Examiner*, July 18, 2000, p. 23.

44. Changas, *The Films of Elia Kazan*, p. 603.

45. Finstad, *Natasha*, p. 242.

46. Wood, *Natalie*, pp. 62–64.

47. Harris, *Natalie & R.J.*, pp. 65, 98–102.

48. Kashner, *Vanity Fair*, p. 226. True-crime writer/biographer Suzanne Finstad calls this incident "unsubstantiated, recycled gossip" in *Natasha*, and gives another version of the night at Chasen's, evidently based on an interview with Tom Bosley, who once had dinner with Natalie at the restaurant. In the Finstad-Bosley version, Natalie arrives at Chasen's alone, having broken off her affair with Warren at the airport. Finstad, seemingly wanting to deny Warren's impact on Natalie's life, may not have taken into account that the couple dined at Chasen's more than once, and that both versions may have occurred, at different times.

49. Harris, *Natalie & R.J.*, p. 117.

50. Ibid., pp. 117–118. Said a friend, "Warren's a terrible user of people. He'd gotten all the publicity mileage he could from the relationship. When it started, nobody ever heard of Warren Beatty. By the time he left Natalie they were calling him the hottest star since Brando."

51. Munshower, *Beatty*, p. 67.

52. Ibid.

53. Ibid., p. 68.

54. Kashner, *Vanity Fair*, p. 118.

55. Ibid.

56. Wood, *Natalie*, p. 66.

CHAPTER THREE

1. The Bunny's name has been changed to protect her anonymity. Cathy Griffin conducted the interview.

2. John Parker, *Polanski*, London: Gollancz, 1993, p. 116.

3. Gretchen Edgren, *Inside the Playboy Mansion: If You Don't Swing, Don't Ring*, Santa Monica, Calif.: General Publishing, 1998, includes the following merrymakers at Hef's mansions: Bernie Cornfield (p. 217), Jimmy Connors (p. 218), Berry Gordy (p. 220), Jim Brown (p. 220), Gay Talese (p. 236), John Phillip Law (p. 284), Barry Goldwater Jr. (p. 284), Joe Namath (p. 243).

4. Roman Polanski, *Roman*, New York: Morrow, 1984, p. 280.

5. Parker, *Polanski*, pp. 99, 190, 224.

6. J. B. White, *Hefner Unauthorized*, a television biography produced in 2000 by Leanne Moore, directed by Peter Werner and starring Randall Batinkoff and Natasha Gregson Wagner.

7. Interview with Karen Bihari, 2001.

8. Thomson, *Desert Eyes*, p. 233.

9. Ibid., p. 147.

10. Kercher, *Warren Beatty*, p. 20.

11. According to Williams's friend Dotson Rader, Warren came to Williams's hotel room wearing a bathrobe, but Williams sighed and said, "Go home to bed, Warren. I said you had the part." See Thomson, *Desert Eyes,* p. 147.

12. Parker, *Beatty*, p. 64.

13. Spada, *Shirley and Warren*, p. 64.

14. Beatty file, Hedda Hopper Collection, AMPAS.

15. Thomson, *Desert Eyes*, p. 147.

16. Radie Harris, *Radie's World*, New York: Putnam, 1975, p. 227.

17. Spada, *Shirley and Warren*, pp. 64, 66. Cathy Griffin interviewed Valerie Allen.

18. Anne Edwards, *Vivien Leigh*, New York: Simon and Schuster, p. 245, writes that Vivien Leigh found him to be arrogant and uncooperative during the shooting of *Roman Spring*.

19. Spada, *Shirley and Warren*, p. 67.

20. Ibid.

21. Ibid., pp. 69–70. His awkward reply to a reporter who'd asked what he looked for in a role: "For instance, if I started working . . . and some of the questions I don't have answers to . . . Something hits me, it hits me . . . I read something and I say, 'Oh, I *know* that moment.' You never know what it is you really look for." Ibid., p. 72: "I don't speak as concisely and articulately as I would like to."

22. Ibid., p. 69.

23. The company made the statement about Warren in an advertisement for an article by Joe Laitin.

24. Spada, *Shirley and Warren*, p. 72.

25. Ibid., p. 83.

26. Peter Biskind, *Easy Riders*, *Raging Bulls*, New York: Simon and Schuster, 1998, p. 25.

27. Biskind, *Vanity Fair*, p. 173.

28. Biskind, *Raging Bulls*, p. 25.

29. Marion Meade, *The Unruly Life of Woody Allen*, New York: Scribner, 2000, p. 64.

30. A.M. Sperber and Eric Lax, *Bogart*, New York: Morrow, 1997, pp. 503–504.

31. Peter Bart, *Who Killed Hollywood?* Los Angeles: Barricade, 1999, p. 192. Biskind, *Raging Bulls*, p. 26.

32. Spada, *Shirley and Warren*, p. 84.

33. Munshower, *Beatty*, p. 38.

34. Ibid.

35. Harry Mines to Hedda Hopper, March 15, 1964, Hopper Collection, AMPAS.

36. Thomas Thompson, "There's Something Awfully Peculiar About Warren Beatty These Days," *Los Angeles*, March 1975 pp. 40, 53.

37. Spada, *Shirley and Warren*, p. 101.

38. Jackson, *The Players*, p. 58.

39. Ibid., p. 57.

40. Thomson, *Desert Eyes*, p. 240.

41. Jackson, *The Players*, p. 55.

42. Cathy Griffin interview.

43. Spada, *Shirley and Warren*, pp. 101, 110.

44. Ibid., p. 102.

45. Munshower, *Beatty*, p. 46.

46. Seymour Hersch, *The Dark Side of Camelot*, New York: Little Brown, 1998, pp. 113, 118–120.

47. Cathy Griffin interview.

48. Ibid.

49. Munshower, p. 41. Hall-Caron marriage, Tim Ewbank and Stafford Hildred refer in *Julie Christie* (London: Andre Deutsch, 2000. p. 160) to "Peter Hall's own admitted adultery with an unnamed woman."

50. Yule, *Life on the Wire*, p. 201.

51. Sheilah Graham, *Hollywood Revisited*, New York: St. Martin's, 1984, p. 242.

52. Finstad, *Natasha*, pp. 248–249, 252, 269.

53. Polanski, *Roman*, p. 258.

54. Parker, *Polanski*, pp. 104, 106.

55. Parker, *Polanski*, p. 173.

56. Polanski, *Roman*, p. 267.

57. Munshower, *Beatty*, p. 46.

58. Parker, *Warren Beatty*, p. 5.

59. Ibid., p. 47.

60. James Spada, *Peter Lawford*, New York: Bantam, 1999, p. 392.

61. Parker, *Warren Beatty*, pp. 48–49.

62. Spada, *Shirley and Warren*, p. 133. Munshower, *Beatty*, p. 75.

63. Biskind, *Raging Bulls*, pp. 27–28, 120. Truffaut's dislike of Beatty: Antoine de Baecque and Serge Toubiana, *Truffaut*, Berkeley, CA: University of California Press, 1999, p. 212.

64. Bart, *The Gross*, p. 192.

65. Mary Murphy, "Don Juan with a Social Conscience," *Los Angeles Times*, May 31, 1974.

66. Thomson, *Desert Eyes*, p. 255.

67. Dunaway and Sharkey, *Looking for Gatsby*, p. 138.

68. Munshower, *Beatty*, p. 58. Thomson, *Desert Eyes*, p. 251.

69 Munshower, *Beatty*, p. 49.

70. Thompson, *Los Angeles*, p. 53.

71. Spada, *Shirley and Warren*, p. 112.

72. Pamela Des Barres, *Take Another Little Piece of My Heart*, New York: Berkley, 1993, pp. 193–194.

73. Thomson, *Desert Eyes*, p. 253.

74. Spada, *Shirly and Warren*, pp. 110, 112.

75. Army Archerd, "Just for Variety," *Daily Variety*, June 21, 1968.

76. Dunaway and Sharkey, *Looking for Gatsby*, p. 120. Tuesday Weld: Eugene Archer, "Give Him Tuesday—Sunday, Monday, Always," *New York Times,* December 13, 1970.

77. Finstad, *Natasha*, p. 270.

78. Fred Lawrence Guiles, *Jane Fonda*, New York: Pinnacle, 1981, p. 153.

79. Dunaway and Sharkey, *Looking for Gatsby*, pp. 11, 25, 71, 96, 121, 123.

80. Jennifer Lee, *Tarnished Angel*, New York: Thunder's Mouth, 1991, p. 54.

81. Munshower, *Warren Beatty*, p. 59.

82. Thomson, *Desert Eyes*, p. 433.

83. Biskind, *Easy Riders,* p. 34.

84. William Goldman, *Which Lie Did I Tell?*, New York: Pantheon, 2000, pp. 88, 221.

85. *Los Angeles Herald Examiner*, August 31, 1975, untitled, unpaged clipping, Beatty file, AMPAS.

86. "Murder on the Run," narrated by Roger Mudd, The History Channel; circa 2000.

87. Spada, *Shirley and Warren*, p. 122.

88. *Los Angeles Herald Examiner*, August 31, 1975, unidentified clip, Beatty file, AMPAS.

89. Dunaway and Sharkey, *Looking for Gatsby*, p. 139.

90. Spada, *Shirley and Warren*, p. 124

91. As a result, the Hollywood Women's Press Club, which had given him the Sour Apple Award, gave him the Golden Apple Award. He became one of the few actors to receive both: Munshower, *Beatty*, p. 64.

92. Yule, *Life on the Wire*, p. 227.

93. Anthony Holden, *Behind the Oscar*, New York: Simon and Schuster, 1993, p. 265. *Bonnie and Clyde* earnings: Jim Burke, *Warren Beatty,* New York: Tower, 1976, p. 173.

94. Dunaway and Sharkey, *Looking for Gatsby*, p. 173.

95. Unsigned, undated *Motion Picture* clipping, p. 66, Beatty file, AMPAS.

96. Dunaway and Sharkey, *Looking for Gatsby*, pp. 123, 144, 187, 234, 319.

97. Graham, *Hollywood Revisited*, p. 80.

98. Rod Gibson, "Stars Rocked by Tinseltown Tell-All," *Globe*, August 8, 2000, p. 41; also see Eszterhas, *American Rhapsody*, passim.

99. "Ladies' Men," *National Enquirer*, undated clip, p. 24.

100. Ibid.

101. Robert Evans, *The Kid Stays in the Picture*, New York: Hyperion, 1994, p. 289.

102. Robert Sam Anson, "The Titan," *Vanity Fair*, April 2001, p. 310.

103. Ibid., p. 421.

104. *Cosmopolitan*, November 1968; *Screen Parade*, June 1969; *Movie World*, June 1969; Shirley Mann to Finstad, *Natasha*, p. 245.

CHAPTER FOUR

1. Polanski, *Roman*, pp. 286, 290.

2. Parker, *Polanski*, p. 128.

3. Parker, *Warren Beatty*, p. 182.

4. Greg King, *Sharon Tate and the Manson Murders*, New York: Barricade, 2000, p. 95

5. Yule, *Life on the Wire*, p. 44.

6. Ibid., pp. 45, 48, 93, 153, 259.

7. Munshower, *Beatty*, p. 110.

8. Jennings Parrott, *Los Angeles Times*, April 26, 1973, untitled, unpaged, Beatty file, AMPAS.

9. Glenys Roberts, *Bardot*, London: Sidgwick & Jackson, 1984, p. 171.

10. Ibid., pp. 189, 224–225, 230–232.

11. Guiles, *Jane Fonda*, p. 154.

12. Donald G. McNeil Jr., "In a City Gone to the Dogs, Bardot's on the Case," *New York Times,* March 2, 2001, p. A4.

13. Tom King, *The Operator*, New York: Random House, 2000, p. 184.

14. Munshower, *Beatty,* p. 110.

15. Unsigned, undated *Motion Picture* article, p. 68, Beatty file, AMPAS.

16. Biskind, *Vanity Fair*, p. 173.

17. Munshower, *Beatty*, p. 89.

18. Evan Thomas, *Robert F. Kennedy*, New York: Simon & Schuster, 2001, passim.

19. Spada, *Shirley and Warren*, p. 149.

20. Munshower, *Beatty*, p. 79.

21. Munshower, *Beatty*, pp. 73, 77.

22. Holden, *Behind the Oscar*, p. 73.

23. Munshower, *Beatty*, p. 77.

24. Biskind, *Raging Bulls*, p. 47.

25. "My Air of Abandonment That Appeals to Men," *Life*, unsigned, undated, p. 66.

26. Graham, *Hollywood Revisited*, p. 177.

27. Munshower, *Beatty*, p. 82. Wycherley, Christy, *Shampoo* connection: Ewbank and Hildred, Julie Christie, p. 203

28. Spada, *Shirley & Warren*, p. 165.

29. Biskind, *Vanity Fair*, p. 173.

30. Thompson, *Los Angeles*, p. 52.

31. James Baron, *Los Angeles Herald Examiner*, December 20, 1974, untitled, unpaged clip, Beatty file, AMPAS.

32. Lee, *Tarnished Angel*, pp. 29–30.

33. Susan Crimp, "Drew Barrymore's Mom," *Star*, June 20, 2000, p. 7; also see Leah and Elina Furman, *Happily Ever After: The Drew Barrymore Story*, New York: Ballantine, 2000, pp. 12–13.

34. Spada, *Shirley and Warren*, p. 140.

35. Sally Davis, "And the Hairdressers Shall Inherit the Earth," *Los Angeles*, undated clipping in Beatty file, AMPAS, p. 54.

36. Munshower, *Beatty*, p. 51. Salaries: Henry Ehrlich, "Warren and Julie: Together at Last," June 1, 1971, *Look*, p. 73. Warren also turned down *Ryan's Daughter*, for a reported three million dollars.

37. L.A. Justice, "Battle of the Aging Superstars," *Examiner*, May 30, 2000, p. 42.

38. George Stevens archive, *The Only Game in Town* files, Margaret Herrick Library, AMPAS.

39. Ibid. Fox memo, August 19, 1969.

40. Ibid. George Stevens to James Martin, September 9, 1968.

41. Ibid. George Stevens to Al Horwitz, Pax Enterprise, Beverly Hills, September 30, 1968.

42. Nathan Fain, "Liz Taylor's Look Is a Little Like Being Electrocuted," *Houston Post*, October 19, 1968.

43. John Knott, "Liquor by the Drink Spurs Construction in Millions," *Memphis Commercial Appeal*, February 10, 1970.

44. Phillips and Jerome, *Papa John*, p. 304.

45. Phillips, *You'll Never Eat*, p. 209.

46. King, *Sharon Tate*, p. 98.

47. Ibid., pp. 113–114. Ira and Julie: Ewbank, Christie, p. 207.

48. Dunne, *Vanity Fair,* p. 278.

49. Parker, *Polanski*, pp. 138–139. "Polanski Was Cheating on His Pregnant wife," *Globe*, June 6, 2000, p. 45. King, *Sharon Tate* pp. 168, 177.

50. Polanski, *Roman*, p. 349.

51. Dunaway and Sharkey, *Looking for Gatsby*, pp. 25, 251–252.

52. Parker, *Polanski*, pp. 106, 108.

53. Ibid., p. 138.

54. King, *Sharon Tate*, p. 180. "Dumb hag," ibid., p. 167.

55. Polanski, *Roman*, pp. 302–303.

56. King, *Sharon Tate*, p. 138.

57. Biskind, *Easy Riders*, p. 78.

58. King, *Sharon Tate*, pp. 152–153.

59. Ibid., p. 174.

60. Marshall Terrill, *Steve McQueen*, New York: Donald I. Fine, 1993, p. 187.

61. King, *Sharon Tate,* pp. 172, 182. Parker, *Polanski*, pp. 157–158.

62. Dunne, *Vanity Fair,* p. 280.

63. King, *Sharon Tate*, p. 221.

64. Parker, *Polanski*, p. 150.

65. Dunne, *Vanity Fair,* p. 282.

66. Biskind, *Raging Bulls*, p. 79. Later, when Polanski was under fire for perhaps having brought on the massacre by his lifestyle, he denied the more gruesome aspects of the killings, and also insisted that Sebring had been fully clothed. Polanski was perhaps reacting to an obvious slap at his male vanity.

67. Polanski, *Roman*, pp. 308–309.

68. Biskind, *Raging Bulls*, p. 78.

69. Ibid.

70. Dunne, *Vanity Fair,* p. 278.

71. Polanski, *Roman*, pp. 318–319.

72. Parker, *Polanski*, p. 160.

73. Polanski, *Roman*, pp. 316–317.

74. King, *Sharon Tate*, p. 239.

75. Parker, *Polanski*, p. 162.

76. Parker, *Polanski*, p. 173. Polanski, *Roman*, pp. 321–322.

77. Parker, *Warren Beatty*, pp. 157–158.

78. Polanski, *Roman*, p. 315.

79. Marie C. Vance, "Death of Innocence," *Examiner*, February 20, 2001, pp. 48–49.

80. Biskind, *Raging Bulls*, p. 79.

81. Parker, *Warren Beatty*, p. 136.

82. Biskind, *Ranging Bulls*, p. 132.

83. Parker, *Warren Beatty*, p. 171.

84. Dunne, *Vanity Fair*, p. 278.

85. Polanski, *Roman*, p. 329.

86. Ibid., p. 330.

87. Ibid.

88. Parker, *Warren Beatty*, pp. 213, 218.

89. Biskind, *Raging Bulls*, p. 160.

90. Polanski, *Roman*, pp. 214, 334, 340.

91. Parker, *Warren Beatty*, p. 177.

92. Ibid., p. 178. Thomson, *Desert Eyes,* p. 349.

93. Ibid. Thomson, *Desert Eyes*, p. 231.

94. Parker, *Warren Beatty*, p. 178.

95. Lawrence Van Gelder, "Pauline Kael," *New York Times* obituary, September 4, 2001, p. A21.

96. Patrick McGilligan, *Robert Altman*, New York: St. Martin's, 1989, p. 345.

97. Biskind, *Raging Bulls*, pp. 103–105.

98. McGilligan, *Robert Altman*, p. 345.

99. Biskind, *Raging Bulls*, pp. 89, 104–105, 190.

100. Peter Feibleman, *Lilly*, New York: Morrow, 1998, pp. 26–29.

101. Parker, *Warren Beatty*, p. 177.

102. Parker, *Warren Beatty*, p. 175. Biskind, p. 104.

103. Biskind, *Raging Bulls*, p. 105.

104. Ibid., p. 109.

105. Spada, *Shirley and Warren*, p. 138.

106. Thompson, *Los Angeles*, p. 103.

107. Sophie Vokes-Dudgeon, "Goldie Hawn and Daughter Kate Hudson's Secret Wild Life," *National Enquirer*, July 3, 2001, pp. 40–41.

108. Spada, *Shirley and Warren*, p. 140.

109. Quirk, *The Films*, p. 171.

110. Justice, *Examiner*, p. 42.

111. Bart, *Who Killed Hollywood?* pp. 188, 193. Bart, *The Gross*, p. 183.

112. Munshower, *Beatty*, pp. 51–52.

113. "Behind the Music," *Globe*, July 3, 2001, p. 67.

114. Meade, *Woody Allen*, p. 65.

115. James Spada, *Streisand and Her Life*, New York: Crown, 1995, p. 291.

116. Ibid., pp. 292, 299, 303.

117. Chris Chase, *New York Times*, June 25, 1975, untitled, unpaged clip, Beatty file, AMPAS.

118. Thomson, *Desert Eyes*, p. 321. Burke, Beatty, p. 45.

119. "Party System," *W*, September 2000, p. 150.

120. Stephen E. Ambrose, *The Wild Blue*, New York: Simon and Schuster, 2001, pp. 161, 234, 245, 251.

121. Judy Klemsrud, "Warren Beatty—Back Where He Belongs," *New York Times*, March 17, 1974, p. 37.

122. Spada, *Shirley and Warren*, pp. 149–150, 294.

123. Parker, *Warren Beatty*, p. 183.

124. Lee, *Tarnished Angel*, p. 66.

125. Frankel et al., *You'll Never Make Love*, p. xvi.

126. Lee, *Tarnished Angel*, pp. 55–56.

127. Bart, *Who Killed Hollywood?*, p. 193.

128. W.A. Harbinson, *George C. Scott*, New York: Pinnacle, 1977, pp. 198–199.

129. Parker, *Warren Beatty*, pp. 183–184. Ewbank, Christie, p. 202.

130. Rachel Abramowitz, *Is That a Gun in Your Pocket?*, New York: Random House, p. 97.

131. *New Times*, October 19, 1974, unsigned, untitled, unpaged clip in Beatty file, AMPAS.

132. Spada, *Shirley and Warren*, p. 152.

133. Ibid., p. 165.

134. Parker, *Warren Beatty*, p. 212.

135. Ibid., p. 211.

136. Lee, *Tarnished Angel*, pp. 31–38, 40, 47–49, 64.

137. Ibid., p. 33.

138. Ibid., pp. 48–49.

139. Ibid., p. 52.

140. Biskind, *Easy Riders*, pp. 156, 190.

141. Parker, *Warren Beatty*, p. 184.

142. Dunaway and Sharkey, *Looking for Gatsby*, p. 252.

143. Interview supplied by by Cathy Griffin on October 25, 2000.

144. Biskind, *Raging Bulls*, p. 107.

145. Ibid., p. 181.

146. Quirk, *The Films*, pp. 15, 42.

CHAPTER FIVE

1. Robert J. Emery, *The Directors, Take Two*, New York: TV Books, 2000, p. 100.

2. Biskind, *Raging Bulls*, p. 365.

3. Ibid., pp. 269–70, 297.

4. Cathy Griffin interview.

5. Edgren, *Inside the Playboy Mansion*, pp. 218, 235, 263.

6. *Los Angeles* magazine, unidentified clip, Beatty file, AMPAS.

7. Abramowitz, *Is That a Gun*, p. 98.

8. Ibid.

9. Patricia Nolan, "I'm Glad Streisand Stole My Hubby," *Globe*, March 20, 2001, p. 6.

10. Bly, *Barbra Streisand*, p. 240.

11. Kercher, *Warren Beatty*, p. 102.

12. Polanski, *Roman*, p. 353.

13. *2001 People Entertainment Almanac*, p. 86.

14. Dorothy Manners, *Los Angeles Herald Examiner*, August 18, 1975, untitled, unpaged clip, Beatty file, AMPAS.

15. Biskind, *Raging Bulls*, p. 107.

16. Ibid.

17. Bill Desowitz, "More Than Soap Bubbles," *Los Angeles Times*, August 31, 2000, pp. 13–14.

18. Parker, *Warren Beatty*, p. 204.

19. Kercher, *Warren Beatty*, pp. 102–103.

20. Hank Grant, "Rambling Reporter," *Hollywood Reporter*, May 30, 1974, unpaged clip, Beatty file, AMPAS.

21. Spada, *Shirley and Warren*, p. 166.

22. Nicolas Kent, *Naked Hollywood*, New York: St. Martin's, 1991, p. 241. Biskind, *Raging Bulls*, p. 191.

23. Biskind, *Raging Bulls*, p. 193.

24. Ibid., pp. 107, 193.

25. Ibid., p. 190.

26. Ibid., p. 305.

27. Goldman, *Which Lie Did I Tell?*, p. 222.

28. Biskind, *Raging Bulls*, pp. 193–194.

29. Munshower, *Beatty*, p. 80.

30. Robin Adams Sloan, *Los Angeles Herald Examiner*, April 16, 1947, untitled, unpaged clip, Beatty file, AMPAS.

31. *Los Angeles Herald Examiner*, June 6, 1977, untitled, unpaged clip, Beatty file, AMPAS.

32. Biskind, *Raging Bulls*, p. 82.

33. Thomson, *Desert Eyes*, p. 326.

34. Spada, *Shirley and Warren*, p. 166.

35. Walls, *Dish*, p. 127.

36. Biskind, *Raging Bulls*, p. 304.

37. Ibid., p. 305.

38. Ibid., p. 304.

39. Ibid., p. 119.

40. Michael Medved, "Emotions, Not Money, Propel Writers Strike," *USA Today*, May 1, 2001, p. 15A.

41. Biskind, *Raging Bulls*, p. 194.

42. "Gene was still a hairstylist when he died in 2001," said Nan Morris-Robinson. "He had a booth in a Beverly Hills shop, with a private clientele, and he lived in Trousdale Estates." In *Shampoo*'s credits, Shacove was listed as technical adviser.

43. Biskind, *Raging Bulls*, p. 303.

44. Ibid., p. 304.

45. Ibid.

46. Leonard Maltin, ed., *Leonard Maltin's Movie & Video Guide, 2001 Edition*, New York: Signet, 2000, p. 1249.

47. *Variety*, September 25, 1975, unsigned, untitled, unpaged clip, Beatty file, AMPAS.

48. Cathy Griffin interview.

49. Abramowitz, *Is That a Gun*, pp. 67–68.

50. Alan Ebert, *Ladies' Home Journal* article quoted in Munshower, *Beatty*, p. 106.

51. Lee, *Tarnished Angel*, p. 56. McGilligan, *Jack's Life,* p. 262. Parker, *Warren Beatty,* pp. 249–250.

52. Liv Ullmann, *Changing*, New York: Bantam, 1977, p. 204.

53. Frankel et al., *You'll Never Make Love*, pp. 23, 41–43.

54. Ibid., p. 99

55. Ibid., pp. 97–101.

56. Ibid., p. 101.

57. Frankel et al., *You'll Never Make Love*, pp. 231–238. Robin Mizrahi, "Heidi Fleiss Hooks 'Pvt. Ryan' Hunk," *Globe*, August 14, 2001, pp. 6–7.

58. Stephen M. Silverman, *Public Spectacles*, New York: Dutton, 1981, p. 43.

59. Biskind, *Raging Bulls*, pp. 194–195.

60. McGilligan, *Jack's Life*, pp. 260–261. Nicholson's height is "five nine and a half," p. 79.

61. Walls, *Dish*, p. 206.

62. Spada, *Shirley and Warren*, p. 211.

63. Ibid., p. 227.

64. McGilligan, *Jack's Life*, p. 238.

65. Biskind, *Raging Bulls*, p. 195.

66. Daphne Merkin, "An Independent Woman," *New York Times Magazine*, January 21, 2001, p. 36.

67. McGilligan, *Jack's Life*, p. 245.

68. Ibid., pp. 44–45, 262–263.

69. Ibid., p. 261.

70. Cathy Griffin interview.

71. McGilligan, *Jack's Life,* p. 262.

72. Ibid., pp. 47, 262.

73. Phillips and Jerome, *Papa John*, pp. 325–326.

74. David Cobb Craig, "Passages," *People*, March 13, 2000, p. 103. Carnie Wilson, "Gaining Control," *People*, April 17, 2000, pp. 55–58.

75. Phillips and Jerome, *Papa John*, pp. 260, 284.

76. Cathy Griffin interview.

77. Lee, *Tarnished Angel*, pp. 77, 82, 85, 233.

78. Munshower, *Beatty*, p. 111.

79. Ibid., p. 112.

80. Robin Adams Sloan, *Los Angeles Herald Examiner*, October 24, 1975, untitled, unpaged clip, Beatty file, AMPAS.

81. *Los Angeles*, January 1978, fragmentary clip, Beatty file, AMPAS.

82. Parker, *Warren Beatty*, p. 252.

83. Phillips and Jerome, *Papa John*, pp. 348–349.

84. Ibid., p. 392. Diane Solway, *Nureyev,* Morrow, 1998, p. 411.

85. Phillips and Jerome, *Papa John,* p. 410.

86. Singular, *Geffen*, p. 32.

87. King, *The Operator*, p. 261.

88. Ibid., pp. 184, 207, 248, 251 (photo).

89. Ibid., pp. 249–250.

90. Spada, *Shirley and Warren*, p. 170.

91. James Bacon, *Los Angeles Herald Examiner*, July 1, 1975, untitled, unpaged clip, Beatty file, AMPAS.

92. Sloan, *Los Angeles Herald Examiner*, September 12, 1975, untitled, unpaged clip, Beatty file, AMPAS.

93. Spada, *Shirley and Warren*, p. 170.

94. Thomson, *Desert Eyes*, pp. 424–425.

95. "A Room of My Own," *Star*, May 15, 2001, p. 42.

96. Vokes-Dudgeon, *National Enquirer*, p. 41.

97. Julia Phillips, *You'll Never Eat*, p. 160.

98. Ibid., pp. 160, 162.

99. Des Barres, *Take Another Little Piece*, p. 137.

100. Julia Phillips, *You'll Never Eat*, p. 175.

101. Evans, *The Kid Stays*, p. 287.

102. Ibid., p. 252.

103. Walter Scott, "Personality Parade," *Parade*, June 20, 2001, p. 2.

104. Terrill, *Steve McQueen*, pp. 220, 316.

105. Alan Hunter, *Faye Dunaway*, New York: St. Martin's, 1986.

106. Terrill, *Steve McQueen*, p. 316.

107. Ibid., p. 315.

108. Evans, *The Kid Stays*, p. 288.

109. Kurt Nikolas, *Corner Table*, Vanity Publications, no publishing information listed, AMPAS.

110. Cathy Griffin interview with Richard Mineards, October 11, 2000.

111. Cathy Griffin interview.

112. Evans, *The Kid Stays*, pp. 288–289.

113. Goldman, *Which Lie Did I Tell?*, p. 178.

114. *Los Angeles Herald Examiner*, September 11, 1976, Beatty file, AMPAS.

115. Gregg Kilday, "Beatty Won't," *Los Angeles Times*, August 11, 1976. See also Gene Siskel, "Warren Beatty: Sex Symbol With Brains," *Long Beach* (Calif.) *Press Telegram*, pp. 9–10.

116. "Actor to Play Howard Hughes," *Los Angeles Times*, November 8, 1976, Beatty file, AMPAS.

117. UHF Channel 68.

118. "Late Show Stirs Debate," *New York*, March 21, 1977, Beatty file, AMPAS.

119. *Los Angeles Herald Examiner*, May 6, 1977, Beatty file, AMPAS.

120. Cathy Griffin interview.

121. Peter G. Bourne, *Jimmy Carter*, New York: Scribner, 1997, p. 329.

122. Bill Boyarsky, "Beautiful People Turn Out, Are Turned Away, Then Turn Ugly," *Los Angeles Times*, July 14, 1976, Beatty file, AMPAS.

123. Bourne, *Jimmy Carter*, p. 339.

124. Ibid., p. 340.

125. Ibid.: "Carter did not need to make such a passionate outburst, but he felt provoked. Although he was barely the nominee, Strauss and Wasserman were already subjecting Carter to wealthy businessmen pushing for self-serving tax breaks."

126. Ibid., pp. 345–346.

127. Ibid., p. 431.

128. Ibid., p. 465: "Reagan would ultimately be diagnosed with Alzheimer's disease, a condition of insidious onset, symptoms of which, including prosopagnosia—the inability to recall familiar faces—were in retrospect present at least as early as his first term. What was then interpreted as dissembling for political advantage now appears to have been, at times, confabulation in which the brain, to cover memory deficits, instantaneously fabricates information that the sufferer does not consciously know is untrue."

129. Joyce Haber, *Los Angeles Times*, November 12, 1974, Beatty file, AMPAS.   Haber wrote that Warren was considering running for president or vice president.

130. Dr. M. S. Swaminathan.

131. Munshower, *Beatty*, p. 104.

132. Spada, *Shirley and Warren*, p. 185.

133. Abramowitz, *Is That a Gun*, p. 68.

134. Thomson, *Desert Eyes*, p. 380.

135. King, *The Operator*, p. 272.

136. Ibid., pp. 275–276.

137. Biskind, *Raging Bulls*, p. 358.

138. Ibid., p. 359.

139. Evans, *The Kid Stays*, pp. 289–290.

140. Spada, *Shirley and Warren*, pp. 186–189.

141. Biskind, *Raging Bulls*, p. 360.

142. Ibid., p. 394.

143. Ibid., pp. 395–396.

144. King, *The Operator*, pp. 293, 295–296, 302.

145. Ibid., pp. 324–325. Biskind, *Raging Bulls*, p. 397.

146. Bobby Shriver, "I'll Bet You Think This Story Is About You," *Los Angeles Herald Examiner*, June 30, 1978, p. B8. Warren's fifteen million *Heaven* earnings: Ewbank, Christie, p. 205.

147. Holden, *Behind the Oscar*, p. 321.

148. Biskind, *Easy Riders*, p. 366.

149. Munshower, *Beatty*, p. 104.

150. "NATO Gives '78 Award to Beatty," *Hollywood Reporter*, October 10, 1978, Beatty file, AMPAS.

151. "NATO Award Winners Beatty, Fonda, Reynolds Sorely Pressed by Press," *Variety*, October 20, 1978, Beatty file, AMPAS.

152. Biskind, *Raging Bulls*, pp. 391, 418–419.

153. October 30, 1978. Christie, Eno: Ewbank, *Christie,* p. 212

154. "Beatty in the Apple," *Us*, November 14, 1978, Beatty file, AMPAS.

155. "Flush Tones," *Us*, December 13, 1977, Beatty file, AMPAS.

156. G. Kilday, *Los Angeles Times*, September 27, 1978, Beatty file, AMPAS.

CHAPTER SIX

1. When contacted by TV show *Entertainment Tonight*.

2. Cathy Griffin interview with source who requested anonymity.

3. Munshower, *Warren Beatty*, p. 3.

4. Ibid., p. 112.

5. Julie Kavanagh, *Women's Wear Daily*, September 9, 1976, Beatty file, AMPAS.

6. Munshower, *Beatty,* p. 115.

7. Anson, "The Titan," p. 328.

8. Munshower, *Beatty,* p. 141.

9. Meade, *Woody Allen*, p. 85.

10. Munshower, *Beatty*, p. 138.

11. Ibid., pp. 138–139.

12. Parker, *Warren Beatty*, p. 312.

13. Spada, *Shirley and Warren*, p. 194.

14. Munshower, *Beatty*, pp. 139, 141–142. McGilligan, *Jack's Life*, p. 320.

15. Cathy Griffin interview with Sarah Porterfield, September 8, 2000.

16. Munshower, *Beatty*, pp. 119, 124.

17. Spada, *Shirley and Warren*, p. 211.

18. Interview with Elaine Dundy, March 3, 2000.

19. Spada, *Shirley and Warren*, p. 196.

20. Abramowitz, *Is That a Gun*, p. 299.

21. Munshower, *Beatty*, p. 140.

22. Meade, *Woody Allen*, p. 161.

23. Interview with Elaine Dundy, March 3, 2000.

24. Holden, *Behind the Oscar*, p. 416.

25. Munshower, *Beatty*, pp. 121–122; Mike Medavoy with Josh Young, *You're Only as Good as Your Next One,* New York: Pocket Books, 2002, p. 110.

26. Munshower, *Beatty*, pp. 123, 143.

27. Ibid., p. 135, Medavoy, *You're Only,* p.236.

28. Holden, *Behind the Oscar*, pp. 158, 330: Orson Welles had done so once, with *Citizen Kane*. Warren had done so previously with *Heaven Can Wait*.

29. Spada, *Shirley and Warren*, p. 339.

30. Ibid., p. 339.

31. Kent, *Naked Hollywood*, p. 51.

32. Ibid., pp. 338, 342.

33. Biskind, *Raging Bulls*, p. 400.

34. Virginia Wright Wexman, *Roman Polanski*, Boston: Twayne, 1985, p. xiv.

35. *Newsweek*, February 13, 1978, Beatty files, AMPAS.

36. Ibid. Parker, *Polanski*, p. 219.

37. Polanski, *Roman*, p. 391.

38. Parker, *Polanski*, p. 222.

39. Ibid., p. 225.

40. Polanski, *Roman*, p. 401.

41. Ibid., p. 402.

42. Parker, *Polanski*, p. 220.

43. Jose Lambiet, "Harrison Ford's House Is Party Central for Strippers," *Star*, June 19, 2001, p. 20.

44. "Polanski Was Cheating on His Pregnant Wife," *Globe*, June 6, 2000, p. 45. King, *Sharon Tate* passim.

45. Evans, *The Kid Stays*, p. 309.

46. Ibid., pp. 310, 312–313.

47. Ibid., p. 321.

48. Ibid., p. 365.

49. Carol Matthau, *Among the Porcupines*, New York: Random House, 1992, p. 236.

50. Munshower, *Beatty*, p. 161.

51. Peter Davidson, "Hollyrude! The Ugly, Nasty Things Stars Say About Each Other," *National Enquirer*, January 30, 2001, p. 35.

52. Gwenda Blair, *Almost Golden*, New York: Avon, 1988, p. 329.

53. Ibid., pp. 298, 319.

54. Ibid., pp. 309, 318, 321.

55. Spada, *Shirley and Warren*, p. 206.

56. Feibleman, *Lilly*, pp. 325–326.

57. "Shirley MacLaine, *Biography* (TV), October 15, 2001. McGilligan, *Jack's Life*, pp. 328–331.

58. Spada, *Shirley and Warren*, p. 208.

59. Ibid., p. 207.

60. Ibid., pp. 112, 210.

61. Yule, *Life on the Wire*, pp. 259–260.

62. Parker, *Warren Beatty*, p. 290.

63. Ibid., p. 291.

64. Eszterhas, *American Rhapsody*, p. 40.

65. Ebert, *Ladies Home Journal* article quoted in Munshower, *Beatty*, p. 132.

66. Parker, *Warren Beatty*, pp. 292–293.

67. Associated Press, "Politics, Sex Get Mixed Reactions," *Gainesville Sun*, July 12, 2001, p. 6A.

68. Parker, *Warren Beatty*, p. 293.

69. Associated Press, "Politics, etc.," *Gainesville Sun*, p. 6A.

70. Ibid.

71. Thomson, *Desert Eyes*, p. 443.

72. McGilligan, *Jack's Life*, p. 168.

73. Ibid., p. 169.

74. Frankel et al., *You'll Never Make Love*, p. 237. Lee, *Tarnished Angel*, p. 71.

75. Thomson, *Desert Eyes*, p. 423.

76. Elena Rodriguez, *Dennis Hopper*, New York: St. Martin's, 1988, pp. 174, 189.

77. Julia Phillips, *You'll Never Eat*, pp. 481–482.

78. Cathy Griffin interview with Richard Sylbert, 2000.

79. Julia Phillips, *You'll Never Eat*, p. 483.

80. Ibid., p. 484.

81. Flo Anthony, "On the Eye Stars," *Examiner*, June 13, 2000, p. 36.

82. Susan Crimp, "Drew Barrymore's Mom," *Star*, June 20, 2000, p. 8.

83. Lee, *Tarnished Angel*, pp. 319–320.

84. Abramowitz, *Is That a Gun*, p. 57.

85. Parker, *Warren Beatty*, p. 281. Some say *Ishtar* cost fifty-one million dollars (see Thomson, *Desert Eyes*, p. 441).

86. Parker, *Warren Beatty*, p. 277.

87. Abramowitz, *Is That a Gun*, p. 299; re: "Fishtar": Bart, *Who Killed Hollywood?* p. 364.

88. Parker, *Warren Beatty*, pp. 282, 287–288.

89. Ibid., p. 295.

90. Eszterhas, *American Rhapsody*, p. 65.

91. Parker, *Warren Beatty*, p. 296.

92. Ibid., pp. 287, 289–290, 312.

93. "Pssst," *Star*, August 22, 2000, p. 13.

94. King, *The Operator*, pp. 395–396, 444.

95. Ibid., pp. 488–489.

96. Evans, *The Kid Stays*, p. 384.

97. Ibid., p. 399.

98. Leon Wagener, "The Night Madonna Seduced Gwyneth," *Star*, July 31, 2001, p. 34. J. Randy Taraborrelli, *Madonna*, New York: Simon and Schuster, 2001, pp. 324–326.

99. Taraborrelli, *Madonna*, p. 24.

100. Cathy Griffin interview.

101. Taraborrelli, *Madonna*, pp. 13–14.

102. Ibid., p. 24.

103. Parker, *Warren Beatty*, pp. 297–298. Boze Hadleigh, *Celebrity Feuds*, Dallas, Texas: Taylor, 1999, pp. 30–31.

104. Christopher Andersen, *Madonna Unauthorized*, New York: Simon and Schuster, 1991, p. 128.

105. Taraborrelli, *Madonna*, p. 150.

106. Ibid., p. 145. McGovern's wrist: Andrew Morton, *Madonna,* New York: St. Martin's, 2001, p. 131

107. Taraborrelli, *Madonna,* p. 106. Morton, *Madonna,* p.148.

108. Andersen, *Madonna Unauthorized*, p. 245.

109. Taraborrelli, *Madonna*, pp. 132–143.

110. Ibid., p. 150.

111. Ibid., p. 153.

112. Ibid., pp. 153–154.

113. Andersen, *Madonna Unauthorized*, p. 259.

114. Taraborrelli, *Madonna*, pp. 156–158.

115. Ibid., p. 169.

116. Ibid., pp. 169–170.

117. Ibid., p. 170.

118. Ibid., pp. 171–172.

119. Ibid., p. 176.

120. Ibid., p. 222.

121. Ibid., pp. 172–173.

122. Ibid., p. 170.

123. Ibid., p. 173.

124. Ibid., p. 172.

125. Yule, *Life on the Wire*, p. 287.

126. "Diane Keaton: I'm Through With Men," *Globe*, July 10, 2001, p. 15.

127. Steve Tinney, "Twin-Credible," *Star*, September 25, 2001, pp. 46–47.

128. Parker, *Warren Beatty*, p. 297.

129. Taraborrelli, *Madonna*, p. 236.

130. Andersen, *Madonna Unauthorized*, p. 274.

131. Julia Phillipis, *You'll Never Eat*, p. 543.

132. Andersen, *Madonna Unauthorized*, p. 254.

133. Morton, *Madonna,* pp. 157, 185. Hadleigh, *Celebrity Feuds*, p. 123.

134. Wagener, *Star*, July 31, 2001, p. 34.

135. Taraborrelli, *Madonna*, p. 177.

136. Ibid., pp. 186–187.

137. *Biography*, October 15, 2001.

138. Parker, *Warren Beatty*, p. 304.

139. Taraborrelli, *Madonna*, p. 189.

140. Ibid.

141. Ibid., p. 191.

142. Parker, *Warren Beatty*, p. 311.

143. Taraborrelli, *Madonna*, p. 188.

144. Kent, *Naked Hollywood*, pp. 111–113. Morton, *Madonna,* p. 168.

145. Walls, *Dish*, p. 185. Newsweek cover: Taraborrelli, *Madonna*, p. 187. Andersen, *Madonna*, p. 302.

146. Walls, *Dish*, p. 257.

147. Parker, *Warren Beatty*, pp. 308, 310.

148. Taraborrelli, *Madonna*, p. 196.

149. Ibid., p. 198.

150. Ibid., p. 208.

151. Ebert, *Ladies Home Journal* in Munshower, *Beatty*, p. 134.

CHAPTER SEVEN

1. Michael A. Lipton, Robin Micheli, and Nancy Matsumoto, "Beauty and the Beatty," *People*, April 6, 1992, pp. 101–102, documented, "First the baby, now the wedding . . . Married? Who knew till after the couple announced on March 12 that they'd tied the knot in a private ceremony?" See also Jesse Kombluth, "The Lady Vanquishes," *Town & Country*, December 1995, p. 187: "After *Bugsy*, Beatty and Bening produced a daughter, Kathlyn. Soon after that, they got married."

2. Biskind, *Vanity Fair*, p. 117.

3. Ibid.

4. Liz Smith, "What She Did for Love," *Good Housekeeping*, March 2000, p. 84.

5. Brad Stone, "Annette Bening Right Now," *More*, January/February 2000, p. 130.

6. Lipton et al., *People,* p. 101.

7. Kornbluth, *Town & Country,* p. 187.

8. Gerard Evans, "Annette Flees," *Woman's Day*, January 29, 1996, p. 15.

9. Ibid., p. 15.

10. Stone, *More*, p. 130.

11. Karen Durbin, "Sometimes You Feel Like Annette," *Mirabella*, p. 149.

12. Sarah Saffian with Christian de la Chapelle, "When Older Men Happen to Younger Women," *Us Weekly*, March 2000, p. 29.

13. Biskind, *Vanity Fair*, p. 117.

14. Marco R. della Cava, "Bening's Deepening 'Love Affair,' " *USA Today*, October 11, 1994, p. 1D.

15. Parker, *Warren Beatty*, p. 318.

16. Biskind, *Vanity Fair*, pp. 117–118.

17. L.A. Justice, "Love Imitates Art," *Examiner*, December 5, 2000, p. 39.

18. Biskind, *Vanity Fair*, p. 118.

19. Andersen, *Madonna*, p. 329.

20. Bart, *The Gross*, p. 191.

21. King, *The Operator*, p. 476.

22. Evans, *The Kid Stays*, p. 287.

23. Edgren, *Inside the Playboy Mansion*, p. 343. Medavoy's conflicts with Beatty and Guber over *Bugsy:* Medavoy, *You're Only,* pp. xviii, 237, 240, 242, 244–245, 275, 283.

24. Eszterhas, *American Rhapsody*, p. 393.

25. Parker, *Warren Beatty*, p. 329.

26. Stone, *More*, pp. 14, 79.

27. Evans, *Woman's Day*, pp. 14–15.

28. Abramowitz, *Is That A Gun*, p. 309.

29. Smith, *Good Housekeeping*, p. 108.

30. Della Cava, *USA Today*, p. 1

31. Evans, *Woman's Day*, p. 14.

32. Ibid.

33. Ibid.

34. Ibid., p. 15.

35. Ibid., p. 14.

36. Ibid.

37. Ibid.

38. Della Cava, *USA Today*, p. 1D.

39. Evans, *Woman's Day*, p. 115.

40. Ibid.

41. Emery, *The Directors, Take Two*, pp. 25–26.

42. Goldman, *Which Lie Did I Tell?*, p. 43.

43. Eszterhas, *American Rhapsody*, pp. 391–392.

44. A. J. Benza, *Fame: Ain't It a Bitch*, New York: Hyperion, 2001, pp. 98, 221.

45. Janet Charlton, "Star People," *Star*, June 16, 1998, p. 14.

46. "Jack Nicholson and *Practice* Beauty's Romance Secret," *Globe*, March 28, 2000, p. 38.

47. Andrew Goldman, "Lara Flynn Boyle's Remote Control," *Talk*, October 2001, p. 146.

48. Kevin Sessums, "Call of the Wild," *Vanity Fair*, February 2001, p. 142.

49. Daisy Garnett, "Life in the Fast Lane," *Talk*, November 2000, p. 110.

50. Deborah Hughes, "Boyle-ing Hot," *National Enquirer*, May 29, 2001, p. 13.

51. Mike Walker, "Boylerworks," *National Enquirer*, 2001.

52. Thomson, *Desert Eyes*, pp. 326–327.

53. Eszterhas, *American Rhapsody*, p. 389.

54. Russ Baker, "At Home With Arianna Huffington," *New York Times*, July 20, 2000, p. B13.

55. Eszterhas, *American Rhapsody*, p. 392.

56. Biskind, *Vanity Fair*, p. 118.

57. Munshower, *Beatty*, p. 152.

58. Bart, *The Gross*, p. 184.

59. Ibid., pp. 187, 192, 200.

60. Caryn James, "A Convention's Worth of (Pretend) Candidates," *New York Times*, August 11, 2000, p. B26.

61. Bart, *The Gross*, pp. 96–97.

62. *The Late Show with David Letterman*, July 17, 2000.

63. Suzanne Ely and Jim Nelson, "Mr. Mom," *National Enquirer*, April 18, 2000, p. 28.

64. George Stephanopoulos, "Behind the Beatty Buzz," *Newsweek*, October 11, 1999, p. 35.

65. Todd S. Purdum, "Coy on Candidacy, Beatty Keeps His Options Open," *New York Times*, October 1, 1999, p. A21.

66. Biskind, *Vanity Fair*, p. 174.

67. Unsigned article, "Primaries," *George*, November 1999, p. 21.

68. James Bennet, "The Cable Guys," *New York Times Magazine*, October 24, 1999, pp. 74, 77.

69. Thomson, *Desert Eyes*, p. 326.

70. Bennet, *New York Times Magazine*, pp. 74, 77.

71. Bernard Weinraub, "Moguls Rattled by Gore's Choice of Critic of Entertainment Industry," *New York Times*, August 11, 2000, p. A15.

72. Amy Wallace, "Hollywood Turns Out in Force for Party in Its Backyard," *Los Angeles Times*, August 18, 2000, pp. U3, U10.

73. Shawn Hubler, "And Now, Let's Go to the Replay," *Los Angeles Times*, August 18, 2000, p. U11.

74. Bennet, *New York Times Magazine*, pp. 74, 77.

75. Biskind, *Vanity Fair*, p. 175.

76. Durbin, *Mirabella*, p. 185.

77. Ely and Nelson, *National Enquirer*, p. 29.

78. Ibid., p. 29.

79. "Say What?" *Examiner*, July 18, 2000, p. 23.

80. Biskind, *Vanity Fair*, p. 118.

81. "Hangin' Out with the Stars," *Globe*, June 20, 2000, p. 46.

82. Smith, *Good Housekeeping*, p. 108.

83. Ibid.

84. Bart, *The Gross*, p. 305.

85. Biskind, *Vanity Fair*, p. 175.

86. Ibid.

87. Ibid.

88. Goldman, *Which Lie Did I Tell?*, pp. 39, 178.

89. Biskind, *Vanity Fair*, p. 175.

90. "Jack's Back in Court," *Globe*, May 30, 2000, p. 37; see also "Gossiping Under the Influence," *National Enquirer*, May 2000, p. 21, and Samantha Stevens, "Jack Nicholson Destroyed My Life," *Star*, May 30, 2000, p. 9.

91. Stevens, *Star*, p. 9.

92. CBS-TV, *Entertainment Tonight*, March 3, 2000.

93. Ely and Nelson, *National Enquirer*, p. 28.

94. "Baby Beatty," *People*, April 2000, p. 92.

95. "Hollywood's Amazing 40-Something Moms," *National Enquirer*, 2000, p. 60.

96. Ibid.

97. "Warren Beatty Plays Tarzan in Bedroom," *Star*, August 8, 2000, p. 14.

98. Maggie Harbour, "Annette Bening & Baby Seat Mystery," *Star*, November 28, 2000, p. 29.

99. "Annette's Big Splash," *Star*, October 31, 2000, p. 13.

100. Janet Charlton, "StarPeople: Uneasy Rider," *Star*, January 16, 2001, p. 12.

101. "Upfront: April 1 Los Angeles," *People*, May 14, 2001, p. 64: "Clinton was caught on tape with sometime critic Warren Beatty, who later stayed mum about their animated encounter."

102. Ibid.

103. Deborah Hughes, "Liquid Magic," *National Enquirer*, June 19, 2001, p. 13.

104. Della Cava, *USA Today*, p. 1D.

105. Halle Berry: Cathy Griffin. Russell Crowe: *Examiner*, February 12, 2002, p. 45.

106. Inside.com quoted in Rick Lyman, "Stumbling Toward a Theater Near You," *New York Times*, April 15, 2001, p. 18.

107. Lynn Hirschberg, "Questions for Michael De Luca, Cast Away," *New York Times Magazine*, February 25, 2001, p. 17.

108. Lyman, *New York Times*, April 15, 2001, p. 18.

109. Lyman, "Villains and Heroes," *New York Times*, May 26, 2000, p. B24.

110. "Warren Beatty: Has He Lost Sex Appeal?" *Examiner*, April 25, 2000, p. 22.

111. Stephen Holden, "If the Sport of Infidelity Had an All-Star Game, Then This Would Be It," *New York Times*, April 27, 2001, p. B10. *Town & Country* gross: Scott Bowles, "Hollywood Flaps its Wings, Despite the Flops," *USA Today*, January 2, 2002, p. 4D.

112. Charlene Tilton, "Soggy Stars Shine On," *Globe*, September 4, 2001, pp. 12–13; Matthew Cole Weiss, "*Seagull* Gets Rained Out," *Us Weekly*, August 27, 2001, p. 16.

113. Flo Anthony, "Eye on the Stars," *Examiner*, August 28, 2001, p. 45.

114. "Star Shots," *Star*, August 7, 2001, p. 1. In *At Sevastopol*, Alphonse Karr wrote in 1849, "The more things change, the more they remain the same."

AUG

2008